FOOD POLICY

FOOD POLICY

The Responsibility of the United States in the Life and Death Choices

Edited with an Introduction by
Peter G. Brown
and
Henry Shue

THE FREE PRESS
A Division of Macmillan Publishing Co., Inc.
NEW YORK

Collier Macmillan Publishers
LONDON

Copyright © 1977 by The Free Press
A Division of Macmillan Publishing Co., Inc.

All rights reserved. No part of this book may be reproduced or transmitted in any form or by any means, electronic or mechanical, including photocopying, recording, or by any information storage and retrieval system, without permission in writing from the Publisher.

The Free Press
A Division of Macmillan Publishing Co., Inc.
866 Third Avenue, New York, N.Y. 10022

Collier Macmillan Canada, Ltd.

First Free Press Paperback Edition 1979

Library of Congress Catalog Card Number: 76-57803

Printed in the United States of America

printing number

HC 1 2 3 4 5 6 7 8 9 10
SC 1 2 3 4 5 6 7 8 9 10

Library of Congress Cataloging in Publication Data

Main entry under title:

Food policy.

   Includes bibliographical references and index.
   1. Food supply--Addresses, essays, lectures.
2. Agriculture and state--United States--Addresses, essays, lectures. I. Brown, Peter G. II. Shue, Henry.
HD9000.6.F59   338.1'9   76-57803
ISBN 0-02-904980-6
ISBN 0-02-905170-3 pbk.

Contents

Preface ... vii

Introduction ... 1

Part One: NEEDS AND OBLIGATIONS

1. World needs: shall the hungry be with us always? ... 13
   Lyle Schertz

2. Reconsidering the famine relief argument ... 36
   Peter Singer

3. Poverty and food: why charity is not enough ... 54
   Thomas Nagel

Part Two: RESPONSIBILITIES IN THE PUBLIC SECTOR

4. Food as national property ... 65
   Peter G. Brown

5. Food aid, commercial exports, and the balance of payments ... 79
   Lawrence Witt

6. The political uses of food aid: are criteria necessary? ... 94
   Daniel E. Shaughnessy

7. A utilitarian framework for policy analysis in food-related foreign aid ... 103
   Joseph D. Sneed

8. Bigotry, loyalty, and malnutrition ... 129
   Samuel Gorovitz

Part Three: RESPONSIBILITIES IN THE PRIVATE SECTOR

9 Food aid and the free market 145
    Charles B. Shuman

10 Intervening in the market 164
    Victor Ferkiss

11 International food reserves 183
    C. William Swank

Part Four: REDUCING DEPENDENCE

12 A new legislative mandate for American food aid 199
    Thomas Reese Saylor

13 Individual needs: nutritional guidelines for policy? 212
    Linda Haverberg

14 Beyond humanitarianism: a developmental perspective on American food aid 234
    John Osgood Field and Mitchel B. Wallerstein

15 Slowing population growth with food aid 259
    Michael F. Brewer

16 Nutritional dilemmas of transforming economies 275
    Norge W. Jerome

17 Distributive criteria for development assistance 305
    Henry Shue

18 Focus on nutrition: who should pay for what? 319
    The Hon. Edwin M. Martin

Index 337

Preface

We began this study in the summer of 1974, when food shortages abroad had acquired an unusual prominence in U.S. foreign policy. Prospects for the autumn harvest of that year were uncertain. Would the world be moving into the winter of 1974-75 with substantial grain shortages? This uncertainty and the unexpected developments in the grain markets of the previous 2 years had produced a situation of mild hysteria. *Ad hominem* attacks were being made on the Secretary of Agriculture. Public officials, clerical leaders, and strident voices from the right and the left were advancing proposals for protecting or changing the life-style of Americans. Some observers stressed the need for very substantial increases in foreign assistance. Others argued that assistance in fact undercut the welfare of those for whom it was intended or their descendants, and thus was irresponsible.

The furor has subsided with 3 years of better harvests in some regions. But, unfortunately, the problems of food shortages and malnutrition are not confined to the years when public attention focuses on them. Malnutrition of millions of people—indeed, hundreds of millions—occurs year in and year out. It is very likely to become worse in the future. What should we, the agriculturally affluent, do? What is fair in the distribution of this vital resource, food?

This book is designed to serve as a foundation for a reflective appraisal of these questions. Like all public policy issues the problem of chronic malnutrition, and occasional starvation, is a complex combination of factual, institutional, and moral elements. The formulation of policy necessarily involves a careful consideration of all these elements. Yet, despite enormous expenditures on research, we seldom if ever find ourselves in a position to consider these factors simultaneously. Philosophers and others trained or experienced in thinking analytically about moral issues often do not concern themselves with broad questions of public policy. When they do, they frequently do not have the appropriate factual knowledge or a realistic appraisal of the institutional constraints on policy formulation and implementation. On the other hand, those well versed in the factual and institutional sides of policy problems often give little analytic attention to moral and conceptual issues.

As is unfortunately the case with many fundamental decisions about public policy, additional facts are themselves indeterminate. In the case of a U.S. policy with regard to world hunger, one great need is for a careful reexamination of the concepts and purposes in terms of which we structure the problem. Such a reexamination, with an eye to the factual situation and institutional constraints, is the purpose of this book.

In order that the reexamination should be untrammeled, no attempt has been made by the editors to enforce a single point of view upon the contributors, and the volume contains lively and, we believe, fruitful debates. Naturally the author of each essay speaks only for himself or herself and neither for the Academy for Contemporary Problems nor for his or her own institution or organization. Essays are included because they express well an important point of view and not necessarily because either editor agrees with them. Nor does the introduction speak for anyone except the editors.

Without the foresight of Ralph Widner, President of the Academy for Contemporary Problems, neither the essays which follow, all written specifically for this volume, nor the Academy's Working Group on Moral Issues in the Distribution of Food, which stimulated the essays, would have been possible. We appreciate his willingness to have the Academy undertake this unusual enterprise. We are also grateful for the continuous encouragement and good counsel of Michael F. Brewer, Fellow of the Academy, whose contributions to the book extend far beyond the essay bearing his name. Extraordinarily perceptive and thorough reviews of the manuscript were provided by Cheryl Christensen and Martin McLaughlin. And for sometimes long days of patient and skillful work and good humor under pressure, we are grateful to Colleen Pobanz and Virginia Smith. Only the editors of course bear responsibility for the final judgments made.

P.G.B.
H.S.
Center for Philosophy and Public Policy
University of Maryland at College Park

Introduction

Peter G. Brown & Henry Shue

Chronic undernourishment of hundreds of millions of people whose lives are permeated by fatigue and without hope of fulfillment is first of all a problem of justice—at least as long as other hundreds of millions sit at bountiful tables. Assisting the hungry to get enough to eat involves, of course, a number of economic, political, and technical problems. Yet to guide these social and technical efforts, we must first decide who has a right to the relevant resources, and why. Recent public debate has not dealt directly with this issue. It often is assumed that the affluent have—for one reason or another—more of a right to food than the hungry.

This volume is concerned with the responsibility of the United States as an agriculturally affluent nation to assist in meeting the food needs of the world's poorer nations. Although not a new concern, it has assumed new importance as the alarming dimensions of the long-range problem have become known. Most projections of future world income, population growth, and patterns of food use suggest that the intensity of the problem is likely to increase. Hence appropriate U.S. policies must be formulated in the next few years.

In the following pages we introduce the four major issues discussed in this book: What is the nature of the problem? What responsibility, if any, does the United States have to respond to it? To what extent can we respond to it through our export policy? And what should be our policy for assisting increases in agricultural production by other countries? In discussing these questions here, we present glimpses into the chapters that make up the book, along with our own assessments of some of the major issues, assessments not all shared by all the authors of individual chapters.

THE PROBLEM: IS THERE A SHORTAGE OF FOOD?

Solutions to the problem of hunger can be evaluated only after the character of the problem is fully grasped. Several features of the "world food shortage" are now widely understood. There is more than enough food for every human being in the world to be adequately fed. By some more equal distributions of food, including distributions which were still far from strictly equal, the amount of food now produced would provide an adequate diet for the current world population. Indeed, instead of an overall shortage of food, there are unjustifiable inequalities in the distribution of food among nations, within nations, and, where the allotment to each family is meager, within families.

The distribution of food consumption among nations, for example, is extraordinarily unequal. And how nations use the food they have varies considerably: more grain is consumed by the livestock of the Soviet Union and the United States than by the entire human population of less developed countries. Over the last decade, the increase in total grain consumption by Eastern Europe, where meat is becoming a more widely available food, was greater than the increase in total grain consumption by India, where population grows by a million a month. Generally, the difference in per capita food consumption between the wealthy nations and the poor nations is not only immense but expanding, with the poor nations failing even to keep up. The major reason for this is that increases in the income of the less poor almost always result in more demand for meat, the production of which often consumes large quantities of grain.

When poor people obtain more money, a large proportion of the additional money goes to purchase food. The distribution of food consumption generally reflects the distribution of wealth and income. The difference in diet between the United States and, say, Mali or Nepal is strongly influenced by the fact that in 1973 the GNP per capita of the United States was $6,200, while the comparable amounts for Mali and Nepal were $70 and $90. These differences in income are, in Thomas Nagel's phrase, "radical inequalities," and they are at the root of the enormous differences in the quality of diet. As Charles Shuman puts it, "Hunger is an economic problem—there are no hungry people where there is money to buy food."

Most knowledgeable people, whatever their differences on other points, would agree with the preceding two general points concerning the total amount of food and the relationship between the distribution of food and the distribution of wealth and income. The two can be summed up together as follows: the basic cause of the "world food shortage" is the high degree of inequality in the distribution of wealth and income both among and within nations. The food needed now is being produced now, but the poor who need it most are not producing it themselves and do not have the money to buy it. In short, there is no "world food shortage," but, most tragically, there is a shortage of food in many places in the world.

Both increased production of food and improved distribution of wealth and income are necessary elements in any effective response to the future threat of hunger. An improved distribution of wealth and income by itself might merely lead to inflation in the price of food, which consequently would still remain beyond the reach of the poor. But increased production of food by itself does nothing to prevent the increases in supply from going to the satisfaction of the preference for meat on the part of the not so poor rather than to the satisfaction of the need for grain on the part of the very poor.

Of the factors contributing to these regional shortages, population growth has until now tended to receive the most attention. But the present shortages of food in many parts of the world are a combination of rising population and rising incomes, though usually not in the same country. The malnutrition of millions is caused simultaneously by rising incomes for others—while the malnourished are left behind—and the high fertility of the malnourished.

Malnutrition is less an acute crisis than a chronic disease. Malnutrition is one aspect of a whole way of life—part of a package wrapped in the bonds of poverty. As several authors, including Haverberg, Martin, and Field and Wallerstein, point out, malnutrition reinforces, and is reinforced by, high rates of population growth, disease, lack of health care, inertia, and—above all—oppressive poverty.

What can be done? Former Secretary of State Kissinger in 1974 called for the elimination of malnutrition within a decade:

> All governments should accept the removal of the scourge of hunger and malnutrition, which at present afflicts many millions of human beings, as the objective of the international community as a whole, and should accept the goal that within a decade no child will go to bed hungry, that no family will fear for its next day's bread, and that no human being's future and capacities will be stunned by malnutrition.

The opening chapter of this volume considers the feasibility of reaching such a goal in terms of global grain supplies, while a later chapter considers how individual malnutrition is to be defined and alleviated.

- How much more grain would have been required annually during the early 1970s to have *cut in half the number of malnourished individuals?* Lyle Schertz calculates that this would have meant increasing annual production—and consumption—by from 86 to 258 million metric tons. To have eliminated malnutrition would obviously have required far more. A decade from now, with a larger population and higher incomes in many parts of the world, reaching this same objective would require increasing production by many hundreds of millions of tons—*if* the demands of the affluent continue to be satisfied in accord with long-established dietary trends and distribution is determined in accord with supply and demand.
- How do we decide who is malnourished? Since, as noted by Linda Haverberg, nutritional standards are culturally relative, and even partly dependent on standards derived from what we mean by "health," they must be carefully used. We can easily make the problem seem better, or worse, than it is by employing misleading standards. Yet careful nutritional planning can be invaluable in making existing food supplies and

monetary resources go further. Where there is simply not enough to go around, it is urged that resources be given to infant and preschool children and pregnant and lactating mothers, ignoring, if necessary, adult workers, so that irreversible harm may be prevented while it can be.

THE RESPONSIBILITY OF THE UNITED STATES IN THE LIFE AND DEATH CHOICES: WHAT IS IT AND WHY?

Do those with the resources substantially to reduce—or even eliminate—malnutrition have an obligation to do so? Many of the chapters of this volume consider whether a negative answer to this question can be sustained: *none offers compelling reasons why transfers of income and wealth directed toward the malnourished should remain at their present low level.* Moreover, several argue convincingly that foreign aid be thought of, not as an act of charity, which is praiseworthy although optional, but as a moral obligation, which is required if one is to live a moral life.

Several chapters consider the nature and source of this obligation. Though coming at the question from different frameworks and premises, all offer essentially the same conclusion: that the United States has a substantial obligation to help meet food deficits in the poorer nations abroad by the most effective means possible. Present policy falls short of this objective.

- Starting from three simple premises—(1) that starvation is bad, (2) that if we can do something about a bad situation, we ought to, and (3) that we can do something about starvation—Peter Singer concludes that assisting those without enough food is morally required. Failure to contribute at least 10 percent of our incomes to the hungry is, on his view, morally wrong. Arguments that the hungry are undeserving, or are acting irresponsibly in continuing to increase their populations, are considered, but, in Singer's view, do not mitigate the immorality of continuing only present levels of assistance.
- In helping the radically impoverished, do we commit ourselves to being brought down to very near their level? Is such a view an attack on differences in wealth as such? Not in the least, according to Thomas Nagel. Radical inequalities should be eliminated, even if one does not favor equality of a more general sort. Since the world economy operates more and more like a fully integrated system, the legitimacy of that system must be judged by reference to the outcomes it generates. The radical inequalities underlying malnutrition, though often taken for granted, demonstrate the illegitimacy of the present world economic system.
- Should we reject the claims of the poor on the grounds that we own the resources in question and can do with them what we wish? Not if we

carefully examine various normative theories of property, argues Peter Brown. Even those views of property which minimize our obligations to others imply a responsibility to share certain proportions of wealth with nonowners. Other, and often more popular, theories suggest an even stronger obligation.

- Should we not give priority to family, friends, and home community over strangers in other nations? Our morality contains a place both for a principle of the equal moral standing of all persons and for special rights based on special relationships. In particular cases much depends, Samuel Gorovitz maintains, on whether what is at stake is the satisfaction of preferences or the provision of what is necessary for the exercise of human rights. While loyalty to one's own has morally laudable forms, self-deception can allow bigotry, selfishness, and insensitivity to masquerade as loyalty.
- Is it morally preferable, as advocates of "lifeboat ethics" maintain, to deny assistance, thus permitting a "small famine" now in order to avoid a possibly much larger one later? Not, according to Henry Shue, after a careful consideration of who is most likely to benefit from the denial of help and how reliable our predictions about the future will probably be. But it would also be irresponsible to concentrate on current needs to the neglect of investment for future generations. Most important, we are not forced to choose between today's hungry and tomorrow's hungry.
- Should we neglect the malnourished because assisting them will involve robbing other individuals of freedom of choice, as expressed through the free market? Only, says Victor Ferkiss (sharply disagreeing with chapters by Brown and Shuman), if we accept a hypothetical and unjustifiable idea of human freedom, and neglect to consider whether people's differential capabilities to participate in the free market are the result of free choice.

If, then, good arguments can be offered for increasing foreign assistance, what can be done about chronic malnutrition? Since there is no short-term prospect that the world will be able to get along without substantial American grain, how should we use it? And since the United States also has the technology and expertise to assist others to increase their own production, what forms of assistance are best for the recipients? A number of chapters address each of these topics.

EXPORTING TO THE DISADVANTAGED: DOES IT REALLY HELP?

What should be done about our grain exports to less developed countries? Some chapters advocate moving toward a free market in agricultural products.

- How much help are direct shipments of food outside market channels likely to be? Not much, argues Charles Shuman, since the primary

concern must be to avoid the tendency of governments to destroy the incentives for farmers to produce as much as they can. Attempts to handle food shortages by government interventions almost invariably make them worse. Moreover, such policies undercut the freedom to contract and to use one's own property, in addition to unnecessarily aggravating the problem of hunger by dampening production incentives. Interventionist policies are simultaneously morally hazardous and counterproductive.
- What about intervening in world markets to the extent of maintaining a reserve stock of grain for use when world production is low? Like the Biblical Joseph, shouldn't we put aside for the lean years? No, a monetary reserve would be better, in William Swank's view, for several reasons—above all, because the fact that a reserve system which actually held grain would make the supply situation worse by depressing production, both in the United States and overseas.

These chapters urge that free markets be relied on to increase agricultural production. Probably, on the supply side high returns on labor and capital will call forth strenuous production efforts. But will these be enough? How much grain would it take to meet human needs for food if most other related policies remained the same?

The currently accepted analysis of the world food situation by the U.S. Department of Agriculture concluded, as Schertz notes, that to eliminate malnutrition would require a production increase in grain of only 25 million tons, a comfortingly small amount (less than 10 percent of the annual U.S. harvest). "But, says Schertz, "Such an estimate assumes that the 25 million tons would reach the malnourished and only the malnourished."

For anyone who would like to continue to rely on the existing markets for the purpose of getting food into the hands of the malnourished, Schertz has made a profoundly disturbing point: much of any increased production will go to those who want meat, not to those who need grain. In his assessment of this question, Schertz took seriously the most important implication of relying entirely on free market forces: that the poorest are always competing for grain with those with more money who prefer grain-fed meat. His conclusion, as already indicated, was that to have reduced the number of malnourished to 226 million people in the early 1970s would have required annually an additional 86 to 258 million tons of grain. And the amount of additional grain needed to eliminate malnutrition for the other 226 million would have been much higher still. Today, of course, the amounts required would already be even greater. Looking to the future, one can only conclude that the end of malnutrition is unforeseeable as long as grain must reach the poorest through normal market channels.

If we believe we are obligated to help end malnutrition, we appear to have no alternative to the building of effective extramarket mechanisms to influence *distribution*, as distinct from *production*. Effective extramarket channels

(Saylor, Martin) and intelligent interventions in the market (Ferkiss) must be used if our moral responsibility to help eliminate malnutrition is to be fulfilled. This is not to deny that agricultural producers, be they Indian peasants or American corporations, will produce only if they have incentives (Shuman), nor is it to deny that interventions in the market, such as the possible creation of grain reserves, should be designed so that production is not impaired (Swank).

But interventions which affect the way people express their wants and how much they are able and willing to pay can shift productive capabilities in ways which do not retard overall production. Two different types of alternatives are possible. First, we can alter the ability of the poor to buy grain, either by lowering its price (if this can in fact be done without discouraging production) or—probably better—by increasing their purchasing power through wider, better-paid employment and direct income transfers or increasing their resources for growing their own food. Until the unpredictable day when some breakthrough in agricultural technology makes possible a vast increase in world grain production, some action is needed to help the very poorest compete successfully in the world grain market with the less poor and the affluent, who can afford to pay more in order to consume grain indirectly in the form of meat.

Second, we can alter the consumption patterns of the more well-to-do. One mechanism for this purpose would be a luxury tax on grain-fattened meat, with revenues to be used in assisting the poorest to achieve a minimally adequate diet. These revenues could be spent on foodgrains so that overall production was not impaired. The moral appeal of this proposal is that those most able to eat well help those least able to eat at all. By merely making the satisfaction of a preference slightly more expensive for some, we could generate funds for reducing the desperation in the lives of others.

Other chapters do not address the free market, but look at various other policy objectives which might govern grain exports.

- Given the fairly complicated moral and economic considerations, we can at least minimize the sort of political uses of food aid which occurred during the Vietnam war, can't we? Yes, Thomas Saylor reports, Congress is already moving to establish a clear ranking of priorities among the various legitimate uses of food aid. No, argues Daniel Shaughnessy, all food aid is inherently political, and the new Congressional criteria designed to make much of it nonpolitical cannot work and will only make implementation inflexible. Moreover, Shaughnessy argues, some criteria employed in the past have excluded those who need food the most.
- As Lawrence Witt observes, food aid is much more expensive now that the surpluses are gone, or at low levels. If we assume we have some fixed level of obligation, then changes in price will have profound impacts—since commercial grain sales help the U.S. balance of payments—on how much we do about world hunger in terms of amounts of food shipped. If

we desire a certain amount of foreign assistance, it is only rational to cut back on how much we provide if the price rises—much as we might eat less steak at $10 a pound, even though we still liked it just as much.
- It is also not obvious, says Joseph Sneed, how to distribute satisfaction among various people and their various demands. If we can decide which desires are to be satisfied and which ignored, we will have simplified policy making considerably. Several alternatives concerning which demands to satisfy are discussed.

BETTER NUTRITION FOR THE POOR: WHAT PRIORITIES SHOULD THE UNITED STATES SET?

Every contributor to this volume would probably agree that it is urgent to improve the diets of the malnourished poor abroad, and each would probably also agree that it is urgent that appropriate steps be taken to slow the growth of population in the countries with severe malnutrition, not to mention elsewhere.

Many chapters allude to the "child survival hypothesis," which provides the theoretical basis for the hope that improving nutrition is one effective means toward controlling population, thereby obviating the need to choose between improving nutrition and controlling population. Michael Brewer's chapter analyzes the hypothesis in detail.

Accepting Brewer's judgment that the available evidence is inconclusive on the questions whether and in what circumstances the hypothesis is correct, we would argue as follows. First, in light of some of the basic and undisputed facts which we do know about demographic change, such as the compound rates at which population grows (for example, a growth rate of 3 percent, which is quite typical of less developed countries, means a doubling of the total every 24 years) and the importance of the percentage of the population which is entering the childbearing years (a percentage which may be very high indeed after a decade and a half if better nutrition does in fact decrease child mortality), a misplaced confidence in the effectiveness of indirect measures to slow population, which diverted resources from genuinely effective direct measures, could have catastrophic consequences which would become apparent only two or more decades after the fateful choices had been made. Even if the probability that the child survival hypothesis is not true, or is misleading, is low, policies based on it should not command undue resources. If it should be off the mark, we will be facing a world of far greater population and, probably, malnutrition of an even greater magnitude than today's. Hence, even if the child survival hypothesis should later turn out to have been correct all along, it need not have been irrational to have hedged one's bets until the evidence was more conclusive.

Second, as Brewer indicates, an improvement in nutrition which is to be adequate for a significant reduction in child mortality cannot occur in isolation from improved sanitation, improved medical care, and perhaps even improved employment opportunities for parents—in other words, little short of general economic development. Such development cannot be either inexpensive or rapid. The programmatic complexity and the financial cost of fully implementing the strategy suggested by the child survival hypothesis must be directly faced.

Third, all that the correctness of the hypothesis entails is a decline in the birth rate, not a decline in the rate of population growth, which depends on the difference between the birth rate and the death rate. This distinction is crucial. Since it is precisely a decline in the rate of death of children which is supposed to lead to decline in the rate of birth of children, the two changes, as Brewer makes clear, *could* simply cancel each other out, leaving the rate of population growth as high as ever.

For these reasons it seems crucial that no increase in appropriations for improved nutrition should come at the expense of appropriations which can be effectively used for population control. The dilemma of this choice between nutrition programs and population programs is tragic and risky only if one begins by assuming that the resources devoted to these tasks should be at or near present levels. But from a number of very different sets of premises good reasons are given in each of several chapters (Singer, Nagel, Brown, Gorovitz, Shue) against treating the current distribution as justified or even acceptable.

Even if fertility rates decline sharply, world demand for grain will exceed the capacity of the United States and other exporters to meet it. In any case, less developed countries want to avoid dependence on external sources for their food. Increased production abroad by those who need the food is imperative. How should we facilitate it?

A long-standing problem in economics and in ethics is, How much should one generation forego in consumption in order to save or, more accurately, make investments for the future? Regarding policies to aid the malnourished to grow more of their own food, this problem has a special poignancy: since the numbers of malnourished in many less developed countries are likely to be larger as each year passes, should we not now be concentrating our resources on agricultural investments which will enable more people in succeeding decades to have adequate diets?

Edwin Martin and John Field and Mitchel Wallerstein challenge the economic and political assumptions of any policy of taking the investments for the future out of the food consumption of the present. Although they give a number of different specific arguments, their basic judgment, phrased as a point about the conceptual framework assumed by such a policy, is that in the case of food consumption by the malnourished, the sometimes useful theoretical distinction between "consumption" and "investment" often collapses. The potential productivity of those who are now malnourished is enormous. Accordingly, one of the best possible "investments" would be in the food "consumption" of the malnourished.

- But can we assist the malnourished without actually undercutting their own productive capabilities? Thomas Saylor suggests that the revenues generated in the less developed countries from sales of U.S.-supplied grains can be used to develop the productive capacities of the disadvantaged countries. Shipping food can effectively put otherwise idle capacity in this country to work and can also back up a commitment by other countries to emphasize their agricultural production until adequate increases in food output are attained.
- John Field and Mitchel Wallerstein argue that if appropriate levels of assistance can be guaranteed and kept free from political manipulation, shipping food can help unleash the productive capability of those who would otherwise remain malnourished. They urge that purely humanitarian arguments for shipping food give way to broader developmental rationales.
- And Norge Jerome warns that many attempts at development of agriculture have ignored—and hence disrupted—healthy balances between human populations and food resources. In the course of delineating stages of development she cites case after case in which nutrition has declined as a result of "improved" agriculture. "Development" will improve nutrition only if it is carefully planned to do so.
- Edwin Martin offers a broad program of aid designed to give first priority to improving nutrition in the poorest countries. And he maintains that, leaving aside consideration of our obligations to others, it is in the long-range national interest of the United States to support such programs.

However, is it not evident that the overlap of "consumption" and "investment" in the case of food for the malnourished is not total and that sometimes the hard choice will still have to be made between the most productive investment for the long run and the full satisfaction of existing needs for food?

Even this seemingly innocuous concession to what is likely to happen is misleading. Once again, this dilemma arises only if we assume that the existing distribution of wealth is just. Several chapters argue, for different reasons, that it is not. To the extent that foreign assistance is increased and the terms of world trade are modified so that the actual distribution of wealth among nations eliminates radical inequalities, the dilemma within poorer nations will be eased, if not eliminated. The dilemma is created by the arbitrary assumption that the less developed countries must continue to operate under the present conditions of extreme scarcity within their borders: a lack of resources simultaneously to improve present diets and to make provident investments for the future. To the extent that resources are scarce within the poorer countries, this is partly a product of the distribution of wealth among countries which human decisions have permitted to arise, and it can be changed by a decision to make a prudent, but significant, redistribution of wealth among and within many of the world's nations.

Part One
NEEDS AND OBLIGATIONS

ABOUT THE CONTRIBUTORS

Lyle Schertz wrote the influential article, "World Food: Prices and the Poor," which originally appeared in *Foreign Affairs* and was then selected for *The World Economic Crisis,* ed. William P. Bundy. Schertz, a USDA research administrator, anticipated the need for "rules of the game" for access to U.S. food by the USSR. His writings have stressed the overwhelming importance of wealth and income as determinants of world hunger.

Peter Singer teaches philosophy at Monash University and has taught at Oxford, New York University, and La Trobe. His most recent book is *Animal Liberation,* and he also wrote *Democracy and Disobedience* and several articles, including ones for *New York Review of Books, New York Times Sunday Magazine,* and professional philosophical journals.

Thomas Nagel is Professor of Philosophy at Princeton and author of *The Possibility of Altruism* as well as of many articles including "Altruism and Economics" and "Reason and National Goals."

World needs: shall the hungry be with us always?

Lyle Schertz

The world will eat better in 1985 than it eats today. But the gains for the poor will be only slight. An overwhelming number of them will still be inadequately fed. It could be different. But it is not likely to be so, for the amount of resources needed to correct malnutrition is overwhelming if the world continues to rely mainly on the traditional approach of income growth to make the correction. Thus a combination of approaches, including larger incomes for the poor, slower population growth, greater equity among and within nations, and substantial increases in food production, is necessary if the food gap between the rich and the poor is to be narrowed and if the number of people who are inadequately fed today is to be substantially reduced within this century.

INTRODUCTION

The world is very much concerned about how who gets what food, when, and why. And justly so. In many foreign lands millions continue to suffer from inadequate diets, and through modern communications they realize that others do not. In still other foreign lands, such as Poland and the USSR, millions would like to add more meat and animal products to their diets and through modern communications they know that others enjoy such diets.

Domestically, millions of us are becoming increasingly aware, again through modern communications and through price changes, that the incomes of

---

This paper draws heavily on exchanges with colleagues in ERS. I am especially indebted to Tony Rojko, Pat O'Brien, John Shields and Christine Collins for assistance in the preparation of the paper. The views expressed here are not necessarily those of the U.S. Department of Agriculture.

American farmers, the budgets of American consumers, and activities such as subsidies for the U.S. maritime interests are closely related to the poverty in northeast Brazil, drought as far away as Africa, decisions in the Kremlin, and empty food bowls in parts of Asia.

This heightened awareness has led an increasing number of Americans and officials of foreign governments to wonder about the prospects for decreasing hunger in the world. To focus on this question, a good place to start is with the record of production in the past several years with special attention to how production has changed in recent years and the role of weather in these changes. Next, we focus on how consumption is dominated by the affluent, whether communist or capitalist, with the poor being the first to suffer in times of restricted overall food supplies. Then we examine the manner in which national markets are insulated from changes in production. The perspective accorded by these situations along with the longer-term record make it easier then to examine the prospects for the future.

There is general agreement that the dependence of the lower-income countries on imports will increase during the coming years. Substantial numbers of people in these countries will still have inadequate diets, however, because of the inadequacy of their incomes. Changes in national incomes necessary to substantially reduce malnutrition, say by one-half, would mean up to 50 percent larger consumption of food.

WHO PRODUCED WHAT

The Longer Run

In general, developed and developing countries have generated agricultural increases almost in step with each other. In both, food production in the mid-1970s was more than 30 percent above levels of the early 1960s and more than 50 percent above the mid-1950s (Figure 1-1).

Unfortunately, the uptrend in developing nations has been almost totally eclipsed by population growth. Over the past two decades food production per capita in the less developed regions increased slightly less than a half of 1 percent per year, compared to a 1½ percent rate of increase in the developed world.

The sharpest long-term increases in per capita food production among the developed countries occurred in Eastern Europe and the USSR. In both areas, per capita food production in the early 1970s has been more than 25 percent greater than in the early 1960s. Increases in the United States have been more modest, at least partially due to the programs restricting production. Production changes in 1975 altered these contrasts somewhat. USSR production dropped sharply while U.S. production reached a new record.

Africa's continuing decline in per capita production and accelerating dependence on food imports was further exacerbated by the devastating drought in

Figure 1-1. Food Production and Population, Developed and Less Developed Countries

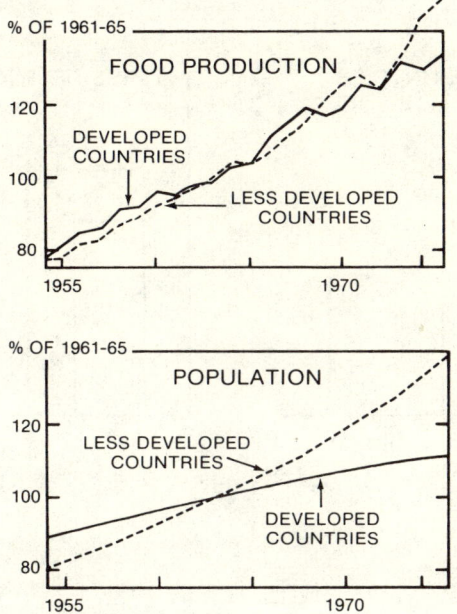
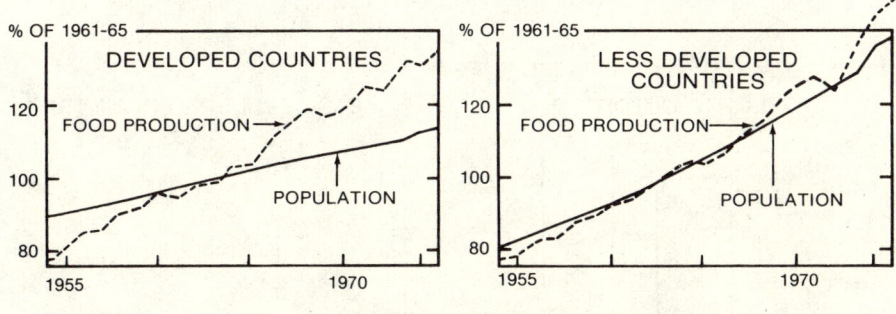

POPULATION EXCLUDES COMMUNIST ASIA

the Sahelian Zone. South America's progress is spotty. Chile has had serious problems, and Mexico has not lived up to forecasts of self-sufficiency. Brazil and Colombia have made considerable gains in food production.

Asia's green revolution improved that area's eating ability. But, even there, as well as in Africa and Latin America, weather variability remains a highly important factor by accentuating crop declines and exaggerating production peaks.

Outstanding as the green revolution has been in aggregate terms in the lower-income countries, it is important to recognize that the biggest green revolution has in fact occurred in the capitalist and communist developed

Figure 1-2. Grain Area (million hectares)

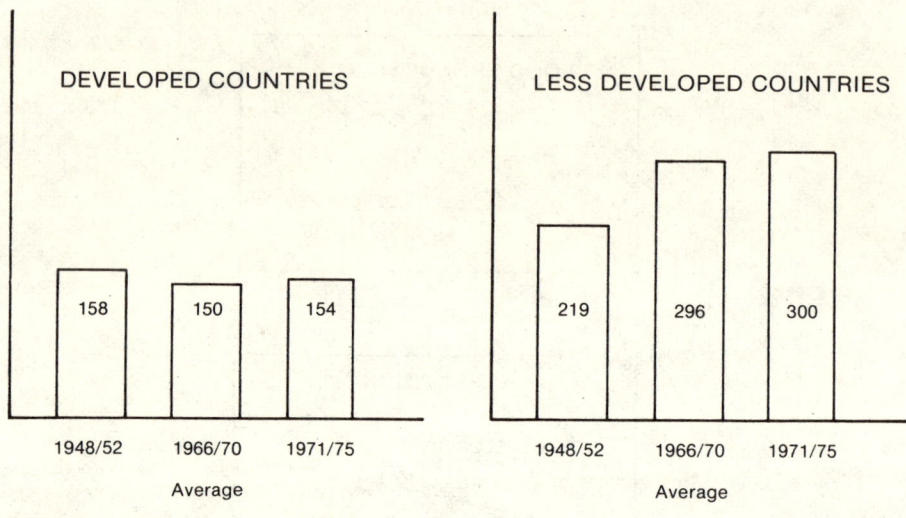

USDA

Figure 1-3. Grain Yields (metirc tons per hectares)

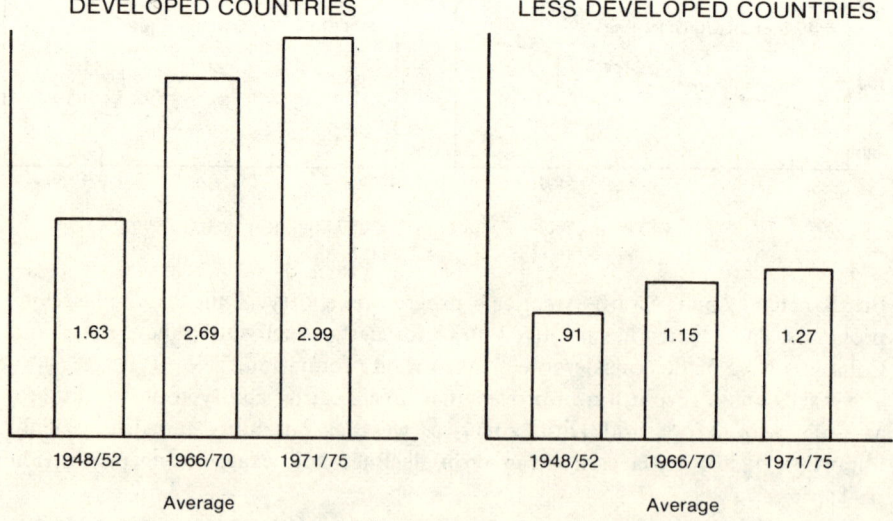

USDA

countries.[1] As indicated in Figures 1-2, 1-3, and 1-4, the area devoted to cereals in the developed countries has hardly changed since 1950. But yields have increased by over 80 percent, so that the 1971–75 average cereal production was 203 million tons above the 1948–52 average production. In contrast, the 180-million-ton increase in the developing countries was due to a combination of yields being up almost 40 percent and area increases of 40 percent. Most of these area increases had been realized by the late 1960s. Thus, while the developed countries increased cereal production by 200 million tons, the lower-income countries with twice as many inhabitants increased cereal production by only 180 million tons.

The Recent Years

On a world basis in most years since 1960, production has exceeded the previous year. Decreases in particular countries have been offset by increases in other countries. The drops in 1972/73 and 1974/75 therefore stand in sharp contrast to the usual (Figure 1-5). But one must be cautious in interpreting the meaning of these developments.

Any farmer in India, the USSR, or America knows that if you don't get rain, you don't get grain. But sometimes professional economists forget; there is

Figure 1-4. Total Grain Production (million metric tons)

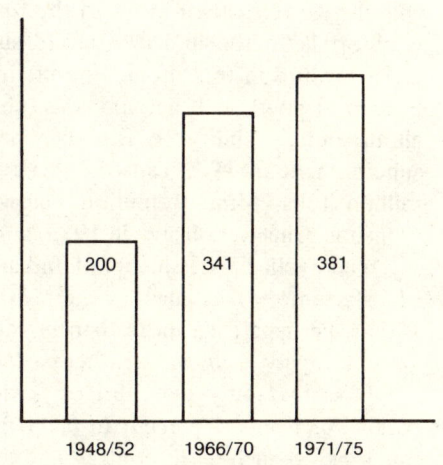

USDA

Figure 1-5. USSR Total Grain Production* (million metric tons)

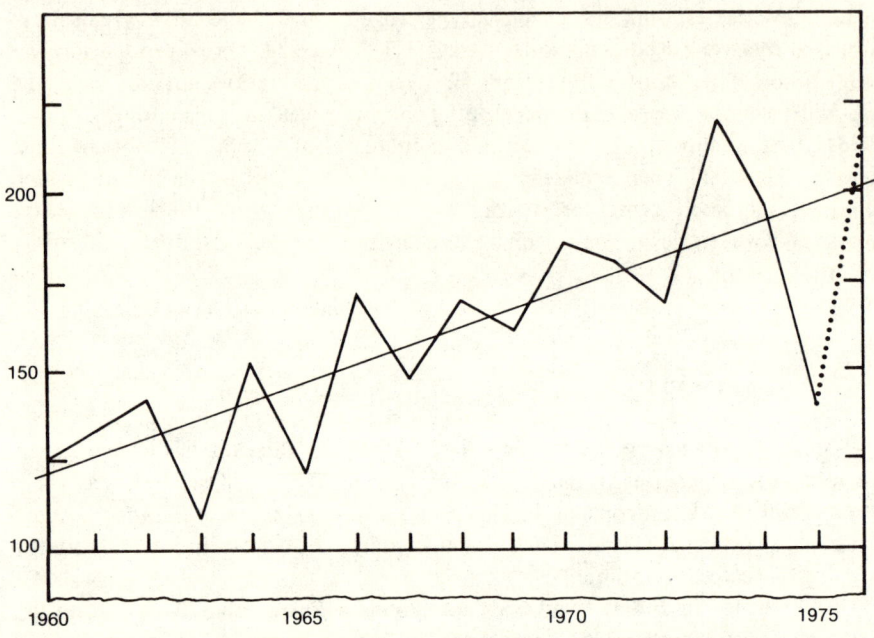

USDA

*Soviet total grain includes pulses as well as wheat, rough rice, the major coarse grains (corn, barley, rye, oats, and sorghum), and the minor coarse grains (millet, mixed grains, etc.)

a great tendency even for experts to assume that recent weather will continue or will change to fit their image of the future. Such thinking generated much of the famine talk in the mid-1960s, and subsequently the abundance talk when the green revolution took hold. For example, if the weather in 1970 had been poor instead of good, as it actually was, observers would not have been so confident about India's ability to feed her people. The poor monsoon in the Indian subcontinent in 1972 caused India's 1972/73 cereal production to drop to 96 million tons, some 9 million below the high of 1971/72. In contrast, the monsoon rains were heavy in 1975, and production reached a new record.

The cyclical assessments of Indian food needs are a special lesson for those of us attempting to guess at the prospective import requirements of the Soviet Union. Perhaps even more than in India, variations in Soviet cereal production are cut largely from the weather pattern. This situation is significantly related to the facts that only one-third of Soviet agricultural land lies south of the 48th parallel and only 1 percent of it lies in areas with an annual rainfall averaging as much as 28 inches. In contrast, almost all of the United States lies below the 48th parallel, and 60 percent of U.S. arable land averages at least 28 inches of rainfall annually. Little wonder, then, that there are frequent and wide changes in Soviet cereal production—such as the drop of 13 million tons in 1972, an increase of 54 million tons in 1973, with 1975 production 82 million tons or over one-third below the record 1973 production. A graph of performance since 1960 shows a marked long-term upward trend, but it is like the teeth of a sharp saw, with the jags almost annual (Figure 1-6).

In the United States wet weather in the spring of 1974 and then an early frost in the fall of the same year further aggravated the supply conditions. In contrast, in 1975 excellent weather over much of the United States permitted record harvests of wheat and near record feed grain production.

Drought in the Sahel over several years and in Argentina and Australia in 1972 added to the difficulties in 1972.

There were five important overall differences between 1972/73 and 1975/76:

- Grain price levels were considerably higher at the beginning of 1975/76 than they were in 1972/73.
- Grain production drops were more widespread in 1972/73 than in 1975/76. Aside from USSR, 1972/73 production was down 18 million tons from 1971/72, and in 1975/76 it was up 70 million tons from the previous year. The United States accounted for 10 of the 18 drop and 44 of the 70 increase.
- USSR in 1975/76 cut back on livestock production. In 1972/73 the Soviets maintained livestock production.

Figure 1-6. World Grain Production (million metric tons)

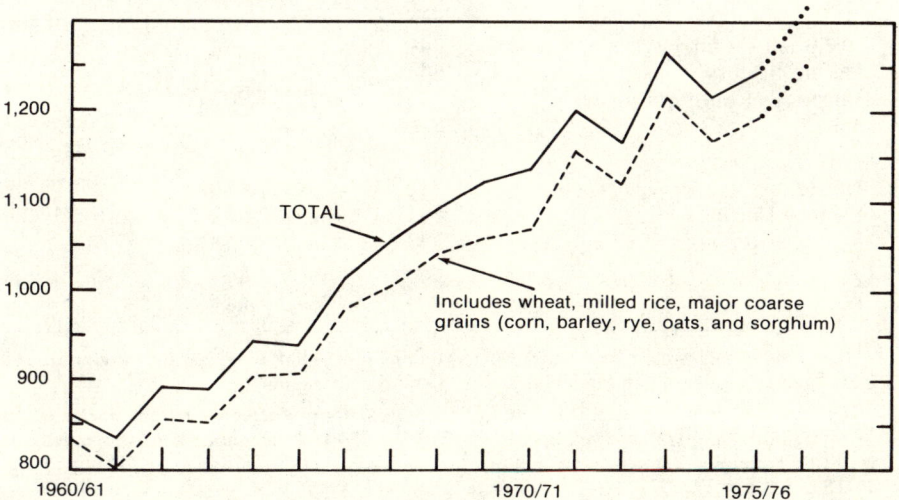

USDA

- Exchange rates were adjusting quickly in the 1972/73 period. They are still flexible in 1975/76, but their changes have been considerably smaller.
- Partially offsetting these conditions, grain stocks of major countries totaled 163 million tons in 1972. In 1975 they were 117 million tons.

WHO ATE IT

Millions of people remain inadequately fed. FAO estimated that the food intakes of over 400 million individuals of the lower-income countries do not meet the "maintenance cost of energy" [1, pp. 65-67].[2] As many as 30 percent of the populations in some areas are subject to food deficiencies.[3] FAO goes on to estimate that one-half of child deaths in the lower-income countries are "in some way attributable to malnutrition" [1, p. 67].[4]

Further, the gap between the lower-income countries and the developed countries has increased. From the early 1960s to the early 1970s per capita cereal consumption (direct and indirect) increased 100 pounds in the United States and 460 pounds in the USSR (Table 1-1).[5] The increases contrast with an increase of 15 pounds for the less developed countries as a whole. In fact, the

Table 1.1. Per capita cereal consumption[1] (in pounds)

	1960/61-1964/65 Average	1971/72-1975/76 Average	Percent Increase
Developed Countries	1,042	1,184	14
United States	1,644	1,750[2]	6
European Community-Nine[3]	893	1,001	12
Japan	500	610	22
Centrally Planned	668	856	28
USSR	1,170	1,634	40
Eastern Europe	1,231	1,634	33
People's Republic of China	398	488	23
Less Developed Countries	392	407	4
India	352	349	–

[1]Includes wheat, milled rice, major coarse grains (corn, barley, rye, oats, sorghum), and minor coarse grains (millet, buckwheat, mixed grains, other grains).

[2]The calculated increase in the United States was sharply affected by the inclusion of 1974/75. For example, the 3-year-average 1971/72-73/74 U.S. per capita cereal consumption was 1,889 pounds. Per capita consumption dropped to 1,476 pounds in 1974/75 and was 1,615 pounds in 1975/76.

[3]Figures for the cereal consumption of the European Community, and to a lesser extent of Japan, are reduced somewhat by the extensive use of noncereal grains for livestock feeding. Japan's figure is also reduced by the fact of extensive direct imports of meat, thus mitigating the livestock consumption of cereals within Japan.

Source: ERS, USDA.

increase in the USSR in the 11-year period was more than the average per capita consumption in the LDCs at the end of the period.[6]

Increased production has made it possible for the United States to become the supplier of large amounts of cereals to other countries. For example, from 1960/61-1964/65 to 1971/72-1975/76 average annual U.S. cereal production increased 67 million tons. Of that increase, 28 million tons were utilized domestically, with the remaining 39 million tons exported.

Wealth and income have had an overwhelming effect on distribution of food and therefore on the incidence of hunger in the world. It is the major explanation of why the developing nations, which include two-thirds of the world's population, eat only one-fourth of the world's protein, mostly in the forms of cereals, and why the pattern of cereal consumption corresponds to that shown in Table 1-1. In countries such as India, people consume less than 400 pounds of cereals per capita each year. On the other hand, in developed countries, large quantities of cereals are converted to protein. The billion people in these rich nations, with tastes for livestock products, use practically as much cereal for livestock feed as the 2 billion people in the low-income nations use directly as food.

While population growth has obviously been a significant factor in increasing world food demand, even more striking has been the sharp recent increase in per capita cereal consumption, especially in the centrally planned economies (Table 1-2).

Table 1.2. Cereal consumption increases from 1962/63 to 1973/74[1] (in million metric tons)

	Total[2]	Attributable to[3]	
		Change in Population	Change in Income
Developed Countries	83	38	45
United States	28	18	10
European Community-Nine	20	8	12
Japan	8	3	5
Centrally Planned	154	55	85
USSR	67	16	51
Eastern Europe	29	6	23
People's Republic of China	58	28	30
Less Developed Countries	92	81	11
India	20	20	0

[1] Mid-year of 5-year averages.

[2] Difference between 1960/61-1964/65 annual average and 1971/72-1975/76 annual average of total cereal consumption.

[3] Allocation of change in total consumption attributed to population and income based upon percentage changes in per capita consumption and percentage income changes. Joint effects were distributed proportionally.

Source: Based on data of Foreign Demand and Competition Division, ERS, USDA.

In considering effects of wealth and income on the distribution of food it is important to distinguish between short-run and long-run periods of time. When the world is dealing with food already produced or about to be produced—the short run—the distribution of income among rich and poor is then a primary determinant of the distribution of food. Regardless of the price level additional amounts are not produced in this time period. Thus incomes bid for that available. In contrast, the response of producers in changing their production over time is an important consideration in the long run. For example, production in the past has been responsive to demand flowing from incomes, especially in the developed countries. Technology, of course, has been a factor. But the responsiveness of production in the long run has also involved adjustments in the use of resources reflecting both private and public responses to the changing demands. Thus, in the long run, low incomes of low-income nations have been a primary determinant of low food consumption levels of these countries.

Diets may vary widely in terms of resource requirements but yet provide adequate nutrients. For example, expert observation of the PRC suggests that the Chinese population is receiving adequate nutrition and that few if any suffer from malnutrition or undernutrition [2]. However, the resource requirements indicated by per capita cereal consumption are sharply below those of the United States or the European Community. The egalitarian approach of the PRC to income distribution and food consumption minimizes the possibility of individuals using income and wealth in commanding a diet requiring the conversion of grain into livestock products. This situation contrasts sharply with the relationships among income, wealth, and nutrition descriptive of most other countries. In turn, PRC per capita cereal consumption is only 500 pounds, with limited if any nutritional problems. In comparison, many other countries have average per capita consumption considerably higher, yet substantial parts of their population experience malnutrition and undernourishment because of uneven distribution.

Political Economic Decisions

Production to an extent, but especially consumption, has been affected by important political decisions such as the United States floating of the U.S. dollar.

In August 1971 important steps were taken to bring about significant realignment of currencies. The devaluation of the U.S. dollar mitigated the effects of the nominal dollar increases in 1972 and later years of the prices of U.S. farm products on the consumers of many importing countries (Figure 1-7). This was especially true when the changes in exchange rates were reflected in consumer prices of these countries. Even when this was not the case, the effect on the actions of finance ministers in allocating foreign exchange should not be overlooked. The Indian situation shows the opposite effect as the value of the

Figure 1-7. U.S. HW Wheat Import Unit Value, North Sea Ports—U.S. Dollars and DM Germany

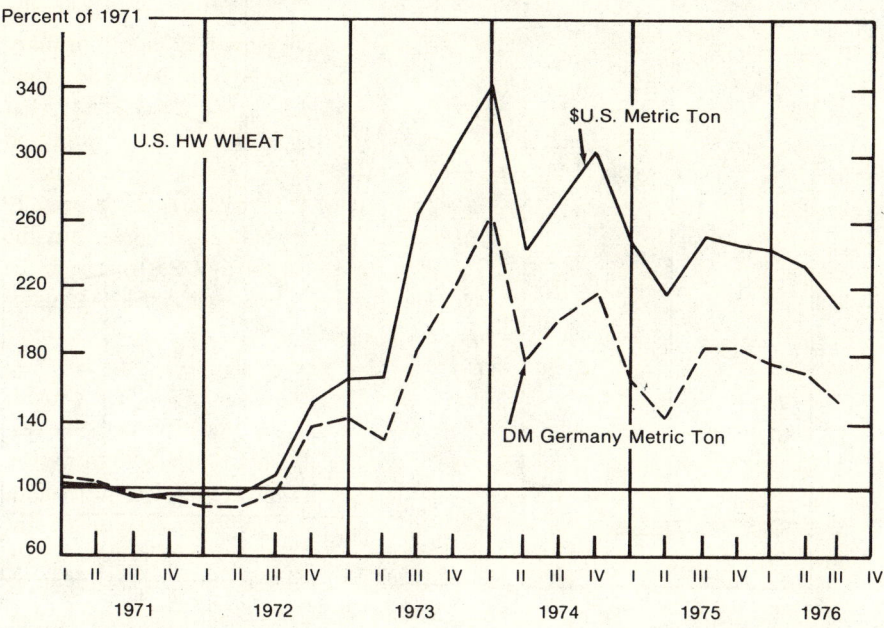

USDA

rupee relative to the dollar deteriorated (Figure 1-8). As a result, in early 1975 U.S. wheat import unit values in terms of U.S. dollars were some 200 to 220 percent of the 1971 levels. But in contrast, in terms of rupees they were 300 percent of 1971 levels.

Traditionally, when the Soviets came up short on production, they tightened their belts and steeled themselves to wait out the shortage. Some of the internal adjustments have included large-scale livestock slaughter. But not in 1972. Winter-kill and dry midsummer weather severed the Soviets from their cereal harvest expectations. In an effort to maintain food consumption and livestock production, they purchased some 30 million tons of cereals, 18 million of them from the United States for delivery that year and the next.

Similar political economic decisions were made by the USSR in 1975 as its cereal crops dropped to 140 million tons. However, indications are that the USSR this time also slaughtered livestock in order to balance consumption needs with availabilities.

The USSR's decision to protect diets in 1972 was felt worldwide by both rich and poor. When the Soviets purchased almost one-fifth of the total U.S. wheat supply (production and stocks) in the 1972/73 crop year, supplies normally available to others dropped sharply. Nations and people reacted by

Figure 1-8. U.S. Wheat Import Unit Value, Indian Ports—U.S. Dollars and Rupees

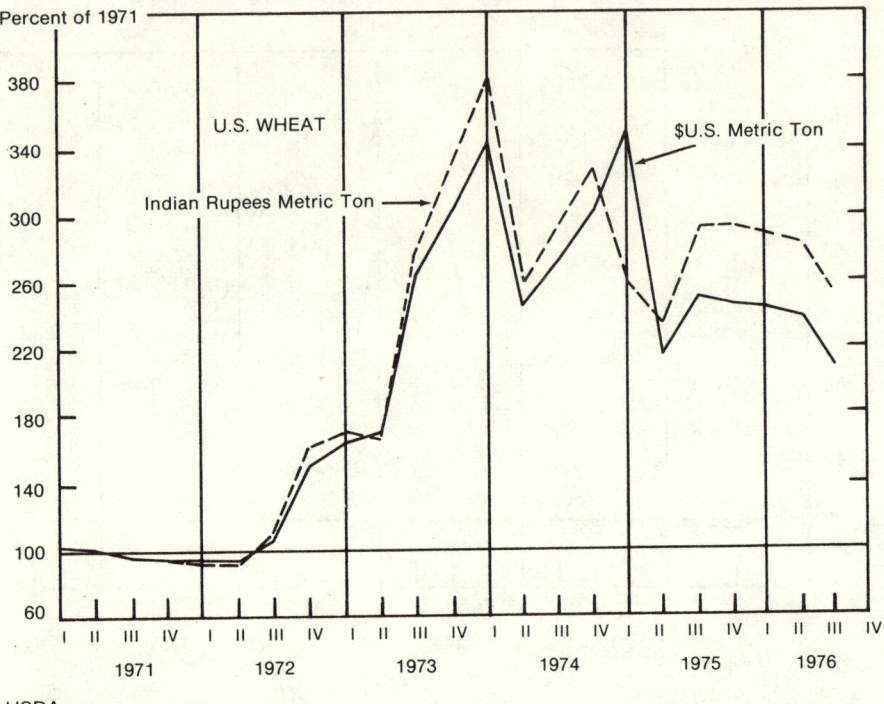

USDA

bidding up the price of the remaining wheat, the more aggressively because currencies of Japan and several other commercial importers of U.S. foodstuffs were worth substantially more in terms of dollars as a result of successive dollar devaluations.

In contrast, the limited wealth and low income of poor countries again determined how well they could compete in food purchasing. In times of sharply increased demand or curtailed supplies impacts can be harsh. For example, the 1972-73 Indian food grain crop dropped from 105 million to 96 million tons. In the tug-of-war between maintaining diets and saving foreign exchange, diets lost and food prices were allowed to increase. In some areas, food grain rations were cut in half in fair-price food shops, which serve many of the lowest-income Indians. Per capita calorie availability dropped toward the critical levels of the mid-1960s.

INSULATION OF DOMESTIC MARKETS

In considering the future, the tumultuous developments of the four years 1972-75 as well as the longer-run relationships of production and consumption must be contemplated in the context of continued insulation of internal markets of rich countries from the effects of changes in food production in their own country and in other countries. For the combination of these factors has brought about a significant cutback in international food aid and a new politicizing of food.

Insulation of Internal Markets

Most countries insulate their domestic prices and food supplies from changes in prices and supplies in international markets and from changes in internal production. The devices are many in number. Trade, exports and imports, is used by many countries including the United States. An example of an importer is Egypt. There, rice farm prices are held relatively low through importations of increasingly larger quantities of wheat.[7] The European Community uses variable levies to insulate internal prices from fluctuations of international prices. Variable export subsidies are also utilized. Taxes on exports are used in Argentina, Burma, and Thailand. Quotas and in some cases embargoes on export are employed in Brazil. In Canada, the Canadian Wheat Board decides whether to offer wheat for sale and at what price. Contracts are not made unless supplies are considered to be available in sufficient amounts that desired domestic prices can be realized. Thus the Canadian actions add up to export quotas, but they are generally not referred to as quotas.

The situation for the United States has become unique. For many years through the 1950s and 1960s the domestic U.S. market was insulated. Export

Figure 1-9. Cereals Fed to Livestock: United States, USSR, Japan, and EC (million metric tons)

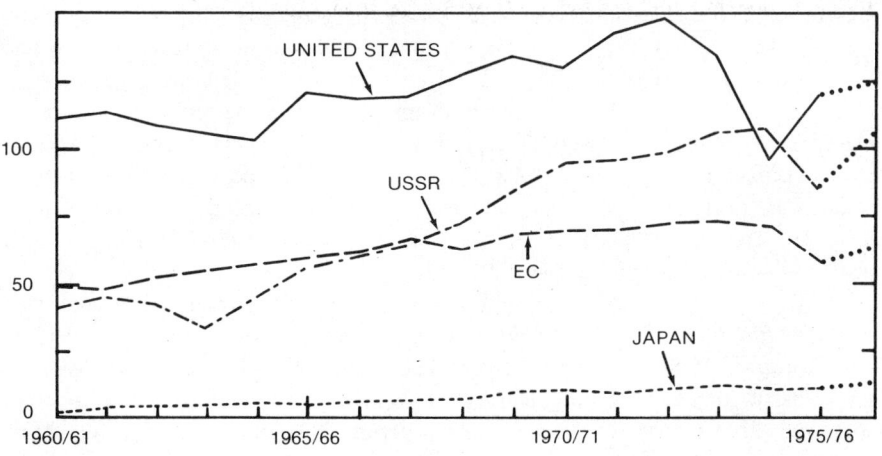

USDA

subsidies, restrictions on land use, price support, and stockpiling of cereals were utilized to moderate price swings nationally and internationally. This moderation also tempered changes in livestock production and consumption of cereals as feed for livestock.

This situation changed completely. Stocks held by the government were eliminated, and land once held out of production was freed for production. In general, any amount of food commodities could be purchased by private traders for export from the United States. Exceptions to this approach involved the export limitation on soybeans and oilseeds during July-September 1973, the fall-of-1974 cutbacks on USSR purchases, and fall-of-1975 arrangements with the USSR for upper limits on its purchases.

USSR prices paid to state and collective farms were increased in 1970. They have not been changed since. Retail prices for bread and meat were increased in 1962 and have not been changed since that time.

One adjustment was in feeding of livestock. The sharp downward adjustment in cereals fed to livestock in the United States in 1973/74 and 1974/75 contrasts sharply with continued increases through 1974/75 in the USSR and relative stability in Japan and the European Community (Figure 1-9).

Food Aid

Recent upward pressure on prices and the potential to export all available cereals in excess of U.S. domestic needs brought significant changes in P.L. 480 programs. Quantities of 1974 food aid dropped significantly. Because of higher prices, value dropped much less. Quantities in fiscal year 1975 increased, but were still significantly below levels of earlier years.

Reduction of international food sharing contrasted sharply with domestic food sharing. The food programs—child nutrition, special milk, and food stamp programs—in the fiscal year ending July 1, 1976, were at record levels and represented almost three-fourths of the Department of Agriculture budget.

P.L. 480 in the past has been a program for U.S. agriculture. For many years, P.L. 480 programs were consistent with commercial objectives for agricultural exports. They permitted charging lower prices to poor countries without undercutting prices to the richer countries. Through adjusting terms—use of local currency, credit, and commercial sales—effective prices were tailored to the customer's financial and security status.

With strong demand, negligible stocks, and high prices, it is not now advantageous to U.S. agriculture or commercial trade objectives to move significant amounts of food under P.L. 480. Therefore, political support for food aid has waned somewhat, although efforts have been undertaken to revitalize the program. But because of the large and growing U.S. import bill for petroleum supplies and the potential of commercial agricultural exports to ease the burden of that bill, concessional sales or grants in a U.S. food aid program will probably not provide the volumes that they have in the past. The significant food gap in developing countries remains to be filled by other means.[8]

The world will need to evaluate trade-offs between food aid and other economic assistance. Most developed countries and international assistance agencies have limited but significant resources for assisting low-income countries. They have never had to closely evaluate trade-offs between food aid and other forms of assistance. In the United States, these kind of considerations could be avoided since the appropriations flowed from different Congressional committees to different executive departments, and there was a strong constituency for food aid based on U.S. farm interests. The international assistance agencies did not finance substantial amounts of food aid, simply because it was in the U.S. self-interest to finance and implement a program of food assistance as a major adjunct to U.S. agricultural programs. This division was complementary. Resources for international assistance could be used for items other than food, and the Department of Agriculture could carry food aid costs.

It is time for international agencies such as the World Bank to ask, "Should food aid be made an integral part of economic assistance programs?" And it is time for the lower-income countries to ask, "Should aid proceeds in times of food shortages be used to buy items such as turbines or to buy grain?"

Food assistance can be a form of investment.[9] Proceeds from the sale of food provided on a concessional basis—through P.L. 480 or other assistance programs such as AID and IBRD—can be used for investment in irrigation facilities, locally made machines, and production facilities. Thus food assistance can lead to productive investments in much the same way that hard-currency loans can be used to provide foreign-made machines, and probably with greater employment and productivity effects in the developing countries. These choices have not been faced because of a combination of institutional factors. P.L. 480 funds were appropriated to the USDA. U.S. agriculture was glad for concessional markets, and thus USDA did not press AID or other assistance agencies to assume responsibility for food aid programs. To have done so may have resulted in less food aid and a different mix. Now higher prices will require more difficult and complex choices by all.

New Politicizing

The conditions of the 4 years 1972–75 have heightened the awareness of food problems among the rich and among the poor, and have led to increased pressure for political decisions about food.

People and governments say they are unhappy with food prices and distribution. Domestically, U.S. government agencies and economic groups which heretofore had paid little attention to food policies are aggressive participants in the debate. International meetings about food attract many participants other than representatives of traditional food and agriculture units of government.

Internationally the 1974 World Food Conference focused world attention on the food needs of the low-income countries and established new institutions to give greater attention to food problems of these countries and to encourage political decisions affecting prices and distribution of food.

Détente with the USSR and the People's Republic of China has added another set of political dimensions to food. In both countries government units conduct the international trade. Political as well as economic considerations undoubtedly influence the timing and amount of their contracts for food imports and food exports. These considerations are part of the total political framework in which world food problems must be examined.

Political decisions have always affected domestic economies and international markets. In some cases effects are direct, as when governments buy and sell commodities and set trade subsidies and tariffs. In the United States restraints on meat imports, marketing agreements, and the food stamp program reflect political decisions affecting food prices and distribution.

Significant efforts have been made over the years to integrate politics with economics in international food trade. The General Agreement on Tariffs and Trade (GATT), for example, has focused on national trade barriers and the overriding influence of domestic food policies on international trade. The International Wheat Agreement, while criticized in many ways, provided a legitimate framework in which the United States and Canada, and to some extent Australia, could cooperate in making government decisions regarding international wheat trade in the 1960s. The current International Wheat Agreement offers opportunities for exchange of information and consultation on matters related to international trade of wheat.

There have been periods in the past, such as in the mid-1960s, when there was increased concern about world food problems with subsequent diminishment of these concerns. Thus it is reasonable to ask, "Is the present situation fundamentally different, and will the current politicizing be more sustained?" One cannot be sure, but there is a greater chance that it is different and the politicizing will be more sustained.

One reason for this expectation is the prospective uneasy balance between supply and demand for food, even though the crisis conditions of 1973-75 will not continue on and on and per capita supplies of LDCs will resume an upward trend. But the gains will be modest, and the masses of low-income people in these countries will experience only limited improvements in nutrition. Further, supplies in developed and developing countries are bound to be affected both by weather variation and by energy prices and availabilities. Levels of demand for imports are highly uncertain. The unpredictable decisions of countries such as USSR and China are involved.

The answer is associated also with the international context in which political decisions will have to be made—new discontinuities in the relationships among nations and challenges to the present situation in which wealth and income overwhelmingly affect the incidence of hunger in the world. These factors have the potential to sustain the current concerns for food and to influence the future more than has been the case previously.

THE FUTURE

Prospects for Great Instability

During the 1950s and 1960s large U.S. grain stockpiles had a moderating influence on price fluctuations—nationally and internationally. As international shortages developed, the availability of U.S. stocks dampened price changes in the international market while discouraging increases in domestic prices. In times of general surplus, the United States chose to stockpile large portions of its domestic production rather than permit prices to drop so that all production would be consumed domestically, exported, or stored by private industry. It also withheld land from production rather than accept lower prices, larger export subsidies, or larger government stocks.

Now U.S. government stocks have essentially disappeared. And owners of land that was once held out of production are not restricted in the use of that land. Thus two of the important food reserves have been wiped out, and major policy thrusts are expanded food production but the avoidance of accumulating government stocks.

Livestock has also been an important food reserve and an adjustor of U.S. food supplies. A portion of livestock production depends on forages grown on land not suitable for food production. Some is also dependent on wastes and other materials that are not appropriate as human food. "Flexibility" is mainly associated with that portion of livestock production dependent on products that can alternatively be utilized directly as food or that are produced with resources that could be alternatively used in the production of products consumed directly as food.

Adjustments of food supplies are facilitated by livestock, therefore, through the increases of livestock production in years of expanded crop production and decreases in livestock production in years of contraction of crop production. Further, food supplies are supplemented with heavy rates of slaughter during periods of contraction of livestock numbers and vice versa when herds are expanded. The 1974-75 contraction of livestock feeding in the United States illustrates this flexibility. Livestock feed consumption dropped precipitously when high cereal prices reflecting scarcity of supplies in relation to national and international demand were not matched by changes in livestock product prices. Adjustments of these types can be painful and often have occurred with considerable time lags.

Without comparable reliance on market prices the Soviets have also depended on livestock to adjust to changing availabilities of food. This was especially the case previous to 1972. Imports of cereals were utilized in 1972-73 to offset domestic production shortfall so that livestock numbers were not adversely affected. However, in 1975-76 livestock slaughter, as well as substantial imports, were required to accommodate to the sharply reduced cereal production.

U.S. farm product prices are expected to be unstable. Factors accounting for this expectation are (1) the lack of government stocks, (2) the direct interfacing of the U.S. and international markets, (3) the price adjustments necessary to stimulate changes in livestock production, and (4) the certainty that weather will change from year to year and therefore U.S. crop production and import needs of other countries will change from year to year.

Prices will allocate U.S. supplies available and guide U.S. resource uses. In years of shortages higher prices will discourage U.S. consumption, exports, and storage, as well as stimulate production in future years. In years of abundance, lower prices will stimulate adjustments whereby supplies are consumed domestically (as food and feed), exported, or stored to be used in another time period. Under these conditions stocks won't be as large as they were in the 1950s and 1960s, and the variability of prices will likely be greater.

The Economic Gap Will Widen

Two points of overwhelming importance emerge in most projections of prospective food conditions in the world. First, the role of the United States as the major supplier of food in international markets is expected to expand. Second, the dependence of the lower-income countries on food imports is anticipated by 1985 to be 2 to 3 times the 1970 level. The two points add up to heavy dependence by the developing countries on the United States as a supplier of food.

The projections for the United States anticipate continued advancement of agricultural technology, as well as policy pressures to use exports of food to help pay for imports which underpin the American standard of living. Moreover, levels of production will depend substantially on returns to farmers. If farm product profits remain at recent high levels, further expansion of production is likely to occur as land not now in production is utilized to grow crops and forages and new technologies are adopted more readily in order to capture these potential profits.

In the poor countries, increases in food production will likely keep up with population and perhaps gain on it. Some areas, such as Brazil, will be able to expand the area devoted to crops; others will develop their cropping capacity through irrigation; hopefully most will have improved technology. However, nutritional improvement efforts, income growth, the use of cereals to produce livestock products, and above all population are expected to push demand ahead of local production increases; hence the prospect that the poor countries will increase their dependence on imports of food, especially cereals, and markedly

Table 1.3. FAO and USDA cereal projections[1] (in million metric tons)

	FAO Base (1969-71)	FAO 1985	USDA Base (1969-71)	USDA 1985
World				
Demand	1,207	1,725	1,062.6	1,502 to 1,644
Production	1,239	NS[2]	1,081.8	1,504 to 1,646
Balance[3]	+32	NS	+19.2	+2 to +2
Developing Countries				
Demand	590	929	466.6	678 744
Production	585	853	443.1	626 721
Balance	−5	−76	−23.5	−22 −78
Developing Market Economies				
Demand	386	629	299.7	467 529
Production	370	544	279.2	419 513
Balance	−16	−85	−20.5	−16 −72
Asian Centrally Planned Countries[4]				
Demand	204	300	166.9	212 214
Production	215	309	163.9	208 207
Balance	+11	+9	−3.0	−4 −7
Developed Countries[5]				
Demand	617	796	596.0	823 900
Production	654	NS	638.7	877 972
Balance	+37	NS	42.7	24 79

[1]The data for FAO and USDA are not comparable because FAO carries rice as paddy and USDA carries rice as milled.
[2]NS–not shown.
[3]Imbalances for USDA between demand and production in base are due to stock buildup, timing of shipments, and missing data on a number of small importers. Projected equilibrium does not allow for building or reducing stocks.
[4]FAO Asian centrally planned includes the People's Republic of China and other Asian centrally planned countries (North Korea, North Vietnam, etc.), while USDA includes only the People's Republic of China.
[5]Includes the USSR and Eastern Europe.
Note: Detail may not sum to total because of rounding.
Source: [3, p. 35].

from the United States to the extent they can pay for them or they are provided on a concessional basis. It is in this context that the specific estimates of demand, production, and trade merit attention.

FAO projections anticipate a net deficit of 76 million tons of cereal for the developing countries in 1985 [3]. In comparison, USDA projections range from 22 to 78 million tons. The difference depends heavily on alternative income growth rates and on efforts of the developing countries to increase their food production (Table 1-3).

Nutritional Gap

But regardless of the particular scenario considered as most likely, the prospective conditions will mean that substantial numbers of people in these countries will still have inadequate diets in 1985. The most optimistic of the FAO and four USDA scenarios in terms of economic demand, as well as production, would involve a 15 percent increase in *per capita* cereal consumption from the 1969-71 base period to 1985 for the developing (market) economies, even though their *total* cereal consumption would increase from 20 to 60 percent. Specific estimates of the absolute numbers of people in 1985 that would have inadequate diets were not included in either the FAO or the USDA studies. However, the 15 percent estimate, along with the prospective increase in population, suggests that the *number* of hungry people in 1985 will be at least as great as it is today.

In the base period 1969-71, FAO estimates that "there is a very high probability that over 400 million individuals have [in 1970] available food in a quantity insufficient to meet their needs" [1].

The specific estimates were 434 million in the developing market economies. In making the estimates, FAO set the critical limit at 1,900 to 2,000 calories per young adult male. These are roughly equal to "the maintenance cost of energy" (1.5 times the basal metabolic rate). Conceptually the maintenance cost assures constant body energy in nonfasting subjects engaged in minimum level of activity needed for dressing, washing, and eating, but not working. Further, the basal metabolic rates utilized are based on healthy populations.[10] Thus "maintenance," "minimum level of activity," and "healthy" concepts suggest that the FAO estimates are conservative (Table 1-3).

FAO concludes that "one-half of child deaths are in some way attributable to malnutrition"; 200 million living children suffer from malnutrition; and as many as one out of three of some populations are malnourished. How much cereal would it take to correct these deficiencies?

One approach to this kind of question reflected in USDA and FAO studies is the "control" approach. Assuming that 500 additional calories per day for each of 460 million malnourished in the world would correct their malnutrition, USDA estimated that 25 million tons of cereals would be needed [3]. However, such an estimate assumes that the 25 million tons would reach the malnourished and *only* the malnourished. FAO made a similar estimate using 250 calories and therefore came up with a 12-million-ton estimate [1]. But the likelihood is extremely low that this type of distribution could be carried out in the developing market economies. In fact, if such distribution could be accomplished, the developing economies could go a long way to meeting current deficiencies by redistributing the supplies they have now.

Another approach, the "income" approach, is more consistent with the organization of most of these economies. Improvements in nutrition come about through higher incomes. This approach assumes that relative income increases are distributed throughout their economies and, in turn, result in higher food consumption levels by those who now enjoy adequate diets as well as those who suffer from inadequate diets. This approach requires large increases of income and, in turn, large increases in grain consumption. A primary consideration is that income and related consumption increases are realized not only by those

Table 1.4. Nutrition and cereal situation, less developed countries, actual and "alternative," 1969/70[1]

	Actual	Alternative[1]
Private Consumption Expenditures per Capita	$155	$385
Population below Lower Nutritional Limit[2]	25% 434 million	13% 226 million
Total Cereal Consumption (annual) by Less Developed Countries	328 million metric tons[3]	414 and 586 million metric tons[4]

[1] Assumed situation in which incidence of malnutrition is one-half that incidence estimated by FAO.

[2] Source of nutritional inadequacy estimates for 1970 [1].

[3] 1969/70-1971/72 average.

[4] "Estimates" were based on the assumptions that (1) average per capita income levels of each major region of the less developed countries were equal to the actual average income of Latin America, and that (2) in turn, the incidence of malnutrition in all major regions of the less developed countries would be equal to the incidence in Latin America, 13 percent.

The 414-million-ton estimate was derived with income elasticities of demand for cereals for food and for feed equal to the income elasticities for "Latin America other than Argentina" presently incorporated in the Grain Oilseed Livestock projection model of ERS. The relatively lower man-land ratios of Latin America in relation to other LDC countries suggest that this estimate is conservative.

The 586-million-ton estimate was derived with income elasticities for cereals for food and for feed equal to the income elasticities for the respective regions presently incorporated in the Grain Oilseed Livestock projection model. These elasticities were generally higher than those applicable to "Latin America other than Argentina." These elasticities gave rise to relatively high per capita consumption levels in a few major regions.

The midpoint between the two estimates is perhaps a more realistic estimate than either 414 or 586. It would imply consumption responses to changes in income midway between the estimated "Latin America less Argentina" income elasticities and the higher income elasticities judged to exist at the present time for these individual regions.

presently with inadequate diets but also by those with adequate diets. In fact, in many countries the largest part of the increases in cereal consumption would be associated with those with adequate diets at the start. Also, significant parts of the increases would be for feed for livestock demanded by the higher incomes.

Estimates of the increase in cereal consumption necessary to reduce malnutrition substantially via an income approach are speculative. Rough estimates can be developed, however, using historic income and cereal consumption levels along with elasticities of demand for cereals used in making projections of the future.

Even with allowance for sizable error, the resource implications are overwhelming. For example, to have reduced by this approach in the early 1970s the incidence of malnutrition in the major less developed regions of the world from 26 percent to 13 percent (the level of Latin America) would have required an additional 86 to 258 million tons of cereals per year (Table 1-4).[11] Under this scenario 13 percent (226 million) of the population of the LDCs would still have been malnourished. Pointing up the resource implications, income levels 2 to 4 times the actual would have been required for specific regions and countries of the less developed countries.

Looking to the future, the present high population growth rates and present rates of income growth suggest that an even larger amount of cereals would be required to bridge the gap between what is likely to be the case and a targeted 13 percent with malnutrition. A target of no hungry people implies an even greater resource requirement.[12]

These type of resource requirements are the central reasons why reliance solely on income growth will mean that many hungry people will be with us always. In turn, the estimates point up the need to give emphasis to income growth but also the great importance of slower population growth, greater equity among and within nations, and substantial increases in food production and development programs that benefit the poor relative to the rich if the number that are inadequately fed today is to be substantially reduced within this century.

NOTES

1. "Green revolution" has been used frequently in recent years to refer to the introduction and adoption in lower-income countries of new varieties of cereals responsive to fertilizer and improved management techniques.

2. Maintenance cost of energy was defined as 1.5 times the basal metabolic rate. These are generally less than the requirements associated with a moderately active reference man.

3. See Linda Haverberg, "Individual Needs: Nutritional Guidelines for Policy?" in this volume for a discussion of why malnutrition problems are not due to food and nutrition inadequacies alone and of some of the inadequacies of nutritional standards.

4. These estimates do not include the Asian centrally planned economies.

5. Trade has been an important means of upgrading the diets in many developed countries and of maintaining diets in the developing countries.

6. The calculated increase in the United States was sharply affected by the inclusion of 1974/75. For example, the 3-year-average 1971/72–1973/74 U.S. per capita cereal consumption was 1889 pounds. Per capita consumption dropped to 1,476 pounds in 1974/75 and was 1,615 pounds in 1975/76.

7. See "World Food Situation and Prospects to 1985" [3] for a more extensive discussion of prices in lower-income countries.

8. See Lawrence Witt, "Food Aid, Commercial Exports, and the Balance of Payments," in this volume for a discussion of how costs of food aid have increased and how this affects the willingness of food-exporting countries to provide food aid.

9. See P.L. 94-161, International Development and Food Assistance Act of 1975, for legislative recognition of the potential utilization of P.L. 480 programs to bring about needed investments.

10. See Linda Haverberg, "Individual Needs: Nutritional Guidelines for Policy?" in this volume for a discussion of FAO nutritional allowances.

11. See footnote 4 to Table 1-4 for the description of the methodology utilized in developing this range of estimates. Obviously, the method has significant implications for the specific quantity estimates.

12. See Hon. Edwin M. Martin, "Focus on Nutrition: Who Should Pay for What?" in this volume for a discussion of ways in which at least limited nutritional improvements can be enhanced without substantial changes in income.

REFERENCES

[1] United Nations, "Assessment of the World Food Situation: Present and Future," E/Conf. 65/3, United Nations World Food Conference, November 1974.

[2] National Academy of Sciences, "Plant Studies in the People's Republic of China: A Trip Report of the American Plant Studies Delegation," Washington, D.C., 1975.

[3] Economic Research Service, USDA. "World Food Situation and Prospects to 1985," FAER-98, December 1974.

 **Reconsidering the famine relief argument**

Peter Singer

I first wrote about the obligations of the affluent to those in danger of starvation in November 1971.[1] At that time there was one major crisis on which the attention of the world—or rather, that small part of the world that is concerned with people in faraway countries—had focused: Bangladesh. In refugee camps across the Indian border, 10 million people were subsisting on meager rations that seemed sure to run out before the people could return to their farms; the affluent nations, though possessed of ample stocks of grain, failed to fulfill the requests for assistance made by the Indian government and the World Bank. It was this situation that made me think that my views about the obligations of the affluent to the starving were worth putting into print.

That particular crisis was resolved dramatically by Indian military intervention, and is now history. In the 4 years that have passed we have had major famines in the African Sahel, and in Ethiopia, as well as a number of minor ones; but, fortunately, as I write now there is no single famine of the magnitude of that which was threatening 4 years ago in Bangladesh. Nevertheless, the world food situation is no less urgent now than it was then. Now we face, not isolated crises, but the prospect of protracted food shortages affecting two-thirds of the world's population. In the underdeveloped countries food production, which kept narrowly ahead of population growth in the fifties and sixties, has now fallen behind the unchecked population increase: in other words, the amount of food available per head has been reduced.[2] Sharply increased fertilizer prices make further reductions probable. Moreover, recent poor harvests in the U.S. and USSR, coupled with increased demand, have meant that the ability of the developed countries to make up the shortfall with gifts or cheap sales of surplus grain has been reduced. The great grain stocks of the United States have virtually gone, and the arable land that until 1974 was held out of production by U.S. government programs is now back in use.[3]

The time is appropriate, therefore, for a review of my earlier article, taking account of the altered situation with which we now have to deal, as well as some objections that have been urged against what I wrote.

It will be best to begin with a brief restatement of the argument, which, essentially, I still hold.

I start from three premises, two moral, the other factual. The first moral premise is that starvation is a bad thing—that is, that a world in which no people are starving is better than a world in which some people are starving, and a world in which few people are starving is, other things being equal, better than a world in which many people are starving. I don't think it is necessary to offer any defense for this premise, other than to point to the suffering, destruction of capacities and abilities, and finally loss of life that starvation involves.

The second moral premise has two versions: the weak version is that if we can prevent something bad happening without sacrificing anything of moral significance, we ought to do so; the strong version is that if we can prevent something bad happening without sacrificing anything of comparable moral importance, we ought to do so. I think the strong version is defensible, and I shall defend it shortly; if so, the weaker version is of course correct too, as far as it goes. I presented both versions only because the weaker version, modest as it is, is sufficient for a far-reaching moral critique of the way of life accepted almost without question by citizens of the affluent nations.

The factual premise is that we in the affluent nations can do something to reduce the number of people starving in the world. We can do something because we are affluent. This means that we have income that we can dispose of without giving up the basic necessities of life. We can, if we choose, use this income to reduce starvation elsewhere in the world. When I wrote my earlier article, it seemed to me quite obvious that this was the case, and I still think it true; but certain objections now seem to me to require more discussion than they did before, and I shall consider these in due course.

From these premises, the conclusion that follows (using the strong version of the second premise) is that we ought to prevent as much starvation as we can, up to the point at which we can do no more without sacrificing something of comparable moral importance. This means that instead of spending our available income on new clothes, cars, dinners in expensive restaurants, or other items that cannot be compared, in moral importance, to saving someone from starving to death, we ought to give our money to those who can most effectively use it to prevent starvation.[4]

If this is sound, the conventional moral attitude to helping the poor must be rejected. In these circumstances giving away money is not an act of charity, the doing of which is praiseworthy, but the omission of which is not to be condemned; it is a moral requirement, the fulfilling of which is as important as the fulfilling of the more commonly recognized moral requirements, like those against injuring others, stealing, cheating, and so on.

Henceforth, I shall refer to this argument as "The Famine Relief Argument." This argument is, of course, based on a consequentialist view of morality.

The second premise states that the fact that an action would prevent something bad happening is a reason for doing that action. Thus this premise directs our attention to the foreseeable consequences of our acts, and makes these consequences relevant in deciding whether the act is right or wrong. (Most consequentialists, including utilitarians, would add that the fact that an action would bring about something good is also a reason for doing it; but since this claim goes beyond the argument we are now considering, there is no need to discuss it.)

Now it seems to me very obvious that the foreseeable consequences of our acts are relevant to their moral assessment, and that the fact that an action would prevent something bad happening is a reason for doing it; I hope it seems equally obvious to others. Yet there have been moralists who have rejected even such mild forms of consequentialism and have asserted that the whole of morality lies either in the conformity of our actions to certain moral rules—rules like "don't lie," "don't kill innocent human beings," "don't steal," etc.—or else in the accordance of our actions with certain principles, of which the principle of justice has figured most prominently.

So we need to consider two kinds of objection to the Famine Relief Argument: those which reject the consequentialist premise from which it starts, and those which accept at least this limited form of consequentialism, but urge reasons of a consequentialist type against its conclusion.

I shall start with the nonconsequentialist objections.

The most popular alternative to utilitarianism today is a moral theory based on, or giving considerable weight to, some principle of justice.[5] Some theories of justice may be regarded as consequentialist theories insofar as the acceptability of a moral rule or institution (if not of an individual act) depends on its tendency to produce a given result that is said to be just, like a more equal distribution of income, or, as John Rawls's theory proposes, an improvement in the position of the worst-off group.[6] The general principles of these consequentialist theories of justice are compatible with, and in some cases even entail, the Famine Relief Argument, so it is not necessary to consider these views in detail.[7] Instead we should consider theories of justice which are not consequentialist, since they do give rise to objections to the Famine Relief Argument.

Perhaps the most widely held nonconsequentialist view of justice is that it involves giving people what they merit, or deserve. It may be held as a corollary that we ought not to give to those who are not deserving, since to do so is to undercut the value of what is given to those who are deserving.

This view of justice does not imply that we should abandon the starving to their fate; only that we must first separate the deserving starving from the undeserving starving, and restrict our aid to the former. What are the criteria for this separation? The Victorians, who seemed more at home with the notion of the "deserving poor" than we are today, thought that the industrious, the thrifty, and those left destitute through accidents or other circumstances beyond their control were deserving; while the lazy, the spendthrift, and the drunkard were undeserving. The rationale for this distinction apparently was that some are poor "through no fault of their own" while others could have risen from poverty, or not fallen into it, and thus deserve what they get for failing to use their opportunities.

If we use this distinction when allotting famine relief, we shall find that our donations will scarcely differ from those we would have made had we simply accepted the Famine Relief Argument; for the individual Indian peasant in an overpopulated, drought-prone region had no opportunity to be anything other than what he is.

Indeed, if we reflect on ways in which victims of famine might be undeserving, we find that the distinction between the deserving and the undeserving becomes difficult to sustain where famine victims are concerned. The clearest case of people *apparently* undeserving of help I have come across is the Ik, a tribe living in the arid northern region of Uganda. According to Colin Turnbull, an anthropologist who lived with the Ik during a year of famine, the Ik were so selfish that the stronger members of the tribe would snatch food from the hands of the weak or elderly. Parents would not share their food with children older than three; four-year-olds had to fend for themselves or starve. When relief supplies became available at a village a few miles away, those who were able to walk the distance collected rations for themselves and those unable to come, and then stopped on the way back to gorge themselves, bringing nothing home for the others. Moreover, when in the following year the rains came again, most of the Ik still did not work their fields. Since wild edibles were readily available, they felt no need to work, and their habits of immediate consumption gave them no inclination to build up a store against future scarcity.[8]

If we assume, for the sake of discussion, that Turnbull's description of the Ik is accurate, our first reaction may well be that such people do not deserve aid. Should we help people who will not help their own villagers, or even their own children? Certainly not!

Can we justify this reaction on the grounds of desert? Consider the situation of an individual Ik family. Do the children, too young to fend for themselves, deserve to starve because their parents will no longer provide for them? Obviously not, so they at least should be aided, although it could prove difficult to aid the children and not their parents.

What of the individual adults? Turnbull's description does not suggest that the Ik practice of feeding oneself immediately and neither gathering nor storing a surplus that might have to be shared with others has been adopted by any kind of conscious reflective choice. It seems, rather, that the social and cooperative bonds that existed in this society in better times were unable to withstand conditions of extreme scarcity. The causes of this collapse of Ik society and the retreat into an overwhelming preoccupation with one's own short-term interests are unclear, but what is tolerably clear is that it resulted from a combination of drought and something fairly deeply ingrained in the Ik culture.[9] If this is correct, we cannot pin the blame for their present situation on individual Ik, since they were formed by the culture of their society and cannot, as individuals, be held responsible for its collapse. It appears, too, that no individual could by his own actions have changed the course of Ik society.

Someone might argue that had one man or woman stood up and exhorted his or her fellows to cooperate, share their food, and work for the future, everything would have been different; but even granting this improbable hypothesis, that person would have had to be a remarkable person, someone with more initiative and vision than all the other Ik. (This follows from the fact that among all the Ik there in fact was no one who actually did this, although, according to the hypothesis, it could have been done.) Can we say that a person deserves to starve because he or she does not have greater initiative and vision than all the other members of his or her society or tribe? This is not at all what the Victorians meant by the undeserving poor.

If we are not clear that famine victims deserve to starve even in so extreme a case as the Ik, as Turnbull portrays them, can we ever be sure that famine victims deserve to starve? I think not. The reason is that since famine, by its nature, affects a large number of people at a given time and place, there is always going to be some cause or combination of causes, whether climate, or overpopulation, or corrupt government, or outdated social customs, or even, to indulge in some Victorian fantasy, innate racial tendencies toward laziness, for which the individual starving person cannot be held accountable.

This conclusion is not, as might at first be thought, a piece of armchair anthropology, a factual generalization which should only be made after examining a wide range of actual cases. The point is a conceptual one, resulting from the juxtaposition of the concepts of famine and moral desert. The former, defined by the *Oxford English Dictionary* as "extreme and *general* shortage of food, in a town, country, etc." (my italics), refers only to situations affecting whole groups of people, and such situations must, if we are to make any sense of them at all, have some general cause or causes. Moral desert, on the other hand, requires individual moral responsibility. When we can ascribe individual acts, however base, to general causes which it is unreasonable to expect an individual to overcome, moral blame becomes inappropriate. Headhunters, for instance, commit acts which, if they were committed by someone living in Kansas City, would be regarded as evidence of either insanity or the utmost moral depravity. If the theory of desert ever makes sense,[10] a sane Kansas City headhunter would deserve harsh punishment; but can the same be said of a headhunter who is a member of a tribe of Amazon Indians, if all the adults of the tribe have been headhunters for as long as anyone can remember? I do not think we can blame such a person, since only a most exceptional person would not be hunting heads under these circumstances, and it would be very odd to blame someone because he or she was not a most exceptional person.

So we should reject criticism of the Famine Relief Argument by those who claim that instead of trying straightforwardly to prevent as much starvation as possible, we should first ensure that the recipients of our aid deserve it. The notion of desert makes little sense in a famine situation. This does not mean that in deciding whom to aid, we should dismiss from consideration factors commonly thought relevant to desert, like the extent to which the group is trying to help itself, or the efficiency and honesty of government; my point is only that these factors are relevant, not to whether people deserve assistance, but to whether assistance is likely to be effective. (For instance, whatever we think about desert, Turnbull's account shows that aiding the Ik by handing out grain rations at a nearby village is a grossly inefficient method of reducing starvation.) This is a point I shall return to when I consider consequentialist objections to the Famine Relief Argument.

There is another nonconsequentialist theory of justice that should be considered: the entitlement theory, proposed by Robert Nozick in his recent book *Anarchy, State and Utopia*.[11] According to this theory, the way to tell if goods and resources are justly distributed is not to measure them against some ideal pattern of just distribution, but to look at the manner in which the present distribution was reached and to see if unjust means such as force or fraud were responsible for this distribution. If they were, there is need for reparation, but if goods were originally acquired justly (for instance, someone took a log, which no one else owned, and made it into a chair) and were transferred by legitimate means (voluntary exchange, gift, and so on), then the present distribution is just.

It is obvious that this conception of justice is compatible with an unlimited amount of inequality. If some are unfortunate in their original acquisitions, or trade what they have for goods that prove to have no lasting value, or give to others in misfortune but are not themselves given to, then they may end up with nothing while others accumulate vast fortunes. A man may feast, make himself vomit, as the Romans used to do, and then feast again, while a child starves to death on his doorstep; and all within the bounds of justice, according to the entitlement theory.

Even so, it is possible to exaggerate the opposition between the entitlement theory and the Famine Relief Argument. While the entitlement theory insists on our *right* to retain property, and rejects the use of compulsory means like taxation to help the poor, it is quite silent on the questions of whether it is *good* for the rich to give to the poor. In several passages of his book, Nozick suggests that we can achieve the ends we deem morally desirable by voluntary means alone. Implausible as I find this suggestion, it does imply that while Nozick would oppose government aid paid for by taxation, he might well accept the Famine Relief Argument insofar as it applies to what individuals ought voluntarily to do. True, Nozick would reject the claim that rich people have an "obligation" to give to the starving, insofar as this can be taken to imply that the starving have a right to our aid, but he could still grant that giving is something we ought to do, and that though failing to give is not unjust, it is—since justice is not all there is to morality—morally wrong.[12]

So important parts of the Famine Relief Argument stand, even if we accept the entitlement theory of justice. In any case, though, we should not accept the entitlement theory. To go into all the difficulties that face it would be too much of a digression, but three points can be made very briefly. First, the whole theory starts from a questionable individualistic theory of human rights. Second, the idea of tracing back present holdings through history to their original acquisition from an unowned state is absurdly unrealistic; yet if this cannot be done the theory breaks down, for it seems reasonable to demand that we start all over again from the original position in which nothing is owned. Third, and most relevant to the question of international aid, the theory accepts so many arbitrary outcomes that it can be doubted if it deserves to be called a theory of justice at all. For instance, in the world as it is now, those whose forefathers happened to inhabit some sandy wastes around the Persian Gulf now possess fabulous wealth because oil lay under those sands; while those whose forefathers settled on better lands in parts of Ethiopia are now starving because rains that fell regularly for many years have failed. Can this distribution really be sanctioned by justice? I do not think it can be, because justice, like other moral principles, must be acceptable from an impartial point of view. One way of testing the impartiality of a principle is by asking if we could accept it even if we did not know how it was to affect us—that is, in this case, if we did not know whether we were an oil sheik or an Ethiopian peasant.[13] If we imagine ourselves ignorant of our own identity in this way, would we accept the principle that oil sheiks are under no obligation to use their wealth for famine relief? I know that I would not, and I doubt that anyone whose choice was not predetermined by a desire to cling to a particular theory of justice would.[14]

Apart from theories of justice, there is one other important nonconsequentialist view of obligations that gives rise to objections to the Famine Relief Argument, and so requires discussion. This is that we have obligations to those near to us, first to our own families, and then to the poor in our own community, which take precedence over our obligations to those overseas. One finds this view both among ordinary people—anyone who has tried to collect money for famine relief, or demonstrated in favor of overseas aid will have encountered the response that we should concern ourselves only with our own poor—and among sophisticated theorists, who suggest that obligations arise out of concrete personal relationships rather than universal moral principles connecting one abstract person with another.[15]

Now it may well be true that we instinctively prefer to help those who are in some sense members of our community, rather than those who are not; but the question we are concerned with is not what we prefer to do, or what we usually do, but what we ought to do; and it is difficult to see any sound moral justification for the view that our obligations cease at the boundary of our own nation or kin.

Consider, for instance, racial affinities. Should we, as whites, help poor whites before we help poor blacks or Asians? Most of us would reject such a suggestion out of hand. If asked to state reasons for rejecting it, we would say that a person's need for food has nothing to do with his race, and if there are blacks who need food more than whites, then it would be arbitrary to allot the food on the basis of a principle which has nothing to do with need.

The same point applies to citizenship or nationhood. While there are some poor citizens in all the affluent nations, the need is greatest in the poorer countries. Under these circumstances, it would be arbitrary to decide that only those fortunate enough to be citizens of our own community will share in our surplus.

We feel the obligations of kinship, particularly those of parents to children, more strongly than those of citizenship, no doubt because these obligations are supported by love and affection. In a famine situation, there would be few parents who would think of giving their last bowl of rice to others if their own children were starving. Indeed, we might well consider parents who did so to be unnatural, and lacking in basic human feelings. But would it be morally wrong to do so, if the need for food was the same? I am not sure that it would be; and in any case, we are concerned not with that situation, but with the one in which our own children have had an adequate meal, and now would like a second helping, while others are starving; or, more realistically, a situation in which others starve while our children are well clothed, fed, and educated, and would now like a stereo set or a car. In these circumstances any special obligations we might have had to our children have been fulfilled, and the needs of strangers make a stronger moral claim upon us than the wants of those close to us.

Family ties, like communal, national, and racial ties, are based partly on sentiment and partly on the utility of a system of definite, assignable responsibilities. I do not use the word "sentiment" derogatively, as people sometimes do when they describe a novel as being "sentimental." Sentiments like love, affection, and community feeling are a large part of what makes life worthwhile. But sentiments are likely to lead us astray in moral reasoning, seducing us into accepting positions that are based, not on an impartial consideration of the interests of all involved, but rather on our own likes and dislikes. We can see this clearly enough if we look at racism. One supporting factor behind Nazism was the feeling of brotherhood that "Aryan" Germans gained when they felt themselves to be part of a group, a "volk" that was united against "aliens." Since we are not racists, we have no difficulty in seeing, in this instance, that this feeling of volkish unity did not justify discrimination against those outside the group. Once this has been understood, we may also be able to see that our own feelings of affinity with our fellow citizens, or even our family, do not justify discrimination against those outside these groups. It will be objected that, unlike the Nazis, we are not actively killing those who do not belong to our group. True, but we are allowing them to die; and if that's not quite as bad, it's bad enough.[16]

The element of truth to be found in the view that our obligations to members of our family or community take precedence over our obligations to strangers lies not in the sentiments that make this view so hard to give up in practice, but in the utilitarian benefits, in certain circumstances, of a recognized system of responsibilities. To stress this point, however, is to make a consequentialist objection to the Famine Relief Argument, and this can be dealt with in the section on consequentialist objections, to which I now turn.

Suppose we accept that starvation is bad, and that if it is in our power to prevent something bad without sacrificing anything of comparable moral importance, we ought to do it. We have then accepted the core of the Famine Relief Argument, but we might still have doubts about its conclusion. Two of these doubts have already been suggested in the preceding discussion of nonconsequentialist objections, when I said there were elements of (consequentialist) truth in the views that we ought to aid only the deserving, and that we ought to help those near to us first. I shall begin with these issues and then go on to other problems.

First, might there be advantages, from the point of view of preventing bad things like starvation, in a system of obligations in which members of families take care of each other before they take care of others in the community, and members of the community take care of fellow members of the community before they take care of outsiders? If so, is this a consequentialist reason for retaining this system of obligations, instead of advocating the view that we have obligations to all who are starving?

In earlier times there were obvious advantages in a strictly limited system of obligations. Each locality had to look after its own poor, if they were not to starve, since communications were so poor that people far away would not be able to help, even if they had wanted to.

Today, under normal circumstances, there are still some advantages in allowing families to look after themselves and allowing local communities to take care of their poor. In this way ties of affection and community feeling achieve ends that would otherwise require a large, impersonal bureaucracy. Those who are living with the needy in the same family or the same community may be expected to know their needs better than an outsider; and individual initiative and a sense of responsibility are encouraged.

For these reasons, as well as some others I leave to the reader, it would be absurd to propose that henceforth we are all exactly equally responsible for the welfare of everyone in the world. But the Famine Relief Argument does not propose that anyway. Its weak version would hardly interfere with our existing system of obligations at all; and even the strong version applies only when some people are starving and others have a surplus. In these circumstances the amount of suffering involved, the impossibility of individual families or local communities caring for themselves, and the improvement in modern communications which makes it possible for people far away to learn of the situation and to do something to help combine to outweigh decisively the utility of restricting ourselves to the usual system of obligations.

Next, what is the significance, on the consequentialist view, of the degree to which people are trying to help themselves, which is usually thought to bear on whether they deserve our aid? What if, for instance, a nation should use the assistance we give it as an excuse for postponing tough population control measures, arguing shortsightedly that as no one is without food now, these measures are unnecessary? I have argued that the notion of desert makes little sense in a famine situation. Does this mean that we should disregard these factors as well?

In my earlier article, I supported the claim that we have obligations to strangers for whose misfortunes we are not ourselves responsible by asking the reader to imagine that a young child had stumbled into a pond and was in danger of drowning. Any passer-by who noticed the child would, I said, have an obligation to wade in and pull him out.

Peter Brown has suggested a modification to this illustration which may serve to clarify the effect of the victim's own actions on our obligations.[17] Winter has come to the little pond and it has frozen over; but the ice is thin, and the authorities have erected a sign saying "No Skating—Thin Ice." Yet a child, 10 years old, has gone skating and fallen through. Do we still have an obligation to rescue him? What if the skater were an adult, and we had rescued him twice before, in similar circumstances?

Intuitively, I imagine most of us would say that we ought to rescue the 10-year-old, despite his disregard of the warning, because death is too severe a punishment for the offense he has committed and the experience will probably teach him a lesson anyway; but in the case of the adult who has failed to learn from his two previous acts of foolhardiness, we may well be less sure.

I suggest that the reason for our hesitation in concluding that we ought to rescue the adult is not that we think he doesn't deserve to be rescued. True, someone who has had to be rescued twice before must be pretty stupid to go skating on the same spot again; but leaving him to drown is, still, unjustifiably harsh treatment for stupidity or recklessness. The problem is, rather, that by rescuing him again, we allow him to escape the natural costs of his stupidity; thus we do nothing to discourage a repetition of the incident; and we can only feel exasperation at the prospect of having to rescue him all over again in the near future. Indeed, the skater may even come to believe that since he will always be rescued, he has no need to heed warnings. So at some point we might properly say that we will no longer rescue him, since this might be the only way to persuade him to be more careful in future.

The example shows, then, that the extent to which a person takes reasonable precautions against being in a situation in which he requires aid is relevant to our obligation to aid him, not because it makes him intrinsically undeserving of aid, but because we can use our aid most effectively by giving it only to those who do what they can to help reduce their dependence on aid.

(Admittedly, in the real world deciding how to use aid most effectively is not always straightforward. In poor countries there are many who are sick, or old, or infested with parasites, whose need for food is great, but whose digestive systems are inefficient at utilizing the food. Younger, healthier people may be able to survive with less assistance. Another way of increasing the effectiveness of aid may be to direct it to those who are themselves involved in producing food, so that they will be able to produce more, and thus multiply the benefits of the aid given. There is no real dilemma here, however, so long as we bear in mind that our goal is to prevent as many people as possible from starving. If the way to do this is to aid those who are actually starving, then we should do so; but if we can save more by employing other criteria as well, that is what we must do.)

The principle of giving aid only where it is most effective would not apply if we had an unlimited amount of aid to give away, so that we could help everyone, however careless they were, at no sacrifice to ourselves. But we are never in this kind of situation. The amount of aid available is always limited, hence the need to use it as effectively as possible.

Having clarified this, we can now go on to consider the actual situation that faces us as we try to aid those facing famine. Are the people who need aid like the reckless skater, bringing disaster on themselves despite the opportunities to improve their position we have provided for them? In most respects there is no parallel here. The poorer nations try to provide sufficient food for their inhabitants; it is the difficulty of the task, rather than lack of will, that limits their success. Yet there is one respect in which it might be said that the poorer nations have not heeded warnings, and so have brought their problems on themselves: population control.

Consider India. If India had stabilized its population in, say, 1950, while improving its agricultural methods as it has done since that date, India would have no overall food shortage today, and would have a food reserve sufficient to meet emergency requirements. But India did not curb its population growth in 1950, nor has it done so to a significant extent since then, despite ample warning about the disastrous consequences of continued increase.[18]

Is India now in the position of the heedless skater? Is our continued aid merely putting off the inevitable day of reckoning? Should we actually cut off aid and allow famine to establish a natural balance between population and resources, as some have suggested?

There is no denying the seriousness of the population problem in India and some other poor nations; and there is no denying the fact that efforts to supply these countries with more food, and to enable them to produce more food themselves, will not reduce the long-term risk of famine unless population growth is checked. On the other hand, it does not follow from these facts that we ought simply to cut off aid to India and countries in a similar situation.

Allowing people to starve to death is a brutal way of controlling population. If there were absolutely nothing else we could do, we would, I suppose, have to resign ourselves to it. In that case the factual premise of the Famine Relief Argument—that we can do something to reduce starvation—would be false. But if there is any alternative, anything at all that we can try that may avoid the horror of widespread and protracted starvation, then we ought to try it.

What else can we do? Let us return for a moment to the problem of rescuing the skater. To make the situation more like the world food problem, imagine that there are a large number of skaters, each of whom, on two or three occasions, has ignored warnings and needed to be rescued. Should we therefore simply give up rescuing them, and let any skaters who fall in drown? Surely it would be preferable to issue a warning, before taking such a harsh step. We could, for instance, agree to rescue a skater only on condition that in future he stay well away from the pond; and if this condition were violated, we might then refuse to carry out a rescue. If the skater did return to the pond and we were forced to carry out our threat, this would, at least, serve as a warning to other skaters that we meant what we said.

This analogy suggests that we might make our offers of aid to countries with rapidly increasing populations conditional on effective steps being taken to halt population growth. I imagine that many people who have agreed with me up to this point will be reluctant to accept this conclusion. It will be said that it would be an attempt to impose our own ideas on other, independent, sovereign nations. And so, in a sense, it would be—but it doesn't follow that this imposition is unjustifiable. I have argued that we have an obligation to prevent starvation if we can; but I have not argued that we have an obligation to make sacrifices that, to the best of our knowledge, will do nothing to prevent starvation. Hence we would seem to have no obligation, of the kind for which I have argued, to give food or other assistance to any country or person if the gift will serve no good purpose in the long run.[19] So long as we are sincerely carrying out a policy of reducing starvation and not merely using the claim that aid may be ineffective as an excuse to reduce our total amount of aid, no country or person can properly accuse us of acting wrongly. A poor country or person has a legitimate claim to aid only if the conditions are such that the aid will be effective.

We have then a right to attach to our offers of aid conditions designed to make that aid effective; but the practical objections to this plan must also be considered. The fact is that we do not really know how to stop population growth, and some of the methods that look promising require expenditure that might be beyond the poorer countries. For instance, many demographers believe that the birth rate drops only when the living standard rises, in which case we need to provide substantial aid as well as contraceptive services.[20] Even schemes which focus more narrowly on contraception and sterilization, perhaps offering incentives to persuade those who have had three children to be sterilized, would be expensive to carry out in a large country of small villages like India. These considerations suggest that the richer nations must help with population control schemes as well as with food aid and agricultural development. Then in consultation with local officials, experimental schemes could be tried in limited areas, and methods that prove successful applied on a larger scale.

This may be an appropriate place to comment on the "lifeboat theory," advocated by Garrett Hardin and others.[21] According to Hardin, we in the rich nations are like the occupants of a crowded lifeboat adrift in a sea full of drowning people; if we try to save the drowning by bringing them aboard, our boat will be overloaded and we shall all drown. Since it is better to save some than none, we should leave the others to drown. Similarly, the rich should leave the poor to starve, or else the poor will drag the rich down with them.

The lifeboat analogy differs from the analogy of the heedless skaters because it assumes that making the rescue attempt endangers our own survival. It is just this assumption, however, that is doubtful. Consider the degree of our affluence—the material goods that we own and the wastage of food involved in the absurdly high meat content of our diet—and then ask yourself whether a substantial increase in our overseas aid would threaten our survival. I cannot see how it would. Without going into the question of how much more food the world can produce, if yields elsewhere are brought up to Western levels, we should note that the world presently produces enough food to give all its inhabitants an adequate diet. Unfortunately that food is very unevenly distributed. *In the United States and Western Europe alone, more food is wasted by being fed to farm animals than the total world food shortfall.* Through his high meat diet, which provides him with about twice as much meat as his body can use, the average American indirectly consumes enough grain to feed four Indians.[22] Under these circumstances the lifeboat analogy seems grotesquely inapt. It is rather as if we in the rich nations were on a luxurious yacht, feasting gluttonously and playing deck quoits to ward off obesity, while we avert our gaze from those drowning in the sea around us.

What is true about the lifeboat theory has already been captured by our discussion of the reckless skaters. Food handouts that only postpone disaster are no use; but the upshot of this is not that we should reduce our aid, but that we should take steps to make it more effective. The Famine Relief Argument still holds. We should give far more aid than we are now giving—but we should not shrink from doing everything necessary to ensure that it brings about a *permanent* reduction of starvation.[23]

There is one more consequentialist objection to the Famine Relief Argument—or rather to the strong version of it—which I find worrying. This is that the standard set by it is so high that no one except a saint can fulfill his obligations to the starving; and therefore it will be counterproductive to demand so much, since people will say, "As I can't do what is morally required of me anyway, I may as well not bother about morality at all." If, however, we were to set a more easily attainable standard, people might strive to do what the standard demanded. Thus setting a lower standard might actually result in more aid.

It is important to avoid confusion about the logical status of this point. Assuming that it is correct as a prediction of human behavior, it would still not follow that the Famine Relief Argument was mistaken. All that would follow is that public advocacy of the strong version of the Famine Relief Argument would be undesirable; indeed, it would mean that the famine relief argument itself, coupled with the facts of human behavior, leads to the conclusion that we advocate some lower standard, since this is the most effective way of aiding the starving. Of course, we ourselves—that is, those of us who accept the strong version—would know that we ought to do more, and we might actually give more than we urged others to give. There is no inconsistency here, since in both our private and our public behavior we are trying to maximize the amount of benefit to the starving.[24]

Is it true that the standard set by the strong version of the Famine Relief Argument is so high as to be counterproductive? There is not much evidence on this topic, but some discussions with my students have led me to think that it might be. On the other hand, the conventionally accepted standard—a few coins in a collection tin if one is waved under your nose—is obviously far too low. Somewhere in between these extremes might make people realize that indulgence in an affluent life-style without making a serious effort to help those in need is morally wrong, without leading people to reject morality as hopelessly idealistic.

What level of contribution, to population control as well as food and agricultural development, should we advocate? Any figure will be to some extent arbitrary, and anything said on this topic will be tentative; but for a middle-class person in an affluent society, there is something to be said for the figure of 10% of one's income. Such a figure is much more than a token donation and, if widely acted upon, would probably go a long way toward ending starvation; at the same time, it is an amount which does not require a degree of altruism that is positively saintly. Indeed, for middle-class families a 10% gift probably does not go beyond the requirements of the weak version of the Famine Relief Argument. It may mean putting off getting a new car, or doing without a stereo set, or buying fewer clothes, or eating less meat—and there are independent reasons for doing the last of these anyway—but it should not involve sacrificing anything that is really needed.[25]

The figure of 10% of one's income has the additional advantage of being reminiscent of the ancient tithe, or tenth of all agricultural produce, which was traditionally given to support the church, whose responsibilities included care of the poor. This aura of a past era, when people accepted that they had obligations to the less fortunate members of their community, may make the idea more acceptable today, when we talk of belonging to a global community but have yet to act accordingly.

I conclude that we can safely say that everyone earning an average or above average income in an affluent society, unless he has an unusually large number of dependents or other special needs, ought to give a tenth of his income to groups working to end starvation. By any reasonable moral standards this is the minimum that we ought to do, and we do wrong if we do less.[26]

NOTES

1. "Famine, Affluence and Morality," *Philosophy and Public Affairs,* vol. 1, pp. 229–43 (1972).

2. *The World Food Situation and Prospects to 1985* (Economic Research Service, U.S. Department of Agriculture, Foreign Agricultural Report No. 98, Washington, D.C., 1974), p. 2.

3. See the chapter by Lyle Schertz in this volume, especially the section entitled "The Future."

4. It should be obvious that I do not accept the view, voiced often during the heyday of "linguistic analysis" but less common now, that moral philosophy is a morally neutral activity, and so the moral philosopher *qua* moral philosopher can have nothing substantive to say about controversial moral issues. In common with some other philosophers who are contributing to this volume (Thomas Nagel, Peter Brown, Samuel Gorovitz, and Henry Shue) I believe that developing, examining, and criticizing moral arguments is within the province of the moral philosopher. I cannot accept the contrasting position, advanced by Joseph Sneed in his chapter, that moral philosophers must confine themselves to the nature of moral reasoning rather than to the issue of what a decision maker ought to do in a given situation. Indeed, I cannot see that Sneed himself succeeds in doing the former rather than the latter—for in telling the decision maker that the method he ought to adopt is the one that maximizes the preferences of his "constituents," Sneed is telling the decision maker what he ought to do, at least to the extent of telling him that he ought to ignore the alternative approach of seeking justifiable moral principles on which to base his decision.

5. Of course, a utilitarian theory like that of J. S. Mill or Henry Sidgwick will also give some weight to a principle of justice, on the grounds that so doing will maximize happiness in the long run; but the reference here is to a theory that gives weight to justice independently of whether so doing promotes some other goal like happiness.

6. *A Theory of Justice* (Cambridge, Mass., 1971).

7. This statement needs qualification, because an incompatibility with the Famine Relief Argument may arise if—as in the case of Rawls's theory—limits are placed on the application of a consequentialist principle of justice. The underlying idea of Rawls's theory is that if we imagine people choosing principles for the regulation of a society when they are themselves ignorant of their special talents, property, position, and so on, they will choose justly because they will have no way of knowing which principles are to their own particular advantage, and they will wish to protect themselves against injustice, whatever talents, property, or position they turn out to have. Rawls then argues that people choosing under these conditions would wish to protect themselves against the worst possibilities and so would adopt a principle of distribution that would maximize the welfare of the worst-off group, but—and here the incompatibility with the Famine Relief Argument arises—Rawls applies this principle of distribution only within each society, or nation-state, and not across national boundaries.

The restriction of the principle of distribution to the society or nation-state, however, cannot be justified consistently with Rawls's own theory, which is based on choice under conditions of ignorance. People who are uncertain whether, when the veil of ignorance is lifted, they will turn out to be citizens of Bangladesh or of the United States of America would surely adopt principles that would do something to reduce the gap between the levels of welfare prevailing in these countries. As Brian Barry has pointed out in *The Liberal Theory of Justice* (Oxford, 1973), pp. 129–30, if Rawl's arguments for principles that maximize the level of the worst-off are sound, they must apply to international as well as national distribution.

8. Colin Turnbull, *The Mountain People* (New York, 1972).

9. Some aspects of Ik culture—for instance, the design of Ik villages, which cuts each family off from the others—suggest that the Ik had fairly weak social bonds even prior to the famine.

10. I have assumed that the notion of desert is coherent when applied to individuals; but the conclusion just reached would receive additional support if this was denied, as it well might be, on the grounds that individuals are not responsible for their character. See *A Theory of Justice,* pp. 103-4, 311-2.

11. New York, 1974. See especially part II.

12. Nozick has confirmed this interpretation in a private communication.

13. Cf. R. M. Hare, *Freedom and Reason* (Oxford, 1963), ch. 6; J. Rawls, *A Theory of Justice,* ch. 3. For an account of the similarity of these and other constraints on the nature of a moral principle, see R. M. Hare, "Rules of War and Moral Reasoning," *Philosophy and Public Affairs,* vol. 1, no. 2, pp. 166-181 (1972).

14. It is on the basis of this kind of test that I would defend my position against those who claim that it goes too far because it forces one individual to make a sacrifice for the benefit of another. Thus Peter Brown asks (this volume, p. 69) if I would be obliged to give one of my two good eyes to a blind person to enable him to see. I would defend my affirmative answer by asking you to imagine that you did not know if you were the blind person or the person with two good eyes, and then to think about whether you would prefer an arrangement in which people were obliged to help others in this manner. Admittedly, some qualifications might have to be made in certain circumstances, for instance, where a person had gone blind because of failure to take simple preventive measures. For a discussion of a still more extreme kind of sacrifice, see John Harris, "The Survival Lottery," *Philosophy,* vol. 50, pp. 81-87 (January 1975); and for some qualifications, see my "Utility and the Survival Lottery," *Philosophy*, vol. 52, no. 199 (January 1977).

15. Cf. Raymond Gastil's comment on "Famine, Affluence and Morality" in *Ethics,* vol. 85, p. 185 (1974-75).

16. Whether allowing someone to die is morally equivalent to killing him or her is a complicated issue. While the case for famine relief would be immeasurably strengthened by an affirmative answer to this question—and I think the case for an affirmative answer is strong—I have avoided an appeal to this position in order to base the Famine Relief Argument on minimally controversial foundations. For recent discussions of the killing-letting die issue, see M. Tooley, "Abortion and Infanticide," *Philosophy and Public Affairs,* vol. II, no. 1 (1972); J. Rachels, "Active and Passive Euthanasia," *New England Journal of Medicine,* vol. 292, pp. 78-80 (1975); R. L. Trammell, "Saving Life and Taking Life," *Journal of Philosophy,* vol. LXXII, pp. 131-7 (1975); and a forthcoming book on the morality of killing by J. Glover.

17. Peter Brown, "Appraising Policies regarding Goods Scarcity" (unpublished ms.), p. 13.

18. Since this was written, the Indian government has announced that it is taking stronger steps to slow population growth, including the restriction of government jobs in certain areas to couples with no more than two children. It

remains to be seen whether these measures will develop into an effective national program. If it does, this and the following paragraphs will not be applicable to India, but there are many other countries to which they would apply. See *New York Times,* February 26, 1976, pp. 1, 7, and March 19, 1976, p. 3.

19. Robert Nozick has suggested (private communication) that it is a mistake to talk of aiding *countries* here; it is *people* we are aiding, and our aid will prevent some people from starving, whatever population policy the country adopts. I agree that it is people with whom we must be concerned, but the basic point stands, for while our aid will prevent some people from starving now whatever the rate of population growth in the country, if the people we save have several children, and so contribute to a situation in which their children, along with many others in the country, are starving in 20 years time, we have not, on balance, prevented starvation.

20. See the chapter by Michael Brewer in this volume.

21. Garrett Hardin, "Living on a Lifeboat," *Bioscience,* October 1974, pp. 561–8.

22. Frances Moore Lappe, *Diet for a Small Planet* (New York, 1971), pp. 4–11; Barbara Ward, "The Fat and the Lean," *The Economist,* November 2, 1974; Boyce Rensberger, "Curb on U.S. Waste Urged to Help World's Hungry," *New York Times,* October 25, 1974.

I cannot accept the claims made by Charles Shuman (this volume, p. 152), that since very little of the principal grains fed to animals (corn and sorghum) is used for human consumption, cattle and hogs do not compete with people for grain. For a start, one would have to add to the feed grains Shuman mentions soybeans. Soybeans are highly suitable for human food, providing good-quality protein. They are an important part of the diet in many Asian nations. The United States produces three-quarters of the world's soybean crop and dominates the world soybean trade to an even greater extent; yet 95% of the soybeans produced in the U.S. are fed to livestock.

Even so far as corn and sorghum are concerned, we would need to ask whether, if the demand warranted it, the land used to grow these crops could not produce crops better suited for direct human consumption. If so, then obviously animals and people are competing. Finally, it should be noted that corn and sorghum *are* consumed directly by people in some of the poorer countries.

Two points that Shuman makes about meat consumption are sound: first, that some meat can be produced from free range grazing on nontillable land, and this can represent an addition to food supplies for humans, though not when the animals are taken off the range to be fattened on grains or soybeans; and second, that a reduction in meat consumption *alone* would reduce the incentive to farmers to produce grain and soybeans, and so might not benefit the poor. What is needed, of course, is a coupling of a reduction in meat consumption with an increased political will to use the food-producing capacity thus released for the benefit of those who need it most, perhaps through an International Food Reserve (see the chapter in this volume by C. William Swank). Thus purchases by government agencies or nongovernmental aid organizations would take up the slack in the market caused by the reduced demand for animal feeds.

23. Thomas Nagel makes another powerful objection to the lifeboat theory when he points out that the theory requires us to allow a *certain* present disaster in order to forestall a *possible* greater future disaster. See p. 60 of this volume, and for a related point, the chapter by Henry Shue at p. 313.

24. For a consequentialist, this kind of apparent conflict between public and private morality is always a possibility. Some may consider it indicative of an elitist or even manipulative attitude toward ordinary people, but this charge has more bark than bite, and should not trouble the consequentialist. If ordinary people will not be put off by the high standard demanded by the strong version of the Famine Relief Argument, all will be well, and that is what the consequentialist will advocate. But if more starvation will actually be prevented by advocating a lower standard, both in the short and in the long term, one would be a fool to continue to advocate the high standard. If that is what is meant by being "elitist" or "manipulative," then we should be elitist or manipulative in this situation.

Like many other objections to consequentialist ethics, this one has rhetorical force because terms which have condemnatory overtones acquired in contexts where they do lead to bad consequences (for instance, when someone falsely believes that "the masses" are too stupid to govern themselves, and therefore rules them by force and keeps them subordinate to a ruling class which exploits them for its own ends) are transferred to superficially similar traits which, in the strictly limited situations in which they would be accepted by the consequentialist, are not based on false premises and can only be beneficial.

25. When I read an earlier version of this paper at a working meeting at the Academy for Contemporary Problems, Washington, Edwin Martin and Lawrence Witt suggested that I was greatly exaggerating the size of the problem of starvation. Actual starvation (as distinguished from poor and inadequate nutrition) could, they said, be eliminated by the expenditure of no more than 1% of the U.S. gross national product; its elimination would therefore not require any serious sacrifices at all.

My initial reaction to these comments was that if this is correct, it is all the more shocking that the necessary steps have still not been taken to prevent starvation. On further investigation, however, I can only conclude that these estimates refer only to the amount of food that would have to be provided to cope with the present level of starvation; they do not include the expenditure required to slow population growth and foster development, so as to prevent greater numbers starving in the future.

26. I am grateful to many people for comments: members of the working group on "Moral Issues in the Distribution of Food" at the Academy for Contemporary Problems, Washington; Robert Young; Robert Nozick; and especially, for very detailed and helpful suggestions and objections, to Peter Brown and Henry Shue.

3 Poverty and food: why charity is not enough
Thomas Nagel

Although the world food situation raises acute problems of distributive justice, they are not comparable to problems about how to distribute a definite quantity of food that is already on hand to numerous hungry victims of a natural calamity. Because of the significant effects of distribution on production, and the impossibility of separating the distribution of food from that of wealth in general, there is no isolable question of justice about redistribution of food from the haves to the have-nots. In a sense, therefore, the ethical aspects of this topic can be discussed only as part of the general problem of global economic inequality. In a money economy, anything can be exchanged for anything else, and the issue of the distribution of food is inseparable from that of the distribution of transistors or power plants.

Nevertheless there is a reason for thinking about the larger question in terms of food. Food is basic. It is the last thing an individual can afford to give up, if he can afford nothing else, and this means that in the current world situation we are not dealing with an abstract problem of inequality, but with something more specific and acute. If everyone in the world had at least a minimally adequate standard of living, there would still be ethical problems about the justice of big differences in wealth above that minimum—as there are, for example, about the distribution of wealth within the United States. But whatever may be said about this general problem, the inequalities that appear in the distribution of food on a worldwide scale are of a very different kind, and raise a different issue. They are, to be sure, basically inequalities in wealth rather than in food; but inequalities in wealth and income which result in starvation or severe malnutrition for some are in a different moral class from those inequalities higher on the scale that result in luxuries and multiple dwellings for some and marginal poverty for others. When the subject is enough to eat rather than a yacht, the difference between haves and have-nots goes beyond the general problem of equality and distributive justice. It is an extreme case, involving extreme needs.

I shall use the term "radical inequality" to describe this situation. A radical inequality exists when the bottom level is one of direst need, the top level one of great comfort or even luxury, and the total supply is large enough to raise the bottom above the level of extreme need without bringing significant deprivation to those above—specifically, without reducing most people to a place somewhat above the current bottom, or otherwise radically reducing their standard of living. The term therefore describes not merely the size of the gap between top and bottom but also the available total and the level of the bottom. The distribution of the world's food supply is a case of radical inequality because in a situation of adequate productive capacity for the world's population over the predictable short term, economic inequalities mean that under a market system millions of people will be undernourished from infancy and their health and life expectancy severely damaged.

The point of separating out this kind of case for special treatment is to forestall or at least weaken the force of a question that tends to arise whenever the rectification of inequalities is discussed: the question "Where do you draw the line?" When it is observed that people in the U.S. and Northern Europe have a high standard of living and people in South Asia are starving or malnourished, and that there is something wrong with this, one reaction is anxiety about the prospect of bringing everyone to a common level only a bit higher than that of an Indian peasant. Now there may be an argument that justice requires such a solution, but it is not one which I am prepared to endorse, and the issue does not have to be decided in order to deal with situations of radical inequality. It does not take a strongly egalitarian principle to indicate that something is wrong in these cases, and that it would be an improvement to raise the bottom even if the resulting distribution were still very unequal.

But even if one decides that radical inequality is unacceptable, that does not tell us what to do about it. If those who are well off had *stolen* their riches from those who are poor, then redistribution would be nothing more than the uncontroversial rectification of past wrongs. But it is not so simple as that. To be sure, there has been substantial colonial exploitation of poor countries by rich ones, in trade, in labor, and in development. But a great deal of the difference in wealth between developed and underdeveloped countries is independent of this, and depends on a big head start in technology, organization, and capital accumulation which would have existed even without colonialism. While this claim may be disputed, it seems important to arrive at a view of the situation on the assumption that it is true. One would concede too much if one tried to base an argument for the injustice of radical inequality entirely on the claim that the inequality arose through wrongdoing. Even if it did not, there is still something wrong with the result, and with the system that allows it to continue. There is something wrong, in other words, with an international market economy in which many people are malnourished while many others live high, when there is enough productive capacity to feed everyone adequately. There is something wrong even if nobody is stealing from anyone else, and even if the inequalities result automatically from the influence of supply and demand, which can produce inequalities of wealth that result in inequalities of distribution.

Such a view challenges the idea that individuals, companies, or nations have a basic right to accumulate wealth and property and to trade with others on whatever terms are mutually acceptable, letting the chips fall where they may. It challenges the idea that if, by industrial and other development, the U.S., the USSR, Europe, and Japan become wealthy enough so that competition between them bids the price of grain up out of the range that India and other poor countries can afford, then there is no moral objection to this outcome because no one has done anything wrong. The position I want to defend is that even if it doesn't involve anyone's *doing* anything wrong, the system that permits this outcome is still morally objectionable. It is true that the moral principles that tell us not to harm other people, by killing or injuring them or stealing the food out of their mouths, are extremely important. But they do not exhaust the moral conditions on personal interaction.

It may seem that the natural suggestion to make at this point is that the worst effects of market inequalities should be dealt with by charity: charity of the rich nations toward the poor. This is a familiar remedy, and seems particularly appropriate when the inequality of wealth is paralleled by an inequality of power. In such circumstances the only motive available for parting the wealthy from their possessions seems to be generosity, if indeed that is available. Perhaps appeal can even be made to something stronger, a *duty* of charity, which comes into force when one can help others in serious distress without excessive cost to oneself. Certainly most people would acknowledge an obligation to throw a life preserver to a drowning man, even if they wouldn't risk their lives to save someone from a burning building. Where in between these extremes the duty of aid to others gives out is not clear. Peter Singer[1] has advocated rectification of inequality along these lines. Governments and individuals are sometimes motivated in varying degrees to engage in charitable aid, and such policies are worth encouraging.

Nevertheless I think it is important to reject charity as a satisfactory solution to the problem. It is important to reject it in this context, not only because of the limits on what it can achieve but because of what it presupposes. Until recently voluntary charity was the major instrument of redistribution *within* countries, and it still has its advocates. It is not threatening to those asked to give, for two reasons. First, it is left to them to determine when the sacrifice they are making for others has reached a point at which any further sacrifice would be supererogatory. Second, it does not question their basic entitlement to what they are asked to donate. The legitimacy of their ownership, and of the processes by which it came about, is not challenged. It is merely urged that, because of the severe need of others, those who are well off should voluntarily part with some of the wealth to which they are morally quite entitled. For this reason people are especially happy to donate help to the victims of a flood, tornado, or earthquake, since the needs created by such natural disasters cannot possibly be taken to cast doubt on the legitimacy of possession of those who have not suffered a comparable calamity. The inequality in these cases, however radical, has not in any sense been produced by a set of social institutions, and a request for rectification by charity cannot therefore be construed as an implicit criticism of the legitimacy of existing wealth.

Radical economic inequalities, however, are not like the results of natural catastrophes. When they persist and tend to reproduce themselves over generations, then the system of political and economic institutions which provides a vehicle for their operation needs to be examined critically. An appeal to charity as a solution, with its implied refusal to challenge the legitimacy of the system of property under which the donors of charity hold title to their possessions, tends to obscure this need. That is why charity has been largely superseded in domestic political arrangements, at least for the most basic requirements of life, by various schemes of redistributive taxation, public benefits, and mandatory social insurance.

The central claim I want to make is that any system of property, national or international, is an institution with moral characteristics: claims of right or entitlement made under it, claims as to what is ours to use as we wish, carry only as much moral weight as the legitimacy of the institution will bear. An institution of property is defined by the mechanisms of acquisition, exchange, inheritance, taxation, and transfer that determine when someone has, loses, or acquires title to something. Moral criticism of these mechanisms may cast doubt on the moral importance of the fact that something belongs to someone under that institution of property—without challenging the claim that it does so belong.[2]

The possibility of such criticism is not limited to any particular point of view. A welfare state will be found illegitimate by a libertarian because it expropriates the well-off in order to support those who have not earned or been given enough to live adequately. A laissez-faire system will be found illegitimate by someone of more egalitarian sympathies, because it permits prosperity to depend too much on the fortunes of birth, background, and talent. My own views are of this second kind. I believe that the provision by sovereign states of a social minimum for their citizens is justified by the fact that morally arbitrary factors can exert so powerful a negative influence on people's lives in the absence of such a policy. For this reason a procedurally orderly system in which no one cheats, coerces, or steals from anyone else can still be morally objectionable because of radical inequalities which systematically arise under it, caused in part by morally arbitrary differences between people in natural endowments, family influence, or access to resources. A society which fails to combat these influences permits the existence of an illegitimate system of property, whose legal conditions of entitlement are morally questionable. The appropriate remedy is not an exhortation to charity, but a revision of the system of property rights to remove its objectionable features. There are more and less radical ways of accomplishing this, but some form of redistributive social welfare is generally accepted as a built-in feature of the operation of modern national economies. It then defines new conditions for legitimate ownership, acquisition, and exchange.

A redistributive tax may be regarded by some libertarians as a form of enforced charity. (Others would call it theft.) But from the point of view I am advocating it is an attempt to build into the conditions of exchange, accumulation, and possession certain safeguards which prevent them from being unjust. Within the United States, for example, a system which permitted one-fourth of the population to starve while the rest were well off would be regarded as unacceptable even if this result arose without coercion or theft, by non-fraudulent economic transactions. The possibility of such a result would generally be taken to undermine the legitimacy of the system, and therefore indirectly the legitimacy of possessions held under it. It wouldn't mean that they were not legal possessions, but only that they were not morally legitimate. Property, in other words, is not a value-free institution. Like political institutions (systems of voting, authority, representation), or judicial institutions, it can possess or lack legitimacy, depending on how it is organized. And the pure workings of market exchange, governed entirely by supply and demand, do not constitute a legitimate institution of property if they permit certain kinds of outcomes. (Just as a system of majority rule would be illegitimate, no matter how impartially applied, if it contained no safeguards against the persecution of unpopular minorities.)

Despite the vast differences in scale and in the political form of the problem, I think these considerations can be applied to the assessment of the international economic order as well. One question about the application of this view is what constitutes a single institution of property in the relevant sense. Why are all the inhabitants of the U.S., for example, participants in one system which can therefore be criticized if it allows excessive inequalities? And what would it mean to call the world economy such a system? If the world contained countries that could not trade or interact with one another, inequalities between them could not be used to criticize the "world economic system." But when a set of institutions governs and authorizes the economic transactions of even a very large population, they become to that extent a community and the effects of the institutions require scrutiny. If the institutions are economic, they govern the lives and require the adherence of practically everyone in their geographical range, and if they play an essential part in creating great wealth in some areas but not in others, then they can be said to contribute to the production of radical inequality even if they do not produce the poverty that is its other aspect. If there are possible alternative arrangements which would reduce the inequality without drastically harming productivity, then such a system is illegitimate.

It seems fairly clear that there is a world economy and that it is illegitimate in this way. Internationally, it is essentially a market economy, with conspicuous deviation toward monopoly in some areas but no significant international taxation, certainly none designed to ensure distributive justice. That kind of thing goes on, to varying degrees, within the boundaries of states. But internationally there is no check to the development of astronomical differences in purchasing power, with disastrous results for the poor countries when the rich countries compete in the market for a limited world grain crop and drive prices out of reach of the poor. These inequalities are largely due to factors of development, resources, population, and history that are morally arbitrary as far as the people involved are concerned. To a limited extent the situation can be mitigated by charity in the form of foreign aid, but it is not an ideal solution. Some internal conditions on the international economy and international markets, to make the whole system of property more legitimate, would be far preferable.[3]

The problem, of course, is that no one is in a position to impose such conditions. It will not be done unless the wealthy countries decide that an improvement in the economic condition of the rest of the world is to their advantage, or at least that it will not cost them much. This is a risky proposition. While redistributive systems do not simply take away from the top what they give to the bottom—since the economy is not like a jar of already baked cookies—still, there is likely to be some effect on the position of the wealthy from any reform that raises the buying power of the poor. Where there are serious problems of scarcity in resources, these effects are likely to be adverse. Moreover, even if it were generally recognized that an international system of taxation would benefit everyone, it would still require forcible imposition because otherwise no nation could be confident that others would contribute if they did. This is the standard problem of coordination and sovereignty familiar since Hobbes analyzed it in the *Leviathan.*

But even though nothing of this kind is likely to occur without a strong international system, it provides a different view of the problem. One cannot take as beyond challenge the fact that each nation owns what it produces and what it can buy on the open market, and that therefore what we have is ours to decide what to do with. Legally this is true, and even if we are moved by the plight of the poor to transfer some of our wealth to them, it is entirely a matter of decision for us, about how to allocate our wealth. Until another system of property is developed, moreover, this will be the main method of combating radical inequality at the international level. But it is useful to keep the illegitimacy of the system in mind, if only for the force it adds to the charitable arguments for foreign aid.

One consequence of the view that radical inequality is an injustice arising from the economic system is that aid should be truly humanitarian. By this I mean that it should be directed at the impoverished purely in virtue of their humanity and not in virtue of their special relation to the donor. Everyone at the bottom deserves help. Perhaps some forms of aid are appropriately influenced by such factors. But aid which simply lifts people off the absolute bottom and helps them to a minimally adequate diet addresses a need so general and basic that it is an inappropriate vehicle for the expression of political preference. Therefore a feature of recent U.S. aid policy that has caused controversy seems clearly objectionable: the preference given to military allies in the allocation of direct aid under P.L. 480. Congress was understandably motivated to impose a requirement that at least 70 percent of food aid under Title I of P.L. 480 go to the most seriously affected countries, independently of their alliances with us. Actually, if the program were truly humanitarian, it would disregard politics entirely. This is not because the somewhat better-off countries that are our allies do not need food aid and cannot use it to serve basic human needs. It is just that the inhabitants of the most seriously affected countries need it more, and if a policy is to be purely humanitarian it must be directed at people in virtue of their humanity alone, and not in virtue of their politics. A humanitarian food aid policy would therefore base allocation solely on nutritional needs.

The trouble is that no aid can be entirely nonpolitical in its *effects*. Aid of any kind permits the transfer of resources from that sector to another, and is therefore equivalent to monetary aid. Food aid to either a friendly or an unfriendly nation permits it to spend more on arms than it could otherwise. There is no aid without some side effects of this sort. Nevertheless, the provision of certain basic human needs can be given priority over political and even strategic considerations, as it is in warfare. The laws of war[4] prohibit attacks on medical personnel and hospitals, destruction of crops, and blockades aimed at starving out the enemy population. Such measures might be militarily useful, but they are prohibited as inhumane. I suggest that the reverse side of this coin is that positive aid, if it is to be fully humane, should not be influenced by political factors when it concerns basic and universal human needs—even when, as is almost inevitable, it has politically relevant effects.

A final point to consider is the one raised by Garrett Hardin in support of what he calls the "lifeboat ethic."[5] He argues that food aid to the poorest countries will do harm rather than good, because by reducing the death rate without altering the birth rate it will result in larger populations and ensure a larger-scale collapse at a later date, when the world's productive capacities are exhausted. This means that the most beneficial policy toward the poor countries coincides remarkably with the interest of the rich—namely not to give any aid at all.

We should be suspicious of a result which coincides so perfectly with our economic self-interest. Certainly population control and internal agricultural development are the most important factors in improving the situation of the poorest countries over the long term. But the immediate problem still exists, and transfers are the only way of preventing starvation and malnutrition for millions of people over the next 10 years. Those people have already been born, and a very powerful reason would be needed to deny them food resources that are definitely available. The reason offered by Hardin is not powerful enough, for it depends on a conjecture about what will happen in the future. We are therefore weighing the certainty of a present disaster against the possibility of a greater future disaster—a possibility to which no definite likelihood can be assigned. While the determinants of birth rate are complex and not uniform, population growth often diminishes following a rise in the standard of living, for good reason. Since the catastrophic results predicted by Hardin are not inevitable, and can be combated directly, it would be wrong to refuse to avert certain disaster in the present on the assumption that this was the only way to prevent greater and equally certain disaster in the future. Sometimes a present sacrifice must be made to forestall even the uncertain prospect of a far greater evil in the future. But this is true only if the two evils are of different orders of magnitude. In the case at hand, the present sacrifice is too great to be subject to such calculations.

While foreign aid is not the best method of dealing with radical inequality—being comparable to private charity on the domestic scene—it is the only method now available. It does not require a strongly egalitarian moral position to feel that the U.S., with a gross national product of a trillion dollars and a defense budget which is 9 percent of that, should be spending more than its current two-fifths of 1 percent of GNP on nonmilitary foreign aid, given the world as it is. The worst-off countries are so poor and unable to compete in the world commodity market that without transfers, millions of individuals in them will grow up malnourished, with short and wretched life spans. We can afford to give substantially more than we do without reducing ourselves to starvation.

Whether the rich should give more than is needed to combat *radical* inequality—whether they should take a more general equality as their goal—is a question I shall not address. It seems in any case that charity is a poor instrument for the achievement of substantial equality, and that alternative institutional arrangements would be required. It is moreover unrealistic to ask the well-off to make substantial sacrifices voluntarily in order to improve the standard of living of others who are merely much less well off, without being wretchedly poor. Redistribution of this kind requires a universal involuntary system that can be enforced, and that does not depend on the sum of individual decisions. Perhaps some day such a system will exist. But till then, there is much to be done to ameliorate the worst effects of those radical inequalities that are produced by the unimpeded operation of the international market economy.

NOTES

1. "Famine, Affluence, and Morality," *Philosophy and Public Affairs,* 1 (Spring, 1972), pp. 229–243. Also see Peter Singer's chapter in this volume.

2. My remarks are influenced by Thomas M. Scanlon, "Liberty, Contract and Contribution," in *Markets and Morals,* ed. by G. Dworkin, G. Bermant, and P. Brown (Washington, D.C.: Hemisphere Press, forthcoming).

3. For a penetrating discussion of this topic, see Charles R. Beitz, "Justice and International Relations," *Philosophy and Public Affairs,* 4 (Summer 1975),

pp. 360–389, esp. pp. 381–382, at which he discusses the conditions of social cooperation and institutional unification that makes requirements of distributive justice apply.

4. The Hague Convention on Land Warfare, of 1907, and the Geneva Convention on the Law of War, of 1949.

5. See "Living on a Lifeboat," *Bioscience,* 24 (October 1974), pp. 561–568.

Part Two
RESPONSIBILITIES IN THE PUBLIC SECTOR

ABOUT THE CONTRIBUTORS

Peter G. Brown wrote *The American Law Institute Model Land Development Code, The Taking Issue and Private Property Rights,* and a number of articles including "The Place of Informed Consent in Social Experiments" and "Ethics and Policy Research." He is the Director of the Center for Philosophy and Public Policy of the University of Maryland.

Lawrence Witt has written several books, including *Agriculture in Economic Development* with Carl Eicher, and many articles. A past president of the American Agricultural Economics Association, he has served as consultant to the World Bank, A.I.D., F.A.O., and to various institutes in this country, Turkey, and Latin America. Retired from Michigan State University, he now works in the U.S. Department of State.

Daniel E. Shaughnessy is Deputy Coordinator of the A.I.D. Office of Food for Peace. He earlier directed the Food and Nutrition Division of A.I.D. in India for 4 years and has participated frequently in international negotiations concerning food and development. A former food policy specialist on the staff of Senator Hubert Humphrey, he was also a member of the staff that coordinated U.S. preparations for the World Food Conference and served on the U.S. Delegation to the Conference.

Joseph D. Sneed's publications include *The Logical Structure of Mathematical Physics* and, with Steven Waldhorn, *Restructuring the Federal System: Approaches to Accountability in Post-Categorical Programs*, as well as articles in *Erkenntnis, Synthese,* and other scholarly journals. He teaches at the University of California at Santa Cruz.

Samuel Gorovitz is senior editor of *Moral Problems in Medicine* and has written extensively in the philosophy of medicine and other areas. He is Professor and Chairman in the Department of Philosophy at the University of Maryland, College Park.

Food as national property
Peter G. Brown

INTRODUCTION

The purpose of this paper is to examine some of the implications of thinking of food as the property of the nation in which it is grown. In developing this perspective about food I concentrate on a justification of property—the labor theory—which minimizes the responsibility that owners have to others. I do not think this theory is free from a number of problems as a justification for property rights. However, I concentrate on it because if it can be shown that we (collectively) have a greater obligation than we are discharging on its terms then—because it minimizes obligations—we can be certain that (for the theories considered) we have at least that much obligation.

Hence, I will show that even in terms of this kind of justification the United States has an obligation to assist in alleviating food deficits abroad. Other theories that are discussed and evaluated would yield even stronger redistributive conclusions. Thus accepting the redistributive conclusions of the chapter does not depend on accepting the theory of property most discussed in it. Put differently, substantial redistributions are neutral, at least among the theories considered. Of course, the amount of redistribution differs according to the theory on which one depends.

This overall conclusion is supported by means of the development of the following thesis: *Present practices in international trade fail to reflect the special rules that ought to apply to oligopolies*[1] *in natural assets.* (I will argue below that natural assets are in some sense common assets.) By way of these arguments I hope to offer at least a general answer to the question of why the United States

---

I am indebted to a number of individuals for help on this chapter. They include Lynn Daft, Robert Kudrle, Martin MacLaughlin, Henry Shue, and Robert Spaeth. Difficulties with the present version are the author's sole responsibility.

has an obligation to assist, and even take the initiative, in meeting food deficits abroad.[2]

I proceed as follows: first, a discussion of meaning of ownership; second, a discussion of types of theories that can be offered as justifications for ownership; third, an analysis of some of the constraints that should accompany ownership of certain natural vital assets; and fourth, a discussion of how these arguments clarify the nature, and the extent, of United States obligations to those in food deficit countries.

THE MEANING OF OWNERSHIP

I offer the following as a definition of ownership: We own something if and only if we may use it, and even dispose of it, when and how we see fit. Since I own my tie, I may throw it away, tie it in knots, or hang it carefully in my closet. I may dispose of it on sheer whim. But this is surely a polar case, for the context in which something is owned normally dictates a number of constraints.

The most commonly advanced set of arguments for restricting rights connected with ownership build on the notion of limiting or eliminating the negative effects of one person's actions with his property on the person or property of others. Perhaps a more adequate definition of property is that property is what we may use and dispose of when and how we see fit subject to the legitimate constraints imposed by society. More precisely, we own something when both of the following conditions are satisfied simultaneously: (1) we may do with it what we wish, subject to the constraints imposed by the institutions of our society;[3] and (2) we have acquired it fairly.[4]

There is no difficulty in asserting that collectivities like corporations and nations can own something in much the same sense in which an individual can. Indeed, most of my argument is directed to the supposition I think underlying a good deal of present policy—that the United States owns, that is, has certain rights to use and dispose of, the food grown within its borders.[5]

Of course, the government has to pay for food secured from private suppliers much as a corporation has to pay for materials purchased from others. But when the government imposes constraints on its food exports—through embargoes or long-term contracts—it imposes constraints characteristic of ownership on the disposition of food. In short, the more the government intervenes in a freely operating market, when the nation in question is one of a few net exporters, the more its behavior can become oligopolistic. These market interventions are sometimes justified by reference to increasing farm income, improving the balance of payments,[6] satisfying various strategic and military objectives, etc. At bottom these policies rest on the assumption that the government may use food policy to maximize the welfare of some or all of its citizens.

While few would doubt that maximizing the welfare of its citizens is *a* responsibility of government, another set of concerns can be raised about the means which should be employed in fulfilling this responsibility. Because the United States is one of a very few consistent net exporters of grain, the more the government consolidates the market on the distribution side, the more its behavior becomes oligopolistic. To the extent oligopolies are undesirable the government has at least a *prima facie* obligation to avoid such behavior.

THEORIES OF OWNERSHIP

While this paper focuses on a labor theory of ownership, the idea that one owns that in which one has invested his labor is not the only account that can be offered of ownership. If one extrapolates from various theories of ownership that have been advanced in the philosophical literature, there appear to be two other general types: those which emphasize accidental acquisition of the asset in question and utilitarian theories of ownership.

Accidental Acquisition Theories of Ownership

In *A Theory of Justice*,[7] John Rawls has raised the question of who is entitled to the fruits of human intelligence. Do the benefits derived from being intelligent, such as increased income, and productivity, rightfully accrue to the person who is intelligent, or should they be allocated according to some other principle to all members of his society? Rawls responds in favor of the view that these are common resources and are not owned by the individuals possessing them. He reaches this conclusion by asking to what we can attribute a person's possession of this capability. "Once we decide to look for a conception of justice that nullifies the accidents of natural endowment and the contingencies of social circumstance as counters in quest for political and economic advantage, we are led to ... the result of leaving aside those aspects of the social world that seem arbitrary from a moral point of view."[8] Intelligence in his view is derived largely from genetic "accidents" having to do with the characteristics of one's parents and to environmental circumstances of early childhood, also largely, if not wholly, beyond the realm of influence of the person possessing this resource. From the point of view of the individual involved, possession of these resources is entirely accidental, since they depend on factors over which he had no control.

For Rawls, this line of reasoning establishes that the fruits of human intelligence, ambition, and the like are accidentally acquired and hence subject to the principles of justice. In particular, for Rawls these assets would be subject to the two principles of justice.[9] This position assigns an all-encompassing role to justice, and perhaps helps to make clear what Rawls means when he says "Justice is the first virtue of social institutions. . . ."[10] In deriving the legitimacy of social institutions, the requirements of justice must precede those of property. (But for reasons sketched below, this may go too far.)

Can similar arguments be made in respect to the possession of agricultural resources? Consider the question first from the point of view of the populace as a whole. To what extent does the present generation of individuals living in the United States, that is, the populace at large, deserve exclusive or even predominant rights to the enjoyment (either directly or indirectly by selling them) of the fruits of our agricultural affluence? The fact that *we*, the present generation, live in the United States is wholly accidental (except for recent immigrants). It would appear that, as a group, we have done nothing to deserve this boon.

Can the same kind of argument be made with respect to at least some of the agricultural producers (farmers and the like) in the United States? Have they not purchased these productive capabilities or inherited them from persons who, in one way or another, earned them? And for these reasons do they not deserve to own them? Divide individuals into two groups in respect to this question. First, consider those who inherited these assets. A general Rawlsian line of argument will still work, since by definition they acquired the assets earned by another if, indeed, the other earned them. Second, take purchasers: though this is not so obvious, a Rawlsian line seems to still work. How did they acquire the assets which made it possible for them to make these purchases? How did they acquire the capital, both human and financial, to purchase these productive capabilities? One could make the argument that this capital accrued in ways which were accidental from their point of view—that is, their education, upbringing, and the acquisitions of wealth depended in large measure on capabilities which were acquired fortuitously.

There are two reasons for not wanting to accept this as an exhaustive account of ownership. First, a difficulty with the Rawls view is that it seems to go too far and leads to the undermining of the dignity that it seeks to preserve. Insofar as it stresses the accidental acquisition of *all* human resources, it appears to undermine the possibility of individuals affecting their own future, and hence a good deal of the dignity normally associated with human choice. In order to support his view that intelligence is wholly accidentally acquired, Rawls is forced to embrace a thoroughgoing determinism.

Second, Rawls argues that the common ownership of resources requires that a benefit for the more advantaged is justifiable only if it improves the condition of the least advantaged. Under certain conditions that Rawls specifies[11] it seems compatible with requiring individuals with rare blood types (since blood types are accidental from the individual's point of view) to constantly give blood to a hemophiliac and seems to give this requirement the status of an obligation. Hence the accidental acquisition view carried too far seems to make one's own body a piece of public property. Perhaps Rawls's position on the ownership of one's talents rests on failing to distinguish between zero-sum and non-zero-sum situations. In the ownership of land, one person's ownership of it is incompatible with others having *the same* relationship toward it. Land is naturally finite, or very nearly so. But one person's being intelligent does not take intelligence away from someone else. Looked at this way, it seems reasonable to attach certain conditions (discussed below) to naturally limited assets necessary for life (though I would draw the line "at the body" or at least "outside the body"), but not to apply them to non-zero-sum characteristics.

Drawing this sort of distinction should yield a "mixed theory" of property and justice. Justice would not be "*the* first virtue of social institutions," but *a* first virtue. While admittedly untidy when compared with a pure theory—where one or the other is prior—a mixed theory suggests that considerations of justice begin, *ceteris paribus,* where those of property leave off and vice versa. The trick of this kind of theory is to specify both what is meant by justice and by property *and* the boundaries between them. Further, an analysis of whether or not there are conditions under which considerations of property or justice become "temporarily" prior and controlling is required.

Utilitarian Theories

The question that a utilitarian theory must *begin* with is, How can the sum total of resources and the capacity for producing them be allocated in a way to maximize human happiness? The answer that one gives to this may involve private ownership, nationalization of the means of production, international ownership, etc. None of these forms is ruled out in advance. Choosing between them is to be decided on the basis of aggregate productive capability maximizing human happiness flowing from alternative ownership arrangements. In this framework, when the community of interest is construed as mankind at large,[12] any special *a priori* claims Americans have to their abundance disappear. U.S. claims, and those of its citizens, become subject to the same utilitarian calculus as everyone else's.

Utilitarian theories are often objected to as an exhaustive account of our moral life because they seem to permit exploitation of one individual to secure greater happiness for others.[13] Moreover, on certain interpretations it seems to give rise to overreaching obligations. Am I *obliged* to give one of two good eyes to a blind person (stranger) on the grounds that this will increase his happiness more than it will diminish mine? Peter Singer's view, for instance, seems to offer no place to draw a line indicating where obligation ceases.[14] His view seems to rule out any personal development which would not assist the needy.

But to the extent that utilitarianism is an adequate account of moral practice, it is doubtful whether certain aspects of present policy reflect its precepts. Utilitarianism, at least in its more recent formulations, offers itself as an account of moral practices of the human race generally.[15] Within this framework it thus becomes incumbent on those setting national policies to show that the pursuit of national objectives based on efforts to maximize the happiness of citizens is the most effective means to maximize happiness overall. It may be possible to sustain such arguments for certain types of practices, where it can be shown that it is more efficient for each nation to "take care of its own." However, policies inhibiting access to vital resources like food will be difficult to prove on any reasonable assumptions concerning the role of an adequate diet in human happiness. On this view, national policies which have oligopolistic effects on commodities vital for human life are *prima facie* suspect.

The very brief arguments of this section are devoted to assessing what appear to be government interventions that can have oligopolistic results—in particular, long-term contracts and other efforts to "centralize" export policy. Of course, centralization of exports does not necessarily encourage oligopoly within domestic markets,[16] but it makes the U.S. government an oligopolistic actor in world market.

At bottom, efficiency-based antioligopoly arguments rest on the idea that ability to control a large portion of the supply of something can, and usually will, cause unnecessarily high prices to consumers and/or result in restrictions of the overall supply. Hence any attempts to limit the number of distributors either directly or through covert or overt manipulations of information on the production side of the market should have a burden of proof against them, requiring demonstration that their arrangements do not have adverse price effects.

What is interesting from the point of view of food exports is that an oligopolistic result can be produced even though the number of private suppliers and distributors is relatively large, and even where new entrants on the supply side are not artificially restricted. As the U.S. government becomes a principal actor in export policy, it sharply restricts the number of bargainers on the supply side. These oligopolistic effects could be intensified by long-term contracts which may have a tendency to create a residual market in grain.

Take a simple example. Suppose the United States was one of ten governments in the world and negotiated export agreements with six of the others. Though these agreements may contain various escape clauses, the more they constitute real contracts, the more they may tend to put upward pressure on prices, though the crucial test would be whether prices were higher on average. Conversely, the broader the escape clauses, the less they constitute real contracts. What are the circumstances of those left to bargain for that portion of the supply not subject to export agreements? Insofar as arguments can be mustered against private monopolies and/or oligopolies for their effect on price, the same arguments can be marshaled against governments for their effects on prices to consumer countries that must make their purchases from the residual market.

Of course, if these and other interferences with trade affect only a small portion of the market, then their oligopolistic impacts would be small (though international trade in commodities is generally far from competitive). To the extent that these effects are not very small, these arguments serve to shift the burden to the government to show that interventions in the competitive system are justified on other compelling grounds. At a minimum it would seem reasonable to require that the government show (as opposed to assert) that these arrangements do not have either of the following effects: (1) that in *short-supply years* the price in the residual market will not be substantially higher than it would be without such long-term contracts, and (2) that the *overall effects* of these arrangements taking an average of prices (over some period) would not be higher in the residual market than prices that would prevail in the absence of such contracts.[17] In the first case, if the creation of a residual market has a large price effect in years of short supply, this would work very substantially to the disadvantage of the poor in food deficit countries and consumers in this nation. For the price then would be even higher than it would have been during a year when it was high to begin with. In the second, such contracts could produce persistent price and quantity constraints to the "residual consumers," not to mention malnutrition and/or starvation to those of insufficient income.

While I admit that the determination of these two effects is tricky and to be left to the trained economist, my suspicion is that these effects could be substantial if long-term contracts, embargoes, or other market interventions became the rule rather than the exception. Minimally fair requirements would demand a showing that these fears were ungrounded, *or* that there were very compelling arguments for excepting these policies from normal rules governing oligopolies because of other beneficial effects they might have. If the price effects do prove to be substantial but the long-term contracts can be supported with strong and compelling other reasons, then the burden should be on the U.S. and other beneficiaries of these agreements to design institutions to mitigate and even reverse their price-elevating and quantity-restricting consequences to those disadvantaged by the policies.

The Labor Theory of Property: Arguments against Oligopolies in Common Assets

What is at stake here can be drawn out by beginning with an example similar to Garrett Hardin's in "The Tragedy of the Commons."[18] Suppose there is a sheep meadow of 10 acres and there are 10 individuals who wish to graze sheep on it. Suppose it could be shown that more sheep of better quality could be raised if, rather than having the 10 acres in common, several individuals appropriated certain proportions of the commons. Suppose further that it turned out that the most efficient size for a sheep pasture was 2 acres, and that five individuals proposed that the common be divided into five 2-acre lots. In order to be fair to the five individuals excluded from the land, some arrangement would have to be made so that the reapportionment of commonly held property did not work to their disadvantage. Otherwise, the appropriation is not in their interest, and becomes an unjustified coercion of them.

Now what is required to show that other people are not disadvantaged by the appropriation is demonstrating that private property does not constitute a net disadvantage to them, but offers *other* opportunities, perhaps even net benefits. There is no presumption against private property on this view, but it does place the burden on those who would appropriate from common assets to show that their appropriations have not worsened the plight of others. Since this point is formulated by Locke I shall, following Nozick, henceforth refer to it as the "Lockean proviso."[19]

In *Anarchy, State and Utopia,* Nozick summarizes the way private ownership can satisfy this requirement as follows:

> Is the situation of persons who are unable to appropriate (there being no more accessible and useful unowned objects) worsened by a system allowing appropriation and permanent property? Here enter the various familiar social considerations favoring private property; it increases the social product by putting means of production in the hands of those who can use them most efficiently (profitably); experimentation is encouraged, because with separate persons controlling resources, there is no one person or small group whom someone with a new idea must convince to try it out; private property enables people to decide on the pattern and types of risks they wish to bear, leading to specialized types of risk bearing; private property protects future persons by leading some to hold back resources from current consumption for future markets; it provides alternate sources of employment for unpopular persons who don't have to convince any one person or small group to hire them, and so on. These considerations enter a Lockean theory to support the claim that appropriation of private property satisfies the intent behind the "enough and as good left over" proviso, *not* as a utilitarian justification of property.[20]

If, in appropriating a common asset, one has simultaneously taken some opportunities away but substituted others of equal or greater value, then the requirements of fairness have been satisfied. It is of great importance to notice that one way this stipulation can be met is to (in some extended sense) permit others to continue to use the asset in question. One way *this* requirement can be satisfied is by selling the products from the appropriated assets; though, needless to say, this way of satisfying the Lockean proviso is perverse if others do not have the wherewithal to purchase these products, and their poverty is a result of the appropriation by others.

As further examples of common assets that have been appropriated by private individuals consider air and water pollution. Those who are polluting them are appropriating what is a common asset for disposal of *their* waste. The view sketched above does not say such waste disposal is to be prohibited, but it does require those who would dispose of their waste in this way to show that the overall result of this appropriation works to the advantage of those previously (or who would otherwise be) enjoying it unhampered. The benefits accruing from this manner of waste disposal must compensate those who are disenfranchised for their loss.

But I want to go beyond these familiar examples and make a somewhat bolder claim: that the natural resources of the earth insofar as they are *natural* constitute common resources. While there are good and even compelling reasons why these natural resources should be appropriated, those who would undertake such appropriations must show that those excluded from the appropriations do not suffer as a result of it.[21] (It is important to note that this assertion is being made about wealth generated by natural resources and not about the wealth generated by the labor of individuals now living.)

Here several complications arise: (1) Under what circumstances would we know that appropriation had adversely affected others? Suffer as compared to what? By what standard do we judge being disadvantaged? (2) What reasons are there for believing that the world's natural resources are common resources? And (3) what do we make of the fact that most natural resources available to the present generation are mediated to some degree or another by labor and capital of preceding generations? Take these issues in turn.

The first question can be broken down into two parts: (a) what sorts of conditions should *give rise to inquiry* as to whether the Lockean proviso is being violated, and (b) by what standard should we decide whether it is being violated?

Certainly one set of considerations that should trigger such an inquiry occurs when one group of individuals is suffering long-term chronic needs and another group is enjoying affluence based to some degree on wealth generated from natural resources. Surely, this is a rough description of circumstances prevailing in the world food market. The more that others are in need, the more heavily the burden rests on those in possession of these resources to demonstrate that their appropriations have not disadvantaged those in need.

There are clearly cases where there could be large numbers of individuals in need and those in possession of common assets could not be charged with having disadvantaged them through the appropriation of these assets. This could be the case in at least two circumstances. The first is where the overall supply of the food in question is simply insufficient for the number of individuals making a claim on it. A second case in which individuals could be in substantial need but the proviso has not been violated is where those in possession of the assets have made redistributions of their income in whatever proportion it flows from the ownership of natural assets. Thus the demonstration of need does not show on its face that the proviso has been violated. My guess is, however, that neither of these cases, where the proviso is inapplicable, is even remotely approximated by the present distribution of world food and related resources.

But by what standard should we judge whether individuals or groups have been disadvantaged through the appropriation by others of a common asset? The example of the meadow, discussed above, presupposes that a historical baseline can be used to answer this question: individuals are disadvantaged by the appropriation if after it, *ceteris paribus,* they are worse off than they were before it. This standard would seem to be applicable to resources not yet, or just being, appropriated, such as the ocean floor. (However, even here we do not get a clean point of departure since what nations are now getting from the ocean floor is, at least in part, a function of their share of other resources.)

Moreover, the case of the ocean floor is the exception rather than the rule—most natural resources of the world come to us mediated by the ownership of many previous generations. Here a historical baseline seems less relevant, and probably is unusable.

Nevertheless, perhaps the root idea of the baseline can be captured by another conceptual net. People should have equal opportunity to enjoy the fruits of natural assets, *insofar as the equality of opportunity can be secured by a redistribution of the wealth flowing from the natural assets. Note that this does not imply equality or even equality of opportunity, but only that the wealth flowing from natural resources should be distributed in the most effective way possible to promote equality of opportunity.* To the extent that this is most effectively accomplished by helping the poorest, this principle provides a rationale for the new emphases in the International Development and Food Assistance Act of 1975.[22]

Perhaps "not advantaged" or "made to suffer" in the appropriation of common assets can then be taken to mean that *insofar* as the wealth and income of some individuals and/or groups flows from natural assets, it should be distributed so as to increase the access of all to the use of those resources. Where an effective production and distribution capability exists, income transfers or means to stimulate indigenous agricultural production can satisfy *this* principle. At a minimum this would seem to indicate that the products derived from natural assets should be distributed to those most unable to secure the preconditions of entry to world markets.

Turn now to the second question: what reasons are there for believing that the world's natural resources are common resources? I think the labor theory of ownership gives a rather clear answer to this question, simply by pointing out that since natural resources are natural, and therefore no work or "art" has been expended upon them, they are not property at all. Rather they are the common "capital" of those who need them to sustain and enhance life.

Since, by definition, they depend upon no human efforts, no one has any more of a claim to them than anyone else. *To the extent* that the income and wealth generated by private ownership of these assets depends upon the naturalness and not upon the effort expended upon them, that portion of the income should be used for the common benefit. Thus the burden of proof is on those nations presently holding assets like petroleum, coal, and prime agricultural land to show that appropriation of these assets has not disadvantaged those not so enfranchised. (This imposes an affirmative burden on nations, such as some in Africa, to make effective use of underutilized agricultural potential.[23]) One way to think about the consequences of the proviso is that whatever income and wealth are generated by natural assets should be subject to a theory of distributive justice. This marks a juncture between a theory of property and a theory of justice.

Third, take the question of assets left to any given generation by its predecessors. I think that these can be divided (perhaps conceptually only) into those secured by effort and those derived from natural assets. Most, probably all, forms of wealth will involve a mix of these two sources. Disentangling them is sure to be a formidable process *at the very best.* But such problems should not impair the conceptual issues addressed by the proviso.

Yet insofar as wealth and income are the results of individual labor and investment, they remain private goods subject to inheritance and the like, though, of course, there may be numerous reasons not connected with the proviso for intergenerational taxes. Yet note that goods that are private for one generation are not necessarily so for another. A patent may make any invention a private good for some time, but after a certain number of years it can become a public asset. Hence, all else being equal, the number of public assets should be greater with each generation. Hence *some* of the private assets of one generation can be thought of as the "natural" or public assets of the next.

I hope this provides an extremely rough and ready but hopefully not totally ambiguous way of classifying factors in the production of food. Consider Figure 4.1:

Figure 4-1. Natural and Artificial Factors in the Production of Food

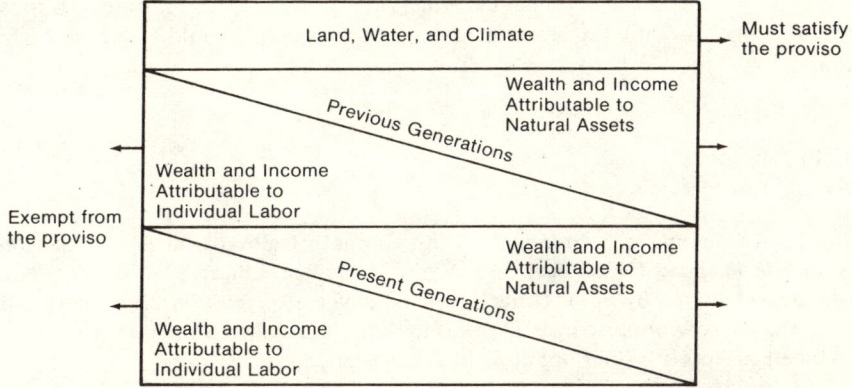

The notions sketched in the figure are obviously in need of further refinement, and problems of empirical disentanglement may be crushing at best. Obviously, no attempt at empirical estimation has been made, nor is the author qualified to do so.

SOME IMPLICATIONS OF THE ARGUMENTS

The arguments sketched before seem both to explicate and give foundation to two widespread sentiments on foreign agricultural assistance: (1) it provides an answer to the question of why we are obligated to provide assistance and why the United States and other agriculturally affluent nations have a special obligation to meet nutritional needs;[24] and (2) it seems to offer (absent other reasons), a stopping point in these obligations by suggesting that once the proviso has been satisfied, wealth is not *prima facie* suspect. It thus seems to offer an escape from one argument against foreign assistance: that once we begin meeting the needs of others, there is no stopping place—that we will be completely impoverished, with our resources and even our lives laid waste. While redistributions based on the arguments advanced in this paper could be substantial, they would not be unlimited. These arguments advanced against foreign assistance may be applicable to other rationales, but not to this one.

Moreover, these arguments suggest at least a structuring of multilateral initiatives with the agriculturally affluent nations forming special assistance groups. Of course, being a net exporter does not exhaust the class of agriculturally affluent nations, since nonexporters with prime agricultural land may also fall under the proviso. Such policies could set an example for other nations, rich in other natural resources, to do likewise.

One way the proviso can be satisfied is to arrange the factors of production and distribution so that those not enfranchised can still enjoy the benefits of the natural assets. Securing the conditions of employment and keeping as fully competitive a market as possible can thus satisfy the proviso in respect to those able to work. In-kind transfers or income supplements should be provided for others.

NOTES

1. An oligopoly is defined by John Kenneth Galbraith in *Economics and the Public Purpose* (New York: The New American Library, 1975), p. 38, as "the market shared by a few firms." *Webster's New Collegiate Dictionary* (1973) states that an oligopoly consists of "a market situation in which each of a few producers affects but does not control the market."

2. While many observers assert that we have an obligation to assist the malnourished, few, if any, go beyond demonstrating that others have a need for resources, and fail to show who, if anyone, has an obligation to meet it. Someone may have a need for sex, but does it follow that I (or anyone?) have an obligation to provide it? In general, even the existence of a vital need does not *ipso facto* demonstrate an obligation. If someone unknown to me needs a kidney transplant, this does not show that I (or anyone) have an obligation to provide a kidney. However, such obligations may exist in the context of special relationships of the sort discussed by Samuel Gorovitz. See Gorovitz chapter of this volume.

3. When we rent something, we own the use of it for a certain period of time. Obviously, our discretionary actions toward it are much more limited than when we own it in a more literal sense. I am indebted to Ilmar Waldner for this point.

4. See Robert Nozick's *Anarchy, State and Utopia* (New York: Basic Books, Inc., 1974) for a detailed, if radical, account of ownership.

5. These arguments are neutral in respect to the question of whether farmers own the food they produce. I take it that farmers have no more or less responsibility to aid in meeting world food deficits than other Americans. Farmers operate in a system of incentives and rules of national and, in some cases, international determination. To single out one group to bear the costs of reforming those rules would be unfair, since the costs of redefining the rules should be borne by all those who benefit from them.

6. See Lawrence Witt's chapter in this volume.

7. John Rawls, *A Theory of Justice* (Cambridge, Mass.: Harvard University Press, 1971).

8. *Ibid.*, p. 15.

9. *Ibid.*, pp. 60-65.

10. *Ibid.*, p. 3.

11. Rawls notes that under certain social conditions liberty is not prior: "(§26). The supposition is that if the persons in the original position assume that their basic liberties can be effectively exercised, they will not exchange a lesser liberty for an improvement in their economic well-being, at least not once a certain level of wealth has been attained. It is only when social conditions do not allow the effective establishment of these rights that one can acknowledge their restriction. *The denial of equal liberty can be accepted only if it is necessary to enhance the quality of civilization so that in due course the equal freedoms can be enjoyed by all.* The lexical ordering of the two principles is the long-run tendency of the general conception of justice consistently pursued under reasonably favorable conditions." (*Ibid.*, p. 542.)

Perhaps Rawls could deal with my counter-example by distinguishing between liberties that could be sacrificed, e.g., never violating bodily integrity, and those that could be violated. (See, for instance, his discussion [p. 247] of the constraints on liberty that may be undertaken in the name of equal liberty.) But, at best, this is going to be a difficult line to draw in such a way that does not rule out legitimate invasions of bodily integrity such as vaccination.

12. In terms of the terminology employed in Joseph Sneed's chapter in this volume the question of whose happiness is to be maximized turns on what one takes to be the domain of the theory.

13. While the distinction between act and rule utilitarianism serves to blunt this objection, it does not remove its force entirely. It still leaves the practice or rule in question open to calculation in terms of its consequences for human happiness, and it is the possibility that certain fundamental rights, or whatever, could be up for grabs that is the source of the disquiet with this view.

14. See Peter Singer's chapter in this volume.

15. For Bentham it was to be a framework for formulating national policy.

16. Indeed, to the extent that farmers rely on other more oligopolistic sectors of the economy (for their inputs) their strict adherence to the free market may place *them* at a comparative disadvantage.

17. Arguments based on adverse price effects of long-term contracts can be brought on behalf of consumers both in the United States and in chronic food deficit countries.

18. Garrett Hardin, "The Tragedy of the Commons," *Science*, December 13, 1968, pp. 1243-1248.

19. This would seem to capture what Locke had in mind with the proviso.

20. Nozick, p. 177.

21. Perhaps "incompatibility of consumption" by more than one individual is a necessary condition for being subject to the proviso. But it cannot be sufficient, for then all private consumption goods (like automobiles, hamburgers, etc.) would fall under it.

22. P.L. 94-161, 89 Stat. 849-869. See Henry Shue's chapter in this volume.

23. I am indebted to Robert Kudrle for suggesting this point.

24. Since, as noted above (note 2), the existence of a need does not show who, if anyone, should meet it.

5 Food aid, commercial exports, and the balance of payments

Lawrence Witt

Three characteristics dominated the world food scene in the 25 years prior to 1972, namely:

- The persistence of excess food production capacity in many of the developed countries
- A growing sense of responsibility and moral concern to help people living near the edge of subsistence
- An expansion in large-scale food aid activities

Declines in food aid after 1972 raise questions as to whether support for food aid is weakening, and if so, whether this change is due to an erosion of moral values, to frustrations stemming from the persistence of serious nutritional problems, or to changes in the economic setting that make new commercial options available.

While some aspects of all three characteristics can be identified over several generations, they were usually expressed in domestic terms, and only episodically in the international arena, until the 1950s. The coincidence of these three characteristics makes it difficult to determine whether the expressed values were newly emphasized, were convenient rationalizations, or were long-held values that could be implemented at modest cost. Additional complications can be introduced by using alternative definitions of steady support for food aid—whether as an amount of money, a constant volume of food, or a constant percent of donor country GNP. Further, as international food aid became

---

Although this chapter was written mainly while the author was on detail from the U.S. Department of State to the World Bank, the views expressed do not necessarily represent those of either the Bank or of the U.S. Department of State.

operational, the institutional structure and feedback from actual programs could have an impact on the attitudes of people in donor countries, often positive but sometimes negative, as a result of dissatisfactions with food aid accomplishments or frustrations because malnutrition was not rapidly eliminated.

This chapter argues that most of the changes in the volume of food aid can be explained by holding moral values on food aid constant in a framework of decreasing excess capacity and rising real costs of food aid. It considers some of the options in a world in which balanced supply and demand make food aid much more expensive, because continued donations draw on food supplies that could be sold or require the investment of capital to enlarge food production and food export capacities.

GROWTH OF SOCIAL CONCERN

Until relatively recently, food and shelter constituted two-thirds or more of family expenditures for most people in most societies. Assistance to other people inevitably was dominated by food; however, the "other people" were at no great distance, culturally and geographically. During the twentieth century, domestic programs to mitigate some of the inequalities in the flow of income became institutionalized in developed countries. Specifically, early programs provided food and shelter to those without income-earning prospects, then expanded to those whose earned income was deemed inadequate. More slowly, the flow of consumer goods and services expanded from food and shelter to a broader, more recipient-selected group of products.

From time to time, severe disasters, such as the aftermath of World War I and the Japanese earthquake, led to temporary programs to assist people in other lands, with food as a principal component. The Red Cross became institutionalized with both a domestic and an international mission. Improved communication accelerated a process of becoming more concerned with low-income, low-consumption people who were farther away culturally, socially, geographically, and consciously. This led first to an increased use of national governments to reallocate goods and services domestically, and in the last half of the twentieth century to the use of both national and international government to reallocate products among nations.

This recent transfer of resources from the more affluent to the less affluent nations has taken many forms, in contrast with the nineteenth and early twentieth centuries. Early economic development was dominated by large commercial loans (with subsequent doubts, at least in recipient countries, as to whether these loans facilitated development or were techniques for long-term exploitation). During the past quarter century, the international transfer has become a complex set of commercial loans, soft loans, in-kind transfers, concessional sales, and donations, and includes a wide range of goods and services. But food continues to play a special role with softer terms, most of the donations, and an important share of investment activities, reflecting its importance in maintaining life.

THE GROWTH OF FOOD PROGRAMS

The Marshall Plan and other precursors of AID developed as broad programs of assistance, including food as one of the commodities eligible for transfer. By the early 1950s, Congressional and public (agricultural) pressures on program administrators were placing high priorities on food shipments, with specific legislation or administrative agreements to increase the proportions of assistance funds spent on agricultural products, culminating in the passage in 1954 of Public Law 480. Under this law, U.S. international food assistance quickly expanded and became institutionalized. Also, the U.S. government now had a capacity to respond more quickly to a disaster, without requiring special legislation, and to respond to small-scale disasters which would not bring enough attention to induce legislation.

Although early food distribution programs were worldwide, U.S. programs shifted focus, during the 1950s, to concentrate on nations in the developing world, and over the next decade were joined by other countries in their own bilateral programs. The World Food Program came into being in 1962, providing a multilateral activity to which many nations could contribute, expanding beyond food exporters and including the use of food, shipping services, and cash. The Food Aid Convention in 1968 became a complementary part of the International Wheat Agreement, committing most members to specified levels of food aid.

FOOD AID WITH EXCESS PRODUCTION CAPACITY

For most of the period from 1929 to 1970, governments in grain-exporting nations intervened in the marketplace in efforts to maintain returns to farmers above what would have been provided by low-equilibrium prices. As simple intervention proved to be inadequate, more complicated programs to reduce acreage planted were created. Whatever their merits, the costs of holding down production and withholding supplies from the market proved to be high. In the late 1950s and particularly the early 1960s, it became evident that substantial amounts of food could be exported at relatively small net additional costs to the exporting economy; if they could be sold at 50 to 60 percent of quoted prices, there might even be a net gain to the exporting economy, as government costs of holding stocks, or enforcing more rigorous production controls, were reduced. The calculations might be something like the following:

1. The cost of a program to retire acreage and thus reduce production could easily exceed 80 to 90 cents per bushel. Similarly, the storage costs of holding a bushel of surplus grain for 3 years or more, until sold, could mount up to a similar figure, with no assurance that the grain could be sold at the end of that period.
2. Shipping the grain to another country in exchange for local currency could realize 20 to 60 cents on the dollar, under Title I, the largest component of P.L. 480 shipments. (The terms were stiffer after 1967, so that more return was realized on each dollar.)
3. Thus the U.S. government might save possible expenditures of about 90 cents per bushel, and receive a net of 35 to 95 cents per bushel through the substitution of local currency for dollar expenditures, for a total return of $1.25 to $1.85 per bushel, less ocean freight, at a time when the export price of wheat at Gulf ports was about $1.65.

Thus it became possible to implement a concern for the nutritional status of low-income people in other lands, at little real cost to the American economy, and similarly for the Canadian economy. The pressures to build large-scale food aid programs came from several sources. Farmers welcomed a program that would make the output of their efforts more useful. They welcomed an activity that would reduce government stocks or slow the rate of increase, and permit them to use a somewhat larger proportion of their production capacity. Religious and humanitarian agencies saw opportunities to enlarge their programs and be helpful to more people. U.S. citizens, restive with the obvious presence of surplus grains while people in other countries were poorly fed, welcomed a low-cost opportunity to bridge the gap. And those in government similarly welcomed a chance to respond to pressures, when most of the extra costs promised to be offset by savings.

Whether these calculations were completely accurate was not important; they do indicate that the cost of food aid to the U.S. was substantially less than the current market value of the grains delivered, *so long as surplus capacity existed*, and the government felt committed to programs to protect grain producers from extremely low prices for their products. For some years, it was possible to implement moral values concerning food aid at costs which ranged from near zero to perhaps half of current market values, plus some part of the freight and local distribution costs.

No wonder that food aid programs approached $2 billion annually, in export market equivalent, during the 1960s. (See Table 5-1.)

The terms under which the U.S. made P.L. 480 shipments gradually became more severe; that is, local currency donations were reduced, later eliminated, interest rates on unpaid balances were raised, some of the freight was charged, etc. This occurred, in part, because the Congress perceived less excess production capacity, a greater ability to control domestic production (as lower support prices became less of a stimulus), and some improvement, before 1970, in the ability of recipient countries to make larger payments.

Table 5.1. U.S. agricultural exports by major categories, 1955 to 1975 (millions of dollars)

Year	P.L. 480	AID	Total Food Aid	Commercial	Total
1955	385	450	835	2,309	3,144
1956	984	355	1,339	2,157	3,496
1957	1,524	394	1,919	2,809	4,728
1958	981	227	1,208	2,795	4,003
1959	1,017	210	1,227	2,492	3,719
1960	1,116	167	1,283	3,236	4,519
1961	1,316	186	1,502	3,444	4,946
1962	1,495	74	1,569	3,573	5,142
1963	1,456	14	1,470	3,608	5,078
1964	1,417	24	1,441	4,627	6,068
1965	1,580	26	1,596	4,501	6,097
1966	1,346	42	1,388	5,359	6,747
1967	1,271	37	1,308	5,513	6,821
1968	1,279	18	1,297	5,086	6,383
1969	1,039	11	1,050	4,775	5,826
1970	1,056	12	1,068	5,650	6,718
1971	1,023	56	1,079	6,674	7,753
1972	1,058	66	1,124	6,922	8,046
1973	954	84	1,038	11,864	12,902
1974	867	76	943	20,350	21,293
1975[1]	1,093	123	1,216	20,368	21,584
Total	24,248	2,652	26,900	128,113	155,013

[1]Preliminary.

Source: *Foreign Agricultural Trade of the United States,* Economic Research Service, U.S. Department of Agriculture, December 1975.

IMPACT OF AN EXPANDED WORLD DEMAND FOR FOOD

Analysts now debate whether excess grain production capacity exists, or whether demand caught up with supply about 1973. Clearly, since the shortfalls in production in 1972, the current supply of grains, and many other food products, has balanced out at a higher price level. Also, production and marketing costs have risen substantially as a result of inflationary conditions during the past several years. Severely adverse weather has affected production in each of the major food-growing regions of the world at least once in the last 4 years. Livestock production has expanded substantially in the USSR, East Europe, and Japan, and to a lesser extent in a number of smaller economies.

Adding up these diverse factors, and without precluding the reappearance of surpluses, it still seems evident that supply and demand, in economic terms, are much closer to balance than during the previous two decades. If this continues to be true, future food aid decisions will be made in a different, more costly choice framework. The following four cases, while not exhaustive, bracket the possibilities for future food aid programs:

1. Embark upon an intermittent food aid program, one that takes effect only following years in which excess production permits low-cost concessional exports and donations. This would permit near maximum commercial sales, tell the deficit nations that they must improve the management of their internal food production and distribution activities, encourage them (and others) to carry larger inventories, and from time to time permit temporary improvements in diets and size of carryover inventories (of their own grain supplies). It would be very disruptive of administrative and organizational structures operating food aid programs, particularly in recipient nations. Short of complete interruption, program size could vary widely, both in terms of volume and in number of countries participating.

2. Continue to operate at about the same level as in recent years, but at higher cost when necessary, saying that bargain foods are not the only reason for food aid. Instead, precisely when prices are high, the nutritional welfare of other peoples requires an increased priority among the people and governments of the wealthier countries, and the production of commodities specifically for distribution as food aid and/or the allocation of funds to increase food production for the same purpose. This program, in effect, becomes equivalent to an income tax on some 20 to 30 nations directed to the procurement of food to be allocated to some 30 to 50 nations that do not have the capacity to pay for appropriate amounts of imported food. Some variation in volume could occur, because some nations will need food aid only occasionally, while others would need smaller amounts in some years when their domestic harvests were good. Such an approach could also include a reserve program to help bridge the gap in years of worldwide small crops. This approach says, "We have tried food aid when the cost was small; we liked the results; we think the program deserves a much higher priority." (A food aid program limited to grain-exporting nations would be a special case of this more general proposal.)

3. The third approach argues that the decades from 1952 to 1972 were a happy accident in the food area, that surpluses will appear again only in the exceptional years of widespread good weather, and that present food recipient nations must find other ways to meet their food deficits. Meanwhile, the wealthier nations should help them develop their internal capacity to produce food (or goods that can be exchanged for food), their capacity to control population growth, and during an interim period will gradually phase out food aid activities.

4. Another alternative stems from analyses of trends in food production and consumption in the developing nations, arguing that the need for food aid is increasing rapidly, perhaps doubling or tripling by 1985.[1] Accordingly, investments need to be made in developed countries to expand production specifically for food aid exports, thus requiring even higher priorities than those found in alternative 2.

It should be emphasized that the above options do not apply to disaster relief. It seems probable that an earthquake, a drought, a flood, or the aftermath of human conflict will still call upon moral values that will bring a sharing of food and other products to aid the suffering—and draw from many sources.

Let us examine these alternatives, in terms of volume, with the United States food aid program as an example:

Alternative levels of food aid (billions of dollars)

	Alternatives			
	1	2	3	4
Initial program in year 1				
Market value	2.0	2.0	2.0	2.0
Real Cost	1.0	1.0	1.0	1.0
Year 3 with a short crop				
Market value	0.4	4.0	3.0	5.0
Real cost	0.4	4.0	3.0	5.0
Year 4 with a large crop				
Market value	2.0	2.0	1.4	4.0
Real cost	1.0	1.0	0.7	2.0
Year 5 with an average crop				
Market value	1.0	2.0	1.2	6.0
Real cost	1.0	2.0	1.2	6.0
Year 8 with an average crop				
Market value	1.0	2.0	0.8	10.0
Real cost	1.0	2.0	0.8	10.0

This table is simply a realistic illustration of how the risks of price changes and the responsibilities for meeting food deficiencies can be shifted drastically, depending upon which of the four alternatives is accepted as the central principle. Under alternative 1, the maximum level of food aid is held constant and attained only in years of a large crop, thus shifting to recipient nations all of the responsibilities for meeting expanding needs for food imports and most of the risks of high prices in a short-crop year. Alternative 2 shows a steady program with the donor country absorbing the risk of price variation, with a resulting fourfold variation in real costs, while recipient countries absorb responsibility for meeting an increase in import needs. Alternative 3 assumes a gradual decrease in food aid, as a result of successful (agricultural) development activities (and additional expenditures) while the donor country absorbs the risks of price changes. Alternative 4 assumes that the donor nation absorbs both the risks of price variation and a responsibility to meet an expanding need for food imports. Thus, in these examples, food aid costs could vary from $1 billion to $10 billion.

WHOSE DECISION?

Most developing countries would prefer the fourth option, since it relieves them of a major food problem and enables them to pursue other economic and developmental objectives. The first option would be preferred by groups opposed to food aid or anxious to reduce its costs. However, intermittent programs are not efficient administratively and organizationally, and could be damaging to recipient consumers as they fall back to minimum diets to which their bodies are no longer accustomed, and politically damaging to donors because ongoing programs are curtailed just when the costs of commercial food imports have risen. Alternative 3 is one compromise position, with a sharing of responsibilities but looking toward an eventual phase-out of food aid as domestic production in the recipient countries expands to take its place. Alternative 2 is another intermediate position, one that recognizes that food aid is likely to be a persistent need but resisting an expansion in program size, perhaps by expanding agricultural developmental aid to assist needy countries in meeting their expanding demands for food.

The determination of the future direction of food aid programs (and associated food activities) will be influenced by peoples' ideas of who has responsibility for food aid decisions. In the past, the initiative has lain with the United States (subsequently joined by other food exporters) spurred by the presence of excess stocks of grain and the particular economics of food aid with excess productive capacity. As this spur becomes less important (or disappears entirely), the pleas or demands of the potential recipients are likely to become more important as they seek ways to ease their deficit problems—deficits of food, of export earnings, and of foreign exchange.

Food aid in the 1950s and early 1960s could be characterized as a marriage of convenience, enabling grain exporters to bypass the problems of excess production capacity and grain importers to avoid facing the problems of inadequate production capacity. With the exporting partners no longer sure that the marriage is convenient, the terms for continued food aid have become harsher, while the importing partners seek alliances and world public pressures to help them maintain the relationship. Thus multilateral relationships and international agencies become participants in decision making, in ways that go beyond the operation of their own food aid programs.

This situation also has made food aid an important aspect of help from rich nations to poor nations rather than help from food surplus to food deficit nations. The ability-to-pay approach would argue for a sharing of the cost of food assistance among all rich nations, not only those that export food products. This, in turn, raises the question of whether food aid should not give way to general economic aid, with the recipient country taking a major role in determining the kinds and volumes of commodities that should be imported. It also is obvious that development choices over time become part of the decision framework—food and other consumption goods now versus tools, equipment, and research which will increase the supplies of consumption goods in the future.[2]

Some of these questions move far from the issues of possible changes in moral values on food aid; however, some comments on the economics of foreign aid are relevant. Generally, it is more efficient to use money aid from rich countries and existing market channels to bring commodities to the recipient country than to use "in kind" contributions of food, ocean shipping, trucks, gasoline or other commodities, always a cumbersome procedure.[3] The World Food Program, for example, in seeking to place sorghum in a drought-ravaged African country, would have to match sorghum supplies in a U.S. or Argentine port with Norwegian or Greek shipping services, and to program them so that the grain arrives in time and in quantities that the receiving port can handle. If all or most of the food aid commitments were in money, sorghum could be purchased at any convenient location, regardless of origin, and loaded on the first available vessel, utilizing normal commercial channels to supervise the operation and to replace the grain by new imports from the U.S., Argentina, or other exporting country. This process could bring more rapid responses, conserve administrative personnel and communications, and probably reduce the amount of transportation and other services required. Some of this efficiency could be lost, however, if the money aid was tied aid, that is, had to be spent in the supplying country, i.e., marks spent in West Germany, rubles in the USSR, yen in Japan, and dollars in the United States.

In-kind or tied aid, however, has at least two appeals. First, it is psychologically appealing in the donor nation since a physical item is being donated or sold on concessional terms, just as food stamps are more appealing than a money or income grant. The donor hesitates to accept the recipients' spending priorities. Second, when an economy or some industrial sector is operating well below capacity, there are national economic advantages in stimulating the output of particular products—to increase the income of grain producers, to decrease unemployment in truck production, to utilize unused space on ocean vessels, etc. In such circumstance, tied aid costs the economy less than the nominal value of the commodities or services, in some cases adding reduced welfare costs or unemployment benefits to the example previously cited.

It seems likely that future food aid decisions will be far more complex than in the past, even if moral values remain constant. The economic incentive for food donors has lessened, at least temporarily, as a result of livestock expansion in Eastern Europe, the Soviet Union, and elsewhere, but economic recession has increased interest in tied aid. The potential recipients are involved in a series of organizations and tactics that make them less pliant and sometimes bring adverse reactions from donors. At the same time, the increase in population, the slowed rate of agricultural expansion, the increased price of grains, and higher payments for petroleum products, upsetting improved exchange earnings, lead some to argue that the need for food aid is greater than ever.

BALANCE OF PAYMENTS, FOOD GRAINS, AND FEED GRAINS

The expansion of livestock production has increased U.S. feed grain exports to West Europe and Japan and appears to be in the same expansion process for East Europe and the Soviet Union, with exports of some 8 to 10 million tons annually committed to Poland and the USSR. While food grains are used sparingly in livestock production in the U.S., larger proportions of low-grade wheat are fed to livestock in Europe and the USSR. In the drier western parts of the Great Plains sorghum competes with wheat for the use of the land, while further east wheat and corn overlap. Also in some countries, corn and sorghum are human foods. While most of the land now devoted to wheat will remain in that crop, unless price ratios change dramatically, there is enough flexibility to increase or decrease U.S. wheat production by 5 to 10 million tons with small price changes, increasing the amount as the price change becomes greater. Thus there is some competition between livestock and man in the use of grains, both directly and over several crop years for the use of land.

Within any one marketing year, the competition between livestock production and the amount of food aid is relatively quite minor; however, the existence of longer-run competition does lend support to the expression of moral indignation at the continued use of grain in fattening cattle. But much of this indignation is misplaced due to a lack of understanding of the complex grain-livestock interrelations. When wheat is in short supply, instead of trying to curtail current use of feed grains, attention should be directed toward stimulating next year's wheat production (improved prices, released acreage, larger food aid budgets, improved technology) and discouraging the future outlook for livestock products (less consumption of meat, eggs, and dairy products, lowered prices).

The expansion of livestock production in other developed countries, coupled with the impact of adverse weather and worldwide inflation, has increased the import of feed grains from the U.S. and other exporters, pressed feed grain prices upward, and brought a substantial lift to the U.S. balance of payments. Should these feed grain exports to support a more "luxurious diet" in other countries be protested?

HAVE FOOD AID PRIORITIES CHANGED?

The argument posed earlier in this chapter is that changes in the size of the U.S. food aid programs are consistent with a relatively steady moral concern with the problems of malnourished peoples, expressed in the real cost of providing assistance. As the cost of food grains doubled between 1972 and 1975—export prices of wheat rose from abut $1.70 per bushel to about $3.60—surplus capacity disappeared and real costs of food aid rose from say $1.00 to $3.60 per bushel. The dollar value of Public Law 480 and AID agricultural exports gradually declined from $1.6 billion in 1965 to $1.1 billion in 1972, dropped to $943 million in 1974, and then returned to $1.2 billion in 1975 (see Table 5-1). The quantities exported, of course, declined by about 50 percent from 1972/73 to 1973/74, then increased by 35 percent in 1974/75 (see Table 5-2). Metric tons of food, however, is a very approximate figure, because the components vary in proportions and in value for weight. Wheat and its products, which constitute nearly half of the total value of food aid exports, dropped from 15.4 million metric tons in 1965 to 6.5 million in 1972, to 4.1 in 1972/73, to 1.7 in 1973/74, and then doubled to 3.5 million metric tons in 1974/75 (see Tables 5-2 and 5-3).

The data to mid-1973 are roughly consistent with the hypothesis; shipments dropped to about one-fourth of the high point as real costs quadrupled. The increased budget from 1974 to 1975 and larger quantities could reflect both an increased moral priority as knowledge of the consequences of smaller shipments became known, and the easing of wheat prices from 1974 to 1975.

An examination of food aid as a percent of national budget, or as a percent of GNP, indicates an attrition in food aid budgets from the early 1960s to 1974; the small reversal in 1975 becomes less significant. This also was a period in which total aid, as a percent of GNP, was declining (though increasing in money terms), and not only from the United States. The increased aid from OPEC countries in 1974 and 1975 is a partial offset (see Table 5-4). Until 1972, agricultural production in the majority of the developing countries was increas-

Table 5.2. Quantities of U.S. agricultural exports by selected groups (thousands of metric tons)

Item	1972/73	1973/74	1974/75
		Food Aid	
Wheat and Products	4,166	1,746	3,484
Feed Grains and Products	1,599	1,052	268
Rice	1,119	611	774
Blended Food Products	269	179	167
Others	525	183	539
Total	7,678	3,771	5,232
		Commercial Exports	
Wheat and Products	28,230	29,512	24,819
Feed Grains and Products	34,204	43,106	34,405
Rice	819	973	1,521
Blended Food Products		Negligible	
Others	22,316	22,441	18,791
Total	85,545	97,530	79,530

Source: *Foreign Agricultural Trade of the United States,* Economic Research Service, U.S. Department of Agriculture, December 1975.

Table 5.3. Quantity of food aid grain exports, 1955 to 1973 (thousands of metric tons)

Year	Wheat and Products	Rice	Feed Grains and Products
1955	4,249	14	1,157
1956	6,492	285	4,738
1957	10,382	979	4,126
1958	6,940	287	2,291
1959	8,394	314	2,412
1960	10,284	581	3,329
1961	12,876	662	3,304
1962	13,741	444	3,658
1963	13,576	630	1,915
1964	13,442	704	1,549
1965	15,369	567	1,388
1966	14,725	450	2,319
1967	8,387	828	3,843
1968	10,754	759	2,064
1969	6,933	999	1,029
1970	7,629	950	1,433
1971	6,646	1,075	1,385
1972	6,469	1,204	1,485
1973	4,108	1,120	1,590

Source: *U.S. Agricultural Exports under Public Law 480,* Economic Research Service, U.S. Department of Agriculture, ERS-Foreign 395, October 1974.

Table 5.4. Net disbursements by OPEC countries for concessional assistance

Country	Millions of Dollars			Percent of GNP		
	1973	1974	1975	1973	1974	1975
Algeria	3.1	42.8	15.8	0.04	0.37	0.12
Iran	2.7	397.4	458.4	0.01	0.89	0.81
Iraq	9.9	403.6	204.8	0.17	3.13	1.35
Kuwait	148.1	274.8	337.7	3.22	2.24	2.82
Libya	41.9	117.5	125.9	0.74	1.03	1.24
Nigeria	5.0	9.9	9.7	0.04	0.06	0.05
Qatar	4.1	91.5	106.9	0.69	4.58	4.65
Saudi Arabia	180.7	861.3	901.4	1.74	2.45	2.59
UAE	85.6	288.9	403.7	3.57	3.86	4.64
Venezuela	1.0	56.0	24.9	0.01	0.21	0.09
Total	482.1	2543.7	2589.2	0.53	1.40	1.28

Source: *Flow of Resources from OPEC Members to Developing Countries,* OECD, Paris, February 26, 1976.

ing per capita—the period of the green revolution. Since then, growth in agricultural output has been less satisfactory in the developing countries, while higher prices for grains and petroleum have had a severely adverse effect upon their balance of payments. One result has been much greater international

Table 5.5 The increasing dependence on North American Grain [1]
(trade in million metric tons)

Region	1934-38	1948-52	1960	1970	1976
North America	+ 5	+23	+39	+56	+94
Latin America	+ 9	+ 1	0	+ 4	− 3
Western Europe	−24	−22	−25	−30	−17
East Europe and USSR	+ 5	—	0	0	−27
Africa	+ 1	0	− 2	− 5	−10
Asia	+ 2	− 6	−17	−37	−47
Australia and NZ	+ 3	+ 3	+ 6	+12	+ 8

[1] Plus sign indicates net exports; minus sign, net imports.

Source: As cited in a review of two papers by Lester Brown, in *Survey of International Development,* Society for International Development, November-December 1975.

concern with the inadequacy of food supplies in the countries most severely affected and efforts to increase the amount of food aid, along with the expansion of domestic production. Much of the pressure from the low-income food deficit countries is applied on the high-income food-exporting countries, in effect asking them to give up some of their opportunities to sell food in commercial markets in order to make larger concessional food shipments. The LDC's have also argued that increasing incomes, stemming in part from higher grain prices, should increase the possibility of assisting nations not so fortunate.

These pressures and the arguments that go with them all accept the view that food producers and food exporters have a special responsibility because their product is so vital for maintaining life, thus placing most of the burden on the U.S., Canada, and Australia (see Table 5-5). But why should a farmer have more of a responsibility than a plumber or a dentist? Or in broader terms, why should the United States have more responsibility to provide food aid than a Kuwait or a Switzerland, after adjusting for differences in population? Past discussions of income inequalities and difficulties in paying for adequate food and shelter have led to support for income taxes to finance programs to help low-income people. Internationally, this concept was pragmatized at 1 percent of GNP for foreign aid, even though there was no way to enforce such a contribution other than a voluntary national willingness to do so.

Following this reasoning, food aid, and all developmental aid, becomes a global responsibility, rather than a function of where the particular resources needed for aid are located; those who enjoy good incomes would be expected to contribute more than those with lower incomes; and both should help those with the lowest incomes. In these terms, a food-exporting nation has the same responsibility as an equally wealthy food-importing nation of the same size. One food exporter might, for political and psychological reasons, prefer to make much of its aggregate foreign aid contribution in the form of food, while another food exporter might prefer to make a cash contribution, meanwhile selling grains to its traditional customers. So long as such "in kind" transfers do not result in more food (or some other commodity) than required in a balanced development program, these preferences pose no serious problem, despite inefficiencies previously listed, provided the commodity is not overvalued to minimize a country's aid contribution. Cash contributions destined for food aid would purchase food in commodity markets, stimulating those prices and, hopefully, leading to greater production of the desired products and smaller nonfood uses of grains. In a short-crop year, with small carryover stocks, these purchases could lead to unacceptable price increases in retail markets, clamors for export controls, grain reserves, reduced food aid, and other measures to avoid a new inflationary spiral. But many of these consequences would occur regardless of the methods by which food aid supplies were obtained; the solution to shortages within the crop year requires a general belt tightening rather than restricting the cutbacks to a few nations whose poverty excludes them from the market, often those most dependent on grains as food supplies.

Some may argue that a steady concern should yield a constant level of food aid performance. A steady concern also could translate to a constant percent of budget or of GNP. In our definition, a steady concern means an equality of national sacrifice, measured in real terms. During the 1960s there were no great differences among these measures. The sharp decrease in quantities and smaller decrease in budgets for 1973 and 1974 can be explained (not necessarily justified) by a steady concern in real costs rather than by a lowering of moral concerns in those two years. Under any of these definitions, an increase in U.S. food aid in and after 1976 appears to require an increased level of national concern, including a willingness to risk higher domestic food prices as part of the cost of helping less fortunate peoples.

Moreover, an increase in public concern could find an outlet in more pressures on other countries, such as members of OPEC, to make substantial financial contributions.

In these readjustments, moreover, there could be increased concern that the recipient target groups should follow certain desired patterns of action. If alternative commercial markets are available, the donors are more likely to use food aid as a reward for positive actions (in areas applauded by the donors), or at least to seek greater discrimination among recipients than in the past. The criteria for such allocations are debated, and clearly some previous allocations are now rejected, e.g., large food aid programs in Southeast Asia. However, other criteria, such as the existence of effective population control programs, are suggested, as are significant internal agricultural development programs.

The thesis presented here is that public concern or moral values supporting an improved international distribution of food supplies became prominent about 25 years ago; increased affluence and improved communications have contributed to this broadened feeling of social responsibility. Until 1972, implementation of these values was facilitated because the real costs of grain exports were substantially below the nominal market prices—due to surplus capacity and governmental costs of controlling it.

With the disappearance (temporarily?) of surplus capacity, the costs of food aid have increased greatly. Implementation of food aid goals at the same quantitative level as formerly requires a substantially greater degree of sacrifice of other goals which individuals and a society hold. This leads to the view that food-exporting countries are not likely to make these larger sacrifices unless there is greater comparability of sacrifice from people in other rich nations. These subscriptions could be in money, petroleum, transportation, or other commodities, but they need to be visible and real. Overall income and well-being should govern the level of contribution to improved nutritional well-being, rather than the importance of food as an export product.

NOTES

1. Food and Agriculture Organization of the United Nations, U.N. World Food Conference, *Assessment of the World Food Situation—Present and Future,* E/Conf. 65/3, p. 89. Also see International Food Policy Research Institute, *Meeting Food Needs in the Developing World,* Research Report No. 1 (Washington, D.C., February 1976).

2. See the discussion of allocation among generations in the chapter by Shue.

3. Compare the position taken in the chapter by Saylor, p. 201.

6 The political uses of food aid: are criteria necessary?

Daniel E. Shaughnessy

POLITICAL ASPECTS OF FOOD AID

This paper will examine the use of food aid for political and strategic purposes. Not only is the subject one which evokes considerable controversy, but it can be an emotional topic and one on which rational examination can be easily distorted. Accordingly, any discussion of the "political uses of food aid" necessarily involves a clarification of terms and some attention to definitions. It must be said at the outset that it is virtually impossible to identify a program that can be classified as exclusively "political." Even the most humanitarian program has a political element to it, and conversely even the most political of programs has its humanitarian aspects. Food assistance to India, for example, is partly motivated by humanitarian concern for its hungry masses; nevertheless, it is also directed toward improving our posture on the subcontinent.

For the purposes of this chapter, "political uses of food aid" shall be construed as the provision of food assistance resources in situations where the primary rationale for assistance is the furtherance of U.S. self-interest to attain foreign policy, strategic, or economic objectives. Further, the self-interest objectives discussed in this paper are confined to those whose attainment may be enhanced by the use of food aid. In part, the basis for this definition of political uses of food aid is derived from United States Public Law 480, which provides for the use of food aid to further foreign policy and market development objectives.

"Political" uses of food are nothing new in the United States. As long ago as the end of the nineteenth century, the United States government considered

This chapter reflects only the personal views of the author and not those of the Agency for International Development or the Executive Branch.

concessional sales of food to friendly governments a method of developing and improving markets. Food shipments to war-torn Europe after World War I may have been motivated by humanitarian concerns; nevertheless, the buying of good will and promoting better intergovernmental relationships had definite political overtones. Similarly, provision of food aid in concert with the Marshall Plan and Point Four Program had its political objectives, i.e., a mutual reinforcement of programs and a building of political relationships with recipient governments. In 1966, changes were made in the P.L. 480 legislation which took food aid out of the realm of "surplus disposal" and brought the "political uses" of such aid into clearer focus. Under the authority of this legislation, food aid to Indochina, the Middle East, and selected other countries openly became an instrument of foreign policy and a means of achieving political or strategic objectives.

It is important here not to stereotype "political food aid" as bad or improper. Current legislative authority provides a clear legal base for such activities, and since most assistance activities rendered by one government on behalf of another are essentially political acts, one must avoid the temptation to automatically classify the "political" use of food aid as evil because it is in the U.S. self-interest.

Thus, as the P.L. 480 program became less of a means of disposing of surplus commodities overseas and budgets became tighter, more distinct rationale and criteria for granting food assistance began to emerge. Humanitarian, developmental, and political considerations had to converge and sometimes compete for budget resources. It was during this period (1973/1974) that the levels of food assistance to Indochina began to attract Congressional and public attention.

An examination of food aid sales agreements over the past 5 years will indicate that a number of agreements negotiated and signed during that period might be categorized as "political." Here a question presents itself: given the premise that the U.S. government uses food aid as a means of assisting in the attainment of its political objectives, is it possible to specify criteria for such uses? The initial consideration of this concept produces a good deal of skepticism; after all, politics, or any manifestation thereof, rarely lends itself to any fixed set of rules, and as decision makers, politicians are notorious rule breakers.

PROJECTED CRITERIA

Congressional response has been to attempt to "reorient" the P.L. 480 sales program in an effort to limit the political use of food assistance and establish some basic criteria.[1] During fiscal year 1975, Congress passed a provision to the Foreign Assistance Act which stipulated that no more than 30 percent of food assistance under Title I of P.L. 480 be directed to nations other than those included on the United Nations list of "most seriously affected countries" (MSAs). The "most seriously affected countries" were defined by the UN as those countries with a trade deficit and low per capita GNP that were hurt the most by the dramatic increases in commodity prices, particularly food, fertilizer, and fuel prices. This list, however, was not necessarily a list of food deficit countries. The most obvious example is Burma, which although an MSA, is a major rice exporter. Many other MSAs are not food exporters, but they typically export commodities like cocoa, tea, and coffee and often are not food grain importers. At any rate, Congress soon discovered the difficulties involved in using criteria for food aid based on a UN-determined MSA list. For example, the UN added Egypt to the MSA list during fiscal year 1975, making the legislated 70-30 split outdated. The resulting final allocations of P.L. 480 Title I food aid in fiscal year 1975 were 79 percent for MSA countries and 21 percent for non-MSA countries. Allowing an international or non-U.S. government entity to establish the criteria used for setting food aid priorities troubled many in Congress and, as a result, was dropped from the law late in 1975.

Discussions within Congress late in 1975 evidenced considerable support for other measures which would attempt to ensure that food assistance be used only for humanitarian assistance. There was continued discussion about developing criteria or formulas which would further define which countries should be eligible for assistance. Here are several examples of such proposed measures: setting a per capita GNP assistance factor, establishing a base amount of P.L. 480 assistance which would have to be distributed before political programs could be considered, requiring that no assistance be provided unless countries were taking vigorous population control measures. These examples, including the GNP factor which was adopted and the others which were not, deserve attention to determine if it is possible or even desirable to direct the allocation of "political" food assistance by establishing criteria or formulas.

A per capita GNP assistance factor was established by Congress in P.L. 94-161 as the criterion for setting a 75-25 poor-to-wealthy-country food assistance allocation. It is too early to see how well this provision will work. Per capita GNP is a widely recognized measure of development, but it is only a crude index at best. Per capita GNP is in no way a measure of either food deficits or food surpluses. It also does not in all cases separate "political" programs from humanitarian. In many cases also it does not reflect real differences in purchasing power. For one thing, in less developed countries and particularly in MSAs, large segments of the economy may be subsistence and not yet monetized. The most recent GNP per capita lists are based on figures 2 or 3 years old. As a result, inflation or changes in currency exchange rates can make them outdated even before they are published. A further criticism of using GNP per capita as a measure is that it does not reflect local differences in income distribution within the less developed countries. Some countries have a relatively high GNP per capita but also have large areas of real poverty and malnutrition because of unequal income distribution. Finally, restrictive criteria legislated by

Congress tend to promote inflexibility in programming food aid. This in turn, could have the effect of making food aid nonresponsive to changing economic conditions.[2]

Attempts to establish definitive criteria must overcome other problems also. The MSA-to-non-MSA ratio or per capita GNP formula on any established P.L. 480 base level may run into trouble with commodity availability. Thus far, the problem has not been significant because commodities have been available in reasonable quantities during fiscal years 1975 and 1976. It is often not recognized, however, that the P.L. 480 program consists essentially of food and not cash. Each year, depending upon production, stocks, commercial demand, and other factors, the Secretary of Agriculture makes specific amounts of food available. These availabilities have to be matched up as well as possible with prospective recipient countries. It may happen (particularly when availability is short and prices are high) that the poorer countries are interested in some commodities and not in others. It is entirely possible, therefore, that MSA countries may not want given commodities, rice for example, while there are non-MSA countries that are eager to purchase them. In this case, administration of food aid programs and attainment of objectives would be blocked as there could be a violation of the ratio, or formula.

The MSA requirement or GNP formula does not take into account the serious downturns that may take place in non-MSA or high-GNP countries. This does not include a full-fledged disaster, because the law permitted an escape clause to provide for that contingency, but applies to a more long-term crop failure over a period of a year or more or reduced prices for major exports whether agricultural or otherwise. These items, while not catastrophic, have a serious effect upon a nation's balance of payments and may set back development for several years. It is this situation to which we would like to respond but may be restricted from doing so by the GNP criterion.

No matter what formula or criterion is decided upon, some countries will be excluded, and this raises a further question. Should food aid be denied to countries that are trying to improve their agricultural productivity but still have large food deficits because they are relatively better off than other poorer countries that are not making sufficient self-help efforts.[3]

Another related measure would be to provide food assistance only to countries that were making acceptable progress on controlling population. This was proposed in the fall of 1975 on the floor of the House. This is perhaps best answered by a similar question: would the United States accept any foreign proposal that carried with it the caveat that we would have to meet birth control criteria? Apart from the infringement upon national sovereignty, the withholding of food to countries without adequate population plans could have a counterproductive effect. It has been found that population curves do not decline significantly until, among other things, adequate food supplies are available.[4] The refusal to provide food assistance might very well perpetuate a high birth-rate curve.

EXISTING RESTRAINTS

This discussion is, of course, with Title I of U.S. Public Law 480 in mind. It is this provision of the law that permits large-scale transfers of grain to other nations on concessional loan terms. It is the size of these sales and the terms that are negotiated that provide a meaningful input to foreign policy relationships in general and specific political or strategic objectives. Title II of P.L. 480, which is a donation program primarily through voluntary agencies and the World Food Program and sometimes on a government-to-government basis, has rarely been accused of being subject to "political" uses.

Therefore, in considering the subject of criteria, it is important to note that there are already restrictions under Title I, even for the most "political" of programs.

- First of all, there must be an evident and specific need for food on the part of the recipient country. This need may not necessarily manifest itself in apocalyptic spectors of famine or a display of starving and emaciated bodies; it could simply be the result of a nation's shortfall in agricultural production or due to shortages caused by war.
- Second, food aid is a form of economic assistance, be it disaster relief, balance-of-payments support or strategic aid; it does fulfill a need for external help. Food aid is not given to countries that have no need for donations or concessional loans.
- Third, food aid as rendered by the U.S. represents the expenditure of a considerable budgetary resource. This fact dictates the existence of a controlled, rather elaborate, and often complex decision-making process.

Thus there are already some criteria for even the "political" uses of food aid: at the very least, a definite need for food must exist; there has to be evidence that the country would find it difficult, at least, to pay for all of its imports on a commercial basis; and finally, the proposed program must be able to withstand the rigors of an interagency review and compete for the allocation of budget resources.

In addition, political and strategic food aid is not immune to "outside" influences, which in themselves impose constraints and help to develop criteria. In 1974, U.S. crop production levels dictated severe reductions in food aid. While these reductions did not significantly affect the levels of "strategic" food aid—i.e., that sent to Indochina—they did, for the first time, clearly delineate priorities for food assistance.

Further, any consideration of criteria for Title I programs must take into account the existing decision-making process. Any attempt to specify new or additional criteria especially for political or strategic food aid programs will require intervention in that process—not an easy task.

Public Law 480 may be a unique phenomenon. There is some justification for this view when one examines what is necessary to obtain decisions on the allocation of its resources. This is a program with an overall value in excess of $1 billion. Its funds are in the appropriation of the U.S. Department of Agriculture; its administration is charged to both USDA and the Agency for International Development, and its activities, both planned and underway, are heavily influenced by the Office of Management and Budget, the Departments of State, Commerce, and the Treasury, and White House interests. To say that Public Law 480 programs require interagency approval is one of the better understatements in the federal Bureaucracy.

As a means of organizing this confusion of interdepartmental interests, there exists what is called the Interagency Staff Committee, or ISC. The ISC is chaired by USDA and operates on the basis of consensus; all members must agree to a proposed Public Law 480 program—or at least, not object—in order to approve the program. Any objection or "reserve" on the part of an ISC member will delay or prevent program approval, and over the past few years different agencies have had varying degrees of influence on ISC decisions. Such influence reflects the concern of each agency and tends to develop various, and at times, conflicting criteria—i.e., the political or security concerns of the State Department, USDA commodity interests, OMB budgetary concerns, and AID developmental interests.

The State Department's criteria for judging concessional food aid could be summarized as promoting our U.S. self-interest. This could include political concerns; for example, the government in power may be friendly to the U.S. while the major opposition party is not; it may include security concerns such as base rights or membership in mutual security pacts. Economic self-interest might also be a consideration, such as promoting trade interests or American investments.

Under the provisions of Section 401 of Public Law 480, the USDA is required to use a commodity availability criterion first in examining concessional food and sales. This provision of the law requires sufficient commodity quantities for domestic consumption, adequate carryover, and commercial exports in determining the quantity of commodities that can be made available for Public Law 480. USDA first attempts to maximize commercial exports in order to maintain farm income and a healthy U.S. farm economy as well as to earn foreign exchange for the U.S. balance of payments. Therefore, the potential for market development is one of the most important criteria for USDA.

AID, on the other hand, uses developmental and humanitarian criteria to examine concessional sales programs. Among the factors AID takes into consideration are the size of the recipient country's food deficit and its ability or inability to finance commercial food imports, the country's balance-of-payments situation, and other economic indicators that demonstrate a need for concessional assistance and the impact of food aid on agricultural production and other development activities.

OMB's role in ISC decisions is largely one of seeing that cost effectiveness criteria are met. OMB attempts to see that each dollar spent has the most impact possible within defined budgetary constraints. Treasury and Commerce concerns are largely the possible impact Public Law 480 will have on the economy.

Obtaining ISC consensus on a program can be viewed as a struggle over which criteria to use or favor or which criteria are the most valid when applied to the particular country program under consideration. This places the burden of proof on the advocate of the program.

THREE CASE STUDIES

Thus far, this chapter has discussed theoretical considerations or criteria. It is particularly important to apply these considerations to specific examples where political factors have played a part in the provision of food assistance. The countries about which most inquiries are received—Korea, Chile, and Egypt—are all usually labeled "political" programs.

Korea has made very significant economic progress in the past 10 years. Its per capita income has risen from $100 to about $400 during this relatively short time. No small measure of this success may be attributable to a large Title I program supplied by the United States. The Koreans have made good use of the foreign exchange savings that the Public Law 480 program has afforded, and much of this needed capital has been ploughed back into the agricultural sectors. As a result, the Koreans hope to reach rice self-sufficiency within the next 2 years. Despite its rapid growth, Korea still has serious financial problems. It faces a record $2 billion current account trade deficit for 1975, it already has a negative net foreign exchange asset position, and sustained recovery is unlikely until the U.S. and Japanese economies recover. Korea still has a large food deficit, and under the best of circumstances will have to import food for years to come. In this regard, it is important to note that Korea has become a large cash customer for U.S. wheat. U.S. economic and military assistance is winding down; however, the Koreans hope that U.S. food assistance will continue for a few more years and appear to have a demonstrated need based on specific requirements.

Chile has lately been the recipient of U.S. food assistance. Much has been made of the fact that the U.S. did not provide food assistance under Title I to Chile during the Allende regime; however, the truth of the matter is that there is a more serious food problem today than there was at that time. The price of copper dropped from $1.50 per pound in 1974 to about 52 cents per pound in 1975. Over 85 percent of Chile's export earnings come from copper, and to give some idea of the copper price impact, a penny per pound change in the copper price makes a plus or minus $20 million change in the Chilean balance-of-payments position (which did not improve). Further, in pre-Allende days, the food input requirement was in the neighborhood of $250 million. During the Allende regime, agricultural production dropped drastically and affected succeeding years. The value of the food gap is now $600 million per year, and Chile has to provide for food imports at the same time it faces a balance-of-payments gap of $300 million to $375 million, and this is after including all proposed assistance. The need for food aid through this "political" program, therefore, appears already to have specific criteria.[5]

Now, both Korea and Chile have rather repressive regimes, governments about which the United States has expressed concern on a number of occasions. Behind the scenes, there are quiet pressures being applied by the U.S. to liberalize. There is, however, considerable criticism of political food assistance to these countries. Yet what useful purpose would it serve to cut off assistance to these countries? Would curtailing food assistance have any impact on the regimes to grant more liberties, or would it lead to more repression as those governments had to deal with a reduced food supply? Ultimately, would not a cut in food assistance only hurt the poor of both countries? I submit that these are some of the questions that should be answered by those who would propose to deny assistance to these countries and impose further limitations or criteria simply because they are "political" programs.

In the case of Egypt, Public Law 480 is tied directly to peace efforts in the Middle East. After years of confrontation and military expenditure there appears to be a genuine desire on the part of President Sadat and his government to deal with the staggering problems of the Egyptian economy. While there is money coming in from the OPEC oil states, it is in no way enough to sustain the Egyptian economy or provide for growth. The Egyptians have a large food deficit and import well over 3 million tons of wheat and flour per year. The U.S. has used food assistance both as a means to help relieve food shortages and as leverage in reaching agreements. The U.S. should not have to apologize about this. To quote a *Washington Post* editorial of last year, "the use of food for more overt political purposes, however, has an undeniable merit of its own. There is no need to shy from it out of an excessive fastidiousness. Food is not only a natural resource but a political one and the proper policy question is not whether to use it but how. In the case of the Middle East," the *Post* went on to say, "it is refreshing to find Food for Peace being used for once in the uplifting spirit of the program's name."[6]

In summary, it would appear that the dangers of the "political" use of food have been greatly overstated. As noted earlier, the political aspects of food assistance are closely intertwined with the other humanitarian, developmental, and market-oriented objectives of the Public Law 480 legislation. With this in mind, it seems inappropriate that additional formulas or fixed criteria beyond those already in place should be applied to food assistance and, particularly, political food aid. The issuance of too complex or inflexible criteria and even the best-intended measures often have results that are far from those expected by their authors. Public Law 480 Title I programs, political and otherwise, already have their criteria, and the decision-making process has its checks and balances.

The enlightened use of food assistance should be continued, not just for short-term expediency, but for long-term gain as well and always keeping in mind the basic humanitarian character of the Food for Peace Program. To quote the *Washington Post* again, "What Americans should be considering is ways to wield this power responsibly—not to punish adversaries or settle historical scores but to serve the common good. Using food to relieve hunger is one way, and using food in the pursuit of peace is another."[7]

NOTES

1. See the chapter by Thomas Saylor in this volume for a detailed description of the Congressional changes in P.L. 480.
2. Compare with pp. 203-204 of Saylor's chapter.
3. On pp. 314-316 Shue notes similar problems in establishing criteria.
4. See Brewer chapter.
5. For a different perspective on the Chile situation, see Stephen S. Rosenfeld, "The Politics of Food," *Foreign Policy,* Spring 1974.
6. *Washington Post,* February 2, 1975.
7. *Ibid.*

 # A utilitarian framework for policy analysis in food-related foreign aid

Joseph D. Sneed

Why is food scarcity a *moral* problem? Things get to be moral problems in three basic ways. First, things can rather suddenly get "worse" for some people in ways that could at least be ameliorated by actions of other people. Famine caused by drought can be ameliorated by direct aid from those who have food reserves. Second, new possibilities arise for some people acting to make things better for other people. Technology can improve, making some things objects of decision that were not objects of decision before. New technologies can open up previously unproductive lands to cultivation. The decision of whether to do so rests with those who control the technology and capital required. Finally, people's attitudes to objective circumstances can change though the circumstances themselves remain the same. Fifty years ago it was at least tolerable to most people in developed nations that a good portion of the rest of the world's population lived at or near the starvation level for their entire, rather short lives. The number of people for whom this is a tolerable situation appears to be diminishing.

A necessary condition for a person, or institution, having a moral problem is facing a decision. There are no moral problems when there are no options—though perhaps there may be "moral anguish." Many believe that another necessary condition for having a moral problem is that the consequences of the decision have some effect on other people. But these conditions are not sufficient. People, and institutions, make countless decisions every day that affect other people. Only a few of these, if any, are moral problems.

Many organization theorists have noted that "standard operating procedures" suffice to take care of most day-to-day decisions an organization makes. People are rather like organizations in this respect. They have pretty standard ways of dealing with kinds of problems they regularly encounter. One might call these standard ways of dealing with decisions "moral principles"—at least when they deal with decisions affecting other people.

Ordinarily organizations and people get along quite well with standard operating procedures and common-sense moral maxims. Difficulties arise, however, in two kinds of situation. First, a decision arises that does not seem to fall within the purview of any standard procedure or maxim. A new situation, completely without precedent, demands action. Second, and apparently more typical, are decisions in which several standard procedures or maxims apply but lead to conflicting results.

It is just this type of conflict situation that provides the problem for the analytic moral philosopher. Moral philosophers are not, in my view, purveyors of expert advice about what is the right thing to do. They are not like lawyers who purvey expert advice about what is permitted by law. Rather, moral philosophers offer expert advice on reasoning about moral problems—decisions where standard procedures break down or conflict. This is quite a different thing from telling a decision maker what he ought to do in such a situation.

One may instructively, though perhaps not accurately, view a good part of the history of moral philosophy as attempts to provide more general moral maxims to resolve conflict among the standard or common-sense rules. One may also note that no attempt has been completely satisfactory. That is, no systematic "ethical theory" seems adequate to resolve all moral dilemmas in an intuitively satisfactory way. But this need not suggest that ethical theorizing is futile. Here, as in climbing a mountain, "all the fun's in getting there." That is, the exercise of trying to construct a systematic way of resolving particular moral conflicts is what counts as moral reasoning. That the product—"the theory"—does not stand up under attempted application to other decisions does not mean the exercise of constructing it was worthless.

What I have, then, to suggest as a way of dealing with moral problems of food distribution is that we attempt to theorize about them. I suggest that we *try* to fit them into an intellectual framework comprehensive enough, *in principle,* to resolve the conflicts that produce the problems. I say "in principle" because no comprehensive theory, moral or scientific, ever has much directly to say about specific applications. I say "try" because success is clearly not a feasible goal here. There may be fundamental moral disagreements among us that would preclude a single theory's systematizing everybody's views. More important perhaps is to push in the direction of systematization far enough to clarify our own views and recognize areas of agreement and disagreement with others.

I do not simply suggest that we theorize *in vacuo.* Moral problems connected with food distribution are a subclass of moral problems connected with the general question how things people care about should be distributed. There is a significant body of lore about these problems which we use. But first we must be a bit more careful about specifying the problem we want to deal with.

Both individual people and institutions can face distributional problems. For individual people the problem may be one of *personal charity*—how much of what I control personally should I give to whom—or *political influence*—what should I do to influence other people and institutions to transfer some of what they control to others. Institutions may face problems of redistribution *among* their *internal* constituents—e.g., should our local buy beer for the Labor Day picnic out of dues even though only 40% of the membership attends—and redistribution *from internal to external* constituents—should our local contribute from dues to famine relief in Africa. Government-financed foreign aid, unless it is seen only as a means to some further end—say, national security—is redistribution from the government's internal constituents to its external constituents. When we consider food-related aid independently of other national objectives, it involves redistribution of this sort.

It is perhaps obvious but nevertheless important to note that a substantial part of redistribution carried out by institutions is not the result of "voluntary" acts of personal charity by an institution's members. On one plausible but rather strong interpretation of "voluntary,"[1] only if the institution has a unanimity decision rule or if the costs of "opting out" of the institution are zero can we generally say that all members "voluntarily" participated. The members who voted against the redistribution programs (or would have if they had had the chance) and still "kick in" do not do so voluntarily unless they could leave the institution without suffering "losses."

One does not have to accept this strong sense of "voluntary" to appreciate the intuitive point here. The costs to an individual of not contributing to private charity are usually far less than the costs of not paying taxes (or dues) to support redistribution programs.

The importance of these perhaps obvious observations is this. Unless we are willing to restrict our discussion to the moral problems of personal charity in food aid, we must consider situations in which some people will involuntarily participate in redistribution. If our interest is more general than personal charity, then a moral theory that, from the very beginning, ruled out involuntary participation in redistribution as morally unacceptable would not be of interest to us. I think it is reasonable to assume that most of us do not rule out, as a matter of moral principle, all forms of redistribution except personal charity. I believe the question for most of us is this: what sort of institutional (governmental and nongovernmental) redistribution should we use our own personal political influence to promote? We countenance the fact that some may participate only involuntarily in the institutional (particularly governmental) programs we decide to promote.

On this assumption it seems reasonable to formulate moral theories for redistribution decisions facing institutions. The intellectual tradition of utilitarianism and classical welfare economics provides us with a conceptual framework for formulating such theories. Within this tradition one can identify several "theories of distributive justice," apparently intended to apply to national economies, that have actually been propounded. A large number of others lack only a proponent. Roughly, one may think of this tradition as providing a "family" of theories of distributive justice indexed by a small number of parameters—morally significant considerations in distribution problems. Specifying "values" of all the parameters yields a specific theory of distributive justice.[2]

My proposal is this. We characterize roughly this family of theories noting the unspecified parameters. Then we try to see how we might specify each of the parameters to yield a theory applicable to food-related distribution problems. Remember, though, this is an exercise in clearing up issues, not an attempt to come up with a unique theory or make substantive moral recommendations. In particular, we should note that the exercise contains some "built-in" flexibility. Two different arrays of specified parameters could yield two theories that were indistinguishable in their recommendations for particular decisions (extensionally equivalent theories). What we really want to do here is achieve an understanding of how the different moral considerations that are important to us are related, not specify a unique theory or recommend a specific policy objective for food aid.

Theories of distributive justice in the family we want to consider tell us generally that decisions about distributing things people care about should be made taking account of the preferences of interested parties. This rather vague prescription becomes more precise when we begin to specify:

- Which interested parties
- Which preferences
- How conflicting preferences should be weighed

Indeed, the parameters one specifies to obtain a specific theory of distributive justice may be conveniently grouped under these headings. It should be noted that even this rather weak formulation of a type of moral theory rules some considerations out as morally irrelevant. For example, considerations like tradition, custom, "natural rights," and scientific, religious, and ideological conceptions of "man's nature" are relevant to distributional decisions *only* to the extent that interested parties have preferences about these matters. Let us now examine the relevant considerations in more detail.

It is perhaps worthwhile to emphasize once again, as we embark on a more specific discussion, the nature of the enterprise. We are trying to become clear about our own moral values—what people or other individuals *we* care about and how *we* care about them. No argument will be offered that one *should* care about certain individuals in certain ways. I know of no way to argue convincingly to such conclusions.

WHICH INTERESTED PARTIES

The usual starting point for constructing a theory of distributive justice is specifying the "domain" of the theory—the individuals whose preferences are relevant to the distributive decisions in question. Traditional theories have usually assumed that the citizens of a nation-state were the appropriate domain and distributional questions were usually restricted to questions of internal redistribution among the nation-state's citizens. Rather traditional problems here are how to deal with the preferences of children, lunatics, and criminals. It is frequently suggested that countenancing preferences of these groups, in any way whatever, leads to counterintuitive results. Another alternative, however, would be to focus on peculiar features of these group's preferences and try to accomplish the same purpose by ruling out kinds of preferences rather than kinds of people.

Less traditional problems are whether other things besides people should be in the domain. Some of those concerned about preservation of the natural environment appear to suggest that the preferences of animals and perhaps even plants and inanimate objects (in some clearly extended sense of "preference") should be countenanced in social decisions about the use of natural resources. Others appear to suggest that the "preferences" of fetuses are relevant in decisions about social policy on abortion. An alternative would be to introduce these considerations as "second order" considerations. Only people appear in the domain. Animals and other entities receive moral consideration only because, as a matter of fact, some people care about them. A consequence of such a theory might be that I am constrained to consume damaged fruit because other people are fond of birds injured by insecticides, though I couldn't care less about the filthy creatures. More precisely, questions of how to treat nonhuman objects are handled as conflicts of preferences among people. If everybody in the theory's domain couldn't care less about birds, then birds receive no consideration.[3]

Conceptually similar to the problem of how to deal with moral considerations involving nonhuman objects is the problem of how to deal with the preferences of people not now living. In principle, one might consider including past and future generations of people, along with the present, in the domain of the theory. Usually the possibility of including *past* generations is not given serious consideration. The prospect of countenancing the preferences of persons long dead in decisions about what to do today has *prima facie* an air of "superstition and irrationality" about it. But it is worth noting that demands by some groups and nations for "reparations" related to injustices suffered by their ancestors, so far as I know, can be derived from a theory of distributive justice only if something like this is done. This is not of course to say that their demands for "more" today *can only* be justified in this way. There may be other, quite straightforward ways of justifying their demands within a theory of distributive justice. It is only that the "reparation" justification appears to require that we countenance the preferences of past generations—something we might generally be reluctant to do.

The preferences of future generations are a different story. Here tradition runs in the direction of including future generations in the domain of the theory. But there are difficulties with doing this. Aside from the obvious empirical problem of predicting what these preferences will be, there are some conceptual problems. We will see below that there are problems with formulating a plausible principle for resolving conflicts between the preferences of members of present and future generations. We should only note that there is available here the same sort of possibility mentioned in connection with nonhuman objects. We could restrict the domain to persons now living and let the "interests" of future generations be represented by those among the living, if any, who care about them. This, together with some constraints about the kinds of preferences about the situations of future generations that were to be counted as relevant to social decisions, could lead to a plausible theory.

The problems we have been considering all arise within the traditional view of theories of distributive justice applying to problems of internal redistribution among citizens of a nation-state. That the domain in principle consists of people is rarely questioned within this tradition, though it is sometimes suggested that "social classes" serve as proxies for people in actual applications of the theories. That is, we apply the theory to distributions of things among social classes simply because we have information about this and not about distributions among individual people. However, there are internal distributional problems for governments (and other institutions) where things are apparently to be distributed among entities that are not people. The problem of "fiscal equity" among units of local government in a federal system is such. Here financial resources are being redistributed among local governments. Such problems could perhaps be handled with a theory whose domain is people, but it is not immediately obvious that this would capture all the relevant considerations.

For many of the distribution problems connected with food-related aid, it is also not entirely clear whether the domain should consist of people, political institutions, or other entities like "cultures." The political mechanics of distributing food aid appear to constrain distributing institutions to deal with national governments as external constituents. From the standpoint of applicability, it would be convenient to have a theory that said something directly about how to distribute food aid to governments. But, for some at least, there is a strong intuitive feeling that individual citizens of these governments are the intended beneficiaries of food aid. To capture this intuition one would have to have a domain consisting of people. Principles for distribution among governments would then be derived from the theory plus factual information about the government's probable effectiveness in implementing the selected distribution.

This effectively amounts to regarding the "preferences" of national governments as "representative" of the preferences of their citizens. We can always, of course, question how "accurate" this representation is. When we do this, our criterion for accuracy is usually a moral one. We have some idea of how government's policies *ought* to reflect the preferences of citizens. Within our conceptual framework this amounts to judging the distributive "outputs" of government policy against our own views of distributive justice. Thus we view client national governments as simply more or less effective means of achieving our own ethical ends. On this view national governments are not the objects of moral consideration *independently* of their citizens.

Views that some kinds of social institutions deserve consideration in food distribution decisions *independently* of the people who participate in them will always be problematic in the "preference-regarding" conceptual framework. The view that preserving a particular "culture" deserves moral consideration independently of the moral consideration its members deserve is precisely analogous to views that other kinds of "nonpersons" deserve moral consideration. We can either explicitly opt to regard them as having preferences like people or incorporate consideration of them via preferences that people have for them. That these views are problematic within this conceptual framework I count as a "plus." If we do choose to give moral consideration to individuals other than people, we ought, I think, to be clear about the full implications of this choice. This conceptual framework at least forces us to be explicit about our choice and our reasons for it.

In the case of K, the last surviving example of a culture of its kind, it seems reasonably clear that—having accounted for the moral consideration due to the present and future participants in K—whatever remains is most naturally dealt with via the first-order preferences of those "outsiders" who have some interest in preserving K. Some may value the findings of anthropological research carried out in K; others may find aesthetic value in artifacts produced in K; still others may like having K around for touristic reasons. I see no intuitive reason why these preferences should not compete on an equal footing with other people's preferences for museums, national parks, and sports arenas.

Traditional theories of distributive justice have had little to say about problems of redistribution from internal to external constituents of an organization. The reason for this is not difficult to see. There are strong intuitive reasons for choosing a principle of resolving conflicting preferences that in some sense "treats everybody alike." The bigger the domain of the theory, the harder it is to come up with a plausible principle that does this. In particular, it is difficult to produce a plausible principle that treats internal and external constituents of an institution alike. Most principles that are appealing for internal redistribution, when applied to internal-external redistribution, appear to demand much more redistribution from "rich" institutions to "poor" external constituents than most participants in the "rich" institutions would accept.

Here we can do any one of three things. We can change our intuitions and accept the injunction to more redistribution from rich institutions to their poor external constituents. We can recognize that our intuitions are best captured by a principle of distribution that does not "treat everybody alike"—internal and external constituents are treated differently. Or, finally, we can simply exclude external constituents from the domain altogether and reduce the problem to the traditional case of internal redistribution. External constituents would receive consideration only because some internal constituents happen to care about them.

When the institution here is a national government, this is essentially the question of whether, and if so how, moral considerations should extend beyond national borders. Analytic moral philosophy cannot answer this question. At best, it can formulate alternative answers and indicate some consequences of these alternatives.

The last alternative above is conceptually similar to the possibility of countenancing the "preferences" of nonhuman objects and other generations *mediated* through preferences of living people. Some features of these possibilities are worth noting. In all these possibilities people within the domain of the theory have preferences about the "welfare" of people and nonhuman objects outside the domain of the theory. The "welfare" of these is essentially a "public good" for the people in the domain of the theory. That is, everybody in the domain "consumes" the "welfare" of people and things outside the domain to the same degree, though they will typically have different preferences about how much they are willing to "pay" for an increment in the level of such "welfare." More common examples of public goods are public protective services and certain aspects of public recreation and transportation. The provision of public goods through institutional activity typically involves redistribution, since preferences about levels of these goods differ.[4] In this sense all these proposals suggest that a problem of redistribution "in the large" be reduced to a problem of redistribution "in the small."

The main problem with the "public goods" approach to the "welfare" of individuals outside the domain of the theory is that it does not *guarantee* that these individuals will receive the consideration we intuitively think is due them. The consideration they receive depends on how people in the domain care about them. They might not care at all. But we have not exhausted all our theoretical possibilities yet. We still have to consider which preferences of people in the domain are to count in institutional (social) decisions and how conflicts among these preferences are to be resolved. There may be choices we can make at this level that will mitigate the difficulty.

WHICH PREFERENCES

Theories in the family we are considering can, in principle, countenance the widest variety of individual preferences. But specific theories in the family may, for substantive reasons, restrict the kind of individual preferences that are relevant to social decisions. For reasons of systematic elegance, at least, the more "heroic" theorists in this tradition try to get along with as wide a class of preferences as possible. But even the most "heroic" of these usually, at least implicitly, make a distinction between fundamental and derived preferences and use this distinction to rule out some preferences from serious consideration.

Roughly, an individual's fundamental preferences are independent of his beliefs about what is likely to happen; his derived preferences are not. Which of these preferences should be used in deciding how to treat individuals? Do you try to be an individual's benefactor with respect to his manifest preferences—give him what *he thinks* he wants—or with respect to your best judgment about what his fundamental preferences are? For example, suppose you are providing agricultural aid to a less developed country. Your technical experts and its technical experts differ about what the specific aims of the aid program are to be. Should you insist on following the advice of your experts, even to the extent of withholding aid if the advice is not followed? Or should you take the preferences of the client country at face value and "let them make their own mistakes"?

I suggest that here it is most plausible to restrict the preferences countenanced by the theory to fundamental preferences. Derived preferences are determined by an individual's fundamental preferences and the "probabilities" he assigns to what may happen. "Honest and reasonable" men may surely disagree about such probabilities. In the face of such disagreements, should I base my benevolent efforts toward an individual on my best assessment of the probabilities or on his? Intuitively, the answer seems clear. To use his probabilities would be irresponsible. Surely, if my best estimate of the probabilities takes account of things he may be in a better position to know than I, then I have given his views their due. This appears to be a minimal and rather plausible form of paternalism.

Two problems with this view must, however, be mentioned. First, it is only plausible as "administrative policy"—as opposed to theory—if those who implement the policy have sufficient incentive to acquire the best factual information their cost constraints permit. In particular, it presupposes that they seriously countenance the possibility that the client may have "privileged access" to certain kinds of factual information. Second, the distinction between fundamental and derived preferences is problematic in application. We almost never have information about an individual's absolutely fundamental preferences—his basic values. At the level where we typically have information, the best we can do is distinguish more from less fundamental preferences. The theory should then be applied by using the most fundamental preferences about which one can get information at "tolerable" costs.

To be clearly distinguished from the question of "derived or fundamental preferences" is the question of what to do about preferences that do, or can be caused to, change over time. Both fundamental and derived preferences may change over time. Derived preferences may change as a result of new factual information or as a result of changes in fundamental preferences. Fundamental preferences may change as a result of experience in ways that have nothing to do with changes in belief. My preference for wine over beer might change when I discover that, in contrast to wine, drinking beer does not result in a "morning after" headache. But it might as well change simply as a result of consuming enough beer to "acquire a taste for it."

That fundamental preferences may change systematically as a result of "consumption" in the broadest sense leaves a question of "which preferences should be countenanced" even after derived preferences have been removed from consideration. Moreover, it raises the question of how to deal with decisions about trying to change fundamental preferences for social ends. For example, preference for animal forms of protein over vegetable may be "culturally determined"—people "learn" the preference from their society. Were we to observe this change of preference occurring in individuals in certain social strata over a short time period as their cultural surroundings changed, we might plausibly question whether the newly acquired fundamental preferences were to be "taken seriously" in deciding questions of nutritional policy. Moreover, *if we knew how* to systematically reverse this change in preferences, we might consider a policy of doing so.

Some kinds of fundamental preferences do not appear "essential" to an individual's character—perhaps because they can be easily changed, perhaps for other reasons. These nonessential preferences may plausibly be ignored, or maybe just given less weight in social decisions. These nonessential, fundamental preferences also appear to be the ones that we might plausibly attempt to change through social action. Though it is not obvious that the class of nonessential preferences we might "denigrate" and the class we might seek to modify are coextensive. The problem is to specify clearly what kinds of individual preferences are nonessential in each of the (possibly) two senses mentioned.[5]

It must be clear that we are speaking here about *kinds* of preferences, e.g., preferences about brands of beer, rather than *specific* preferences, e.g., a preference for Schlitz over Coors. That specific preferences, even rather general ones like "poetry over pushpin," be identified as essential is a possible solution to this problem that has usually not been acceptable to theorists in the tradition we are considering. Views in which an array of specific, though perhaps quite broad, preferences, is taken as an "image of man" to be pursued through social policy are a kind of limiting case of "extreme paternalism" in which the theory's recommendations may be completely unresponsive to differences in individual preferences. Such diverse historical figures as Plato, Marx, and St. Augustine appear to have held views like this. This view is mentioned here only to emphasize that ruling out *kinds* of preferences as irrelevant to (perhaps, only certain kinds of) social decisions does not necessarily commit us to such an extreme paternalism.

The problem of characterizing an individual's essential preferences is usually considered only when the individuals are people. Here the intuitive idea is that some kinds of preferences (perhaps different kinds for different people) are essential to their "personality" and thus we must take them seriously and dare not tamper with them. It appears, though, that the same sorts of considerations appear when the individuals are "cultures" or nation-states that "represent" cultures. One might claim that an aid program to a less developed country (or a domestic minority culture) need not respect all fundamental values (preferences) of the client culture—only those that are "essential."

The real problem of course is giving operational meaning to the concept of *essential* fundamental preferences of people and cultures. With this problem philosophers (so far as I am aware) now have little assistance to offer. Clearly psychological, sociological, and anthropological facts are relevant here. But how one processes these facts is not, in general, clear. Generalizable examples do not abound here. Preferences about religious practices appear *prima facie* to be fundamental and essential. But my insisting that an aging relative whom I assist financially spend the assistance on medicine rather than donations to a Hari Krishna monastery does not appear illegitimately inconsiderate of his preferences.[6]

Attempting to change the preferences of cultures and individuals therein with respect to population control may be within this problem area. Of course, it is not entirely clear that preferences about "population policy" at the individual or national level are fundamental preferences. Population policy may be only a means to some further end—security in old age, social prestige, national economic and political power. If these are derived preferences and the benefactor is honestly convinced that they arise out of factual misinformation, then they may legitimately be "denigrated." If they are fundamental, then one must ask if they are essential. It is at least conceivable that a family structure based on large numbers of children is so central to a culture and/or the people in it that changing it would effectively "destroy" the culture and replace it with another as the "price" of eliminating malnutrition. This might be rather like "curing" a chronic alcoholic with a lobotomy.

Finally, we should consider another broad area where attempts are frequently made to rule out some kinds of preferences from consideration in matters of social policy making. This area overlaps to some extent the "natural rights" tradition in political philosophy. The basic idea is that some matters of individual concern simply *ought not* to be matters of social concern. Some have tried to regard preferences that one person may have about some things that other people may do "in the privacy of their homes"—say, smoke marijuana or practice sodomy—as socially irrelevant preferences. For example, should the fact that some prefer that *others* do not practice contraception be relevant to deliberations about population policy? In this vein one could also rule out preferences about other people's preferences. This would rule out social policies whose fundamental goals were changing preferences, but not necessarily preference change as a means to some end only contingently connected with preference change.

After having considered, in turn, whose preferences are to count and which of their preferences are to count, we will now proceed to the question of how conflicts among the preferences of different individuals are to be resolved.

HOW CONFLICTING PREFERENCES SHOULD BE WEIGHED

Theories of the sort we are considering are designed to deal with moral problems about distributing things that individuals—people or institutions—care about. Distributing X is a moral problem only when there is not enough X to give everyone the amount of X he prefers—that is, when preferences conflict. A principle for "aggregating" conflicting preferences among individuals is usually called a "social welfare function." Formally, this is a function from arrays of individual preference orderings to single preference orderings. It summarizes our intuitive ideas about how the "admissible" fundamental preferences of individuals in the domain are to be "aggregated" into a fundamental preference ranking that is to guide some "actor." In our case the "actor" is the institution whose policy we are seeking to influence. The "output" of the social welfare function is to be conceived as the basic policy objectives we urge upon this institution. How the institution might best pursue these objectives depends on factual questions. A moral theory does not aim to provide guidance on these operational questions.

Two things about social welfare functions should perhaps be reemphasized. First, different social welfare functions generally lead to theories with substantively different recommendations for particular decisions. Which function one chooses depends on how he judges the consequences of the function. Second, other things besides the social welfare function—the domain of individuals and the admissible preferences—determine the "output" of the theory. For the moment, let us ignore these other ingredients of the theory and focus on the choice of a social welfare function that might capture our intuitive ideas of justice in the distribution of food resources.

To get some idea of the kinds of alternatives available as social welfare functions, I suggest that we look at one particular such function and then view this function as a member of a family of similar functions. The social welfare function I have in mind is closely related to one that has recently received some attention in John Rawls's book *A Theory of Justice* and related discussions.[7] Rawls calls this function "the general principle of distributive justice." It appears to capture, in its consequences, a good part of the moral stance of nineteenth-century liberalism or "social democracy." The Rawls-function is "moderately" egalitarian, but it can be naturally embedded into a family that contains both more and less egalitarian functions.

The first thing to clarify about the Rawls-function is whether it is to be understood as a principle for distributing commodities like food, refrigerators, or diamond rings or as a principle for distributing the satisfaction that individuals obtain from such commodities—"utility" in the technical jargon of this tradition. Applying the principle directly to commodities is generally unsatisfactory since, even at a crude intuitive level, it is clear that different individuals—say, a meat eater and a vegetarian—will have different attitudes about the "satisfaction" to be obtained from the same quantity of tinned beef. Differences in satisfaction accruing to individuals receiving the same commodities become even more significant when we come to decide about how several commodities are to be distributed among them—as "commodity bundles." Nations may be plausibly seen as having perhaps different preferences about the mix of food and nonfood consumption among their population. To take account of this difference in preferences in distribution decisions based on the Rawls-principle, one needs to view the principle as applying to "satisfaction" or "utility" derived from consumption. Distributions of commodities are recommended only indirectly as those leading to the recommended distribution of satisfaction.[8]

Taking Rawls' function as a principle for rank-ordering distributions of satisfaction, the recipient of its recommendations is enjoined to produce the highest-ranking distribution feasible within his resource constraints. There are two equivalent formulations of the function. One formulation says that equal distributions are to be ranked above unequal distributions unless the unequal distribution affords greater satisfaction to at least one individual and less satisfaction to no individual ("Pareto-superior" in the technical terminology). From this it follows that, if we have an equal distribution, we should depart from it to improve some individual's lot just when no other individual is thereby injured. A second and fully equivalent formulation is that distributions of satisfaction are to be rank-ordered by the amount of satisfaction accruing to the worst-off individual in the distribution. For a two-individual domain, this function is illustrated in Figure 7-1. All distributions along a single "chevron" are ranked together. Higher-ranking distributions are on "chevrons" to the upper right.[9]

As stated, this principle is rather crude. It can be refined to tell us what to do in case the worst off are equally badly off in two alternative distributions,

Figure 7-1.

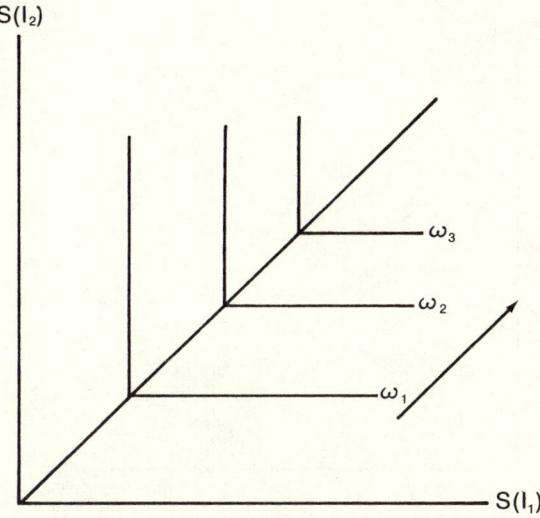

what to do when only the numbers of worst-off individuals differ, and what to do when individuals receive different "weights"—say, the individuals are countries with differing malnourished populations. We will not consider these details here.[10]

To get an intuitive idea of what the Rawls-function entails for distributive problems, let us consider a highly idealized example. Suppose the individuals are countries and the domain consists of all countries in the world. Suppose further that we have a concept of "satisfaction" appropriate to countries with the following properties: Per capita annual food consumption is so important to a country's "satisfaction" that, to a first approximation, all other consumption may be lumped together and "satisfaction" regarded simply as a function of food and nonfood consumption. A single country's preferences with respect to food and nonfood consumption may be represented by an "indifference map" (Figure 7-2). All configurations of food and nonfood consumption along the same curve represent the same level of satisfaction. Food and nonfood consumption "trade off" in the sense that along the same indifference curve the country will accept less per capita annual food consumption for more per capita annual nonfood consumption without being "damaged." Increasing "satisfaction" is represented by indifference curves toward the upper right.

We must also suppose that indifference maps of different countries are comparable. This means, roughly, that we can "number" the indifference curves in each country's map in such a way that curves with the same number in the maps of country A and B represent situations in which countries A and B experience the same "satisfaction."

Finally, we assume that each country may divert resources from nonfood consumption into food production. Roughly, sacrificing nonfood consumption may be regarded as "effort" put into food production. This means we can view

Figure 7-2.

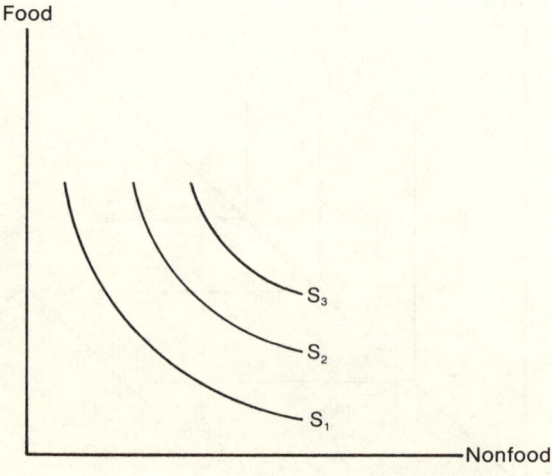

A utilitarian framework for policy analysis in food-related foreign aid 117

the indifference maps (Figure 7-2) as plots of "effort" versus food consumption, with "effort" on the horizontal axis and *decreasing* toward the right. Generally the "productivity" of a given amount of food production effort will be different for different countries. That is, the same amount of resources taken from nonfood consumption and put into food production will yield annually different amounts of food in different countries. This may be represented by a "world production function" for food where total world food output is a function of different countries' nonfood resource inputs (Figure 7-3 for a linear, two-country world).

Note that, among other things, the idealized example ignores the internal distribution of food among citizens of countries and the possibility of long-term investment of resources in food production. "Effort" here is simply the *annual* amount of nonfood consumption "foregone" for the production of food. Clearly the amount of food this produces in a given country depends, among other things, on the existing amount of capital equipment—tractors, irrigation canals, fertilizer factories—in the country's agricultural sector. There might be some (probably, quite unequal) distribution of capital equipment across countries which would lead to equal (per capita) annual food output for equal (per capita) annual food effort. The question of investment in capital equipment is ignored in this simple example. It could be introduced via some "intergenerational" distribution principle. (See below, p. 123.)

Introducing consideration of the internal distribution of food into this simple model is problematic. In countries where there is significant malnutrition

Figure 7-3.

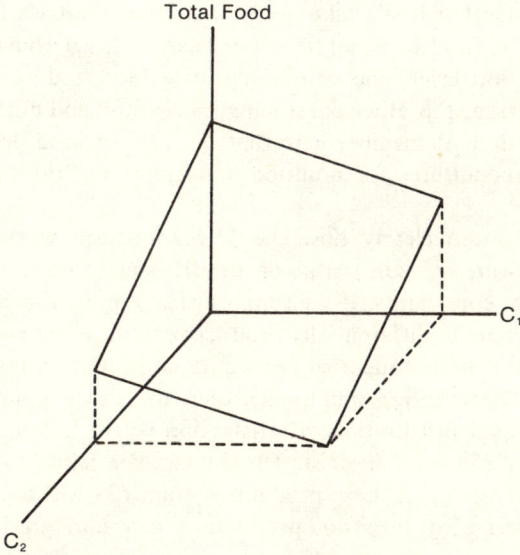

together with a national government economic policy behaviorally compatible with rather strong "preferences" for nonfood consumption, it is simply difficult to see that this policy could result from a "just" consideration of the preferences of its citizens. Suppose the national government "could" in some sense be using the country's foreign currency reserves to purchase food or fertilizer and instead is using them to import luxury consumer goods. This would indicate a national indifference curve favoring nonfood consumption which, on this model, might put this country behind others in consideration for food aid. One does not have to be too subtle to question whether the preferences of the country's malnourished are justly countenanced in the formation of economic policy. This suggests that the concept of "national effort" is only significant in food aid decisions when we are willing to assume that the level of effort resulted from a just—in our eyes—mediation of conflicting preferences within the client nation.

What does the Rawls-function recommend in this idealized example? The second formulation of the function—rank-order distributions according to the satisfaction of the worst off—is most easily applicable here. Here the recommendation is simple. Transfer resources to the country with the lowest satisfaction level up to the point that any further attempts to transfer resources would reduce some other country's satisfaction level below that of the initial country. This is a rather egalitarian recommendation. The only reason for stopping short of transferring resources to produce complete equality in satisfaction is that technological and political constraints might operate in such a way that an equal distribution of satisfaction was not Pareto-efficient.

This strongly egalitarian consequence of the Rawls-function may be unacceptable to many. But before dismissing the recommendation we should remember that what is being distributed here is not food resources themselves, but satisfaction. Satisfaction levels take account of the country's food production effort as well as its food consumption. For example, two countries could have the same satisfaction level, one consuming little food and putting little effort into food production, the other consuming much food and putting much effort into food production. Remember here that "effort" in food production always comes out of expenditures for nonfood consumption—"prestige" airlines, for example.

To see even more clearly how the Rawls-function works, let us ignore political and institutional constraints on the transfer of resources and consider only technological constraints. If we suppose that inputs of resources into food production are generally differentially productive in different countries, but that food productivity is independent of per capita consumption (perhaps only true above a certain consumption minimum), then the Rawls-function will always recommend an equal distribution of satisfaction levels. But this equal distribution will have the following inegalitarian feature. Per capita food consumption generally will not be equal. Less productive countries will be both consuming less and putting less effort into food production than more productive countries.

Less productive countries are, in effect, "paid off" in reduced food effort instead of food consumption.

Even with this understanding of the Rawls-function's recommendations, I suspect many will still find them too egalitarian. Suppose we view some single "rich" nation (the U.S. perhaps) as the recipient of the theory's recommendation. Under any intuitively plausible "rough and ready" comparison of "satisfaction" among nations, this rich nation—even operating under "real world" external political constraints—would in fact be able to bring about, unilaterally or with help cajoled from other rich nations, quite a lot of redistribution before there was any danger that a "rich" nation might become worse off than a "poor" nation. It is not clear that any rich nation's internal political consensus would support such a redistribution policy.

That such radical redistribution is likely to be politically unfeasible does not of course mean that it is unacceptable as a goal of political action. Those of us who find such a policy morally appealing may surely promote it in the political arena with reasonable expectations of moving policy incrementally in this direction—if not of complete success.

There are several ways one might weaken the redistributive implications of our theory to accommodate those whose enthusiasm for redistribution is more limited. First, one might simply adopt another social welfare function. The Rawls-function may be regarded as one of a family of social welfare functions indexed by the angle θ between the "chevrons" (Fig. 7-4). The Rawls-function is characterized by $\theta_{Rawls} = 90°$. More egalitarian theories have $\theta > 90°$. These theories are willing to sacrifice Pareto-efficiency for movement toward equality. Less egalitarian theories have $\theta > 90°$. Classical utilitarianism is characterized by $\theta_{Bentham} = 180°$ where distribution is irrelevant. For $\theta > 180°$ the theories will sacrifice Pareto-efficiency for inequality. Interesting for those who favor less

Figure 7-4.

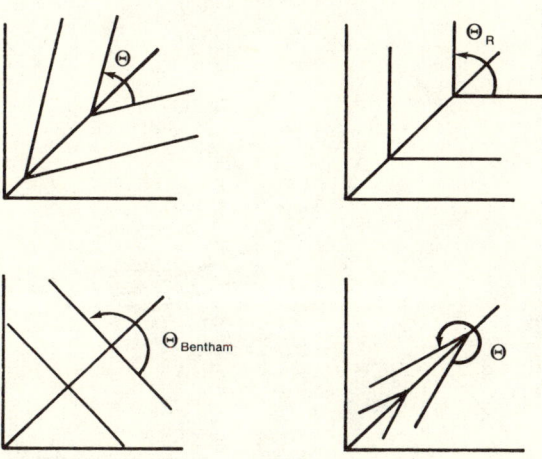

redistribution but have no interest in inequality *per se* are those theories with $180° < \theta < 90°$ (Fig. 7-5). These theories will always recommend a Pareto-efficient distribution, but they allow that one individual may "sacrifice" amount X to benefit another individual by amount Y when $X/Y = \tan(\theta - 90°)$. For small $\theta - 90°$, these social welfare functions recommend that the "poor" sacrifice a "little" to benefit the "rich" a "lot."

Perhaps the most direct way to capture less egalitarian intuitions about redistribution is simply to choose a social welfare function with $180° < \theta < 90°$ that matches these intuitions. With appropriate refinements in the functions, corresponding to those mentioned in connection with the Rawls-function, it appears that a function could be fashioned to capture a wide variety of intuitive moral judgments about a variety of situations. Such a function would admittedly be "contrived" to fit the "data" of specific moral intuitions. But the function would at least systematize this body of intuition into an "implicit" commitment to a "principle of distributive justice" and perhaps "support" extension to situations where intuitions were less clear.

One fact about this approach should be noted. A "theory" that captures less-than-Rawls-egalitarian intuitions in a social welfare function of this form will always depict these intuitions as an "implicit" commitment to a principle that recommends the poor to sacrifice to benefit the rich. Of course, one who resists the egalitarian consequences of the Rawls-function may not be thinking of his views about distributive justice in this way. He may, for this reason, be quite uncomfortable with this way of capturing his intuitions. Maybe it is the intuitions that need reexamining, or maybe we need a better theory to capture them—one that does not have such uncomfortable "side consequences." These

Figure 7-5.

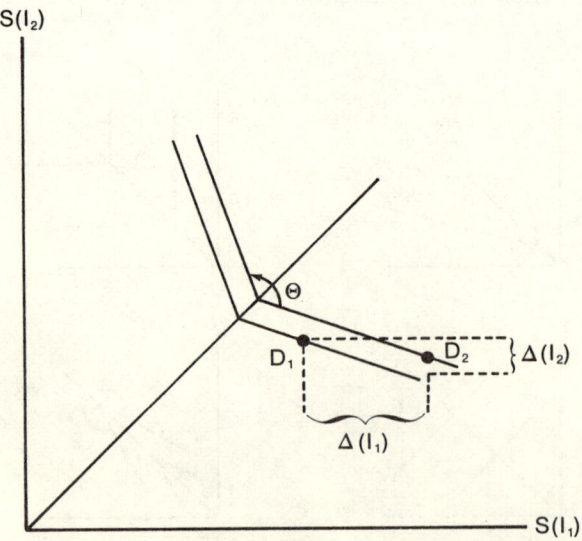

NOTE: I_2 "sacrifices" $\triangle(I_2)$ to secure a gain of $\triangle(I_1)$ when we move from D_1 to D_2.

kinds of considerations might lead some people to more egalitarian views. But they do not provide an argument for Rawls-egalitarianism.

A second way to capture less egalitarian intuitions has already been mentioned in our discussion of the choice of the theory's domain (p. 109). There it was noted that for internal-external institutional distribution problems one might restrict the domain to the internal constituents of the institution and introduce consideration for the external constituents via the internal constituents' "first order" preferences about the welfare of external constituents conceived as "public goods." This suggestion can now be made more explicit by including a specific social welfare function for dealing with *internal* distributions.

In our example this might be done in the following way. We are considering country X's distribution problem for food-related aid to other countries. The individuals of our theory are the citizens of X. They are willing to contribute to aid for countries Y, Z, W, ... in varying amounts. A "food aid" package—aid allocations to Y, Z, W, ... —is a public good in X. Generally, financing public goods by taxation in X involves some internal redistribution."[11] Roughly, the proposal we are considering invites us to rank-order food aid packages by the way internal distributions associated with them are ranked. For example, we might choose the Rawls-function to rank-order the internal distributions. This would mean roughly, "Rawlsian justice at home determines public charity abroad."[12]

Some consequences of choosing the Rawls-function to rank the internal distributions associated with food aid packages are interesting to note. Suppose that the internal distributions of "satisfaction" among citizens of X are ranked by the Rawls-function. Further suppose the "feasible" distributions are just those produced by a market economy plus redistributions from the market allocation produced by the provision of "public goods." That is, the public sector cannot produce individually tailored transfer payments; it can only produce "public goods" financed through taxation of market-produced allocations. Among these public goods are external food aid packages. Suppose the public sector of X, thus constrained, tries to redistribute internally in the direction recommended by the Rawls-function. It is not difficult to see intuitively that the public goods preferences of those poorly treated by the market will receive more emphasis in public sector activity than the public goods preferences of those well treated by the market. The rich will be taxed to provide public goods favored by the poor.

Let us further assume that, as a matter of fact, the "rich" care more about external food aid than the "poor." Though this clearly need not be so, it is not difficult to imagine that X's poor *could* care more about increased public medical care, transportation, and recreation facilities that *they* can use than about providing food for the victims of famine abroad. This might be even more plausible if we focus on the *really* poor in X—those, if any, who are faring almost as badly as the citizens of famine-stricken Y, Z, and W. Under this assumption a *less* egalitarian internal social welfare function would produce more external food aid.

Thus we are led to a rather paradoxical situation. Our purpose in investigating the "public good approach" to internal-external distributions was to find a theoretical systematization that had somewhat *less* egalitarian implications than one using the Rawls-function. What we find roughly is that, under some not too implausible assumptions, *more* egalitarian internal principles produce less egalitarian overall internal-external principles. Very, very roughly, the better we treat the poor at home, the worse we treat the poor abroad.[13]

This does not show conclusively that the "public goods approach" is unsatisfactory. In fact this approach points up an important relevant consideration. When the recipient of the theory's recommendation is a country, the "satisfaction level" of the poor within that country is an important factor in evaluating internal-external redistribution proposals. More generally, there is a problem with taking countries as the individuals in our theory, since we thereby ignore the distribution of food (and other things people care about) within both the "rich" and "poor" countries. For example, suppose X and Y are both about equally "rich" countries in terms of per capita income but have different internal income distributions, such that the poorest people in Y are better off than the poorest people in X (X=U.S.A., Y=Sweden is perhaps an example). Then it may be plausible to think that Y should be devoting a larger percent of its GNP to foreign aid than X. "Redistribution begins at home." Similarly, if Z and W are about equally "poor" countries in per capita terms but the worst-off in Z are poorer than those in W, it appears that our concern should primarily focus on the worst-off people in Z.

This suggests that more appropriate individuals for our theory are people. One could simply take the domain to be all people in the world—ignoring at the theoretical level the problem of obtaining information about the "satisfaction level" of individual people—and ignore the internal-external distinction. Then a country (or other institution) would be enjoined to redistribute within its resource constraints toward the poor in accord with the Rawls, or some more or less egalitarian, function beginning with the *worst-off people* (in the Rawls case) regardless of whether they happen to be at home or abroad. This of course does not avoid the problem of choosing a social welfare function with just the right commitment to egalitarianism. It just lumps domestic and foreign redistribution into the same decision.

On this proposal, whatever degree of egalitarianism we finally settle on, all people are treated alike. The poor at home receive no "special consideration" in redistribution. This will be unacceptable to many. Consider a small but rich nation X, where even the poorest are pretty well off by world standards, deciding how to spend a fixed percent of its GNP on "redistribution." Spent on internal redistribution the effects within X would be substantial. Spent externally where the impact on the poorest people would be greatest, the effects would be negligible. It is not clear that any principle that looks only at people's "satisfaction level" will be able to capture the commitment of X's citizens to "take care of their own."

Thus far we have been considering applications of social welfare functions to problems of distributing things among individuals at roughly the same time. When we come to consider intertemporal distribution problems, new difficulties arise. The problem is easiest to see when we think of the individuals as "generations"—groups of people living at different times—within the same family, firm, country, or the entire world. A common-sense moral intuition is that earlier generations ought to sacrifice some "satisfaction" to increase the "satisfaction" of later generations. If we rank-order distributions of satisfaction among generations by the Rawls-function, it is clear that this intuition can never be captured, for no sacrifice (in the sense of Figure 7-5) by one individual for the benefit of another is countenanced by this principle. Less egalitarian functions do countenance sacrifice, but they don't care which individual it is that sacrifices. It could just as well be later generations sacrificing for earlier.

I know of no plausible general principle that justifies intergenerational sacrifices. To my knowledge, the closest we can come to this, reasoning from general principles, is that the present generation should not make future generations "pay" for its excesses. This is recommended by the Rawls-function. Within this broad constraint, it appears plausible to suggest that the "first order," nonmoral preferences of the present generation *should* determine the amount of sacrifice it makes for the benefit of future generations. Roughly, members of the present generation usually care something about what things will be like in the future. Within the broad constraint that "things should not get worse," these present preferences "aggregated" by an appropriate social welfare function should shape the range of "consumption" possibilities open to future generations.

It is easy to see that many things about future generations that members of the present generation care about are public goods for the present generation. They are broad features of future situations like the availability of resources for food production and outdoor recreation, the average or lower bound on "satisfaction," the continued existence of certain cultural traditions, religious and ethical ideas, the population level. Almost everybody in the present generation cares to differing degrees about at least some things of this sort. Further, they do not admit of "individual consumption" by members of the present generation. To the extent that we have information about what it will be, we must all "consume" the same prospective population level in the next generation. For purposes of a moral theory of "just saving" we might regard only preferences about broad features of future generations as "socially relevant."

This suggests that the "public goods" approach to internal-external distribution problems is appropriate here. We might regard one generation G_0 as the recipient of the theory's recommendation and future generations $G_1, G_2, \ldots$ as the external constituents of G_0. We may leave open what these are generations of—a family, the world, or something in between—as well as how generations are to be divided into members—people, countries, etc.

Certain properties of $G_1, G_2, \ldots$ are conceived as public goods for the members of G_0. Members of G_0 care to differing degrees about some broad features of other generations. Among the features they care about may be something like the "overall satisfaction level" in G_1. We need not be specific yet about what the features are. But what is important is that consumption levels of the usual kinds of things by members of G_0 are causally connected with the features of other (at least future) generations they care about. That is, G_0 must decide among an array of feasible "commodity bundles" consisting of the usual kinds of public and private goods plus public goods associated with the features of future generations which members of G_0 care about. Typically, ordinary "current consumption" commodities will "tradeoff" against features of future generations as will these features among themselves.

The "public goods approach" suggests that the choice among these "extended" commodity bundles for G_0 be made by reference to the satisfaction distributions in G_0 associated with them rank-ordered by some social welfare function—perhaps the Rawls-function. This determines (neglecting uncertainties about the future) the features of future generations that members of G_0 care about.

This gives a pretty weak theory. It still may not recommend conservation of resources or capital investment by G_0. Whether it does depends on the preferences of members of G_0 about future generations and how these preferences get honored in redistribution in G_0 according to the chosen social welfare function. But a stronger and perhaps more plausible theory can be obtained by placing some restrictions on the features of future generations that are to figure in socially relevant preferences of members of G_0. (Remember, our theory need not countenance *all* preferences as socially relevant.) For example, one plausible restriction would be to countenance only preferences about the satisfaction level of the worst-off members of future generations and the total number of people in these generations. We might further suppose (or simply only countenance that) members of G_0 always prefer the worst-off being better off and more people to less in G_1. This imposes a bit of Rawlsian justice on judgments about the future as well as a "more the merrier" view about population.[14]

This simple restriction of socially relevant preferences about future generations highlights two features of future generations that might "trade off" against each other and with ordinary consumption in G_0 in both the "satisfaction function" of members of G_0 and the technological production function. That is, suppose members of G_0 can always be compensated for taking less of one of these "commodities" by being given more of the others. Further, suppose that for a fixed level of ordinary G_0 consumption, the more people in G_1, the lower the level of satisfaction of the worst-off member of G_1. Reducing the level of ordinary G_0 consumption raises the curve along which G_1 population and worst-off satisfaction trade off.

Under these assumptions and a Rawls-like social welfare function operation in G_0 we would still not necessarily get a recommendation that G_0 sacrifice for G_1. The best we can do here appears to be to constrain G_0's choices to rule out making the worst-off in G_1 worse off than the worst-off in G_0. Whether there was any positive sacrifice by G_0 for G_1 would depend on the specific preference configuration of members of G_0.

This simple example may, however, illuminate some issues in food distribution policy. Consider a specific "poor" country. Suppose the satisfaction level of the worst-off in G_0 in this country is related causally to the population in G_1 in the following way. The better the position of the worst-off in G_0 is, the more people there are in G_1. Suppose further that resource limitations are such that the more people there are in G_1, the worse will be the position of the worst-off in G_1. If we think of the members of G_0 and G_1 as social classes, then perhaps the mortality rate from malnutrition is closely related to "satisfaction." Under these circumstances, it follows from the theory just sketched that there is a point beyond which the satisfaction level of the worst-off in G_0 should not be raised—unless the connection with the population in G_1 can be severed.

It should be noted, though, that this analysis has assumed throughout "perfect certainty" about the future. Many will intuitively feel that we ought to aid the starving in G_0 and let the future take care of itself. This view is not obviously irrational, nor even incompatible with moral intuitions underlying the theory just sketched, when future uncertainty is incorporated into the analysis. To the extent that we are uncertain about the connection between the satisfaction of the worst-off in G_0 and the population in G_1 and other relevant facts, it is rational to "discount" the satisfaction level of the worst-off in G_1 in our deliberations. This will have the effect of raising the "cutoff" point for assistance to the worst-off in G_0. But it will not eliminate the "cutoff" point.

CONCLUSION

This attempt to fit the moral problems of food distribution into a general theoretical framework is, at best, a mere sketch. It indicates what kind of theoretical apparatus is available and how it might be applied to some examples. Those with more detailed knowledge of these situations will surely find the examples oversimplified and perhaps naive. If, however, they find the conceptual framework in the least appealing, I would urge that they test it against *their* knowledge of the factual situations. I do not think they will thereby find simple answers to their moral dilemmas. That I did not suggest "answers" was not simply a consequence of the crudeness of my information. Here, I think, answers

NOTES

1. To develop fully a theory of rational participation of social organizations would take us far afield. Suffice it to note that the theory lying behind these remarks uses "voluntary" in a sense so strong that cases of voluntary participation in social organization are rather rare.

2. I speak rather loosely here of a "utilitarian tradition." In the technical jargon of philosophers, theories of the sort we will consider are called "preference-regarding." The term "utilitarian" is usually reserved for theories containing the so-called "Bentham principle of distributive justice."

3. Note that, on the second approach, the theory gives us no guidance about what anyone *should* prefer with respect to the treatment of "nonpersons." Preference-regarding theories attempt to capture all moral considerations in terms of principles for honoring preferences of individuals that "have" preferences. Such a theory will clearly never capture a first-order moral attitude toward individuals that cannot be plausibly regarded as having preferences. This may be a defect of such theories. But it may simply reveal an important boundary on the application of our concept of "moral consideration."

4. M. C. McGuire and H. Aaron. "Efficiency and Equity in the Optimal Supply of a Public Good." *Review of Economics and Statistics*, 1969, pp. 21-39.

5. In introducing the notion of an "essential" preference, I part company with purists in the preference-regarding tradition. They would regard *all* fundamental preferences as essential in the sense that they are worthy *prima facie* of consideration. Most purists, though, I think, would follow me in ruling out derived preferences from those being *prima facie* worthy of consideration. Even though a great deal of what we regard intuitively as an individual's personality may rest on factual beliefs which we believe mistaken, it nevertheless remains plausible to deny preferences based on these beliefs moral consideration. It is worth noting that even very "perverse" preferences may still be "essential" in my sense. Someone may just like torturing people for the intrinsic pleasure of it. Though the theory under consideration countenances such preferences as worthy of moral consideration, their gratification will typically be ruled out by most plausible principles for mediating between conflicting preferences. Considering the preferences of most people to avoid pain, it will simply turn out to be "unjust" to honor the sadist's preference for wanton torture. But should a masochist conveniently turn up, then honoring both sorts of "perverse" preferences might be Pareto-optimal.

6. The notion of an essential preference has some resemblance to what some social theorists have called a "natural individual right." Natural individual

rights are "inviolable" preferences of individuals roughly in the sense that it is *always* unjust to fail to honor such preferences. Essential preferences are *not* inviolable in this sense. It may well be unjust to honor someone's essential preference—say to eat his grandmother. Essential preferences are inviolable in the sense that they always deserve moral consideration—in the technical sense of being incorporated into the chosen principle of mediating conflict—and in the sense that attempting to modify them through social action is not permitted. "Essential preference" is a much weaker concept than "natural individual right."

7. John Rawls. *A Theory of Justice.* Harvard (1971).

8. In opting for this interpretation of the Rawls-function, I should mention two points. First, this interpretation presupposes a rather strong concept of "utility" that is comparable across individuals. The difficulties with such a concept are well known. I will simply ignore these here and concentrate on the intuitive content of principles presupposing this concept. Second, my interpretation of the Rawls-function apparently diverges from that of Rawls. He views the function as applying to the distribution of "primary social goods—liberty and opportunity, income and wealth, and the bases of self-respect" (Rawls, p. 303). These "primary social goods" are commodities in an extended sense, and applying the social welfare function to their distribution appears to avoid the problem of utility comparisons among individuals. But Rawls argues for his favorite distribution of (at least some of) *these* commodities on the grounds that they are the chief *means* to securing *other,* more mundane commodities that provide satisfaction to individuals. To make his argument explicit on this point appears also to require a strong concept of satisfaction. Indeed, a not too far-fetched interpretation of Rawls is that as a basic value judgment his principle applies to the distribution of satisfaction. From this basic value judgment, together with empirical facts about individual preferences and social organization, we *derive* its application to primary social goods.

9. To obtain the equivalence asserted here, one must define the "chevrons" in the diagram with some care. Roughly, they are not precisely right-angle chevrons, but approach right angles (from the bottom right) arbitrarily closely.

10. For a discussion of these problems see A. K. Sen. *Collective Choice and Social Welfare.* San Francisco. Holden-Day (1970).

11. See McGuire and Aaron.

12. The force of the following example clearly comes from taking a social welfare function whose arguments are subjective preferences of internal constituents as the *only* criterion for evaluating internal distributions of satisfaction, and indirectly commodities. To consistently do this requires that we regard internal political institutions—like majority voting—as *means* to achieving the recommended distributions. Such a strong version of a "preference-regarding" theory would clearly be unacceptable to Rawls, who has argued that some political institutions are not to be regarded simply as means to economic justice.

13. One might object that this discussion ignores an important distinction between "subjective preferences" and "objective needs." What we have assumed to be the subjective preferences of the poor at home are being treated on an equal footing with the objective needs of the poor abroad. While it is true that

strong preference-regarding theories do not make such a distinction, this is not the source of the counterintuitive result. Were we to include the poor abroad in our domain, adopt a somewhat egalitarian social welfare function and make some plausible assumptions about how subjectively unpleasant starvation is in comparison to, say, waiting hours for barely competent medical care, we would obtain a more intuitively plausible result without appealing to a concept of "objective need." What is illuminated here is a possible pitfall in the restricted-domain, public goods approach, not the need for an additional concept of "objective need."

14. Rawls's own solution to the problem (Rawls, pp. 284–289) is to introduce a "principle of just saving" which leaves open the rate of saving but requires that it be at least enough to raise the level of the worst-off.

# Bigotry, loyalty, and malnutrition
Samuel Gorovitz

Bigotry and loyalty seem to me two sides of the same puzzling coin. I want to examine the puzzle and explore how it bears on the question of what it is to act in a humanitarian way. There are connections between these concepts and some questions of foreign policy determination. In particular, there is a connection with the administration of P.L. 480, the Food for Peace legislation. But before seeing these connections, we must review some philosophical points.

Two major traditions in moral philosophy—different viewpoints in thinking about ethical questions—divide over the issue of whether and to what extent the actual or expected consequences of an action are determinant of its moral quality. One tradition includes those who hold that the moral character of an act is a function of its consequences in whole or in part. We call such a position consequentialist. This view is exemplified by the utilitarian theory of right action, most notably associated with Jeremy Bentham, John Stuart Mill, and a long line of Mill's intellectual descendants. Utilitarianism holds that actions are right if and only if they produce the greatest happiness for the greatest number of persons. Other views can be consequentialist, too. For example, the (erroneous) view that those actions are right which maximize, say, beauty in the world, quite apart from the amount of human happiness or benefit associated with that beauty, would be a consequentialist, but nonutilitarian, theory.

The other tradition comprises ethical theories which hold that the determination of the moral status of an action is independent of its consequences. This sort of moral theory is exemplified by the views of Immanuel Kant and those who write in his tradition. In Kant's view, actions are right or wrong on grounds wholly independent of the consequences; an action to be right must have been done from a certain sort of motivation. Moral theories that categorize certain classes of action as right or wrong, such as is done by any list of commandments or prescriptions, also are typically nonconsequentialist. Thus some traditional orthodoxies admonish us to refrain utterly from acts of certain

129

kinds, such as killing, stealing, and lying, on the grounds that they are wrong in virtue simply of the kinds of acts that they are.

Much of the history of moral philosophy deals with the tension between these two basic points of view about the moral importance of consequences, and the attempts on the part of moral theorists to resolve the dispute or strike some plausible balance. Clearly we do have strong temptation to hold the consequences of actions to be relevant to their moral status, and thus consequentialist moral theories have substantial and sustained appeal. However, they have not become fully dominant precisely because we also believe that there is something morally lacking in an approach that focuses solely on consequences, and refuses to acknowledge that certain kinds of action are wrong, *simpliciter*.

Both consequentialists and nonconsequentialists typically share the view that each person is of equal value as regards that elusive cluster of issues that constitute the subject matter of moral philosophy and that we refer to with the language of justice, moral worth, human rights, etc. Thus, for Mill and the utilitarians, it is the productivity of happiness and the avoidance of pain that counts, but everyone's happiness is equally important and everyone's pain equally lamentable. And for Kant, the test of a moral action is closely linked with the question of whether one can logically will that each other person be guided by the same moral maxim or rule that guides one's own action. Indeed, it is widely taken to be a criterion of adequacy for any moral theory that it apply equally to all similarly situated persons. Thus if lying is wrong regardless of the circumstances, then it is wrong not merely for you, but for me and for anyone else. And if there are some circumstances under which, on utilitarian grounds or on any others, it is morally permissible to tell a lie, then it is as permissible for you under those circumstances as for me or for anyone else. Further, if I wish to justify my treating two distinct persons differently in some fundamental way—such as in the extent to which I respect their rights—I must be able to cite some relevant difference between them as a basis for the justification of the difference in my treatment of them.

More importantly for our present purposes, if I wish to treat two distinct classes of persons differently in some fundamental way, it is incumbent upon me to be able to cite relevant differences between the two classes of persons in virtue of which my different treatment of them can be justified. In short, moral theory, like justice, is no respecter of persons in their particularity. Rather, it is a respecter equally of all persons, no matter what their individuating characteristics. That is why questions of moral worth and human rights are so sharply distinguished from questions of personal competence, social utility, market value, social position, and the like. Indeed, a large part of what we mean by speaking of all persons as equals, when it is undeniable that people are not equal in their descriptive characteristics, is that as a bearer of basic human rights and moral entitlements any person is the equal of any other.

We thus find frequent explicit endorsement in moral philosphy of the requirement that to be taken seriously as a moral principle, a principle must be applicable equally to all persons as moral agents. That is, what one may do (or is prohibited from doing) all may do (or are prohibited from doing) under circumstances similar in morally relevant respects. This requirement serves to test the moral acceptability of principles concerning how people may, must, or are forbidden to act.

The same requirement also applies to principles of human rights. I shall not here enter or even report on the controversies that exist about the scope, origin, or nature of human rights; suffice it to say that human rights are those, if any, which persons have simply in virtue of their humanity, in contrast to such rights—call them special rights—which particular persons have in virtue of special arrangements, such as their having undertaken contractual relationships or having been made promises. If any person has a human right, all persons have that right, whatever the extent may be to which circumstances result in violation of the right for some people. (In this essay I shall simply take as acceptable the assumption that some such rights exist. I believe that most people involved in consideration of international food distribution problems would grant that assumption, and I will therefore want to focus on the consequences of that assumption for U.S. food policy.)

I call this requirement, both in its application to human actions and its application to human rights, the requirement of the equal moral standing of all persons. It should be clear that this requirement involves a substantive moral claim. One might hold, for example, that the members of an aristocracy are subject to a set of moral rules and enjoy a set of fundamental human rights that differ from the rules and rights that apply to the peasantry. But no such position can be accepted by anyone who accepts the equal moral standing of all persons.

Thus far, I have emphasized equality as regards moral constraints on action and as regards human rights. But what of the *interests* of people? Is it morally required to consider the wants, preferences, and aspirations of all people to be of equal moral importance? Classical utilitarianism holds that happiness is the sole good, and that each person's happiness is as important as any other's. But what contributes to personal happiness goes far beyond what people are entitled to as a matter of right. Jefferson realized this, and hence wrote not of a right to happiness, but merely of a right to its pursuit. The question of the moral standing of interests is even more complex and difficult than that of the standing of rights. Fortunately, we need not be concerned with it here. For our immediate concern is with the alleviation of starvation and chronic malnutrition, and that concern can be addressed usefully at the level of rights.

A recurrent theme in the language of social and political organization is the identification and protection of human rights. The founding documents of American democracy are explicit on the issue, and the *Universal Declaration of Human Rights*, adopted by the General Assembly of the United Nations in 1948, goes substantially further in specifying conditions of human existence that should be guaranteed to all persons whatever their individual characteristics. Yet no right has meaning or value once starvation strikes. It is an ultimate deprivation of rights, for without food life ends, and rights are of value only to the living. Further, the need for food, like that for water and oxygen, is pervasive. All persons, everywhere, need it for survival virtually all the time. It is unlike medical treatment, shelter, clothing, tools, and the like; the need for it is a universal precondition of the exercise of human rights for all people at all times. Moreover, without adequate nutrition, the value of rights is greatly diminished, for the rights that are most often claimed as human rights are those that facilitate growth, the development of personal capacities, and the identification and pursuit of rational life plans. But malnutrition curtails growth, constrains physical and mental development, and limits the possibilities of action. Thus a regard for the value and protection of human rights seems to require a concern for basic problems of survival, and prominently among them, for starvation and malnutrition. And if human rights are held equally by all persons everywhere, it seems that a commitment to human rights—to any of them at all—would require a concern with hunger equally wherever and whomever it strikes. But is this correct?

Consider how our reactions to such events as auto fatalities vary with the location of the event in question. When we read of the death of a child 3,000 miles away, we may incline toward an acknowledgement of unpleasantness, but typically we ward off the blow to our emotional equanimity rather easily. If the accident occurs in our city, we seem rather more concerned. This may be because the event tends to get more attention, and hence we become made more fully aware of it in its detail. But even with the same amount of information we are likely to shudder a bit more deeply when it is a local event. The accident a continent away is a statistic, but across town it is a significant misfortune. And when it takes place on our street, it is a tragedy that reverberates in our lives for quite some time, even if we have no personal acquaintance with any of the principals. Other things being equal, as spatial proximity diminishes, so too does the intensity of our response to people and their plight.

Time, too, has its effect. If we learn that a thousand people died in an earthquake, our distress may be substantial, but will be allayed with the news that the event took place in the twelfth century. And anyone involved in fund raising knows the special effectiveness of appeals to contribute to "one's own kind," whether that kind be defined in terms of ethnic heritage, school affiliation, or some other principal of identification.

This tendency is widespread throughout our reactions to the circumstances of others. As we increasingly identify with other persons, in whatever way, the intensity of our response to their circumstances increases. And when we perceive others as being very distant from ourselves, in location, time, or characteristics, we tend to think of them as somehow less than full persons—as historical or statistical figures, perhaps, but not quite as fully human persons with hopes, needs, and aspirations of their own that are as important to them as our own are to us.

This phenomenon provides one part of the basis for bigotry. Several examples illustrate the point. Few practices are as puzzling as the institution of American slavery. For it is simply not the case that American slaveholders were all moral neanderthals. Many of them were sensitive, self-respecting, reflective, and literate persons, some of whom, like Jefferson himself, were articulate spokesmen in defense of human rights. Yet they embraced, and in some cases defended, a moral abomination. How is this possible?

One answer is simple: No self-respecting person can knowingly treat another person as one treats a slave, but those who become slaves are not fully persons. Once the slave is reclassified out of full human status, then the constraints on interpersonal relationships no longer apply, and the slave owner can maintain a self-image of human decency. He has achieved an emotional distancing from the slave by dehumanizing a whole class of persons of which the slave is a member.

This same psychological move is useful in wartime. I am reminded of an incident during our shameful engagement in Vietnam. American troops had backed enemy forces to the sea and obliterated them. One war-weary soldier, interviewed after the battle, said that it was "just like a Tennessee turkey shoot." Many viewers thought this comment to be evidence of the inhumanity of the soldier, of his callous insensitivity to the horror of killing. But perhaps instead it is evidence of his very human revulsion at the notion of killing other persons. It is one thing to engage in a turkey shoot; it is quite another to slaughter an array of fleeing persons. If one can come to perceive the enemy as less than human—indeed, as analogous to turkeys—the business of killing becomes much easier. For many people, it may become possible where it otherwise would not be. Soldiers, too, have a need to maintain a sense of themselves as decent human beings.

The rationalization making possible the institution of slavery, and facilitating the institution of war, is the partitioning of the population into multiple classes, only some of which we see as enjoying full human status. To some extent, we may also maintain our sanity and our functional ability to respond to tragedy by distancing ourselves from most of the world's problems, choosing to single out just those people and problems that we see as close to us in some way and hence as warranting our care and attention. And sometimes we resort to a denial of full human standing to some subset of humanity when we do not wish to acknowledge their plight, just as when we wish to own or slaughter them.

Yet the principle of the equal moral standing of all persons admonishes us to count all persons as being of equal value. Bigotry, which is the groundless downgrading of some selected subset of humanity, is morally repugnant precisely because it flies in the face of that principle. It depends on and arises from failure to count each person in equal measure. But should everyone count in equal measure?

To varying degrees, in varying ways, we see loyalties of one sort or another as worthy of praise. I do not refer to the unreflective and morally blind loyalties of the hard-core Nixon henchmen, or other such instances of loyalty that have almost made a mockery of the concept. I refer rather to such phenomena as devotion to family and friends, special concern for one's community, and such species of patriotism as will bear moral scrutiny. I do not claim that all instances of loyalty are laudable. It suffices that there be some instances of laudable loyalties. For what is loyalty, if not a special sort of favoritism—the singling out of a subset of the population that one is justified or perhaps even obligated to count as being of greater importance than persons generally?

Loyalty, like bigotry, seems to require a violation of the principle of the equal moral standing of all persons. Indeed, Peter Singer holds that there is no moral justification for such loyalties as favoring one's own children, except insofar as such preferential treatment may be a part of "a recognized system of responsibilities" which is defensible strictly on the basis of its utilitarian benefits to mankind as a whole.[1] Singer goes on to dismiss in one paragraph the view that such a system of obligations and responsibilities can be defended in the context of present world food distribution problems, which in his judgment "combine to outweigh decisively the utility of preserving the usual system of obligations." But this view does not square with the widespread belief that loyalties, and the preferential treatment they foster, are sometimes acceptable and even laudable.

Bigotry depresses the value of some persons, loyalty elevates it; both reflect the partitioning of the population into various groupings, the members of which receive differential treatment depending upon which group they are in. If we then agree that bigotry is repugnant and that loyalty can be laudable, how can we justify condemning the one while praising the other? Or is it, as Singer suggests, an error not to condemn both?

We behave differently toward different people at least in part in virtue of the special relationships we have toward them. For example, if I have promised or contracted to feed you, my obligation is stronger than it would otherwise have been even assuming you are starving. This is not to deny that I might have obligations toward you in virtue of your starving—for if I have extra food and an awareness of your hunger, I may indeed have some obligations toward you on that account. It is to say simply that my having promised or contracted to feed you creates a special relationship between us and concomitantly a special obligation. Not all special relationships yield special obligations. For example, if I know your name, or if you and I wear indistinguishable neckties, then special relationships exist between us. But no obligation seems to flow from such relationships.

Consider some of the other relationships in which I may stand to another person. Some are simple. I may be a relative, friend, neighbor, or colleague. Some are more complex: I stand in special relationship to the parents of the friends of my children. Some special relationships are explicitly obligating in intent and effect, such as contractual relationships. Some may result from precedent. Thus in *On Liberty* Mill writes:

> When a person, either by express promise or by conduct, has encouraged another to rely upon his continuing to act in a certain way—to build expectations and calculations, and stake any part of his plan of life upon that supposition—a new series of moral obligations arises on his part toward that person, which may be overruled, but cannot be ignored.[2]

Spelling out just how some special relationships lead to special obligations, especially in contrast with those special relationships which do not, goes beyond the scope and the needs of this essay. It may be useful, however, to review two kinds of defense that can be given in behalf of preferential treatment on grounds of special relationships.

First, some special relationships are intrinsically the undertaking of obligations. This is obviously true in contractual situations and in promise making. But it also seems plausible that, at least in a significant proportion of cases, familial and other relationships lead to obligations in related ways—via explicit or conventional undertaking of obligations inherent in those relationships. The single, explicit, contractual relationship is not exemplary of all relationships that result in obligations. Indeed, it represents one end of a continuum the other end of which is difficult to discern. For our patterns of interpersonal relationships comprise not only those that we invent by explicit agreements but also those that we assume as we participate in social roles that are antecedently defined to varying degrees.

One cannot undertake the role of home-plate umpire without thereby also undertaking a clearly defined set of responsibilities and obligations, the rejection of any of which is tantamount to a rejection of the role, and perhaps of the game itself in the context of which that role has meaning. Roles like those of parent, spouse, friend, and neighbor are not so well defined. We have wide latitude to shape them to suit our individual circumstances. But that does not mean that such roles can be whatever we choose to make of them. On the contrary, there are constraints the violation of which constitute the rejection of the role as surely as in the example of the umpire—even though it is much less clear what those constraints are. For instance, if I deceive you for my own profit, avoid you when I can, and abuse you otherwise, I may still want to claim to be your friend, but the claim is indefensible. My assertion that I define the role of friend rather more loosely than others do is to no avail. I simply cannot be your friend if I treat you in such a manner; the relationship of one friend to another, though it admits of many shapes and forms, does not admit of that one. To be a friend is to have certain obligations in regard to the object of one's friendship; to reject such obligations is to reject participation in that form of association known as friendship. That rejection is possible, of course. But at what cost?

Each of our established patterns of interaction with one another constitutes a thread in the social fabric. Some are more peripheral than others; some are central. We can perhaps reweave the social fabric to good advantage by replacing or rearranging some of those threads, but to tamper with too many at once may unravel the whole thing, at a cost that cannot be foreseen. A pervasive feature of that fabric of social relationships is that family and friends have special responsibility to attend to the needs and protect the interests of one another, that representatives have obligations to represent their constituents, that communities must maintain a level of mutual trust and concern, and the like. We simply do not know how great the cost would be, or how widespread, of radical tampering with the patterns of interaction that structure our relationships with one another. Of course there are costs associated with maintaining the presently existing patterns of social responsibility; these may include a tendency toward bigotry, narrow and imprudent patriotism, and unnecessarily great insensitivity to the needs of others. But the determination of which course of action—substantial preservation or substantial overhaul of the status quo—leads to greater utility is complex, difficult, and utterly undone. Thus Singer's willingness to override the "usual system of obligations" seems too facile, even from the point of view of utilitarian grounds. He may be right in the final analysis, but to show that would take some doing.

Further, his account presupposes the correctness of a purely utilitarian moral analysis. It is open to the objection that nonconsequentialist considerations support the maintenance of some forms of preferential treatment. One might hold, for example, that to enter into certain forms of relationship with others is to undertake commitments, including some of a protective or nurturing sort, the violation of which can take place only at the cost of one's honor and integrity, quite apart from considerations of utility.

A second kind of defense of the sort of preferential treatment associated with loyalty is the argument based on claims of psychological necessity. Since it is clearly impossible for any individual entirely to apprehend, let alone respond to, the full range of human needs, one who responds with intense concern to the plight of others requires some sort of protection against overexposure. If we were immobilized by an awesome array of problems, we would achieve less even than would result from an effective pursuit of quite parochial concerns. Perhaps the justification of our favoring some segments of the population lies in the observation that few of us indeed are in any position beneficially to affect the population as a whole. This view is reinforced by the observation that as individuals move into positions where it is possible for them to affect the circumstances of increasingly large numbers of persons, we expect their sensitivities and commitments to expand correspondingly. Thus, whereas a senator can be forgiven a certain degree of favoritism toward his own constitutency, a president is expected to be even-handed with respect to the citizenry in its entirety.

It is useful here to bear in mind the distinctions among special rights, human rights, and interests. Obviously, one cannot in general be faulted morally for giving money, say, to the man who painted one's house under contract and who is claiming compensation, rather than to a more needy person with whom one has had no dealings. But if it is a matter of human rights—those rights which exist independently of the character of special relationships among persons—then it seems reasonable to hold that one should be as concerned with the stranger as with the friend.

Nothing follows from this position regarding obligations in respect to the interests of various persons when those interests go beyond the protection of basic rights. Thus one can hold without inconsistency that preferential treatment on the basis of loyalty has no justification when the preferential treatment involves matters of basic rights, whereas preferential regard for the interests of family, friends, and community is morally acceptable when those interests do not involve matters of rights.

This view suggests a basis for distinguishing between the moral status of bigotry and that of loyalty. For bigotry and the dehumanization of others are typically manifested in some violation of the rights of their victims. But loyalty can coexist with a respect for the rights of all, if the favoritism it fosters is restricted to the protection and nurturing of the interests of those to whom we have special obligations and responsibilities in consequence of the social roles we fill in regard to them—can coexist, that is, unless that favoritism can be maintained only at the expense of the rights of others. But if the consequence of my providing incremental advantages to my well-fed children is the denial of food and, therefore, of rights to another, then that manifestation of familial loyalty may well be outweighed by my obligations to combat starvation.

Yet is it not the case that any expenditure on advancing the interests of the well-fed is competitive with, and therefore must give way to, the purchase of food for the hungry? Those few nations which are in a position to be major net exporters of food are affluent, highly developed nations with a high standard of living. They could reduce their production and purchase of luxury goods in order to channel more resources into international food aid, but it is not likely that they could radically alter the basic features of their economics to the point of diverting resources entirely from the production of nonessential goods to international food aid without thereby so weakening the economic basis of their national affluence as to undermine their ability to remain food-exporting nations. This fact in no way exempts the acquisitive from the need to respond to the existence of hunger. But it does call into question whether the most effective way to respond to hunger is to divert resources maximally into production, purchase, and distribution of food. The economic realities are such that a certain level of pursuit of nonessential interests may be essential for the maximization of our ability to meet the essential needs, and hence to protect the rights, of others. Thus expenditure on advancing the interests of the well-fed is not necessarily wholly competitive with the provision of food to the needy, and there may be a utilitarian basis on which individuals can justify maintaining a life-style that seems self-indulgent in the context of world hunger.

There are also nonutilitarian arguments in defense of some expenditure on nonessential interests. For the relationships that bind family and friends include more than a mutual concern with survival. They include as well some rights to be respected as autonomous persons in a context of others who have undertaken obligations to be nurturing of one's interests, and from whom one can claim, as a matter of right, some furtherance of one's interests. One can have such a right to something one does not need or even want, and the force of such rights is unclear when they are in conflict with the survival needs of distant persons. Still, although they may be overridden, they may not be ignored.

Thus far, we have considered primarily questions pertaining to the actions of individuals. It is time for some observations about the relationship between nations and persons. We use the word "nation" ambiguously, sometimes to refer to the government of a country ("The signing of the Border Accord constitutes the first agreement in a decade between the two nations") and at other times to refer to the population of a country ("The nation is starving; disaster relief is urgently needed"). What is true of a nation in one sense is not necessarily true of that nation in the other. Note also that we sometimes speak of a nation as having a characteristic in virtue of the policy of its government ("That is a totalitarian nation" or "That nation is a member of the Arctic Defense Alliance"). But we also speak of a nation as having a characteristic in virtue of the persons or institutions it comprises having that characteristic ("That is a beef-eating nation"). Nations can have many characteristics not shared by their citizens, but a nation is starving only in virtue of the fact that its citizens are starving.

Just here, we must distinguish among governments, the electorate, and persons in need as the objects of our action. Insofar as our objective is political—say, to gain favor with a foreign government or to establish our credentials as humanitarians in the eyes of the domestic electorate—it may make little difference whether or not the aid we give to another nation results in relief of the malnutrition of the persons in that nation. To the extent that our objectives are humanitarian, however, nothing else matters but whether or not the aid relieves the hunger. Thus, insofar as our aid is genuinely humanitarian, its objects should be construed not as nations in the sense of governments, but nations in the sense of populations of hungry persons. A government of the recipient nation may of necessity play a role in the distribution process, but it is hard to see how any characteristic of that government other than its distributional effectiveness can have any bearing on the relationship between the United States as a humanitarian donor and the hungry persons toward whom aid is directed.

Of course, food aid can be motivated by political and developmental reasons, as well as by humanitarian reasons. Public Law 480 and the legislative history surrounding it since 1954 make frequent and explicit reference to each of these three kinds of motivation. But an internal tension exists within that history, for the scope of humanitarian concerns is constrained by explicit exclusion from benefits of nations out of favor with the United States—Cuba and North Vietnam in particular, and hence potentially any nation in principle.

Thomas Nagel, granting that political and humanitarian aspects of food aid are linked perhaps inextricably, has argued that in the face of radical inequality, it is incumbent upon affluent nations to engage in humanitarian food aid programs which respond to the nutritional needs of starving populations simply in virtue of their humanity, and not in virtue of their politics.[3] This assertion seems at variance with the received interpretation of prevailing United States practice, under which ostensibly humanitarian food aid under P.L. 480 is given primarily to nations that are eligible not only in terms of need, as indicated by inclusion on the most seriously affected list, but also in terms of a presidential determination of friendly-nation status. The Foreign Assistance Act of 1961 places no such constraint on presidential action in response to human suffering caused by natural and man-made disasters. But serious malnutrition in the poorest nations is not always attributable to disaster; more commonly it grows out of chronic impoverishment.

That food aid is always in part political in motivation and in effect seems clear; with Nagel, I see no possibility that it could be otherwise. Knowing this, it would be difficult and perhaps impossible to exclude political considerations from our motivation. Thus humanitarian and political aspects of aid do seem bound together. Still, if we are committed to a humanitarian response to human need, an awareness that our actions would have political consequences need not deter us from acting on humanitarian motives. Indeed, so long as we claim to have a humanitarian policy of providing food aid in response to nutritional need elsewhere, we may view undesirable consequences of our food aid—such as strengthening an unfriendly government—simply as part of the cost of, rather than as a barrier to, humanitarian action.

It is worth noting here that much of the language we use to describe relationships among nations is a metaphorical extension of the language we use to describe interpersonal relationships. Thus we speak of nations as friends, neighbors, customers, perhaps even as ancestors and offspring. Nations, of course, can have traditional associations, can sign contracts or treaties, can make promises publicly or privately, can identify with one another on religious or other grounds, and can have complex subset relations such as are exemplified by the business interests of citizens engaged in international trade. But it is not obvious, nor should it be assumed, that what is true of interpersonal relationships is also true of those international relationships that are described in the same or similar language. For example, among persons, some special relationships and the obligations that they entail are subject to constraint or enforcement in virtue of the larger context in which they arise. Contractual relationships are a case in point, subject as they are to regulation by positive law. A somewhat different example is provided by familial obligations, which are enforced not solely by law but by social pressures external to and within the family. What analogues exist at the level of nations? Some international transactions, such as monetary exchange, take place in a highly structured context which makes violation of obligations costly and thus unlikely. But what of such obligations as may exist in regard to disaster relief, environmental protection, or development assistance? Some pressure is perhaps generated by such organizations as the World Court or the United Nations, but on the whole there seems little effective or comprehensive world law to enforce such special obligations among nations as may arise out of special relationships among them. Of course, there is some force in the appeal to world opinion, and there are various kinds of prudential considerations which support the fulfillment of obligations. But on the whole, as regards that subset of special interpersonal relationships that give rise to special obligations subject to external enforcement, there seems little analogue at the international level.

But enforcement is not the issue. Contractual obligations may be *honored* more frequently because their violation can lead to legal sanctions, but such obligations could arise even in the absence of any prospect of such sanctions. That no effective enforcement mechanisms exist for some international obligations surely does not entail the absence of such obligations. In fact, it is all the more important to be clear about such obligations, and to focus public attention on them, precisely because their fulfillment cannot be presumed to be assured by mechanisms of external enforcement. Recall that one defense of what might be called our moral parochialism is the claim that it is a psychological necessity; that the scope and complexity of the world's population of individuals is such that a person would likely become dysfunctional in attempting to deal with more than a restricted subset—indeed, a very carefully restricted subset—of that population.

At the level of nations, the situation appears quite different. Even now, the number of nations is minute compared to the number of persons. It is possible for one individual to know them all, and to know a bit about each of them, and it is comparatively easy for an institution such as a national government to keep abreast of what nations there are, what their needs and aspirations are, and whether they are flourishing or declining. The fragmentation of attention that besets an individual trying to comprehend the personal problems of the world does not entail the impossibility of our constructing social institutions, within or without government, that can attend to the problems of nations. The tenability of the psychological justification for special obligations among persons is thus not apparently relevant to special relationships among governments. The world's persons are beyond the capacity of every individual to maintain individual personal relationships. The world's nations are not beyond any nation's capacity to maintain individual international relationships.

In any case, there is a sense in which questions of food aid in response to world hunger are not questions of international relationships in the same way as, for example, questions of tariff negotiations. It is individuals who starve, and food aid aims at alleviating the hunger of individuals. Our government can be an effective mechanism for facilitating food aid, and the governments of hungry nations can be effective mechanisms for distribution of needed food. But we need not look to the history of our government's relationship with their governments to know that no one should starve because of his nation's politics.[4]

All this speaks mainly to objectives rather than to mechanisms. I have emphasized the moral aspects of the juxtaposition of hunger and affluence in the context of U.S. food aid under law, whereas Peter Singer has emphasized the moral argument for voluntary individual action. There is no incompatability. Without widespread concern on the part of individuals there is unlikely to be significant government action, and without government action, there is unlikely to be a sufficiently systematic or widespread response on the part of individuals to resolve the problems of world hunger in a way that distributes the costs of such resolution equitably.

It is time to take stock. I have argued that morality requires an equal respect for the moral standing of all persons, and that in consequence it is necessary to respect equally the basic human rights of all persons everywhere. I have suggested lines of defense of the position that preferential treatment of family, friends, and community may be justifiable on grounds of loyalty, but only when such treatment is not purchased at the cost of violating the human rights of others. I have argued that adequate food is essential for the exercise of human rights, and for the maintenance of their value, for all people everywhere. But I have not argued or claimed that there is a right to food. My argument is less tight than that. Rather, it is my position that a purported respect for human rights is strange and unconvincing when it is not accompanied by a regard, manifested in behavior, for those conditions which are necessary for the exercise of such rights. Just as the bigot is guilty of hypocrisy when he pretends to a concern with human rights while dehumanizing a subset of the population, so too are the affluent guilty of hypocrisy if they pretend to a commitment to human rights without manifesting in their actions a deep concern with the problems of those whose rights are eroded by disease, oppression, or hunger—unless, that is, they either are ignorant of the relationship between human rights and basic needs or else are victims of self-deception. Perhaps the unhappy refuges of self-deception and hypocrisy are safe from the force of our argument about world hunger, but it is the hope of contributors to this volume that ignorance will become more difficult to plead.

NOTES

1. P. Singer, "Reconsidering the Famine Relief Argument," above, pp. 36–49. (My reference is to a previous version of Singer's paper, which has lately been revised to refer not to preservation of the usual system of obligations, but to "restricting ourselves" to the usual system. My arguments are obviously aimed at defeating facile objections to preservation of the usual system of obligations; I hold no brief for restricting ourselves to such a system.)

2. J. S. Mill, *On Liberty*, Bobbs-Merrill Co., Inc., 1956.

3. T. Nagel, "Poverty and Food: Why Charity Is Not Enough," above, pp. 54-61.

4. Of course, humanitarian considerations do not always dominate. Just as we could justifiably withhold food from a terrorist, we could in some cases justifiably reject the humanitarian case for responding to an instance of severe hunger. But the justification would not be simple. It would require recourse to factors such as clear aggression or culpability of some other strong sort, rather than to such diffuse notions as a general disposition to "unfriendliness." A complete theory of the moral dimensions of food aid would have to specify the conditions providing such justification; I have attempted here only to sketch a general viewpoint the deviations from which would be at issue in developing such a theory.

Part Three
RESPONSIBILITIES IN THE PRIVATE SECTOR

ABOUT THE CONTRIBUTORS

Charles B. Shuman was national president of the nation's largest organization of farmers, the American Farm Bureau Federation, from 1954 to 1970. He serves on the Advisory Council of the Chicago Mercantile Exchange and the board of trustees of several Midwestern universities.

Victor Ferkiss is author of *Technological Man* and *The Future of Technological Civilization,* among other books, and many essays. He is Professor of Government at Georgetown University.

C. William Swank, Executive Vice President of the Ohio Farm Bureau Federation, has made thousands of speeches and television and radio appearances and has written a column for the *Buckeye Farm News* for 20 years. He frequently represents American farmers on trade missions and other delegations sent throughout the world.

 Food aid and the free market
Charles B. Shuman

High-quality food is so universally available in such abundance and at such low cost in the United States that it is difficult for the average citizen to realize that hunger is a real and constant threat for many millions of human beings in other parts of the world. American families who pay out less than 16% of their average income for food often do not realize that they have a good bargain as compared to food costs for most other people in the world.

While malnutrition is fairly common in this country, it is usually caused by ignorance of a proper diet, prejudice against certain foods, pockets of poverty, or the time constraints which lead many people to demand the well-advertised but somewhat less nourishing snack and fast-serve foods. In many other countries, adequate food supplies are physically unavailable. However, despite this degree of isolation from the more serious problem, the United States has done quite well in providing food and food-related aid to relieve hunger and starvation in the world; from 1965 through 1973 we have given 80% of the total contributed by all nations.[1]

The American people always respond to the emergency needs of hungry people, but the real challenge is to correct the basic causes of inadequate food supplies. Food aid is, at best, a temporary expedient. In searching for permanent remedies, it is imperative that we seek facts rather than listening to emotion laden propaganda.

The population explosion is one very visible cause of world hunger, and yet here is a clue to a solution of the food problem. The birth rate is declining slowly in the more highly developed industrial nations while it rolls on unchecked in most developing countries. It may be that economic development is more effective than government-promoted birth control programs in checking excessive population growth. The concepts and techniques of family planning are apparently more readily accepted by those with moderate or high incomes than by the poor. Social and economic progress may help relieve population pressures as well as improve the ability to purchase food. This situation may be due in part to the incentives for large families that are built into those welfare programs in any nation that pays benefits in proportion to the number of children. Old Malthus was wrong—a short food supply does not curb population growth. However, a reduction in the birth rate in the developing nations would hasten the day when starvation might be banished from the earth.

The knowledge that chronic hunger and starvation are largely confined to the economically less developed nations gives some basis for confidence that these historic plagues of mankind can be cured. Perhaps all that is needed is for the developing nations to catch up in industrial and agricultural productivity with the developed countries, but that is a big order.

There are ample natural resources in the world to provide an adequate diet for all of the people here now and for all who will be here in the next few decades. A recent UN survey concluded that only 45% of the tillable land in the developing countries was being utilized for crops.[2] An Iowa State University study estimates that of the 7.8 billion acres of land suitable for crops in the world, only 3.4 billion are presently in use.[3] The developed nations have brought a higher proportion of their tillable land into production than have the developing areas, probably because more capital was available for clearing, drainage, and reclamation. The developed nations also obtain higher yields from their farm land. During the last 20 years, grain yields have increased 63% in the developed countries, while yields were up only 32% in the hungry lands.[4] The question is not, "Can the world feed itself?" but "Will it?"

Practically all areas of the world have the potential to increase food production. Many nations produce more than they consume, but due to inadequate distribution and transportation systems, or inability of the needy to pay, the food supplies do not move to those in need. During a recent food crisis in India, starvation was imminent in several states while others nearby had large quantities of grain with few buyers. Hunger is an economic problem—there are no hungry people where there is money to buy food. Food is available, but it is bulky and expensive to move great distances. Dr. John Hannah, former administrator of AID sums it up: "The only practical solution is to substantially increase food production in the poor countries."[5]

The World Food Conference in Rome in November of 1974 helped focus attention on world food problems. It did very little in finding solutions for these problems as the participants were most interested in advancing their own personal political ambitions by making speeches for home consumption. However, the staff researchers of the FAO, the USDA, and others, in preparing for the conference, surfaced some valuable information.[6] The general conclusion seems to be that the developing nations, with assistance from the developed countries, could achieve the necessary increases in food output to meet their own food needs.[7] Dr. D. Gale Johnson comes to the following conclusion after his study of world food problems:

It is generally agreed that there is enormous potential for increasing food production in the developing countries. The cultivated area could be substantially increased, and yields per unit of land could be doubled within two decades if sufficient effort were made.... There are no reasons based on limitations of resources or on the technology and biology of food production that will prevent the population of the world from being more adequately fed a decade hence than in the years immediately before 1972.[8]

As we turn now to analyze the causes of the food problems of the developing nations and to propose corrective action, it may be helpful to capsulize the complex dilemma that confronts those who seek solutions:

1. There is chronic hunger and starvation in the world, but it is concentrated in the developing nations.
2. The natural resources of land, water, and climatic conditions are adequate to support much greater food production in the developing nations.
3. Food production has been increasing in both the developing and developed countries. However, during the 20 years 1954–73, the 8% per capita gain in the food-critical areas is far surpassed by a 33% gain in the industrialized nations. This slower rate of improvement is largely due to the very rapid population increase in the less developed areas.[9]
4. Chronic underemployment and low income of a large segment of the population is a common characteristic of most areas where hunger is a major problem.
5. Unless the population explosion is slowed and at the same time agricultural productivity materially increased, the developing nations will continue on the borderline of starvation for many decades.
6. Food aid programs, while necessary for emergency relief, cannot permanently solve the food shortage problems of the developing nations and may actually worsen the situation.

The purpose of this chapter is to examine some of the causes of hunger and to consider the possibility of using the free market approach toward correcting the trouble. In doing this, it will be necessary to critically evaluate some of the food aid programs now being used and determine how they could be modified to encourage greater free market action. For the purposes of this paper, the free market may be defined as the willing exchange of goods and services at prices determined by voluntary negotiations between buyers and sellers with a minimum of government supervision and regulation. Since there are no completely free marketing systems, the term "free market" will be used to refer to those markets that are relatively free, as in the United States, as contrasted with government-managed systems of pricing and distribution, as in Russia. It is also recognized that there are probably no market systems that are completely government-controlled.

Since the causes of hunger in the world are varied and sometimes complex, obviously the solutions are not simple. It is not the intention of the author of this chapter to claim that the application of free market remedies will automatically solve all food problems of the hungry nations. However, it will be proposed that all other approaches will be ineffective if the free market with its automatic checks and balances is rejected or unduly restricted. Finally, after considering the economic and political aspects of the hunger problem, an attempt will be made to discuss some of the moral considerations.

Why are people hungry in one part of the world and well fed in other places? This is the key question. In some cases it may be a temporary situation that can be relieved by massive shipments of food. However, in most instances it is a chronic problem associated with low agricultural productivity, low per capita income, inadequate transportation and distribution, unchecked population expansion, and an unfavorable balance of trade with other nations. All of these illnesses except the population explosion are due to economic maladjustments and can be relieved by enlarging the role of the free market while reducing dependence on governmental activity. The high-birth-rate problem also involves economic factors to some extent. Present programs to relieve world hunger have too often approached the problem as if it were a temporary phenomenon. We have learned many things from our experience with food aid and technical assistance programs.

The Food for Peace Program was launched in 1954 by an act of Congress—P.L. 480. Its announced objective was to relieve hunger and facilitate the economic development of the low-income nations. The hidden agenda of P.L. 480 was to get rid of the embarrassingly large surpluses of grain that had accumulated as a result of the price supports and subsidies of the U.S. government farm programs. In the 22 years since Food for Peace was launched, it has provided $23 billion of food aid for the developing countries. It was relatively easy to get appropriations of $1 billion per year from a Congress which was seeking desperately to cover up its farm program mistakes by dumping the surpluses on the developing nations under the guise of humanitarian hunger relief. Today there are no government-owned surplus grain stocks, so the surplus-dumping phase has ended. One of the specific goals of P.L. 480 was to help encourage self-sufficiency through industrial and agricultural productivity in the recipient nations. It is apparent that this goal has not been achieved. In fact, P.L. 480 dumping has probably depressed grain prices and discouraged production in the "beneficiary" nations.[10]

While P.L. 480 concessional sales (Title I) and donations (Title II) have undoubtedly helped relieve the suffering of many unfortunate people, it is also probable that government-to-government aid has helped perpetuate corrupt dictatorships whose economic controls and interventions have been a major cause of low agricultural and industrial productivity. Despite the humanitarian intentions of the administrators of P.L. 480, the long-term net effect may have been to worsen the hunger problem. For example, the *New York Times* of

January 12, 1975, reported on the then current negotiations to send 300,000 tons of American grain to India: "It remains unclear, however, whether the United States has in return received assurances that the food will be used to feed hungry people in India and not be resold by India to other countries. . . . Indian officials refused to promise not to resell the food because, they said, it would represent an American intrustion into the decisions of their government."[11]

If India did in fact resell the grain, either in India or on the world market, it would tend to depress market prices and discourage future production in the area. In any case, a donation of grain to any nation that insists on reselling it rather than feeding hungry people has the same effect as a cash subsidy and helps perpetuate the government policies which contributed to the food shortage. If, on the other hand, an equivalent sum of money were distributed directly to hungry people, they could purchase food on the market and exert a price-strengthening effect which would stimulate greater production.

Public Law 480 programs have benefited many thousands of hungry people, and we have learned some valuable lessons. One of these lessons is that the United States cannot feed the world—we cannot guarantee freedom from hunger any more than we could guarantee freedom from oppression to the people of South Vietnam. However, we do know how to produce food in abundance, and perhaps we can convey this knowledge to those who can be most effective in ending starvation—the farmers in the developing nations.

The key to hunger relief is increased food production in the areas of need, but it can be argued that these more abundant supplies will not automatically reduce hunger and malnutrition. This dilemma would ensue if the increased production were induced by government decree and no further action were taken to assure the distribution of food to low-income people. However, if the free market system were permitted to operate throughout the economy, capital would flow from both foreign and domestic sources into industrial expansion as well as agricultural improvement. More people would find jobs, and their improved income would increase the market demand for farm products.

The free market remedy applied only to agriculture will not correct income and distribution deficiencies—it must be introduced in all sectors of the economy, including industry, transportation, distribution, and capital markets. The free market will not necessarily make food available at lower prices, but it will encourage the flow of capital to job-producing activities and thus permit many underemployed workers to enter the market with their earnings. Income supplements and welfare payments to the unemployable and handicapped will further strengthen the free market and thus stimulate increased food production and more efficient distribution. It is worth noting that in a free market economy substantially all food that is produced is consumed.

A comparison of the major motivating forces behind the farm production explosion of the last 40 years in the U.S. with the viability of the corresponding factors in the developing areas may give some clue to the solution of world food problems.

Modern agriculture is a capital-intensive industry. While American farmers have been handicapped by periods of low income, they have generally prospered under free-choice competitive market capitalism. Taxation, while a serious burden, has not prevented capital accumulation by farmers, and they have not been limited in the size of their farms. The government farm programs made some attempt to limit the volume of production but fortunately were not very successful. Feeble attempts have been made to impose price controls, but they have usually been ineffective and of short duration. United States farmers have been free to sell to the highest bidder and free to work and to save and to invest in their own businesses. The capital (including the value of land) invested in farming is approximately $500 billion and exceeds that of any other business in the nation.[12] Capital will not flow to or accumulate in any business that is unprofitable—profits are the wages of capital. While marginal at times, the profitability of farming in the U.S. has been sufficient to generate or attract and hold the necessary capital, but this has not been the case in the developing nations. It may not be practical or desirable to duplicate the highly mechanized large-scale U.S. farming methods in many of the overpopulated food-deficient countries. However, practically all of these nations have the potential to increase agricultural production dramatically if their farmers were given the freedom and the incentives to plan, work, and invest in free market-oriented farm businesses. Inadequate capital is one of the important causes of low farm productivity in the developing nations. Government policies which discourage capital formation must be changed or many people will continue to starve.

Agricultural credit is an important source of capital for farming, but it too depends upon sufficient profit to pay interest charges (rent on the use of the money) plus a realistic repayment plan. Soft or subsidized credit has been used to some extent in the United States, but, compared to the total credit and capital needs of agriculture, the amount from this source has been insignificant. One of the most serious roadblocks to increased food production is the banking and credit structure in the developing countries. Many of the food deficit countries are ruled by socialist dictatorships which place the allocation of capital and credit under political control instead of permitting investment funds to flow to the areas of greatest need as reflected by market demand. No amount of outside aid or technical assistance will increase production in a nation that persists in policies which limit the profits and income of farmers or turns the allocation of capital and credit over to politicians.

It is sometimes argued that large corporate farming, labor union boycotts and grain trade manipulations place similar constraints on production and marketing in the U.S. However, these and other attempts to develop monopolistic power are usually quickly corrected by antitrust prosecution or by the normal pressures of competition. Most segments of U.S. agriculture are highly competitive. While our agricultural marketing and pricing system is not completely free of outside interventions (governmental or private), it is relatively so and responds more rapidly and accurately to the needs of consumers than in any other nation.

Another important factor responsible for the spectacular explosion in farm productivity in the United States is research. The beginning impetus for agricultural research came with the Morrill Act in 1862, which established the land grant Colleges and the agricultural experiment stations. There is a long time lag between the start-up of research and its application on the farm. The developing nations have a tremendous advantage here, as the result of many years of basic research are available for their use. However, years of applied research are needed for each new soil and climatic area. (Example: the hybrid corn adapted to the Corn Belt will not do well in South America or India.) Rockefeller Foundation research in Mexico triggered the green revolution, but adaptation research must continue in every nation and the funds available at the present time are very inadequate. More of the AID funds should be used to finance agricultural research in the developing areas of the world.

Currently, much of the applied agricultural research in the U.S. is conducted by commercial companies interested in expanding markets for seed, fertilizer, machinery, and supplies. These great service and supply corporations and cooperatives that are so essential for a productive agriculture would move quickly to help develop the food-producing capacity of other nations if they could see any opportunity for a free market agriculture to come into being. Under present bureaucratic management, there are too many political palms to be greased.

One other important essential input for a productive agriculture, sadly lacking in the developing countries, is high-caliber, well-trained management. The American farm production revolution depends upon the blending by skilled management of capital, chemical, biological, technological, and marketing inputs so that a profit can be realized. Farm management in some of the developing areas consists of getting the maximum amount of labor from low-paid workers. In the U.S. the typical farm operator-manager runs a business with many thousands of dollars invested with little or no hired labor. Custom, social pressures, and lack of alternative employment opportunities tend to cause the inefficient use of labor in many nations. Freedom for prices and wages to change, and freedom for capital to earn a favorable return, would increase nonfarm employment opportunities and alleviate the wasteful labor surplus which is a burden on agriculture.

Once they are given the opportunity and incentive, the farm operators in any nation will quickly develop management skills. One of the lessons we have learned from experience with the Peace Corps and other technical assistance programs is that uneducated, unproductive farmers respond to the profit incentive. High taxes, price controls, size-of-farm limitations, and a controlled market discourage capable, energetic, ambitious people in the developing countries from making agriculture their life work. They are more apt to enter the government bureaucracy "where the action is." There is a great need in these developing nations for improved general education and training in business skills as well as in technical agriculture for potential farm managers and operators.

Many casual observers believe that hunger and starvation can be ended by supplying modern machinery, seed, fertilizer, chemicals, and irrigation equipment to the poor farmers of Africa, Asia, or South America. Of course, these inputs are essential for maximum crop yields, but they will not be used extensively until the economic and political climate is changed so that there is the opportunity for their profitable use. The poor farmer in India cannot afford a tractor as long as the threat of a cut in the maximum farm acreage permitted by the government hangs over his head. Restrictive land tenure laws and customs have the same production dampening effect. While there have been temporary shortages of farm supply inputs, most are readily available. There is something very wrong with a political system that penalizes production while millions of citizens do not have enough to eat, but that is exactly the situation in most of the developing nations. The essential ingredient necessary for abundant food production that is lacking in the socialist countries is the profit incentive.

More widespread application of present scientific and technological knowledge, especially in the developing countries, would result in tremendous increases in food production. But there is more to come as research and discovery continue to open doors to further gains in crop yields. It is entirely possible that corn yields of 300 to 500 bushels per acre will be as commonplace in the future as the 150 bushels of today or the 75 bushels of 20 years ago.

At the World Food Conference, Secretary of State Henry Kissinger said, "The profound promise of our era is that, for the first time, we may have the technical capacity to free mankind from hunger." Mr. Sterling Wortman, vice president of the Rockefeller Foundation, echoed this note of hope: "We've reached the point where, for the first time, we can manage the world food problems—if only we will." And that seems to be the rub—"if only we will."

The tenor of the World Food Conference was not encouraging; most of the representatives from the developing nations made speeches placing the blame for their troubles on the U.S. or other so-called affluent countries. They also proposed a variety of panaceas from world food reserves to cash grants. Unfortunately, some of the delegates from the United States had not done their homework and apparently accepted the propaganda at face value. Senator Hubert Humphrey suggested that every American eat one less hamburger per week so that there would be more food available for hungry people. The good senator evidently agreed with the statement by Harvard nutritionist Dr. Jean Mayer, "If Americans would decrease the meat they eat by 10%, it would release enough grain to feed 60 million people." Neither statement is valid. Cattle and hogs do not compete in any substantial way with people for grain, as very little of the principal livestock feed grains (corn and grain sorghum) are used for human food and, conversely, very little food grain is fed to animals.[13] It is, of course, true that a large proportion of the grains fed to livestock could be processed into some form of food, but the cost would be prohibitive. If the American people were to reduce meat consumption substantially, or if hog feeding were banned, the demand for feed grains would collapse and hundreds of thousands of acres of both grain and forage crops would be without a market. This would make grain even less plentiful, and the cushion of feed grains that could be used for human food, if absolutely necessary, would be reduced. Beef cattle and sheep convert grass and other roughage that grows on nontillable land into valuable human food. Approximately 64% of the earth's surface is not suitable for the production of crops, but much of this land can produce grass or hay for cattle or sheep. Contrary to the Mayer-Humphrey advice, increased meat consumption would make better markets for livestock, and the utilization of these otherwise waste lands for food production would be increased.

Another panacea that was given the super sales treatment at the Rome Conference was the proposed world food reserve. The United States has had more experience with food reserves than any other nation, and that experience was mostly bad. At one time the Commodity Credit Corporation (CCC), which is the U.S. government surplus commodity storage agency, held food "reserves" valued at several billion dollars. These reserves were not intentional, as they were acquired in the government farm program price support activities. Being government-owned, these stocks were more highly visible than privately owned stocks and had a greater price-depressing effect on the market. Furthermore, the release of publicly owned stocks is controlled by politicians who respond very quickly to consumer pressures for low food prices. Forty years' experience with reserve grain stocks in the U.S. has demonstrated that they tend to distort production by interfering with market price signals to farmers. During the relatively brief periods when surplus production is being transferred from commercial channels to government storage bins, there is a modest price-supporting effect; but most of the time the accumulated supplies dominate the market and depress prices. Following a short crop, reserves are normally fed onto the market to "stabilize" prices. The result is lower farm prices than would otherwise be expected. This is not the way to correct a shortage.

Low prices not only discourage increased production; they stimulate liberal use and do not sufficiently penalize waste. Food reserves, especially if they were located in the developing countries, would hang over the local market like a wet blanket and reduce food production in much the same way as did P.L. 480 shipments. Some food reserve proponents insist that safeguards against producer price penalties can be designed and that small reserves would not adversely affect prices. The suggestion that reserves can be held at low levels or that producer safeguards will be effective ignores political reality—the voter appeal of cheap food. The World Food Conference document states, "Such an agreement would be able to influence world prices through holding and regulation of stocks designed to maintain world prices in a given range."[14] It seems clear that one of the principal purposes of the food reserve is to manage prices; and managed prices are a principal cause of low farm productivity and of hunger.

There is another negative aspect of food reserves that largely nullifies any supposed benefits for hungry people. When the government maintains a reserve of grain, all privately held stocks tend to disappear. D. Gale Johnson concludes, "Whenever governments have a strong influence over the prices of farm products, the private holding of stocks is minimized because of the reduction of potential gain and the increased uncertainty about future prices when they rest on political decisions."[15] Grain storage is costly, and farmers, handlers, exporters, processors, and speculators all gladly shift the burden to the government, especially when politicians elected by consumers control the release of the reserves. For the first time in 30 years there is very little grain in U.S. government storage, but present estimates of the carryover into 1977 indicate that the reserves held on farms and in the channels of trade will be equal to if not greater than the reserves in many of the CCC years.

World food production varies very little from year to year; therefore, reserves are not needed because of worldwide short supplies. For two decades before the short-crop year of 1972 world food production expanded each year at an average annual rate of approximately 3%. Unfavorable weather caused modest declines in total world food output of 1.6% in 1972 and very slightly more in 1974.[16] There were somewhat greater declines in the production of specific crops and of certain nations; however, 1974 world grain production was only 4% below the 1960-73 trend.[17] These relatively minor dips in grain production relative to trend production were not large enough to explain the sizable increase in prices, especially in view of the large 1973 and 1975 crops. Most of the price increases occurred in the relatively small segment of the world's market for grain that moves in international trade. Prices were regulated in Russia, the EEC, and most of the developing nations, so that most of the price response came in the world market. D. Gale Johnson concludes, "The International Market could have absorbed the production shortfalls with a rather modest increase in prices if producers and consumers in all nations had been given the proper price signals."[18] The logical response to the desire for greater price stability would be to permit market prices to perform their function of signaling for changes in production and, at the same time, to reduce all types of trade restrictions. Politically managed reserves discourage both production and trade because of the impossibility of predicting how they will be used.

Publicly held reserves are needed only because government policies either discourage domestic production and storage or because they prevent ready access to available supplies in other areas. The best food reserves are those which are stored in the soil, in productive livestock, and in the normal channels of trade. A government held reserve is a seemingly innocuous form of market intervention, but it will, in the long run, reduce the incentive to produce food for hungry people.

There are only two systems for ordering production, marketing, and distribution—state control and direction, and the free competitive market. Most nations use a combination of state direction and market pricing to guide food production and marketing. In the United States, competitive market prices generally prevail, but most of the developing nations control prices and direct the marketing of farm crops. The purpose of farming is to produce food for hungry people, and the objective of the marketing system is to deliver that food to consumers at the lowest possible cost. It should not be too difficult to measure and compare the results of the different systems.

The Foreign Agricultural Service of the USDA recently made a survey to determine to what extent food-short nations are "aggravating their problems by government policies and programs that act as disincentives to agricultural production." Of the 50 countries studied, 46 were found to have interventionist policies that directly or indirectly discourage domestic farm production. The government policies which interfered with farm production included direct controls of the prices of farm crops and of retail foods, export controls, export taxes, subsidized imports, exchange rate controls, restrictions on credit, limitations on land tenure and farm size, noncompetitive buying by government agencies, and restrictions on the domestic movement of farm products from one area to another.[19] Of these disincentives, only farm price controls and regulation of farm size, land tenure, and credit are applied directly to the farm business. All of the others are interventions in the marketing or distribution of food, but they have the effect of reducing the price and profit incentives that are necessary to stimulate needed production.

Market intervention by government is usually justified by politicians as being necessary to hold food prices at low levels so that poor people can live better. However, it should be obvious that any interference with the market for food which causes lower prices for farm products almost automatically reduces output and makes it more difficult for poor people to get sufficient food. If long continued, price controls or other market interventions result in shortages and black markets. Eventually, costly subsidies must be paid to cover farm operating costs or food production is nationalized and becomes a function of an all-powerful state, as in the USSR. In a democracy, "cheap food" policies are usually schemes to gain political support for the next election. Politicians are well aware that 96% of the voters in the United States are consumers while only 4% are farmers. It is axiomatic that most political candidates will aim to please the most voters (96%), and campaign promises to control food prices have a popular appeal for those who do not bother to look at facts.

There are other reasons for the political popularity of market interventions. Any government market action benefits some people and penalizes others. Political candidates consider both groups as good prospects for campaign contributions. Those who benefit will pay to keep the favored status, while those who may suffer can be tapped for "protection." The recent huge campaign contributions to both political party candidates by an American milk producers' association were undoubtedly intended to "buy" favorable government pricing decisions for dairy farmers. Government market interventions also have a built-in tendency to become self-perpetuating because the administrators of the programs are usually political patronage appointees, and as in any bureaucracy, they work assiduously for the continuation of their jobs. Most politicians like the feel of power and influence that goes with having jobs to dispense. Jobs in the government market management bureaucracy also provide suitable rewards for campaign workers. Then, too, as a staff worker in one of the federal price and wage control agencies remarked to the author, "It's real fun to manipulate prices."

Years of experience in many nations with government intervention in the marketing and distribution of food demonstrates beyond question that this is not the way to reduce hunger and starvation. However, the failure of one authoritarian scheme to replace the free market usually brings the demand to try yet another panacea. American agriculture was subjected for nearly 40 years to a series of complex price and production control devices, all of which failed. After each failure, the blame was placed on faulty administration and a new set of politicians took over the operation with similar unsatisfactory results. Production, marketing, and distribution are economic functions that respond quickly to market forces but reluctantly to political decisions.

Perhaps the most important cause of the failure of government intervention to get the desired result is the fact that political decisions invariably differ substantially from market decisions. Market decisions are made in response to human need as reflected in effective demand and signaled by price changes. It must be recognized that low-income people may not have the money to buy food on the competitive market and thus their needs would not contribute to "effective demand." This is not an indictment of the market system. Rather, it indicates the need for income transfer or welfare payments to low-income people so that they can participate in the market to satisfy their needs. The market system is not designed to correct income inequities.

Dr. Victor Ferkiss, in another chapter of this book, makes the point that existing and past distributions of economic wealth and power place many of the world's people at such a severe disadvantage that they are not free to participate in the market. This is a fairly accurate summation of the carryover effects of government and other interventions. However, two wrongs do not make a right—further authoritarian action can only aggravate the problem. Corrective action should be taken to remove all government interventions that discourage production while at the same time providing income transfer payments to those whose earnings are inadequate to meet their essential needs so that they can be "free" to participate in the market. The free competitive market will not redress or eliminate past inequities, but it will supply the needed food and other human needs more quickly and efficiently than any other system yet conceived because it rewards those who produce. The free market stimulates the release of creative human energy, which is responsible for all production.

In contrast to market decisions which respond to human needs when translated into effective demand, political decisions are weighed and determined on the judgment as to which course will attract the most votes in the next election. The same voters who go into the meat market and vote with their dollars for pork chops at $1.50 per pound might very well cast their ballots in a referendum for a price ceiling of 50 cents per pound. However, they would complain bitterly when pork chops disappeared completely from the market, as they would with the price below the cost of production. Political decisions must be popular or the politician who makes them will not survive. Therefore, except under an authoritarian dictatorship, human needs can only be satisfactorily filled by a relatively free competitive market.

Food aid and the free market 157

Political decisions differ from market decisions in many ways. Not only are they made in that never-never land of what "ought to be" rather than in the real world, but they are more apt to be in error since only a few people are involved in their making. Market decisions, by contrast, reflect the needs of many thousands of people, and the judgment of the many is superior to that of the few. Consumers are the rulers of the free market, as they make the decisions. In government-managed marketing, producers, processors, or handlers with political or financial power find that it is relatively easy to influence bureaucratic decisions. Bureaucratic decisions are also notoriously slow, as procrastination is a common defensive device used by most politicians. Government intervention and management of marketing and distribution are terribly costly. Price and supply allocation decisions that are made rapidly, automatically, and with little or no cost by the competitive market must be threshed out with innumerable conferences and high level political clearances when undertaken by a government agency.

There is a role for planners in a modern economy, but their usefulness depends upon the type of planning to be undertaken. Architects, budget officers, tour directors, and many other planners for private business concerns must accept considerable responsibility for their actions. Government social planners, on the other hand, are in the more pleasant situation of planning for people in some remote area or in some later time frame, and they are seldom held responsible for the results. The rallying cry of the government planner is "social justice" or "distributive justice." Here again, as in the case of political decision making, the directions of the planners are more likely to be faulty than marketplace decisions, because they are not held responsible for their failures and the judgment exercised is by a few bureaucrats rather than the multitude in the market. Placing the planning function in government invariably results in a large bureaucratic operation that slows rather than facilitates change.

Another reason for the failure of government interventions to achieve their goal of cheap food is that subsidies of one kind or another must be provided as a substitute for price incentives if production is to be maintained. The subsidies must be paid for by taxpayers, and when the cost of the bureaucracy is added, it always totals more than would the free market price. India is an example of the failure of attempts to redistribute income by manipulation of markets. India was well on her way toward agricultural self-sufficiency in 1972, thanks to the green revolution and incentive prices, when Mrs. Gandhi and her socialists won a big electoral victory. Since then, taxation of farmers has increased, farm crop prices have been fixed at low levels, and all grain produced must be sold to the government. The maximum farm size was cut from 30 irrigated acres to 13, and while this law is not strictly enforced, the peasants, who have good reason to mistrust the government, operate under the constant threat of further intervention.[20] The resulting sharp drop in production has forced the government to buy millions of tons of food from an already short world market at prices considerably higher than domestic farmers receive. The net effect of continuing heavy United States AID shipments is to prop up and perpetuate this and other sagging socialist economies throughout the world. Russia, once a grain exporter, is another example of a planned economy where food deficiencies caused by government interventions are concealed by large imports of grain at higher prices than domestic farmers receive. World food shortages are thus aggravated by the competition for available supplies by the managed economies which cannot produce enough for their own needs. The use of subsidies in lieu of price not only reduces food production where needed most and disrupts world markets but distorts production patterns. American farm subsidies stimulated the production of unneeded short-staple cotton and types of wheat suitable only for storage and for livestock feed while, at the same time, people were hungry in other parts of the world.

Perhaps the most misleading argument of the planners and advocates of a politically managed economy is that the free market is unstable and thus contributes to the food problems of the developing nations. The proposed world food reserve is thus offered as a stabilizing device. In practice, the free market is the best stabilizing mechanism as it speedily and automatically transmits information as to changes in effective demand and supplies to those who can take corrective action. At the same time it activates the incentives that will guarantee that distortions in supply and price are eliminated. Government policies that interfere with market price movements are the principal destabilizing factor in world markets. So long as food prices are controlled in much of the world, the full impact of changes in supply and demand will be reflected in the international markets. Since the international market includes only 10% of the world's grain, it is little wonder that the price of wheat and rice has acted like a Yo-Yo during recent short-crop years. If prices in all nations had been free to respond to the variations in production, the price changes in the world market would have been much more moderate.[21]

A few advocates of "a little" intervention argue that wide swings in market price should be prevented by setting minimum and maximum prices. Any degree of price restriction slows the corrective action that is needed and will delay the response of producers. An old but true axiom is that the best remedy for high prices is high prices. Any action, no matter how limited, in any nation that reduces the incentive to produce for its own needs will have a destabilizing effect on world prices. No one but traders and speculators on the world market can gain from government "stabilization" operations. Consumers may seem to have cheaper food in the areas where subsidies or price controls are used to "stabilize" prices, but they actually may be paying more when the hidden costs and higher taxes are included. Secretary of State Henry Kissinger put it very well when he said, "Either societies create the conditions for savings and investment, for innovation and ingenuity, for enterprise and industry which ultimately lead to self-sustaining economic growth, or they do not. There is no magical short cut and no rhetorical substitute."[22]

The most common intervention in the marketing and distribution of food is direct price control, either of farm products or of food at the retail level. The result is the same—serious disincentives for farmers and less food for hungry people. Another very serious disincentive results when the government becomes the sole market, either by decree or by fixing handling margins so low that all other markets disappear. A government monopoly is no more virtuous than any other monopoly, and production is usually stifled when there is no competition on the buying side of the market.

Many developing countries discourage food production by interfering with export sales of farm products. Exports are sometimes taxed to provide revenue for the government. However, interference with export sales is ordinarily for the purpose of keeping food cheap for poor people. A recent example was the U.S. embargo on grain sales to Russia in 1975 at the behest of a powerful labor union. In that instance, the objective was cheap food and a requirement that more export grain be carried in U.S. flag ships which employ the union's members. Embargoes, export quotas, and export taxes penalize foreign sales and channel surplus production to the domestic market, thus lowering farm prices and discouraging efforts to expand output. Often the developing nations follow a low-farm-price-cheap-food policy because they are trying to attract industrial concerns by offering low-priced labor. They reason that labor wages can only be kept low if food is cheap. There is no evidence that any nation has built a viable economy on the basis of cheap food and low-paid labor. Regardless of whether the intervention in export sales is practiced by the developing countries or by the United States, it should be condemned and identified as a serious hindrance to alleviating hunger in the world.

Export taxes, quotas, and embargoes keep domestic farm prices low and discourage the production of needed food in many developing countries. Import taxes or tariffs would seem to have the opposite effect, but since they are often applied to feed, fertilizer, and farm machinery imports to protect domestic industries, the result is increased costs of farm inputs and less incentive to produce. They also protect inefficient farmers from competition.

International trade is essential to agricultural prosperity in both the surplus-producing and the food deficit areas. Very few nations are entirely self-sufficient as far as food is concerned, and most produce an exportable surplus of some commodities. The industrial nations have made considerable progress in reducing trade barriers between themselves, but they have not been as willing to remove restrictions on imports of agricultural products and manufactured goods from the developing countries. One excuse often given for this discrimination is that goods produced by workers who receive poverty-level wages should not be allowed to compete with products made by well-paid labor. This is an unfair attitude as "poverty level" wages cannot be remedied until more foreign exchange can be earned by the developing nations through greater export sales.

Sufficient food can be produced in the world to end hunger and starvation, but poor people must be given the opportunity to earn an adequate income to purchase their food needs. International trade barriers thwart this objective and should be removed as rapidly as possible. The agenda for the relief of hunger must include the promotion and encouragement of trade between nations. Freedom to trade ranks in importance with freedom to produce.

There is a world market for almost all farm products when it is free from trade barriers and subsidies. The open competitive market is an efficient and rapid means of stimulating production when needed as well as causing consumers to eliminate waste and voluntarily reduce their demands when goods are scarce. The major function of a free market is to serve the interests of consumers by supplying their needs. The free market is less kind to producers as it forces them to undergo the rigors of competition—to produce what consumers want and at a price as low as any competitor will accept.

The successful operation of the competitive market requires a relatively free flow of goods, money, and production information. The communist bloc countries have been slow to exchange information on crop conditions, and the other socialist states have generally followed trade restrictive policies. The United States, although not always consistent, has been the world leader in removing restrictions on the international movement of goods, money, and information. Here, too, the free competitive market operates with fewer controls and other impediments than in most other lands. It is not by accident that the people of the United States are the world's best fed; and, at the same time, they far exceed any other nation in their food aid gifts and in the volume of food export sales. The developing nations might do well to ask themselves why the United States produces food so abundantly.

The free competitive market price system works far better than government-managed systems in getting more food produced and distributed to hungry people because it provides incentives for increased productivity, functions rapidly at a low cost, and responds more readily to human needs than to political pressures. However, there are several other important requirements that must be met if the world's hungry people are to be fed. Perhaps the most important is an increase in public and privately financed agricultural research so that new avenues for increased productivity and for more efficient marketing and utilization may be explored. Extension education programs to help farmers learn how to use these research findings should be expanded. More young people in the developing nations should be encouraged to seek education and training in business skills and technical agriculture as a basis for assuming farm management responsibilities. Crop-reporting and production-estimating services should be improved and the exchange of information between nations facilitated. Agricultural credit should be more readily available to farmers in the less developed countries, but it must be allocated on a sound business basis rather than as a political reward. Finally, despite all reforms and incentives there will be handicapped and poor people who cannot enter the marketplace with money to fulfill their needs. It is much better to make welfare or income transfer payments to these unfortunate people so that they can purchase food in the market where their demands will influence production than to isolate them through some type of direct food aid program.

All of these changes will help improve the operation of the market system, but they are costly. Perhaps the United States and other industrial nations would get better results from the funds presently allocated for foreign aid by spending more on programs of this kind and limiting food aid to serious emergencies. Perhaps it is time that the free world stop apologizing for the successes of capitalism and the competitive market system and begin to promote their use as the only adequate answer to hunger.

Solving the problem of hungry people involves a complex mixture of political, economic, and moral considerations. The moral imperative is to relieve hunger throughout the world by helping poor people find the means of satisfying their food needs. Population control, stimulation of greater domestic food production, and industrial development to increase earnings are superior to long-continued food aid programs as the answer to hunger because they approach the problem on the basis of improving the ability and the motivation of people to help themselves. It is well established that the free market will induce greater production and more efficient distribution than any government-managed system, but it may properly be asked if justice will be served. The founding fathers of our nation enunciated the basic assumption that "all men are endowed by their Creator with certain inalienable rights. That among these are life, liberty and the pursuit of happiness." Apparently they believed that individual rights and the freedom of choice were essential to justice. The free market is based on freedom of choice, while a state-controlled system depends upon coercion.

Many economists would insist that the free market is not concerned with value judgments—with justice. However, Ludwig von Mises, in his book *Human Action,* states that economics is not merely the study of physical wealth but is the study of human choice and preferences.[23] The free market permits each individual consumer to negotiate and contract for his needs, and at the same time producers too are free to accept or reject the terms offered. A government-directed system must limit or deny the right of choice and the right to contract because a bureaucracy cannot cope with a multitude of ever-changing decisions.

With state-controlled production, marketing, and pricing, another essential individual freedom is jeopardized—the right to own property. Government control of the output of land or other property is, in effect, a limitation on its value. Of all human rights, the two which generate the greatest incentives to produce are the right to own property and the right to contract for the purchase or sale of goods and services. Both of these important human rights are essential to the free market system, and both are abridged by authoritarian direction of production and marketing. The free market system is a better defender of human rights and values than is the government allocation system.

Moral values vary in different cultures, but almost universally freedom of choice and voluntary collaboration are considered to be "good" while coercion is "bad." The Judeo-Christian religious heritage is based on individual freedom and responsibility. When the state directs the pricing, marketing, and distribution of food, individual responsibility erodes very rapidly. It would seem that in solving the hunger problem the higher moral responsibility would be to provide sufficient food by correcting the causes of inadequate production while at the same time helping mankind to take a small step away from bondage to a dictatorial state or to abject poverty. The free market is the best hope for attaining this objective.

If it were agreed today that the free competitive market system should be substituted for the state-directed system now used by most of the developing nations, there would need be drastic action taken by the governments involved.

1. A complex assortment of disincentives for maximum food production must be eliminated in all nations.
2. Government intervention in the distribution of food must be ended. Every effort should be made to move toward free trade between all nations.
3. Capital formation should be encouraged and restrictions on its flow between nations should be removed, so that more jobs will be created for low-income people.
4. Welfare and emergency hunger relief programs should provide financial assistance rather than direct food aid so that the needy can buy food in the market.

There is a strong basis for hope that hunger and famine can be banished from the earth. Most of the deaths from starvation in the last 50 years have been due to war, unwise government policies, or poor communication, and not to crop failures. Total world food production varies little from year to year and has been increasing slightly faster than the population. The free competitive market is the only device that will provide the discipline and the incentives necessary to cause undernourished people to solve their own problems. The potential for abundant food is here—the question is not "Can we?" but "Will we?"

NOTES

1. Don Paarlberg, USDA, statement quoted in *Successful Farming*, January 1975, and in *Illinois Farm Bureau Family*, July 1975.
2. F.A.O., "Provisional Indicative World Plan for Agricultural Development," vol. 1, 1969.
3. "World Food Production, Demand and Trade," Iowa State University study reported in *Farm Journal*, June 1975.
4. Sterling Wortman, Vice President of the Rockefeller Foundation, address to American Society of Agronomy reported in *Farm Journal*, February 1975.
5. John Hannah, "Opinion," *Farm Journal*, January 1975.

6. ERS, USDA, "The World Food Situation and Prospects to 1985," Foreign Agricultural Economic Report No. 98.

7. "The World Food Problems: Proposals for National and International Action," World Food Conference, E/CONF 65/4 1974. Cf. Schertz chapter.

8. D. Gale Johnson, "World Food Problems and Prospects," American Enterprise Institute for Public Policy Research, Foreign Affairs Study No. 20, June 1975.

9. Lyle P. Schertz, "World Food: Prices and the Poor," *Foreign Affairs,* April 1974.

10. *Ibid.*

11. *New York Times,* January 12, 1975.

12. *World Book encyclopedia,* Vol I, 1972, Agriculture—U.S.

13. Don Paarlberg, "The World Food Situation in Perspective," *American Journal of Agricultural Economics,* May 1974. Also see ERS, USDA, *op. cit.* Cf. Witt chapter, p. 88.

14. Ray Vicker, "The Search for More Food," *Wall Street Journal,* November 4, 1974. Editorial comments and quotations.

15. D. Gale Johnson, *op. cit.*

16. ERS, USDA, *op. cit.*

17. ERS, USDA, "World Agricultural Situation," WAS 6, December 1974.

18. D. Gale Johnson, *op. cit.*

19. Abdullah A. Saleh, "Disincentives to Agricultural Production in Developing Countries," *Foreign Agriculture,* FAS, USDA, Supplement March 1975.

20. "India Muddles Through," *Forbes,* February 15, 1975.

21. D. Gale Johnson, *op. cit.*

22. Henry Kissinger, address in Milwaukee, *Wall Street Journal,* July 17, 1975.

23. Ludwig von Mises, *Human Action,* 3rd ed. (Regnery, 1966).

10 Intervening in the market
Victor Ferkiss

Should society—national and international—intervene in the market in order to assure that all human beings are adequately fed? This question, like most questions beginning with the word "should," has two aspects—empirical and normative—which are inextricably intertwined. If a certain course of action is advocated in any context one must simultaneously ask: (1) Are the means advocated likely to produce the desired end? (2) Is the desired end ethically justifiable, and are the means considered necessary to secure it themselves ethically justifiable? These questions of "fact" and "value" are analytically separate but operationally interdependent in discussions of public policy. The answers to both questions involve uncertainties and dispute, but uncertainties of different character. The validity of any answer to either question does not directly depend on the validity of an answer to the other. One can separate the questions of whether or not John should be killed and whether or not a particular blow to him will be lethal. On the other hand, we know that all actions have secondary consequences and means condition ends. For instance, capital punishment can be defended as a necessary deterrent to arbitrary personal violence but attacked as leading to a diminution of respect for human life which in turn encourages the crimes of violence against which it is directed.

While it can be argued that acceptable answers to our dual questions about the desirability of intervening in the market are equally difficult to come by, the ethical aspects are capable of discussion in a form which, however problematic, can be considered valid and/or useful over extended periods of time, while any proffered answers to the empirical questions are inherently more contingent than remarks addressed to ethical aspects. Therefore the ethical aspects of the question will be discussed first and at greater length; the practical conclusions drawn from ethical considerations will be discussed later and in more summary fashion.

It is obviously impossible to discuss adequately any particular question of social ethics outside of the context of an overall theory of society and ethical values. It is equally obvious that no such theory can be comprehensively explicated, much less established, in the course of a short essay. What can be done at best is to indicate the differing assumptions about the nature of social and moral values upon which differing ethical propositions rest, leaving to the reader the decision as to which ethical system he or she wishes to adopt.

Contemporary Western (especially American) society simultaneously, or alternately, operates according to two different and often clashing theories of the nature of society and attendant moral obligations.[1] The fist can be described variously as the utilitarian, liberal, social contract theory of society. The second can be described as the "organic," traditional, or conservative theory. Though to this writer's knowledge no adequate social survey data exist to delineate which groups in society are most attached to either of these two theories, impressionistic evidence indicates that the former is especially beloved of philosophers and secularized intellectuals, the latter of ordinary citizens and the religiously inclined. (This division corresponds roughly to the upper-class-liberal–lower-class-conservative dichotomy which polls delineate with reference to "social" as opposed to "economic" issues.)[2] What will soon become apparent should perhaps be noted at the outset; the author of this paper finds the latter a more congenial philosophical position.[3]

The liberal theory—as it shall be called here for convenience's sake—usually combines the following premises. Men (and women also, though this is both historically and perhaps intrinsically a "masculine" theory) are free by nature. Freedom consists of the absence of coercion on the part of other human beings.[4] Freedom is the primary human value and good. The only binding obligations are those freely and consciously entered into. Society is the result of a social contract, entered into in order to protect freedom, that is, the ability to pursue autonomously generated desires without any social compulsion. Freedom exists prior to and, in some sense, outside of society and includes life, liberty, and "estate."[5] Such a definition of presocial rights must of course assume that the existing distribution of property rights is intrinsically just, either as a result of the justice of presocial distributions based on hypothetical presocial consent and ratified by the social contract (the purpose of the Lockean labor theory of value is to bolster this position) or, alternatively, that existing distributions at any point in time subsequent to the original social contract result from the operation of mechanisms of property allocation which are freely accepted by all concerned. Various forms of social contract theory also postulate the equality, freedom of action, and/or rationality of the participants in the process of property distribution and its acceptance. Sometimes, ironically, rationality includes ignorance, as in theories which require parties to the formulation of social rules to be unaware of how they personally will be affected by them.[6]

For the purpose of this paper, the major ethical conclusion to be drawn from the liberal theory is that no person has any moral obligation to another save one entered into with his/her consent. Since governments exist in order to preserve basic rights, including property rights, they cannot legitimately act as if noncontractual obligations existed. Individuals are capable of freely deciding to feed the hungry by accepting higher food costs or through other means, but no government can impose such obligations upon them.

The major alternative theory of society is what is called here the organic theory of society, the major proponents of which have been thinkers such as Plato, Aristotle, Burke, and—inconsistently—Calhoun.[7] Among its premises are the following. Human beings do not preexist society, but are socially created. There is an objective order in the physical and social universe capable of being grasped by human reason. This existent order, these theorists assert (denying the modern fact-value dichotomy), imposes moral obligations upon individuals to maintain it. Freedom consists in doing—and being able to do—what is "objectively right." Desires, which are subjective, have a lower priority than needs, which are objective.[8] Human beings are unequal and often irrational. Justice, which involves conformity with patterns laid down by nature, is difficult to ascertain and varies with time and place. Consensus based on rational consent is a desirable underpinning of governmental actions but not a necessary one. Property as such may be a basic human right in the abstract, but all particular distributions of property are socially created and may be socially altered in conformance with social and individual human needs. Nothing "belongs" to anyone except as society says it does; "mine" and "thine" are socially determined.

The major ethical conclusion relevant to our present concerns which can be drawn from this theory is that there is no ethical barrier to the government taking food from some and giving it to others or forcing some to endure sacrifices or disutilities for the benefit of others if society as a whole decides a redistribution of social assets is in conformity with objective social needs.

Needless to say, both of these theories have their adherents among decent and reasonable human beings. If the first asks us to make unrealistic assumptions about human rationality and the nature of history, the latter puts us in the difficult position of trying to achieve consensus about the objective world among humans with different perceptions, and assumes that whatever groups exercise power in society can usually, or often, or at least sometimes be trusted to act on behalf of common rather than selfish ends.

Also, as noted earlier, both these theories have been and are widely held in American society, often simultaneously (if inconsistently) by the same people. Any political decision to act in accordance with the conclusions of either theory—whether partially or completely—will be regarded by large sections of the population as in some sense unjust. Americans have always vacillated between or combined selfish and altruistic motives, and we cannot expect the problem of world food shortages to be dealt with any differently than other domestic or foreign policy questions. At the same time it must be remembered that any decisions made in dealing with world food problems will not only affect these problems directly and/or affect other aspects of our economic and political life but will affect the general ethical tone and moral consensus of our society as a whole.

It can readily be seen that these two conflicting approaches to the nature of society and social ethics are correlated with, and indeed derive from, two differing concepts of freedom. For the liberal philosopher freedom consists in the ability of individuals to choose among alternative means of fulfilling desires which—in some manner not explained—originate within individuals, and any attempt by social actors external to the individual to determine which desires should be fulfilled and in what manner constitutes a dimunition of freedom. For a classic liberal the term "libertarian" is increasingly coming into use to describe this position.[9] Abolition of the private right to own firearms is a dimunition of freedom of choice, as are tax systems which force the individual to surrender money for use by the government to promote education, public housing, or any other governmental activity except the basic protection of citizens against domestic or externally generated acts of coercive violence.

For the organic philosophy freedom consists in the ability to actualize potentialities given in nature. Desires are subjective spurs to the fulfillment of potentiality, but they are conditioned if not created by society and may—indeed must—be channeled by society to their natural ends. The individual can maximize his or her freedom by choosing to create or conform to a collective ordering of social activity designed to make possible the creation of chosen future states for the individual or society as a whole, even if such choice necessitates the surrendering of individual ability to choose among particular alternatives at any point in time. For the adherents of organic philosphies of the state, communal action—implicitly based on coercion—is justifiable in order to provide a climate of minimal potential violence (hence "gun control" is a desirable alternative to simply punishing the illegal use of guns) or in order to achieve the goals of a more educated and/or egalitarian society. If certain social measures are not taken, the desires of some (a possible numerical or political majority) to live in societies having certain characteristics cannot be implemented. My freedom is maximized to the extent that I am able to fulfill my needs, including the need to act "justly" according to whatever self-image I possess. Political action (coercive social action) which induces me to cooperate in a process of getting food to those who need and desire it—through nonmarket mechanisms if necessary—is not a dimunition, but a support of my basic "free" choice to act justly.[10]

This discussion has of course focused upon the citizen-taxpayer as such. The producer of food is in a somewhat different position. Public action to produce food and ultimately give it away can lead to the farmer's receiving lower prices than he might receive in a theoretically free market. The same effect can result from government intervention in international marketing operations, for instance, embargoes on sales to unfriendly nations (e.g., Cuba), embargoes designed to coerce nations which pursue internal policies we deplore (e.g., Rhodesia), embargoes designed to maintain lower domestic price levels (e.g., recent temporary suspension of soybean exports), and government participation in long-term trade agreements with other nations (e.g., the Soviet Union). But purely free markets—especially international markets—are a rare historical occurence. Food producers confront government activity affecting their industry as another external condition to which they must adjust, as in the case of price supports. As long as entry into the industry is voluntary and no direct command functions are exercised by the government, farmers can still be considered to be as basically free as any other producers who operate in a market conditioned by government activity. Teachers, physicians, lawyers, and automobile manufacturers operate in the same kind of quasi-controlled markets, which are endemic to industrial capitalism in the age of the welfare state.

Thus it is impossible to decide whether a system which allocates scarce utilities such as food (either on a national or international basis) by means of the market is more or less conducive to freedom of choice than one which involves intervention in the market without first presuming acceptance of either the liberal or organic theories of society and their conflicting concepts of freedom. At least this cannot be done on a general, abstract basis. But throughout modern history the struggle has not been between these philosophies in their pure form. Whereas there has always been an important strain of doctrinaire liberalism (one might even call it utopianism) in the Western world, especially in the United States, which aims at the almost total maximization of freedom of choice (in its usage), virtually no one—even in most socialist societies—advocates the minimization of freedom (even in the liberal usage) for its own sake. The argument is normally between those who absolutize the liberal notion of freedom of choice—including its alleged incarnation in the market system—and those who argue that while such freedom is intrinsically desirable, it is not an absolute and must be modified in order to permit the achievement of various substantive social ends selected through a process of collective choice.

Implicit, however, in the organicist critique of liberalism is an attack on the claims of liberalism's proponents that their power to choose is a given which must be accorded the status of a natural right, since the organicist assumes and postulates that the individual and his attitudes are a social product rather than "his" in an absolute sense.[11] Insofar as the individual and his attitudes or attributes or possessions are social creations, his right to dispose of them or to control his own actions cannot be absolute. The implications of this difference of view are most easily illustrated by the problem of property rights, the cornerstone of the market system. If you or I do not "own" anything with clear title, the question of whether market exchange is the only legitimate way in which rights can be transferred becomes moot. If one accepts the Lockean premise that property rights existed in a state of nature, the claim to ownership is automatically validated. If one denies this premise and asserts the contrary, that property rights (more specifically the rights of particular individuals to control particular properties) are created by society, ownership systems and individual titles to property can be modified by society.

The question then arises as to how property rights—including rights to the elements involved in the production of food—have in fact originated.

Both liberals and organicists are agreed on the starting point that originally (whether in logic or historical time is irrelevant) the earth belonged to mankind collectively. In the Lockean tradition of liberalism property rights arise because through their labor certain individuals (or, by logical extension, groups or nations) give value to what is originally presented by nature, taking advantage of natural opportunities. In the natural state nothing has value. Land is valuable only because it is cultivated; otherise it is a "waste."[12]

But what enables some to be able to utilize the potentialities presented by nature? Nations and individuals are differentially endowed with the means of agricultural productivity by natural circumstances; that is, some are more talented and powerful than others, enabling them to take possession of desirable agricultural resources, to exclude others, and to better utilize such resources as they control. Peter Brown in his chapter makes the double assumption that the establishment of the property rights of some to the exclusion of others can be ethically justified if the others are better off (or as well off?) as they would be otherwise and that therefore (a big "therefore," since it assumes a certain standard of justice and rationality on the part of the excluded) they accept this exclusion.[13] This paper assumes the contrary, that in fact all existing and historic distributions of wealth and power are the result not of free rational agreement, but of various combinations of coercion and lack of knowledge, thereby voiding the assumption of free consent among equals which underlies the assumptions of free market theorists.

There are several qualifications which must be made to the above generalization. Many human beings have historically accepted unequal ownership of goods and differences between the rich and poor as being just because they reflect the will of God, like unequal health or mental endowment. In such cases, however, it can be argued that this involves not so much an acceptance of the rational justice of the distribution as a suspension of consideration of questions of substantive justice in favor of a divine arbitrariness which is assumed to be *ipso facto* just in any and all cases, even when the good suffer and the wicked prosper. In such thinking institution of substantive justice is usually postponed to an afterlife. In other societies individuals may regard the existing distribution of goods as unjust but give rational consent to it, explicit or implicit, on the grounds that the only alternative is social disturbance, chaos, or revolution which will lead to substantive evils outweighing those of the unjust distribution. In this case, as in the former, it can hardly be said that the liberal premises about free rational consent are fully met. Finally, there are many people in modern liberal societies who believe that inequality is intrinsically desirable and that the competitive process enables the best—among whom they usually but not always include themselves—to rise to the top. Whatever distributive pattern emerges from competition (which may involve other than market mechanisms, including the use of fraud and force) is considered just. But no claim is made by such people that those at the bottom are benefited by others being at the top (as in the Brown-Nozick position), save insofar as all have had the fun of playing the (zero-sum) competitive game.

The difficulty with the classic liberal position is intrinsic to its basic method of argument, which moves from the hypothetical state of nature (or beginning of things, a state out of time and space) directly to existing distributions which it seeks to justify. The abstract and eternal enters the particular and contingent by a historical act of immaculate conception. But particular property rights are not primeval in origin; rather they have arisen in the course of a long history of human development. We do not know who the prehistoric fathers (or mothers) of present tribes or nations or property owners were, but we can assume they were not gods. Property rights arose after human groups came into existence. ("When Adam delved and Eve span, who was then the gentleman?" as a medieval couplet inquires.) Thus, while it might be stated that apeman A, endowed by nature with more energy than apeman B, had a right to a larger pile of bananas collected by his energy (a proposition by no means self-evident), it is a different matter to argue that Harvard-trained MBAs have a right to own more property than black high school dropouts. Insofar as differentials in acquisitive ability are socially created or conditioned, differentials in ownership resulting from them are not justifiable by reference to presocial natural rights.

Not only may talents be the result of social forces, but the ability to use them on the land may be the result of force—either embodied in the laws of a particular society or extralegal. Does the first occupier of a given piece of land have the right to exclude others from its use? Do later arrivals in an area have the right to eject or dominate the original occupants by force? Biblical precedent exists, but many would hardly regard it as governing.

But suppose one makes the assumption that the greatest good of all justifies control by those best able to exploit the land. Americans historically justified the displacement of the Indians and, later, the Mexicans by the argument that they were not fully utilizing the continent's resources. If this argument is valid, the occupation of land by a group making less use of it than another potential occupier would be an injustice. How then could the United States consistently bar unlimited immigration of Mexicans (or Japanese or East Indians) to the United States today if it is accepted that they will use our land more intensively than we are now using it, now that the tables of utilization seem to be turning?

If one accepts the argument that occupation of land by those best able to maximize its production is self-justifying, it is impossible to deny that if others can use land better it should be given to them. Whether the labor-intensive techniques of one group might be more productive than the capital-intensive techniques of another is of course an empirical question which can be argued.

But the argument that more efficient groups should displace less efficient is, if anything, even more abstract and unrealistic than the argument that more efficient individuals have prior claims to land and raises a host of problems which liberal philosophy essentially ignores. Liberal philosophy, as one commentator on Rawls notes, takes individuals as its exclusive counters and says nothing of groups and their rights.[14] Whether the behavior and rights of individuals and groups can be discussed in a parallel fashion is a much mooted question. But certainly, whatever objection can be made that it is psychologically unrealistic to expect individuals to accept unequal division of property simply because division is conducive to maximizing production applies with additional force in the case of groups, where claims of loyalty, tradition, and altruistic devotion to others can be used to bolster what might otherwise be viewed as selfish claims. As noted by many commentators, men in groups often have even lower standards of morality and rationality than they do as individuals and can rarely be expected to accept perceived disadvantages whatever claims are made for their justification.[15] But whether one speaks in individual or group terms, it is not self-evident that first occupation of land gives ethical title to the fruits of such power or occupation, given the absence of free consent of the less advantaged. It is a fact that individuals and nations have retained advantages of access to agricultural resources through coercion—legal or otherwise. It is not self-evident that their ability to do so is justified ethically in the absence of the consent of the disadvantaged. The argument raised by liberal thinkers such as Nozick and accepted by commentators such as Brown is that if preemption of property by a few maximizes productivity and thus redounds to the benefit of all, therefore the nonproperty owners can be presumed to consent in a situation which is to their advantage.[16] This argument can be faulted on two counts, even leaving aside the implicit assumption that normally those who have managed to possess the land are in fact those best able to maximize its productivity. The first is psychological. In general human beings resent (envy) the greater wealth and power of others. Even if it can be presumed to be contributory to their welfare, they will not consent to it, however rational it might appear that they do so. The second reason for rejection is empirical. There is no evidence to indicate that inequalities in property ownership contribute to greater economic productivity.[17] Private ownership *per se* may do so, but this is another matter. Thus even if envy could be discounted, there would be no reason to assume that unequal distributions of property result from consent rather than coercion.

Thus insofar as possession of the means of agricultural production—land, capital equipment, access to skills, etc.—is not necessarily the outcome of the free consent of the community at large—domestic or international—the existing distribution of food resources is not the result of free choice. Use of political mechanisms responsible to the free political choice of citizens in order to allocate food resources may actually serve to maximize the extent to which patterns of food distribution are freely chosen.

ETHICAL TITLE TO FOOD CONSUMPTION

It is assumed as a premise that all of the resources of the earth belong to all mankind collectively and each living individual is entitled to an equal (adequate) share.[18] The original collective ownership of the earth is of course a premise of

Locke and most liberals as well, though some would prefer to regard the original situation as one in which the term "ownership" was a misnomer, ownership being associated with division. The problem of equal shares is also complex. In the first place many definitions of equality exist. But if one assumes that in the original state the resources were sufficient for the needs of all, then various concepts of what equal access would mean can be accommodated.

It is from this original or primal collective claim to the world's resources that the obligation of those who have control over their allocation to distribute them to all peoples originates. The organic philosophy as it has evolved historically regards the unity of mankind and its identity as a species as one of those primal facts of nature which form the basis of obligations which every right-thinking person wishes to fulfill, however confused he or she might be as to what these obligations are in any given case.

Short of theological presuppositions (which many Americans would accept but which our argument does not require), the collective ownership of mankind cannot be demonstrated directly. But—as its acceptance by Locke and other liberals indicates—the burden of proof rests on contrary assumptions. All discussions of private property ask the question of how private property can be justified. The most primitive situation is presumed to be one of undifferentiated access (as among animals). Species solidarity is a common ethological phenomenon. Territoriality exists, and animals (including birds and fish) fight each other for feeding opportunities.[19] Evidence can be adduced that conflict over these and related ends existed among prehistoric mankind. But, despite this, hunger is a common enemy of the species. When territoriality leads to exclusion of other members of the species from feeding opportunities, it can be presumed (under evolutionary theory) to serve survival values. But unless exclusion of others from food can be shown to have survival value for the species (as is assumed under "lifeboat" or "triage" theories), such exclusion must fall before the prior claim of species survival through prolongation of the life of its members.

But while the earth belongs to mankind collectively, resources, including those used in producing food, cannot be utilized collectively either on a national or international basis. The actual process of food production, distribution, and consumption must take place through social subsystems down to the individual level. Even in socialist states someone has to be responsible for different productive tasks and food is consumed individually. Even in a socialist world, community allocations of food would have to be made to regions, groups, and (inferentially if not administratively) individuals.[20]

Thus any society, national or international, is inevitably faced with the problem of how to decide on what basis food—like any other good—shall be allocated among individuals or groups. The decision as to who is entitled to what—the problem of justice—is a political decision, however much it may be possible to philosophically rationalize any particular basis of allocation. The decision that "free market" exchange processes will be used to allocate resources—and the extent to which they will be used—is ultimately just as much a political decision as would be a decision to move to complete socialism in a society. Various societies from time to time decide—according to various concepts of justice, and usually in an eclectic manner—how allocations of social goods will be made. Some of these bases are:

1. *The contribution of the individual or group to the productive process.* This can be regarded as a matter of moral right as in the labor theory of value or of utilitarian considerations as in the belief that giving greater shares to more efficient producers acts as an incentive to maximize the total social product. In actual practice the contribution of individuals to the production process is difficult to measure. If I catch five fish for the village's use, this can be considered to be a greater contribution than the two fish you have caught. But what if I have been allocated first choice of fishing grounds (or time of day), use a better boat (made by the group), or have been taught greater skills at the expense of the group? Anyone familiar with labor economics will readily recognize the various factors that go into determining what people earn, even in a free market situation. The contribution of the individual or group to any process of economic production can be measured in various ways, since the marginal product of any worker is a function of previously created skills, the capital equipment available, and managerial decisions. Society to a great degree predetermines who will be more efficient.

2. *Existing patterns of domination.* The unequal legal status of slaves or the unequal political or economic power of peasants or workers forces them to give the lion's share of what they produce to masters, landlords, capitalists, etc. Socially sanctioned monopolies of scarce and necessary skills or positions plays a similar role; physicians and teamsters may make larger than average incomes in some societies. The issue, of course, is not whether "exploitation" and/or injustice takes place in society, but simply whether exchange rates for goods and services are ever the result of completely free bargaining among equal individuals.

3. *Socially perceived needs of society as a whole.* This criterion, of course, assumes that social goals exist in addition to individual goals. Such perceived needs can lead to distributing utilities among nonproducing elements in society in order to promote social survival. Thus food and other goods are made available to nonworking women, children, old people, the infirm, etc. It can be argued that the housework of females is an unremunerated productive service to male breadwinners in some cases and should not fall into this category, but that part of it which may be devoted to child care certainly does. Similarly, some of the goods given to the old may be regarded as a reward for past services, but much falls into a more general category of maintaining social stability, morale, etc.

4. *Compassion.* Compassion may stem from either religious or humanitarian norms. The criterion of compassion requires distribution of food and other goods to persons simply because they exist and their existence is presumed to be

of value in itself. Thus women who neither work nor are mothers are fed, as are the infirm or old who have no claims on society based on past or prospective services. Obviously in many cases motivations of compassion and social survival overlap. Children may be fed both because society presumes the need for successor generations and because people feel sorry for hungry children, but these motivations are separate, from an analytic point of view. Also, insofar as the distributor of food is remote from those to whom it is given, and perhaps is a member of a different national subgroup of world society, the incidence of these two differing if sometimes parallel motivations will vary. I may be slightly more likely to give food to a starving Asian child because of compassion than because I believe that the next generation of mankind should be fed.

5. *"Negative" allocation.* In applications of this criterion certain individuals or groups are deprived of food or utilities in the belief that they have forfeited some or all of their rights to share in the social product because of conduct which is either socially harmful in general or harmful to the process of producing enough goods to satisfy social needs. Wastrels may have their supplies cut off. The overly fecund may have their living standards reduced. (Theoretical objection is sometimes raised that measures to this end often penalize children who are innocent of the social misconduct [having too many children] which such measures seek to discourage. But this is equally true of the fate of children of jailed criminals, disgraced politicians, the incompetent and lazy, etc.)

Societies can and do use all of these criteria for allocation of food and other goods in various combinations in order to achieve what they collectively regard as just patterns of distribution. This is a matter of political choice. Means of inducing certain patterns of allocation are varied and include taxes, subsidies, controls and regulations, price and credit manipulation, fiscal policies, confiscation, etc. The choice of mechanisms will depend on various factors including perception of negative economic, social, or political side effects of various means, as well as considerations of ethical justification, political power relationships, and administrative capacities. But no particular means can be ruled out as *per se* unjustifiable as a net diminution of freedom if freedom is defined as consisting of the ability of the members of a society to decide what its future state shall be. Various means of allocation will be perceived by individuals or groups within societies as more or less arbitrary or unjust depending on their cultural backgrounds and how they are specifically affected (slaveholders regarded abolitionists as the enemies of their freedom as well as the enemies of their property rights), but societies cannot avoid exercising their collective freedom to choose their own futures through determining what standards of resource allocation they shall adopt.

It follows from the above that, insofar as is necessary, market mechanisms can and should be interfered with by whatever means are most operationally functional in order to ensure that all existing human beings are guaranteed the minimal dietary standard (however defined) necessary to sustain life and health. This is a matter of right for the individuals involved and a primary ethical obligation on the part of those who have the power to allocate food resources nationally or internationally. It does not, of course, argue for interference in the market as an end in itself but merely as a legitimate means to the end of a just pattern of food distribution.

HUNGER AND ITS CAUSES

Populations in various parts of the world are today subject to food shortages or dietary deficiencies (long or short term), involving famine and malnutrition as a result of several causes. Among these causes are:

1. The inability to produce enough food due to basic long-term lack of physical resources—arable land, proper climate conditions, etc.
2. Long-term lack of physical infrastructure—roads, ports, irrigation facilities, etc.
3. Lack of skills and technology with which to produce food.
4. Improper social structures—land tenure systems, class privileges, corrupt government, etc.—which inhibit food production.
5. Short-term disruptions of normal patterns of food consumption and nutrition, including cultural barriers to production and/or consumption of alternative diets.
6. Ignorance leading to improper patterns of food consumption and nutrition, including cultural barriers to production and/or consumption of alternative diets.

Population is not in itself a factor leading to hunger or malnutrition. There are highly populated areas which are well fed and sparsely populated areas which are hungry. All other things being equal, the more mouths to feed, the greater difficulty in feeding them. But, while it can be argued that a population-food problem exists on a global scale in the long range (though this is debated by experts), all things are not equal in the case of individuals or nations. The food-population problem always appears as one of how a given number of human beings are going to be fed at a given time with a given amount of resources. It is assumed that when we speak of a food deficiency problem in a particular national unit we are assuming that feeding the existing population (including projected population over the short run) is the problem at hand.

The causes of food deficiency often operate in combination. In addition, they are associated with the inability of nations to solve the food production problem by the most obvious and simple means available, buying food on the world market. Obviously, if sources of income to purchase food are available within some countries which cannot feed themselves directly as a result of these countries possessing mineral resources, manufacturing plants, skills, etc., no problem exists. We are not concerned with the ability of Great Britain, Japan, and Kuwait to feed themselves. But save for a few highly privileged industrial nations and a few mineral-rich underdeveloped countries, lack of ability to produce food domestically is usually directly correlated with lack of ability to earn income with which to purchase food.

We have argued that where food deficiencies exist, it is justifiable to interfere with the market process in order to remedy these deficiencies. Nations and international bodies have been engaged in such interference. It must be recognized that any aid given by one nation to another through public means (excluding, by definition, private charity) involves interference in the world market process. This applies to loans to buy food, cash grants to buy food, loans to upgrade agricultural productivity (including support for development of economic and physical infrastructures), loans or grants to stimulate industrial production to make later food purchases possible, technical and educational assistance, etc. All of these actions transfer resources from the people of one nation to those of another as a result of collective political decisions (even in nondemocratic states) rather than as a result of a bargaining process between willing buyer and willing seller. It should also be recognized that all tariffs on agricultural products, all tariffs on manufactured goods (most saliently those originating in food-deficient nations), and all export taxes on food or other goods (to say nothing of trade embargoes) interfere with the market process. So do all measures which restrict immigration from food-deficient areas to food "surplus" or "sufficient" areas. These too constitute interference with the free movement of the factors of production postulated by classical economic theory.

Thus if obligations exist to relieve hunger, their fulfillment may take the form of a myriad of possible interferences—or removal of interferences—with normal market processes. Fixing prices or interfering with their normal operations through public gifts of food is only one such form of intervention, though it has received the lion's share of attention in discussions of American policy toward feeding the hungry.

Which means will be chosen by public bodies aiming at solving world food problems will be based on various calculations both of operational functionality and second-order consequences for food-deficient areas, food producers, and other consuming nations. The argument that provision of food to consumers at "artificial" prices inhibits the maximizing of food production both in recipient nations and in the world at large is a serious one which must be taken into calculation within the total context of the world economic scene. So would policy makers have to consider the disruptive effects of uncontrolled imports upon particular domestic economies or the effect of liberalized immigration possibilities upon economic and social structures in both the nations receiving and those sending immigrants. Not every measure which immediately relieves hunger or promises to do so is necessarily wise. It is impossible to set out in advance a series of norms for actions to relieve hunger based either on ethical principles and/or theoretical economic or political concepts and then systematically and ruthlessly apply them across the board. This kind of ideologized policy making is characteristic of liberals (at least when out of power) as well as often characterizing those of their opponents who happen to be socialists. But those organic philosophies of society which are not Marxist-oriented tend to derive from a philosophical tradition which accepts the possibility and necessity of what philosophers from Aristotle to Burke have recognized as the virtue of prudence, the intellectual and moral ability to relate unchanging principles to changing situations, to take shifting and relevant contextual factors into account, and to act to achieve desired ends through flexible means. Prudent action toward relieving hunger assumes that different measures may reasonably be taken to interfere with the market in order to feed the hungry depending on both the causes of hunger and the consequences of possible actions in particular circumstances.

Keeping in mind the general caveat that it is difficult to prescribe in advance what can or should be done in hypothetical future situations, what can be said about the most just and effective ways of dealing with the problem of hunger stemming from various causes?

In the case of nations wherein hunger is due to a long-term shortage of basic resources, food aid should be given on a subsidized basis to the extent necessary to prevent starvation and malnutrition. In return, it is appropriate to insist that recipient nations take reasonable measures to curtail population growth so as to reduce population-resource imbalance, and that their populations evidence a willingness to take advantage of whatever existing opportunities obtain to emigrate to other areas. In addition, reasonable measures to develop sources of income with which to purchase food at market prices should be instituted. What does "reasonable" mean in these circumstances? That of course cannot be stipulated, but there are obvious differences between allowing a nation to continue to double its population each generation, pressuring it to zero population growth within that time span, and aiding it in feeding a growing population if the rate of growth is being steadily reduced. What are reasonable measures to develop income? Again, this is a matter of judgment. Many of the most crowded and resource-poor nations are islands with tourist potential. Should they be forced to turn their beaches over to strangers and their population into busboys and waitresses in order to survive? Should a nation possessing coveted oil or bauxite be forced to sell it cheaply at a rate which will exhaust reserves within a generation in order to qualify for assistance? Obviously these are questions which can only be dealt with on a case-to-case basis.[21]

In cases where the inability to produce adequate food—or to earn foreign exchange with which to purchase it—is due to deficiencies in economic and social infrastructure, food aid can be justified during the period such deficiencies are being remedied, but it should be accompanied by aid in other forms which will assist directly in the development of economic capabilities. Care should be taken, however, that food aid does not become a substitute for food production while other forms of aid are channeled into prestige or overly grandiose industrial projects.

What applies to countries where physical infrastructure limits food production also applies to nations where lack of skill and technology are the causes of insufficiency. A combination of food and technical assistance is called for, but so is vigilance that improving food production and/or real export earnings is central to government economic planning.

Countries where inadequate domestic food production combined with inadequate export earnings results from failures of the indigenous political, social, or economic structures are perhaps the most difficult to prescribe for in the abstract.[22] Food aid can and should be provided on a short-term emergency basis; those who are starving are almost certainly not those responsible for their plight. On the other hand, long-run aid can be objected to on various grounds. One is that in nations where—to put it most succinctly—the cause of poverty is inequality and oppression, aid is likely to go astray and/or be ineffective in raising production because of these very structures of inequality. In many nations the only way to economic—especially agricultural—self-sufficiency lies through radical social reform, including revolution and bloodshed. Nothing else will work. But there may be cases where aid from donor nations can avert hunger while economic development takes place which enables the rich ruling classes to remain so. What this amounts to is a situation where the populations—including many relatively poor taxpayers—of donor nations are engaged in subsidizing the rich of developing nations. This constitutes a regressive form of redistribution throughout the world masked as humanitarianism or the remedy of injustice. Such a situation is as unjust as asking a relatively poor man to feed the starving child of a millionaire who refuses to meet his parental obligations.

But what are the alternatives? Shall social change be enforced by coercion from outside—in whole or in part—say through aid to domestic forces of insurrection? Practical political considerations will generally outweigh whatever ethical appeal such a program might have. Shall outside nations refuse to feed the hungry in "diseased" polities in the hope that they will become so desperate that they will revolt against their rulers, the outsiders acting like physicians trying to starve a tapeworm out of a human being? This would mean the deliberate imposition of hardship upon many over a long period of time before a revolution occurred. Yet such a program is not so different from the suggestions of those who wish outside powers to boycott and carry out economic warfare against the Republic of South Africa until it changes its internal racial policies. And such a program of pressure might not even succeed, making the net results for the oppressed less than zero. Obviously potential donor nations will have to deal with each case in terms of particulars. What are the possibilities for change? How much would radical social change coincide with donor nations' other international goals? To what extent can aid—including food aid—be used as a wedge to encourage social change which will not only raise food productivity but affect political and social structures for the better? If (as will almost certainly be the case) the candidates for aid are many, should not such "diseased" nations simply be given lower priority than others whatever one's absolute judgments as to whether aid to them can be justified? (And conversely, cannot the priority given to these countries be raised if social and political changes justify this?) Certainly in the case of such nations prudence must take precedence over abstract prescription.

Similar considerations apply in the less numerous and dangerous cases where dietary insufficiency is caused by cultural patterns. One can try to persuade peoples to change their eating habits, but persuasion is a slow process and often meets with limited success, and if rice eaters will starve rather than eat wheat, that is a decision which must rest with them. Here respect for human integrity would counsel forms of food aid—whether direct or to increase domestic production—which respect traditions, which are often basic to cultural survival. On the other hand, if priorities must be established among a variety of possible aid recipients, it is difficult to justify devoting two acres or two units of fertilizer to feeding 20 people with crop X when the same expenditure of resources could feed 40 people who eat crop Y. Again, prudence is called for.

Identifying which areas of the world are food-deficient for which reason or reasons is an empirical task too vast to deal with satisfactorily in this chapter, to say nothing of attempting the task of prescribing exactly what kinds of food aid programs will work best in particular national circumstances.[23] Though certain factors leading to relative hunger are long range in nature (one can be sure that it will be at least several generations before diets in the United States and India are comparable), others are short range and can change within the time span in which books are written and published. The same is true, though to a lesser degree, of the social, political, and structural economic factors which affect ability to produce food. Despite this, one can make some broad generalizations. Bangladesh and various countries in the Sahel region of Africa would appear to fall in the category of more or less permanently food-poor nations. So would many of the new ministates of the world, many of which are islands (Barbados, Cape Verde, Mauritius) with small areas, high population growth rates, and increasingly restricted opportunities for emigration. Some chronically hungry nations such as India fit into more than one category when the causes for their hunger are examined (though India would appear to suffer much less from basic lack of resources than is generally believed). Judgments will have to be provisional and subject to constant revision, especially if world climatic conditions are in for long-term change as some argue.[24] A recent report[25] listed Bangladesh, Yemen, Somalia, Tanzania, Rwanda, Burundi, Malawi, Mozambique, and possibly Kenya and Sri Lanka as danger spots. These nations run the gamut of our categories, and many of the fears expressed are already outdated, while new nations are appearing on the latest lists of the hungry. This being the case, the problem of action would seem to be twofold—establishing the principles which, guided by intelligence and common sense, should be applied in dealing with problems of hunger and devising mechanisms and understandings which will make possible a flexible response to changing conditions wherever they occur.

High on the list of response mechanisms would be the creation of world reserve stocks to provide an emergency food supply and act as a warehouse for continuing aid programs. How large such stocks should be—10 million tons of wheat, 50 million, 100 million—what rules should govern movement of these stocks into and out of reserve status so as to both help stabilize world food prices and not inhibit production, what mix of national and international or public and private control should be exercised over them, what kinds of mechanisms would have to be created to move and distribute food from such stocks as the need arises—all these are complicated and often technical questions. Consensus as to the need for such a world reserve is growing, and international agencies are now seized of these various questions involved in its creation. But the principle of its desirability and necessity must be established.[26]

At the same time international economic planning and assistance programs must generally seek to create the conditions in which peoples can feed themselves or buy food. Stabilization of exchange rates or prices of key commodities related to agriculture, such as oil and fertilizer, and removal of barriers to trade and immigration where desirable enter into the picture. The problem of feeding the hungry is not an isolated one, and—it should be underlined—justifications for intervening in the market apply to the whole range of food-related economic questions, not to food alone.

CONCLUSION

If the earth belongs to all its inhabitants collectively, then a moral obligation exists to ensure that all its inhabitants are adequately fed, assuming that this is possible at any given population level and without unacceptable ecological side costs.* Insofar as it is not, various political, economic, and natural causes can and will reduce population levels to a supportable range over time. Fulfilling this obligation will involve various interferences with classical free market allocations of resources by means of taxation, regulation, transfer payments, foreign monetary and technical aid, domestic and international economic planning, etc. Subsidized provision of food for groups which are needy—the provision of help to buy or produce food—is only one in a large arsenal of measures needed to feed the hungry and involves various possible counterproductive effects.[27] But it is a measure which can be justified philosophically as enlarging rather than diminishing freedom and it cannot legitimately be faulted on normative grounds.

NOTES

1. To some extent the classification of theories on liberty used in this paper overlaps with that of Isaiah Berlin in his essay "Two Concepts of Liberty";

---

*The ramifications of this question are outside the scope of this paper. Most classical economists tend to argue that the earth's ability to feed ever-increasing populations is virtually limitless; proponents of government intervention and economic planning are divided, but most probably accept the basic premises of the "limits to growth" theorists.

see his *Four Essays on Liberty* (New York: Oxford University Press, 1970), pp. 118-172.

2. On this division of attitudes regarding liberalism see Herbert McClosky, "Conservatism and Personality," *American Political Science Review* LII (March 1958), 35.

3. My own basic political philosophy is set forth in Ferkiss, *The Future of Technological Civilization* (New York: George Braziller, 1974).

4. Berlin, *op. cit.*, p. 122.

5. See Locke, *Second Treatise on Civil Government*, sec. 87.

6. As for instance in John Rawls, *A Theory of Justice* (Cambridge, Mass.: Harvard University Press, 1971). See especially pp. 18-19, 146-148. For a brief summary of Rawls's ideas see Samuel Gorovitz, "John Rawls' Theory of Justice," in Anthony de Crespigny and Kenneth Minogue (eds.), *Contemporary Political Philosophers* (New York: Dodd, Mead & Co., 1975), pp. 272-289.

7. Calhoun manages to begin with conservative premises and end up with liberal conclusions. See Louis Hartz, *The Liberal Tradition in America* (New York: Harcourt, Brace & World, 1959), p. 159.

8. The movement from need to desire as the basis of politics in the modern world and its negative consequences are suggestively discussed in Samuel Beer, *Modern Political Development* (New York: Random House, 1974); see especially pp. 62-64.

9. For an exposition of libertarian philosophy see John Hospers, *Libertarianism: A Political Philosophy for Tomorrow* (Santa Barbara: Reason Press, 1971).

10. As Burke puts it, "the presumed consent of every rational creature is in unison with the predisposed order of things." Quoted in Berlin, *op. cit.*, pp. 147-148.

11. This contention is a major strand—explicit and implicit—in the American naturalist tradition. See especially George Herbert Mead, *Mind, Self, and Society* (Chicago: University of Chicago Press, 1934).

12. See *Second Treatise on Civil Government*, sec. 42.

13. See Peter Brown, "Food as National Property," this volume, p. 71; and Robert Nozick, *Anarchy, State and Utopia* (New York: Basic Books, 1974), p. 177.

14. On the problem this presents especially for Rawls's version of liberalism see Vernon Van Dyke, "Justice as Fairness: For Groups?" *American Political Science Review* LXIX (June 1975), 607.

15. See for example Reinhold Niebuhr, *Moral Man and Immoral Society* (New York: Charles Scribner's Sons, 1932).

16. Brown, *op. cit.* See also Peter Singer, "Reconsidering the Famine Relief Argument," this volume, p. 41; and Thomas Nagel, "Poverty and Food: Why Charity Is Not Enough," this volume, *passim*.

17. On patterns of distribution and productivity see Lester Brown, *By Bread Alone* (New York: Praeger, 1974), p. 14. Also see Jonathan Powers, "Alternative to Starvation," *Encounter* XLV (November 1975), 11.

18. Compare Singer, *op. cit.*, pp. 41-42.

19. In humans territoriality plays a distinctly secondary role to social hierarchy among other factors. See Roderic Gorney, *The Human Agenda* (New York: Bantam Books, 1973), pp. 78–84, 109.

20. Various patterns of distribution to family groups, etc., can be based on personal needs of individuals without their being direct participants in distributive arrangements.

21. Compare Singer, *op. cit.*, pp. 45–47.

22. For a related argument see *ibid.*, pp. 39–40.

23. For an introduction to the empirical data see Lester A. Sobel (ed.), *World Food Crisis* (New York: Facts on File, 1975), also Lester Brown, "The World Food Prospect," *Science* 190 (December 12, 1975), 1053.

24. See Nigel Calder, *The Weather Machine* (New York: Viking, 1975). For somewhat differing views see Louis M. Thompson, "Weather Variability, Climatic Change, and Grain Production," *Science* 188 (May 9, 1975), 535.

25. Boyce Rensenberger, "Food Experts See Countries in Greater Peril of Hunger and Possible Starvation than Last Year," *New York Times,* June 3, 1975.

26. For opposing views on this issue see Charles Shuman, "Food Aid and the Free Market," this volume, pp. 153–154; and C. William Swank, "International Food Reserves" in this volume, pp. 183–194.

27. This is stressed in Shuman, *op. cit.*, pp. 148–149, 155–159.

International food reserves
C. William Swank

The idea of international food reserves has come into general discussion during the last 2 or 3 years. Pronouncements made at the World Food Conference gave both encouragement and hope to those interested in establishing international food reserves.

Higher food prices in the U.S. markets have consumers wondering if a food reserve might lower and help stabilize food prices, plus provide comfort by assuring that no shortage could exist. There is also interest among grain farmers who would enjoy stabilization of grain prices rather than the wide fluctuations that occur in a free market subject to erratic demand pressures. In addition, livestock producers who purchase a substantial proportion of their grain supplies would benefit from stabilized prices. Not to be minimized, there is an interest among many people, especially religious leaders, concerning the moral obligation of countries blessed with an abundance of food to help countries where food supplies are short. However, even those primarily interested in moral obligations have differing perspectives on the need, structure, and operation of food reserves. Some of those views are included in this book.

While many people believe some kind of food reserve is needed, they all approach the problem with different rationales. The self-interest of each proposing group would make agreements on international reserves a very controversial thing.

When the cost and complexity of reserves are examined carefully, interest may be dimmed. And, if there are counterproductive aspects involved in international reserves, these too should be examined and will result in some diminution of interest.

At first blush, the notion of any kind of grain reserve is quite appealing. Proponents quickly harken to the Bible story of Joseph, who convinced the Pharaoh to store grain in anticipation of the lean years. Television and radio have brought accounts of severe malnutrition and starvation into the living rooms of millions and millions of people. This is not the first time in history there are documented accounts of hungry and starving people, but it is only recently that people in developed countries experienced, through vastly improved communications, the pangs of hunger felt by others.

At the World Food Conference in Rome in 1974, many nations supported a resolution that would establish a system of grain stocks on a national basis. The rationale was to create "an international undertaking on world food security." The following year, in 1975, the International Wheat Council began discussions on an international wheat agreement that would include a system of grain reserves. Later in 1975, at a meeting of the Ministerial Council of the Organization for Economic Cooperation and Development, the U.S. outlined a proposal for an international system of reserves. The proposal was presented in detail at the September meeting of the Wheat Council the same year.

The following year in Geneva, the General Agreement on Tariffs and Trade (GATT) also considered establishing international agreements to stabilize world grain markets in part through "concerted stockpiling policies."[1]

Thus it's clear that the question of international grain reserves cannot and will not be ignored. It's under discussion by the leaders around the world. The compelling question, then, is what kind of consideration should be given to the proposals for international food reserves.

PROPOSALS

While there are as many ideas for establishing food reserves, or programs with comparable impact, as there are people thinking about them, most concepts narrow to a few choices. Since grain is the most easily stored and widely utilized food commodity, virtually all reserve programs center around edible grains. The method proposed by the United States Department of State is for an international reserve (similar to an insurance program) with each participating country providing, and holding nationally, a portion of the reserve stocks. In this proposal, reserve stocks would be holdings in excess of normal working stocks. Normal working stocks are usually considered 10 percent of the national production or consumption, whichever is the larger. The State Department estimates that 100 million metric tons of all grains comprise current worldwide working stocks. It is in relation to this normal or traditional amount of production that a percentage would be contemplated as reserve stocks. A reserve adequate to meet 90 percent of shortfalls is believed to be sufficient to meet needs and to be less costly than a larger reserve. A reserve of 30 million tons of wheat and rice would be sufficient to provide supplies that could be made available when there was a drop in world production.

Reserves would be held by participating nations and would be shared according to some internationally agreed rules or guidelines. Each participating nation would be obligated to acquire either, from its own production, or in world trade, sufficient stocks to build the reserve allocated to it. Action to release reserves within a nation would be triggered by a quantitative indicator based on stock levels and shortfalls.

In the State Department proposal, participants in the system would receive assured access to reserve stocks at market prices. Nonparticipants or participants not complying with the agreement would not be assured of obtaining access to reserves held by others. In years of severe shortage, countries applying export restraints would either get or give preferential treatment by action of complying participants in the reserve system. The developing countries would be given special assistance to help them achieve their obligation to hold a portion of the global grain reserve. The administrative costs for monitoring and servicing the international grain reserve would be borne by the participating countries. Members of the reserve system would bear the cost of managing and storing their own reserve supplies. Thus the reserve stocks would be theoretically scattered throughout the world and be available to countries in need of them at market prices.[2]

An analysis by Philip H. Trezise, writing for the Brookings Institution, suggests a 60-million-metric-ton grain reserve divided equally between wheat and coarse grains might be sufficient for the onset of a reserve that would satisfy virtually all shortfalls in worldwide conditions. His proposal would increase the size of the reserve by 1980 to a 75-to-80-million-metric-ton supply. The estimated cost of a 60-million-ton reserve would be $6 billion for acquisition and about $640 million annually in 1976 constant dollars for storage and interest. All countries would contribute financially to this proposed reserve. The management of reserves would be national in nature but would occur in line with an agreed-upon formula and guidelines.[3]

Another proposal for an international grain reserve is that it should be held in the U.S. by the U.S. This concept recognizes the strategic value of food, both from a military and a diplomatic point of view. Since the U.S. is by far the biggest surplus grain producer, the logic is that stockpiles could be built in the U.S. and then dispensed throughout the world at market prices or on concessional terms depending on the country involved, its needs, its wealth, and perhaps its political makeup. In such a reserve system, the cost would be borne by the U.S. taxpayer, with partial recovery to be made through sales and the remainder to be considered a contribution to our international aid efforts.

B. F. Jones of Purdue University includes a 41-million-metric-ton reserve in his analysis for food reserves held by the U.S.A. This proposal would be made up of 23 million metric tons of wheat, 17 million metric tons of coarse grains, and 1 million metric tons of rice. It is estimated that this level of reserve, coupled with what is normally expected to be held in the private channels of trade, would provide reserves sufficient to make up any production shortfalls in 19 out of 20 years. To establish reserves higher than this would be too expensive to justify. Jones estimates that the private trade could be expected to carry 23.5 million metric tons and therefore the established reserves plus the amount in private hands would total 64.5 million metric tons and would be equivalent to the average level of stocks from 1963 to 1972 in the U.S. The estimated cost to acquire this level of reserve would be $4.7 billion, with an annual carrying cost for storage and interest of $705 million.[4]

Writing for the Congressional Budget Office, staff member Lynn Daft and others put forth the proposal for a more modest food reserve which would mitigate against shortfalls in crop production but would not be so costly or so cumbersome. In this proposal, it is suggested that a 10-million-metric-ton domestic reserve could be established at a cost of $1.2 billion for acquisition at 1976 grain prices and an annual carrying charge of $180 million.[5]

If, through the United Nations or some other international agreement, the U.S. State Department proposal for a 30-million-metric-ton reserve is created and the U.S. portion is to be 20 percent of that total, Daft estimates the U.S. cost of that total grain reserve to be $900 million for acquisition with an annual carrying charge of $100 million per year.

The differences in the amount of reserves necessary or desirable are based on subjective judgments by the various authors of the amount of insurance or stability to be achieved. The variations in estimates of reserve costs are explained by the different assumptions as to the cost of grain stock acquisition, storage, and carrying charges. Jones assumes a storage and carrying charge of 15 percent annually of acquisition costs. Daft's estimate for storage and interest is close to the same. Trezise, however, assumes a much lower interest rate of 3 percent annually and tends to minimize the carrying cost.

Another possibility for international grain reserves is to have a stockpile owned and held by the United Nations or some other international body, with the stockpile to be placed in whatever locations the international authority might designate. This would give the international authority obvious control over the grain reserve and would transfer to the international authority the difficult problem of allocation and administration. It is assumed that UN members would financially support the establishment of the reserves and agree to the drawdown of the reserve on the basis of need at current market prices. Whether or not there would be equity and justice to all participants in such a system would depend on the inner workings of the international body, the strengths and weaknesses of participating nations at a given moment in time, and the political situation throughout the world.

Still another proposal would be an international monetary reserve put together specifically for food emergencies. A monetary reserve could be supported by all developed and developing nations, whether or not they had excess supplies of grain and even if they had traditionally avoided any involvement in food aid. The monetary reserve would be handled by an international authority and allocated to countries that had a production shortfall or an emergency. The recipient countries would then come into the market and buy the kind of grain preferred or the kinds that would achieve the most nutrients for the money spent. It is presumed that they would purchase from the nearest supplier at terms as favorable as could be negotiated. The grain to be purchased would come from the private channels of trade and from stocks normally carried in such private channels. Presumably, private stocks would be increased in amounts if an international fund was established for purchases by countries experiencing severe shortfalls in their domestic production. Each country would carry whatever reserves in whatever manner might seem best to its own self-interest. There would be no systematic buildup of actual grain stocks in any one country, or in a diffused manner in several participating countries. Countries such as the U.S. would only be asked to ship grain if, in fact, the U.S. was the lowest-priced supplier of the preferred grain when all costs were considered. In order to assure adequate supplies for consumers in the U.S., the private trade would bid to keep sufficient supplies within the country.

EVALUATION: DO WE NEED RESERVES?

Before evaluating the various reserves suggested, the more basic question should be raised of whether or not food reserves, as a matter of policy, should be established. There is no question that there are hungry people in the world. Likewise, there are few, if any, hungry people in the world who have the money or goods with which to pay for food or the natural resources with which to produce adequate food supplies. In other words, there is an unequal distribution of wealth accompanied by a maldistribution of food. The unequal distribution of wealth may be in the form of natural resources or in the form of wealth created by the productive use of natural resources made possible by technology, skill, and enterprise. We are becoming aware that, if everyone in the world had sufficient monies to buy the amount of food that is normally consumed by affluent people, there would suddenly not be enough food to go around. While this is easy to demonstrate, it is only a matter of conjecture, since few are seriously considering a redistribution of wealth throughout the world on the basis of need rather than productivity.

In addition, it should be clear that a reserve system would be a futile way of assuring plentiful food for everyone throughout the world, since it could quickly be depleted and only painfully rebuilt. To consider a grain reserve as a means of supplementing the diets of chronically food deficit nations would nullify the grain reserve concept. Such a system, rather than being used for disaster relief or for supplementing severe shortfalls in production, would simply be a scheme to feed all the hungry people of the world to the extent possible. While this has noble and lofty overtones, it is not seriously contemplated by the pragmatic leaders of the world. The amount of redistribution of wealth and resources required to make such a scheme workable is unacceptable. Much of the food aid to India, extended for a number of years through P.L. 480, was no doubt carried on for domestic political and economic reasons, rather than humanitarian ones.

If the purpose of a food reserve isn't to solve the problems of widespread malnutrition or to assure an adequate food supply for starving peoples, then what is the purpose? A more commonly held view is that wide price fluctuations can be avoided by a food reserve. Thus, the so-called "ratchet effect" of escalating prices throughout the economy because of increased food prices might be avoided.

The fact remains that fluctuating prices mean prices go down as well as up. For example, the price for food commodities received by the farmer in late 1975 and early 1976 was significantly lower than in the period 1974-75. Grain prices dropped by 33 percent during the period from mid-August to mid-November 1975. Cattle and hog prices also declined in this period. Since the cost for services added on after these products left the farm (labor, transportation, heat, light, etc.) suffered inflationary price increases during the same period, most people did not notice that the price of food itself was cheaper. It is obvious that retail food prices would have been even higher if prices to farmers had not declined in this period.

Admittedly, the fact that prices will later go down if market forces are allowed to operate cannot undo any permanent damage suffered by those who were unable to purchase food when prices were high. This is a serious problem. But the solution does not lie in the use of reserves to hold prices artificially low. Income transfers of some sort would be a better long-range solution than disruptions of the market system with its built-in incentives for all-out production. Income transfers could also be supplemented, if necessary, by feeding programs designed to ensure that food actually reaches infants and pregnant and lactating mothers who might otherwise be malnourished. Such programs can avoid the sort of interference with the general level of prices involved in the use of reserves to hold prices down for everyone.

Income transfers are better because they go to the root of the problem, which is inadequate buying power. In any case, since many of the world's malnourished cannot afford to pay even a price equivalent to the production costs of food, a reserve system used to depress prices could not possibly hold food down to a price which they could afford. If the gap between buying power and food prices is to be closed for the world's poorest, it must be closed by increasing their buying power or targeting assistance directly to them.

Artificially stabilized prices to farmers still result in steadily increasing consumer food prices in an inflationary economy. Unless great care is taken, farmers in this situation incur increased costs for virtually all production inputs, as well as for family living, but are denied commensurate increases in prices received for their products. The disincentive for expanded production for such a system is clear.

There is also the idea of aid and comfort to a sense of security and people's feeling of well-being when there is not only food for the table and more in the store. This self-interest in an assurance of plenty may motivate more strongly than the humanitarian idea of making sure no others go hungry, although both considerations are possible. A reserve would most likely allocate reserve stocks for feeding people already well fed. It applies to a country that has suffered a production shortfall or a crop failure. This type of nation could either afford to buy from the reserve or would most likely be participating in an international food reserve system. The question here would be whether or not the value of such an insurance policy would be worth both the cost and the trouble. It is conceivable that it very well might be worth the cost and the international deliberations necessary to make it function. The more developed nations might also find their economies well served to allocate monies for food purchasing only when the need was obvious to everyone within their country and to use these same monies for further development in years when food purchases were not necessary.

Countries that are less developed and whose people are often subject to malnutrition or starvation, would likely need more assistance than could be provided by a food reserve. Again, those countries with marginal incomes could purchase more food when prices were low than if prices were stabilized at somewhat higher levels because of an international reserve. If the assumption is made that international reserves will keep prices lower in sum total than would be the average of fluctuating prices, then this would be good for nations with limited incomes. It would also, by definition, be to the economic detriment of those nations with grain to sell. If the decision is made to establish an international reserve in spite of this, the question of which group of people in the exporting country bears the cost becomes critical.

EVALUATING SPECIFIC PROPOSALS

Each of the reserve ideas mentioned previously has strengths and weaknesses. The system of nationally held stocks proposed by the U.S. State Department has many points of merit compared to other systems. It would be an international agreement among participating nations. The cost of each country's stocks would be borne by the country itself, and presumably there would be less propensity in this system to create counterproductive pressures on the suppliers of food. Reserves in any country have a dampening effect on market prices. The stocks are present, and the market forces take these stocks into account in the bidding and selling process. However, the more modest-size reserves that would be in any given country, if reserves were scattered throughout the world, would have a less dampening effect than a huge reserve subject to the control of one single legislative or regulatory body.

As with any international agreement, the proposal would be subject to disagreements and even to unresponsiveness based on political or other international constraints. Unless such a system were operated in an open and voluntary way, it could easily fall into disrepair and disrepute. While it might be easy to assume away the problems of international disputes, experience thus far indicates that without a true working and responsible world government, a great deal of international hassle could be anticipated.

The concept of an international reserve held by the UN or a similar international body with grain stored and controlled by the international body has the same merits and demerits as any UN effort. If the cost of such a program were borne by all members, as other programs are supported, then many nations would make very small contributions and a few would make very large contributions. Unless the veto power of the U.S. or the USSR were used in a very unpopular way, many of the developing nations could easily vote to distribute stocks of the UN to developing nations or others based on desire rather than production shortfalls. In the short run, and from a humanitarian standpoint, this might be a very popular use, but in the long run it would prove to be self-destructive. The stockpile would be dissipated with little incentive for its rebuilding on the part of those with grain contributions to make. The merits of a UN stockpile are only as strong as the UN itself. The most accurate evaluation of this grand idea is embodied in the word "impractical." It is only by controlling the policies of all member nations that such a system could be made to be practical, and that, of course, is not a viable proposal at this time.

A huge reserve held by the U.S. in the U.S. has many good features for U.S. consumers, but may be less attractive in other countries. From the U.S. point of view, it would be grain from U.S. producers that would build the reserve in the first place. It would clearly be under the control of the U.S. and, therefore, could be made available to friends and be withheld from enemies. It might also give great feelings of comfort to those people in the U.S. who somehow feel daily concern over running short of food. It would likewise have a strong leveling effect on price fluctuations, since it would be fairly simple to withdraw stocks when supplies were tight and theoretically to add to stocks when supplies were plentiful.

There are specific problems with this proposal, if past history of the U.S. surplus programs is remembered. Mechanics of storage and distribution and the obvious cost that would be borne by taxpayers are two. During the many years that the U.S. government held surplus stocks of grain simply because export markets were not available and market prices dipped to unprofitable levels for farmers, the storage costs alone for grain were more than $1 million per day. The additional cost of grain that went out of condition and had to be destroyed or disposed of at considerable loss to the government has never been fully revealed. The public's hue and cry in objecting to these storage costs is well remembered by those closely associated with agriculture. The problem of international agreements also looms large. There is often controversy on the sharing of very nonstrategic items. What kind of agreements would be adhered to on something as vital as food?

A compelling and so far unanswered question is, Who should pay for reserves? The most acceptable answer may not be practical or even possible. The first answer, of course, is that the cost of reserves should be borne by those countries desiring such reserves or access to reserve stocks. That is simple enough except when you recognize some of the nations that need this stability the most are least able and/or least willing to pay the cost.

Another answer is that those countries with the ability to pay should maintain a reserve system for those whose needs are great but monetary resources are limited. This is not a new idea and too frequently in the past has been used as a leverage for consideration of other matters—political, social, or economic. What would be the impact, for example, if the U.S. refused grain shipments to a country such as Russia until the Soviets permitted the Jewish professionals wishing to leave the country total freedom for their exodus? International agreement can easily be subject to international pressures.

Another answer is to require the countries that have surplus grain to carry a reserve and make it available at market prices simply as a moral obligation to the rest of the world. Since there is an obvious unequal distribution of natural resources, and especially food production resources, some feel that those countries well blessed should share with those less fortunate as a matter of moral commitment. While this loads the cost on the country with the resources, there are many who feel this kind of sharing is a matter of justice and equity in the affairs of the world. In his chapter, Peter G. Brown contends that there should be a sharing on an international basis of those items of wealth that exist because of natural phenomena. These include the natural resources associated with land and climate which are vital to food production.

The problem with this contention is that the resources alone do not produce wealth and are of little value until treated with enterprise, skill, and management. Therefore, it is difficult to support the necessity for international sharing based solely on the location of natural resources. Taken to its extreme, such logic completely eliminates the market system or free enterprise system and allocates all wealth on the basis of population or the square miles of land within a nation. Such arbitrary allocation would do little for equity or justice.

Shlomo Reutlinger, writing in the February 1976 *American Journal of Agricultural Economics,* puts forth an extensive analysis of the economic impact of a worldwide buffer stock of wheat. The analysis clearly shows that while consumers benefit from the accumulation of stocks, it occurs at a loss to the producer. The producer loss not only of income but also of incentives to continue production should be carefully noted and evaluated by those who would try to manipulate the industry of agriculture.[6]

Finally, great care must be taken or any system of reserves, other than monetary, loads the cost of the backs of farmers who made the production possible in the first place. Both economic theory and recent history in the U.S. prove that food reserves have a dampening effect on prices for grain, since there is always the threat that reserves will be dumped on the market, thus quickly converting a tight supply situation to a long or surplus situation.

The surpluses accumulated in the U.S. after World War II occurred because the economic adjustment that would have taken place in production agriculture without the system of quotas, loans, and Commodity Credit Corporation stocks was deemed politically unacceptable by the U.S. Congress. The market anticipates what can happen with "the stroke of a pen," and grain producers suffer prices stabilized at a low level, or declining prices, while their costs increase along with the rest of society's costs. This not only results in a disincentive for additional production but also exacerbates misuse of production resources. More than 30 years' experience in the U.S. with government-held stocks of grain shows that not only do prices fail to fluctuate sufficiently to give signals for changes in allocation of acreage or resources to the different commodities to meet the demands of the market, but these stocks also stabilize prices to farmers below the cost of production. Governments are then forced to step in with quotas, subsidies, and other administrative remedies to keep farmers in production while also carrying a huge public cost for keeping surpluses in usable condition. The result satisfied no one at the time.

Farmers in the U.S. comprise less than 5 percent of the population. They should not be expected to carry the primary cost of food reserves through outright provision, as would be the case if they donated the extra production or made it available at low prices. Even worse is the straitjacket effect of having the market plagued with a potential surplus, thus keeping all grain prices at the farm level depressed below equilibrium. This lessens the incentive for increased production in future years. If the lessened incentive actually resulted in production decreases, then prices would rise in spite of all government planning. Then comes the question of price ceilings and more political manipulation. While the self-discipline inherent in the market system is sometimes cruel and history has shown sometimes must be mitigated, it has the obvious merits of being self-correcting and totally impartial.

There is also the cost of storage and conditioning of grain as well as administration of the program. In the 1950's, when huge stocks were held by the U.S. government (then called "surplus"), the hue and cry from the public was that the tremendous public expenditure for interest and storage costs was a waste of taxpayers' money, enriching the producers and private companies that had storage capacity. The total costs of any storage-of-food-reserve program are difficult to assess beyond the actual and obvious storage and administrative costs. The other costs to society in general, and farmers in particular, can only be estimated and then rather inaccurately. Recent studies by the Rand Corporation[7] and by Fred H. Sanderson, writing for the American Association for the Advancement of Science,[8] seriously question whether or not the cost justifies the benefits to be derived from a food reserve. Some discount the cost factor in favor of other values such as moral obligations, prudence, or stability.

It should be clear from the outset that there is always a reserve of grain in the "pipeline" of the production, distribution, and processing system. By common usage the term "pipeline" means the amount of grain stored on farms, in country elevators, in terminals and warehouses, at international ports, on railroad cars, and in the storage facilities of processing companies that convert grain into consumer products. While it varies from country to country, a similar pipeline exists for all developed countries. The flow through the pipeline is speeded or slowed by price changes. Increased prices accelerate the flow of stocks through the pipeline and signal the need for increased production of a particular grain or all grains. A decreased price causes those storing grain to continue storage waiting for a price increase, and also signals producers to change to alternative crops where they can.

While people object to price fluctuations, these fluctuations are quite necessary in a market system. Without these signals all decisions for change in price, quantity, and even commodity would have to be made administratively. Since the market is quite sensitive and the demand for grain is inelastic in the economic sense, market price changes can be quite erratic and substantial. Thus the confusion, the concern, and the conversation about international food reserves. While no one advocates abandoning the market system entirely, the continual tampering with the system is part of the problem in causing people to wonder whether or not it works. How much can you modify the market system and still have it perform its function?

If a system of international reserves is deemed necessary, then careful examination should be made of the concept for an international monetary reserve rather than a grain reserve. The monetary reserve can be supported by all nations rather than just those that have excess supplies of grain. The OPEC nations could reinvest some recent oil profits in an international monetary reserve which would be designated specifically for purchase of food in time of need. Industrialized nations such as Japan, Russia, Great Britain, and others could participate by contributing money to such a program even though they are on balance net importers of food supplies and grain.

Under this system, each nation would decide what it considered to be an adequate reserve of actual grain stocks for that nation. This reserve would be available for use in the nation itself or for sale to other nations whose needs were greater. A nation could consider the amount of grain in the Marketing System "pipeline" as its reserve, and thus leave it in private hands, or could create a modest reserve to be held and controlled through its government. In addition to this small reserve of actual grain stocks, each participating nation could draw from the international monetary reserve in times of production shortfall or economic or national disaster.

With the money thus acquired, a receiving nation could buy the type of grain preferred in the diets of its people and could buy its supply in the most economical way. If the system could be compared to an insurance program for automobiles, it should be remembered that auto insurance companies keep a reserve of money so that their insured policyholders can go out and purchase another vehicle, instead of stockpiling automobiles against the time when accidents occur and replacements are needed. While food supplies are more vital to survival than the auto, there are many parts of the analogy which hold. Many people in the U.S. fail to recall that agricultural production takes place on a continuing basis throughout the world. Thus the possibilities of expanding production in time of need exist not only in the United States but also in South America, in Europe, and no doubt in the Far East. While no area of the world can match the combination of land area, climate, and technology that exists in the Corn Belt of the U.S., it should not be concluded that the Corn Belt provides the only area for either expansion or consistent grain production.

Obviously, an international monetary reserve is subject to some of the same concerns and criticisms as an actual food reserve. An international body would need to control the money, establish guidelines for borrowing and for supporting, as well as to establish what use could be made of the funds until they were disbursed. Such a fund would differ from other international banking systems primarily because allocation and distribution of funds would have been predetermined. This, plus an assurance of access to funds for specific food needs, would be its primary asset.

Perhaps more important than what this system does is what it does not do. It does not cause disincentives for the farmers providing grain. It does not cost for storage and administration of product. It does not spoil as actual grain can do. And it does not foist types of grain on countries on the basis of availability rather than cultural preferences or nutritional needs. It does not require uneconomic shipping from point of storage, and it does not facilitate the wasting of large amounts of precious grain. In addition, it should be easier to monitor whether or not the monies were actually used in an appropriate manner than it is to monitor the shipment of grain itself.

One last merit that deserves mention is that while the use of reserve money, rather than tons, might change prices in both supplying and receiving countries, the disruptive impact on markets for both supplying and receiving countries would not be as great as would the impact of actual grain aid.

It seems as if the idea of international food reserves may have a great deal more emotional appeal than economic substance. There is no evidence that a reserve can be established without grave economic harm to the farmers and the economies of both the supplying and receiving countries. The possibility of price improvement is the best incentive for maximum production. The reserve system severely limits this incentive in both supplying and receiving countries. A great deal of further analysis is called for before such a system should be considered. A long-range hope for needy countries is still the hope for increased production in relation to total population. There is no pleasure in rationing shortages. Hope lies in the potential for production of plenty by all nations.

NOTES

1. Congressional Budget Office, *U.S. Food and Agricultural Policy in the World Economy*, April 26, 1976.
2. *Ibid.*
3. Philip H. Trezise, *Rebuilding Grain Reserves toward an International System*, The Brookings Institution, Washington, D.C., 1976.
4. B. F. Jones, "Grain Reserves in Agricultural and Food Policy," *Station Bulletin*, Purdue University, no. 124, May 1976.
5. Congressional Budget Office, *op. cit.*
6. Shlomo, Reutlinger, "A Simulation Model for Evaluating Worldwide Buffer Stocks," *American Journal of Agricultural Economics*, vol. 58, no. 1, February, 1976.
7. John P. Stein and Rodney T. Smith, "The Economics of United States Grain Stockpiling," R-1861-CIEP (draft), Rand Corporation, Santa Monica, Calif., 1975.
8. Fred H. Sanderson, "The Great Food Fumble," in *Food: Politics, Economics, Nutrition and Research*, ed. Philip H. Abelson, American Association for the Advancement of Science, Washington, D.C., 1975, p. 6.

Part Four
REDUCING DEPENDENCE

ABOUT THE CONTRIBUTORS

Thomas Reese Saylor is an economist on the professional staff of the Senate Committee on Agriculture and Forestry and works closely with the Subcommittee on Foreign Agricultural Policy. He is the chief foreign affairs advisor to the Committee and has responsibility for programs and legislation concerning international trade, foreign food assistance, and the international aspects of U.S. food and agricultural policy. He has conducted recent reviews of U.S. programs in Bangladesh, Tanzania, and elsewhere.

Linda Haverberg has been the author or coauthor of more than a dozen articles on nutrition. A nutrition analyst in the International Nutrition Planning Program at the Massachusetts Institute of Technology, she is currently studying the nutritional status of a Guatemalan lowland plantation population, as well as lactose intolerance in American children.

John Osgood Field is an Associate in the International Nutrition Planning Program at the Massachusetts Institute of Technology. Of several articles on development, his most recent was "Nutrition and Development: Dynamics of Political Commitment."

Mitchel B. Wallerstein is a doctoral candidate in political science at MIT and coauthor of *Protein Malnutrition and the Search for a Technological Panacea: The Case of Fish Protein Concentrate* (forthcoming).

Michael F. Brewer is former president of Population Reference Bureau and editor of *The Population Bulletin* and former vice-president of Resources for the Future. His other publications include *Carrying Capacity: Guide for Community Growth and Regional Development*. He is now a Fellow of The Academy for Contemporary Problems.

Norge W. Jerome is a coeditor of *Nutritional Anthropology* and has written numerous articles, including "American Culture and Food Habits." She is an Associate Professor (Nutrition Anthropology) in the Department of Community Health, School of Medicine, the University of Kansas Medical Center, Kansas City.

Henry Shue has written articles on distributive justice, including "Liberty and Self-Respect" and "Justice, Rationality and Desire." He taught at Wellesley College and the University of North Carolina at Chapel Hill. A former Rhodes Scholar, he is the Chairperson of the National Executive Committee of the Society for Philosophy and Public Affairs and a Research Associate at the Center for Philosophy and Public Policy of the University of Maryland, College Park.

Ambassador Edwin M. Martin's diplomatic service included the positions of Assistant Secretary of State for Economic Affairs, Assistant Secretary for Inter-American Affairs, Ambassador to Argentina, and Coordinator of U.S. Participation in the World Food Conference. He is now the Chairman of the Intergovernmental Consultative Group on Food Production and Investment in Developing Countries, established by the World Food Conference.

12 A new legislative mandate for American food aid

Thomas Reese Saylor

Since the absolute magnitude of world food requirements increases at an accelerating rate and the year-to-year variability in food availability becomes ever more dramatic, food aid has played a diminishing role in providing a margin of nutritional security to the indigent throughout the world.

Per capita food production in developing countries increased nominally between 1964 and 1974. Yet the volume of American food aid in 1974 was 21% of the 1964 level, despite the fact that demand for basic food commodity imports of these nations roughly tripled over this period due to increased population and rising affluence.

Furthermore, the basis for allocation of the resources available for American food assistance was becoming increasingly dominated by the use of food aid to support specific short-term foreign policy objectives defined by the Department of State, further limiting the food available for distribution to meet strictly humanitarian requirements.

Finally, the probability of food shortfalls at some future point in developing nations, of a magnitude beyond the capabilities of the donor or recipient nation to either physically or financially provide for, led to greater attention to the problem of increasing food production in the developing world. Yet there is little evidence that the additional resources made available to the recipient government through highly concessional sales of agricultural commodities have resulted in more effective food production policies or contributed to increased assistance to indigenous agricultural production.

An awareness of future threats to food security in the developing world, the dwindling volume of American foreign food assistance, and the allocation of available food aid resources, on what might be termed "political" grounds, led to increased attention both by the public and the Congress to Public Law 480, the legislation under which American foreign food assistance programs are authorized.

A RATIONALE FOR FOOD AID

The near- and intermediate-term "world food problem" is primarily a problem of distribution rather than supply. Assuming trend-line growth in production and demand, supply and demand for food grains worldwide should retain a rough balance, at least until the last decade of this century. However, the problem of assuring food availability to those in need is likely to intensify in the years ahead. The documentation of the world food problem prepared for the recent World Food Conference suggested that the current cereal deficit of the food-importing market-economy-developing countries will grow from the present level of 40 to 50 million metric tons to 100 to 120 million metric tons by 1985.

Simplistically stated, there will always be available supplies for those able to pay the price. However, the cost of such transfers of food will most heavily burden developing countries, most of which have recently experienced an abrupt and significant deterioration in their terms of trade over the past 2 years. Therefore, the problem of food deficits in developing nations must be addressed in a combination of the following ways:

1. Increased indigenous production to replace potential import requirements
2. Improved terms of trade with the food exporters and larger real export earnings
3. Greater share of food imports provided on a grant basis or under highly concessional financing

The macroeconomic problem of food distribution is replicated in the internal distribution of food within developing nations. The market food ration system leads to great inequities in the distribution of available food supplies within those nations. This is particularly acute for the urban poor and rural landless and unemployed, who have insufficient resources to provide adequate subsistence, either from what food they might produce directly or from their competition for available supplies on the market.

One strategy which governments have pursued in alleviating the inequities of the market food ration system has been to establish a "dual marketing" system for food. Under such a system a portion of domestic production is purchased by the government and redistributed to low-income consumers at subsidized prices. Several problems have been chronic with such a strategy. The first problem has been the difficulty in administering such a system in the face of scarce food resources and a propensity for political manipulation. Most frequently the subsidized food ration system has reached only a limited portion of the indigent population. Governments have found the costs of subsidization a heavy burden on their budget and, to the extent this burden is shifted to the producer by mandatory government purchase prices, below the "free" market rates, tremendous difficulty has been encountered in attempts to obtain the government share of a producer's output. Producers, lured by economic advantage, rather have channeled supplies, insofar as possible, into the "free" market. The mandatory government allotment of an individual's production becomes, then, a form of taxation which, in practice, results in a progressive burden on the smaller farmer. To the extent to which subsidization policies result in real or perceived loss of income on the part of the producer, either through inequities of the system or a large share of the subsidized market being supplied through concessional imports, the incentive for food production may be significantly reduced. Finally, even subsidized food prices require at least some resources for exchange, which may be essentially unavailable to the very poor.

An argument for food assistance emerges then from these inequities of the market mechanism in the distribution of available supplies. While recognizing the requirements for attention to raising the level of income and therefore the ability of the individual and nation to participate in domestic and international markets, respectively, and the urgent need to increase indigenous food production, the short and intermediate problem of food distribution must largely be met through extramarket and concessional market channels. On an international level, this means that countries with "surplus" food and financial resources must be able to provide or finance the transfer of agricultural commodities on a concessional basis. This also means the creation of nonmarket food delivery systems for distributing food supplies to those individuals without appropriate access to internal developing country markets.

The longer-term solution to the food problem is increased indigenous food production and greater economic opportunity for the poor and unemployed. This requires greater development of internal resources, but this, in turn, will require a greater transfer of external productive resources.

By virtue of its extraordinary wealth, the United States is in a unique position to provide these resources to the developing world. And since the U.S. is the world's most important producer of food commodities, it makes sense for it to transfer a substantial portion of these resources in the form of food either directly through grants of food or by extending concessional credit arrangements to purchase U.S. agricultural commodities.

Almost a third of U.S. food production is in excess of domestic requirements. Since food represents one of the most basic necessities of life, its real value is enormous to the hungry in a food deficit society. The transfer of food resources from a food surplus to a food deficit nation, this in the most simple economic terms, is a highly efficient resource transfer insofar as the transfer costs are small in relation to the cost of the commodity involved. It is not surprising, then, that U.S. foreign assistance has been dominated by food aid over the last 20 years.

A HISTORICAL CONTEXT FOR AMERICAN FOREIGN FOOD ASSISTANCE POLICY

Current foreign food assistance legislation was formulated in the early 1950s during a period of chronic and burdensome farm surpluses.

Under programs to support domestic farm prices, the federal government was mandated to purchase agricultural commodities to relieve glutted commodity markets. The rather sizable commodity stocks which the federal government accumulated, as a result of such price support operations, led to criticism from farmers, whose fear that the government might release such stocks depressed market prices, and from taxpayers, who viewed the costs of holding the stocks as an unnecessary public expense. The distribution of surplus farm commodities to needy nations abroad was viewed as a unique way to relieve domestic farm surplus and reduce the cost of government-held inventories. It was also intended that grants and concessional financing could be used to develop new commercial markets abroad for our farm exports.

Public Law 480 consists of two operational titles. Title I is the authority to enter into sales to developing countries of American farm commodities under long-term low interest credit arrangements. Title II provides authority to the federal government to make food commodities available for distribution through nonprofit voluntary agencies, the World Food Program, and, to a much lesser extent, foreign governments.

Since Title II grants are distributed through networks largely designed to meet the nutritional needs of individuals with limited or no access to commercial markets, this part of Public Law 480, which represents a third to a quarter of the resources made available under this program, has been viewed almost exclusively as a vehicle for humanitarian assistance. The purposes of Title I, on the other hand, are not as clear. In addition to meeting humanitarian food requirements and helping to remove farm surpluses, Title I concessional financing is viewed as a means of developing foreign markets for American agricultural commodities and of complementing the foreign policy objectives of the United States.

The net effect of extending Title I financing to a developing nation is to provide revenue to the recipient government, increase the domestic availability of food, and relieve the drain of foreign exchange which would be required in the absence of concessional credit arrangements to finance imports. The terms of Title I financing are at 2% to 3% interest for 20 to 40 years (the 40-year loans incorporating a 10-year grace period). Frequently, but not always, recipient governments must make an initial payment.

The concessionality of such terms discounted at a rate of 10%, the cost of capital normally assumed by the U.S. Treasury Department in relation to such uses, results in a grant element greater than two-thirds of the face value of the loan. When a recipient government is extended this highly concessional financing, with which it purchases U.S. agricultural commodities which in turn are sold on the domestic markets of the recipient country, the proceeds of this sale become support.

In the 1960s, within a context of domestic economic expansion and modestly declining farm surpluses, Public Law 480 became an increasingly important component of the United States programs of development assistance to the underdeveloped nations of the world. Extensive use was made of the provisions of the act which permit the United States to accept the foreign currency of a recipient country in payment on the loan obligation, which then could be loaned or granted back to the participating country to be used for economic development and social welfare programs.

However, the United States began to accumulate sizable foreign currency accounts under this procedure, which were unlikely to be distributed without significant inflationary impact on the economies of several nations. As a result, the "foreign currency" provisions were severely restricted during the late 1960s. And presently, foreign currencies are accepted as Title I loan repayment only to the extent that they can be used for U.S. government expenses incurred in that country. The additional resources for development and social welfare represented by these grants and loans were thereby reduced and with them the developmental impact of Public Law 480.

While Public Law 480 clearly mandated the use of food aid to strengthen our relations with friendly nations, until the early 1970s the use of the program as an adjunct to specific foreign policy objectives had been less overt. Occasional exceptions, such as President Johnson's direct role in Title I sales to India in the mid-1960s, had involved the allocation of food aid as a means of influencing certain actions of a developing nation's government, but it was not until the volume of agricultural commodities available for distribution was severely constricted in fiscal year 1974 that the allocation of food assistance for foreign policy and strictly humanitarian assistance came into readily apparent conflict with each other.

Notably, the market development uses of Public Law 480 generally were not in competition with the humanitarian uses of the program for available commodity supplies, since when commodity availability is tight, the need for encouragement of exports is minimized.

As food aid became a legitimate form of development assistance, the Department of State's interest in P.L. 480 grew noticeably, particularly as other funds available to the Department for foreign economic and military aid declined.

The Department of State gained primary control over the allocation priorities of P.L. 480 in the early 1970s. As the Congress placed increased limitations on military and economic assistance to Southeast Asia, foreign policy strategists began to view P.L. 480 as a resource transfer to replace the other forms of aid restricted by the Congress.

During fiscal year 1974, over 66% of Title I commodities, or almost half of the commodities shipped under P.L. 480, went to Cambodia and South Vietnam. Essentially all of the Title I loan obligation was granted back to these recipients to make available resources for internal security and paramilitary supports. Such procedures led to the Congressional restrictions on Title I sales in the Foreign Assistance Act of 1973.

The predominance of foreign policy concerns was again reflected in the P.L. 480 Title I allocations for fiscal year 1975. During the first 6 months of fiscal year 1975, 30% of the total value was proposed for Cambodia and South Vietnam, 19% for the adversaries of the Middle East, and 15% for Chile and Korea.

As the World Food Conference approached in the fall of 1974, the debate over U.S. foreign food assistance policies intensified. Congressional leaders took an active interest in the United States position on food aid at the conference. But budgetary caution led to a decision of the Ford administration to refrain from new commitments to increase American food aid flows despite the possibility that such an announcement might have led other present and potential donors into new commitments to increase their participation in food assistance or the financing of food assistance. At the conference itself, Congressional advisers to the U.S. delegation, with the initial support of the Secretary of Agriculture, unsuccessfully called for a reconsideration of the United States position, and specifically suggested that the United States offer a commitment to increase present levels of food aid by 1 million metric tons.

Disappointed by the failure of the United States to increase food aid shipments, several members of Congress began to explore ways to direct a larger share of existing levels of food aid to the neediest nations. Senator Hubert Humphrey offered an amendment to the Foreign Assistance Act of 1974, which directed that during the fiscal year 1975 not less than 70% of the concessional sales program be allocated to those countries which were determined to be "most seriously affected" by the current economic crisis, a United Nations determination based upon a per capita gross national product and balance-of-payments difficulties. This amendment was subsequently adopted by both Houses of Congress and signed into law.

THE FORMULATION OF LEGISLATION TO RESTRUCTURE PUBLIC LAW 480

While the allocation formula provided for under the Foreign Assistance Act of 1974 went far to reorient U.S. foreign food assistance policy, its direct impact extended only through one fiscal year. Shortly after the enactment of this provision, interested members of Congress began looking at more basic structural reform of foreign food assistance legislation.

Early in 1975 Senator Humphrey directed the staff of the Committee on Agriculture and Forestry to begin a comprehensive review of several years of hearings and the current operations of the programs conducted under Public Law 480. This review, which comprised field inspections as well as extensive consultation with several panels of experts, suggested that effective food aid legislation should provide for four basic objectives: (1) the clarification of program objectives and priorities, (2) supply continuity to ongoing programs utilizing Title II commodities, (3) a strengthened relationship between food aid and agricultural development, and (4) an improved mechanism for disaster relief.

On the basis of this review, Senator Humphrey in May 1975 introduced a bill, S. 1654, which provided for the most comprehensive restructuring of Public Law 480 since 1966. Many of the proposals contained in S. 1654 were subsequently incorporated in Title II of the International Development and Food Assistance Act of 1975.

Until the recent tight supply situation, there did not seem to be significant competition between the four traditional objectives of the earlier program: (1) surplus disposal, (2) market development, (3) complement to foreign policy, and (4) humanitarian assistance. However, over the past several years there has been considerable conflict over whether priority should be given to humanitarian food assistance or to foreign policy uses of available P.L. 480 commodities.

As has been mentioned earlier, over 66% of Title I commodities, or almost half of the commodities shipped under P.L. 480, went to Cambodia and South Vietnam during fiscal year 1974. Had not the 30% limitations on the political uses of food aid been enacted, the administration was planning to ship up to two-thirds of the program to countries of Southeast Asia, countries in the Middle East, or other countries such as Chile with which the Department of State had made special foreign policy commitments. While each of these nations represented humanitarian needs to some degree, the issue which was at controversy was whether humanitarian need should be a secondary criterion to strategic foreign policy uses and the concentration of concessional food assistance in only a few such nations.

Significantly, humanitarian food assistance does not seem to conflict with the surplus disposal and market development objectives of the program. It is generally the case that when supplies are tight, humanitarian need is the greatest and market development-surplus disposal requirements the least, and vice versa. To deal with the conflict between humanitarian and foreign policy uses, the proposed legislation would modify the statement of policy to ensure that the foreign policy uses of P.L. 480 are not inconsistent with the humanitarian objectives of the act.

Also, proposed amendments to Title IV of Public Law 480 would provide for a minimum volume commitment to humanitarian programs and an ordering of priorities in the distribution of food supplies available for distribution under the act. Public Law 480 commodities would be allocated first for disaster relief, then for established Title II programs, then for agricultural assistance programs under Title III, and finally for market development, foreign policy use under Title I.

Such a reordering of priorities would in no way deny the utility of any of the original objectives, but simply establish a mechanism to adjust the distribution of agricultural commodities on the basis of general commodity availability and current needs. While it is recognized that criteria cannot be rigorously assigned under each such purpose, the balance of and, wherever possible, complementarity of objectives will enjoy significant improvement if the allocation process encompasses first a global assessment of humanitarian need, domestic commodity availability, potential for commercial markets for U.S. agricultural commodities, and long-term as well as short-term foreign policy interests of the United States. Each allocation then can be weighed by such criteria.

One of the premises in the construction of S. 1654 is that multiplicity of objectives is one of the most important strengths of the program. The multiple objectives and accompanying multiple constituencies provide a much broader base of support than other foreign assistance programs provide. To undermine this would be to severely weaken P.L. 480 and leave it much more vulnerable to the budget-cutting process. Therefore, S. 1654 attempts to prevent conflicts between objectives with the smallest possible disruption in slated program purposes.

The fluctuations in commodities available for shipment under P.L. 480 have a very disruptive impact on the long-term benefits of food aid. Food shipments have varied from an average of 9 million metric tons annually during the period 1969–72, to 3.3 million metric tons in fiscal year 1974, to 5.5 million metric tons in fiscal year 1975. Uncertain supply conditions make long-term program planning and coordination with programs' agency staffs, the local counterpart agencies' personnel, the host country government, local volunteers, and food recipients difficult or impossible.

This fluctuating supply level is particularly disruptive for Title II, under which distributing agencies have considerable capital resources and personnel committed to the delivery of Title II commodities and programs. Since Title I is primarily an export-financing program, it has been argued that it, rather than regular ongoing program operations under Title II, should absorb the precipitous changes in total commodity availability under P.L. 480.

The major factor affecting the volume of shipments under Public Law 480 has been commodity prices. The level of funding for Public Law 480 has remained at about $1 billion annually over the past 6 years. Therefore, as the average price of commodities rises, the absolute volume of shipments is decreased.

In view of the likely increases in relevant farm support prices above those authorized by the Agriculture and Consumer Protection Act of 1973, necessitated by substantial increases in production costs, the average cost of shipment of a given unit volume of commodities under P.L. 480 can be expected to be substantially above the average over the past 10 years.

The average price per ton of all shipments from 1968 to 1972 was about $110. In fiscal year 1973 it rose to $130 and in fiscal year 1974 to $290. While commodity prices have declined from their 1973 peaks, it is not likely that they will fall to those characteristic of the period 1968–72. Assuming that the Congress is not going to substantially increase the funds available for P.L. 480, we can expect total average annual shipments of from about 6½ to 8 million tons in the coming years.

However, consumption has steadily expanded without a relative expansion of world cereal stocks to buffer production shortfalls. In the absence of commitments to build and maintain reserves capable of moderating the potentially larger fluctuations in world trade, it is increasingly likely that prices may again reach the highs experienced in 1973-75.

Recognizing the need for a minimum commitment to foreign food assistance in times of tight supply but also a strong opposition within the Congress to variable cost commitments, 4.2 million metric tons was selected as a fiscally defensible but reasonably appropriate combined minimum for P.L. 480 Title I and Title II food assistance for humanitarian purposes under the Humphrey proposals. In the consideration of a minimum volume of food assistance, recognition was also given to the opposite problem of using food aid as a mechanism to dampen our agricultural surplus, regardless of the impact on agricultural production in the recipient countries.

Certainly, each developing nation has a finite capacity to absorb concessional and grant food assistance, the primary limitations being the physical capabilities of the port and marketing facilities of the recipient nation and the distribution capabilities of cooperating sponsors of Title II programs. Furthermore, the experience in the operation of P.L. 480 over the past 20 years brings into question the judiciousness of a food aid program based primarily upon moving a maximum volume of food commodities through concessional channels. Rather, experience has suggested that the needs, distributive capabilities, and impact on indigenous production capabilities of the recipient country should be taken into account in determining the proper volume of food aid for a particular circumstance.

There is evidence that our food assistance in some countries may be leading to a form of dependence which relieves the recipient government of normal pressures to direct more resources to increasing its own food production. This is not to disagree with the valid and immediate humanitarian food needs. However, to the extent that a developing country government can count upon a substantial share of its food import requirements being covered through food aid from year to year, the recipient government may be relieved of internal pressures to give more attention to increasing its own agricultural production. By a careful assessment for each potential recipient of what might be a reasonable share of the food input needs which might be met through food assistance, the negotiation of meaningful commitments from the recipient governments to afford greater attention to the development of indigenous agricultural capabilities can reduce the chances that food aid might become a disincentive to efforts by the developing country to increase food production.

Reflecting the priority coming out of the World Food Conference to mobilize resources for assisting the developing world to increase its own food production, an entirely new program was proposed under P.L. 480 to provide for a transfer of highly concessional sales of food commodities which then would be sold by the recipient country governments to generate funds for agricultural development.

Presently, under Title I, the recipient government sells commodities which it has received on a highly concessional basis on its domestic market. The net proceeds which accrue to the recipient government represent a form of budget support. Since the overall effect of Title I financing is to make available additional resources to the government, S. 1654 would create an incentive for the recipient government to use those additional resources for development purposes.

While concessional loans under Title I would still remain available but under somewhat less favorable credit terms, countries taking steps to use resources made available under P.L. 480 to develop their agricultural sector would be eligible under a new Title III for the very concessional terms similar to those presently provided for under development loans of other foreign assistance programs.

Countries choosing to participate in an agricultural assistance program would develop a multiyear agricultural development plan providing for the specific use of proceeds from sales of P.L. 480 commodities. The United States government would assure these countries a stable volume of food commodities over the agreement period and would credit specific uses of the proceeds for agricultural development against the loan repayment. There would be specific safeguards against the accumulation of large currency balances and comprehensive reporting requirements.

It is the intent that such an arrangement be applied with caution and a high degree of selectivity. Such a program would not replace food assistance through the present arrangements, but would represent an option exercisable upon the mutual agreement of the United States and the developing country government. In most cases the food assistance provided under the agricultural development option might represent only a modest portion of total food assistance. The effective application of this alternative will certainly require much more active services, and the extension of such agreements in the future would be heavily based upon prior performance under this arrangement.

Past efforts to strengthen the self-help dimension within P.L. 480 have been largely ineffective. Self-help provisions are routinely written into Title I agreements with little monitoring of their actual implementation or integration of such self-help measures into a comprehensive development plan. The intent of such a new procedure is to provide a way of encouraging greater attention to agricultural development and to the integration of resources available for such development into a medium-to-long-term development strategy.

With respect to the appropriate limit of national sovereignty, S. 1654 is premised upon the belief that if the United States is going to extend highly concessional financing of agricultural exports, our government has a responsibility to ensure that the resources made available to the recipient nation are used efficiently and in such a way as to improve the welfare of the underprivileged in that country.

The specific planning and budgeting requirements provided for under S. 1654 would encourage more active attention and a greater sense of accountability on the part of recipient country governments in the use of concessional resources provided through Public Law 480 for social development purposes than are currently being exercised under the self-help provisions of Title I.

The new procedure proposed under S. 1654 would extend the humanitarian benefits of the U.S. foreign food assistance programs by supplementing the resources available to developing countries for economic development, and particularly for alleviating the longer-term problems of food availability through efforts to increase indigenous production.

A major problem impairing the long-term benefits of food assistance is the disruptive drain of food commodities from ongoing program efforts in order to meet emergency and disaster relief needs. Not only do such emergency needs require reallocation of resources within the country struck with a disaster, but it also requires the United States to reallocate supplies between nations to meet the food emergency.

Often when massive emergencies strike, a large portion of the supplies available for food assistance may have already been allocated. A more orderly and effective means of meeting such emergencies would be to have in place a logistical scheme for distributing food relief, and contingency reserves from which to draw to meet such needs without draining away commodities servicing ongoing programs or forcing a time-consuming and politically sensitive debate on whether to increase food aid to meet needs created by unforeseen disasters at a time when such an increase might strain supplies or inflate commodity prices at home.

Two approaches to deal with this problem were explored in the formulation of S. 1654. The first approach would be to establish what might be termed a "static commodity reserve." Under such a system commodities would be purchased and held by the Commodity Credit Corporation for dispersal in the case of disasters and other emergencies. Since such commodities would be released through extramarket channels, the effective insulations would be essentially complete. However, the costs of storage and the flexibility in meeting disasters anywhere throughout the world in a timely manner pose serious disadvantages to such an approach.

In order to meet such deficiencies, the present draft form of a revised version of S. 1654 would establish a "dynamic" emergency and disaster relief reserve. This system would require essentially no government-held inventories. Rather, a policy would be established whereby normal Title II programs would maintain a 3-month inventory of commodities. In this way, in-country supplies or supplies in transit could be drawn from the "pipeline" without disrupting normal program operations. In fact, until recently 3-months-forward programming had been maintained as normal administrative policy, this period having been found to represent both a reasonable time and volume to cover contingencies affecting Title II programs. Such a volume would represent a quarter of Title II programming and as such should cover most immediate relief needs as historically provided for through Title II. Since this "reserve" would be spread throughout the world, it could be drawn upon to meet emergency needs on a regional basis, thereby providing flexibility and timeliness in the delivery of relief.

It should be noted that the "reserve" discussed above is designed to meet only immediate food relief requirements necessitated by an emergency or natural disaster. The much larger and longer-term requirements resulting from crop shortfalls could be provided for by physically held cereal stocks, which could significantly reduce the burden upon developing nations to meet food import requirements resulting from periodic production shortfalls.

It has been suggested that reserves to cover the exceptional food import requirements of developing countries should be in the form of a cash fund which would be used to purchase cereals from world markets.[1] The basic problem with such an approach, however, is the increased premium which would be encumbered to cover a given level of risk under this arrangement. Crop shortfalls tend to affect major regions of the developing world, particularly South and Southeast Asia. The demand on world markets for covering such shortfalls can have a significant inflationary impact on world commodity prices. If, as has been the case in more recent years, crop shortfalls in developing nations coincide with shortfalls in other major producing areas, high commodity prices and the resultant increase in the costs of covering a given volume of food import needs become even more significant.

Assuming storage and interest costs do not exceed the premium which would be paid to purchase stocks in years of tight supply and high prices, as opposed to accumulating stocks in years of normal supply, a significantly greater crop shortfall insurance can be purchased with a given amount of money. Furthermore, physically held stocks would provide a measure of stability in world cereal markets. Domestic consumers, including livestock feeders, would not be forced to bid against the purchases for meeting the food import requirements of developing nations under a scheme where physical stocks are held. In years of abundant supply, purchases of such stocks would benefit cereal producers by adding strength to weak cereal markets.

Several key features of S. 1654 were incorporated into the International Development and Food Assistance Act of 1975, the bill to authorize and extend foreign assistance programs. Title II of the 1975 foreign aid legislation expanded the statement of policy within Public Law 480 by clarifying the humanitarian intent of the program. The allocation formula provided for under the 1974 foreign assistance legislation was extended in somewhat modified form, providing that no more than 25% of P.L. 480 Title I loans may be allocated to other than the neediest nations. A minimum volume of grant food aid was established at 1.3 million metric tons to assure supply continuity to ongoing programs.

Finally, the rudimentary authority was provided to establish an agricultural assistance program similar to that embodied in Title III of S. 1654. This latter authority, which has been termed the "grant back" or "forgiveness" provision, differs from Senator Humphrey's original proposal in the breadth of discretion left to the administering agency in the establishment and operation of the procedure.

S. 1654 provides that the development uses of Title I sales proceeds be credited against loan repayment only as a part of an explicit and comprehensive agreement which would be worked out in advance of the Title I sales agreement. Furthermore, S. 1654 requires the participating country to be responsible for specific accounting of the proper implementation of this arrangement. The analogous provisions of the 1975 Foreign Assistance Act, in contrast, provide broad authority for the President to "forgive" loan repayment if a country agrees to use the loan proceeds for agricultural development.

The amendments contained in the Foreign Assistance Act of 1975 represent the most comprehensive changes in Public Law 480 since 1966. Yet many of the original proposals in S. 1654 were not addressed in this legislation or were only provided for in their most basic form. Currently S. 1654 is being revised to reflect the changes which were accomplished in the Foreign Assistance Act. However, having just completed legislation to amend P.L. 480 and with the basic legislative authority for food assistance coming up in 1977 for renewal, it is unlikely that additional legislation to amend P.L. 480 will be enacted in this session of Congress. Senator Humphrey, Senator Clark, and other members of Congress who have provided leadership in the revision of food assistance legislation have made clear their intention to continue to study ways to strengthen and improve the Food for Peace Program and to closely monitor the provisions which were recently enacted. In any case, it appears clear that these recent amendments to P.L. 480 were only a beginning and that the process of devising and defining a food assistance mandate appropriate to the needs worldwide and our own ability to respond to them will continue in the years ahead.

NOTE

1. See the chapter by C. William Swank, especially pp. 193-194.

13 Individual needs: nutritional guidelines for policy?

Linda Haverberg

INTRODUCTION

While supply and demand projections for food grains are useful for U.S. agricultural production planning, balance of payments, international trade, and as indicators of potential food deficit and surplus areas, such macro-level information does not provide an accurate picture of world nutritional needs. Aggregate figures of supply and demand tend to overlook the groups with low effective demand, namely the poor, who are the malnourished in developing countries. Focusing on the national level may miss the specific nutrient needs of and the effects of food policy on the nutritionally vulnerable members of a population. In order adequately to address the food and nutrition problems of subgroups or individuals in a population, such factors as food quality, food distribution, and food availability based on purchasing power must be assessed at the micro-level in terms of individual nutrient needs. Thus, besides economics and statistics, nutritional considerations should enter into the formulation of both U.S. food policy and the food policy of governments in developing countries if world malnutrition problems are to be attacked.

This chapter evaluates the potential role of nutritional criteria in establishing guidelines for food and nutrition policy and in assessing possible alternative strategies to meet the nutritional and health needs of populations in developing countries. The discussion focuses on the nature and magnitude of nutrition problems in developing countries with particular reference to several factors unique to the developing world and emphasizes the need to specifically address these problem areas in the formulation of policy. Both the limitations and practical applications of nutritional standards as tools for assessing the problem and implementing programs are examined. The conclusion reached is that specific nutrition and health objectives should be incorporated into food and nutrition policy as part of an overall scheme of development planning. The moral implications of nutrition policy are also evaluated. While nutritional and moral considerations converge, their significance in policy decisions must unfortunately be determined by political and economic concerns.

THE MALNUTRITION PROBLEM

The term "malnutrition" has been used to describe various conditions. (a) *Starvation* implies almost total lack of food and therefore rapid development of severe undernutrition, marasmus or inanition. (b) *Undernutrition* results from the intake of an inadequate amount of food over an extended period of time and in its severe form is defined as marasmus and inanition. (c) *Specific deficiency* results from relative or absolute lack of a single nutrient. (d) *Imbalance* refers to a disproportion among essential nutrients that has pathological consequences. (e) *Overnutrition* results from the consumption of an excessive amount of food over an extended period of time.[1] All these forms of malnutrition, including overnutrition, exist to different degrees in the developing world. While the first four are generally due to poverty and ignorance, the last is associated with affluence and failure to accept or apply nutrition knowledge.

In *Assessment of the World Food Situation,* prepared for the World Food Conference, it is estimated that 94% of the people in the world who receive inadequate calories and protein live in developing countries. Conservative estimates indicate that 61 out of 97 developing countries had a deficit in food energy supplies in 1970. Approximately 460 million people in the developing world are said to suffer from malnutrition, and this figure excludes the centrally planned Asian economies for which insufficient information is available.[2] The incidence of malnutrition is not evenly distributed among developing countries or throughout the population of a country. Whether viewed by countries or families, however, nutritional deficiencies are concentrated at the lower end of the income scale.

Whole-country estimates mask significant differences in the nutritional status of the population within countries. For example, the World Food Conference *Assessment* states, "In such widely dispersed countries as Brazil, India and Tunisia, the 20 percent of the population with lowest income has *half* the per capita energy intake of the top 10 percent."[3] Thus the extent of malnutrition of these population subgroups is much greater than would be predicted from national averages for the countries. The per capita protein consumption for Sweden and Chile in the 1960s was the same, and yet the former represented one of the best-fed populations in the world, while the latter had one of the highest rates of infantile marasmus. In general, the urban poor suffer more than the rural poor, since most of the latter produce at least some food.

Pregnant and nursing women and infants and preschool children constitute the most vulnerable groups in populations. Their nutritional needs are greater than or different in quality from those of the general population, and they often if not always suffer most severely in times of food shortage. It is these groups who do not have their nutritional needs met when large shipments of wheat or rice are sent to developing countries, primarily because of distribution problems and lack of basic nutrition knowledge. One such distribution problem is that of reaching those in need with an inefficient or nonexistent distribution infrastructure; this can take the form of poor roads, lack of transport vehicles, or, in a different vein, the existence of an urban market economy which is inaccessible to the rural poor. More significant is the problem of unequal distribution of food due to differences in income or purchasing power of different socioeconomic groups. Equally important is the problem of intrafamily distribution where young children and pregnant/nursing women receive lowest priority in the distribution of available food; traditional beliefs and social customs combined with lack of basic nutrition knowledge are responsible for this problem. Whereas regional distribution problems can be addressed by building roads and purchasing vehicles, the inequitable distribution problems between socioeconomic classes and within families require major socioeconomic changes such as an increase in purchasing power and a change in attitudes, social customs, and traditions, respectively.

Pregnant and nursing women require an intake of nutrients considerably in excess of their normal diets in order to satisfy the additional physiological demands of their condition. In addition, many of these women in developing countries must maintain their normal level of physical activity in and around the home; their nutritional needs are thus increased over and above the physiological needs of pregnancy and lactation, which are based on estimates of Western women, who often become sedentary during pregnancy. If these women cannot increase their food intake to sufficiently cover their increased needs, not only are they left in a depleted state nutritionally, but they may be unable to provide adequately for the growing fetus or breast-fed child.

Malnourished mothers have a reduced quantity of breast milk, which, depending on the nature and extent of the malnutrition, can also be of poor quality for specific nutrients. This can have severe nutritional consequences especially in cultures where there is prolonged breast feeding without adequate supplementation of the infant's diet. Malnutrition of pregnant women can lead to low birth weights, which have been associated with increased susceptibility to infectious disease in the infant. The evidence suggests that malnutrition of pregnant women may cause impaired physical growth of the offspring *in utero*, poor nutritional status at birth, poorer growth and development in the first year of life, and thereby possible damage to mental development. This problem is severely compounded by the large number of closely spaced pregnancies, which are very common among women in developing countries.

Infants and preschool children, namely those under five years of age, comprise another nutritionally vulnerable group in developing countries, primarily because this period of life is one of rapid physical and mental growth and development when the requirement for many nutrients is substantially greater on a body-weight basis than that of adults. Many children in low-income families die before their fifth birthday, and a significant proportion of these deaths are attributable directly or indirectly to malnutrition.[4] The most severe forms of malnutrition in children are kwashiorkor, which is due primarily to a deficiency of protein relative to calories, and marasmus or partial starvation, which is especially common among young children who are weaned early; moreover, kwashiorkor is usually superimposed on some degree of marasmus. About two-thirds of the preschool children in the "Third World" are estimated to be suffering from mild and moderate forms of protein-calorie malnutrition, which are manifested as growth impairment or thinness.[5] Evidence is rapidly accumulating which indicates that severe PCM, in particular, marasmus, in early life can cause irreparable damage to both mental and physical development. While the relationship between the milder forms of malnutrition and mental development is less clear, it is apparent that the malnourished child interacts less with his social environment than does a normal child.[6]

The etiology of PCM can vary from one community to another. Its cause is due to a number of different interdependent social, biological, and environmental factors including lack of medical care, low income, unsanitary living conditions, high illiteracy rates, inadequate food intake, ignorance of basic nutrition knowledge, and inadequate distribution of the available food. Thus where massive shipments of food as well as medical supplies to a drought-stricken or famine area would probably constitute the most appropriate action to prevent large numbers of deaths, such food shipments alone will not solve the malnutrition problem in the developing world since inadequate food supply alone is not the cause.

The interaction of malnutrition and infection contributes significantly to the development of protein-calorie malnutrition. An "aggravation of disease" or synergism results from nutritional deficiencies which reduce the capacity of the host to resist the consequences of infection.[7] The presence of infection itself exacerbates an already poorly nourished individual by decreasing food intake and nutrient absorption and by increasing metabolic losses of nutrients. Malnutrition-related infections are responsible for high rates of mortality in early life; the common communicable diseases of childhood are much more severe and often fatal in malnourished children. Such children are more likely to be exposed to these infections because of unsanitary environments and poor personal hygiene. An inter-American investigation of mortality in childhood carried out by the Pan American Health Organization in 13 Latin American countries indicated that nutritional deficiency was an associated cause of 60.9% of the deaths from infectious diseases as compared with only 32.7% of deaths from all other causes.[8]

The decline in breast feeding in the developing world has also exacerbated the malnutrition problem. The value of breast feeding lies in the nutritional content of the milk, which is often adequate as the sole source of food for an infant for the first 3 to 6 months after childbirth. Also, breast feeding represents a safeguard against infection both because the milk is uncontaminated compared with that given in a bottle and by virtue of the mother's antibodies, which are transmitted to the child in the milk.

In addition to PCM, the most prevalent world malnutrition problems are vitamin A deficiency, iron- and folate-deficiency anemias, endemic goiter, and inadequate energy or caloric intake. The "classical" deficiency diseases (pellagra, beri-beri, scurvy, and ariboflavinosis) are rarely seen today as isolated deficiencies of population groups but have been replaced by moderate and less clearly defined signs of malnutrition.[9] Vitamin A deficiency is a major cause of blindness in many countries including India, Indonesia, Bangladesh, the Philippines, northeast Brazil, and El Salvador. Iron- and folate-deficiency anemias are widespread in both developed and developing countries. In Latin American countries, between 5% and 15% of the men and 10% and 35% of the women have significant anemias, and in some communities more than 50% of the children have been classified as severely anemic.[10] In most populations, pregnant and nursing women, children 6 to 18 months of age, and adult males appear to be the most vulnerable groups. Endemic goiter due to iodine deficiency is a problem in almost every developing country and, where severe, is associated with an increased frequency of feeblemindedness, deaf-mutism, and mentally defective cretinous dwarfs. It is important to point out that both adults and children adapt to a chronic shortage of calories as well as to anemia by reducing their physical activity. Thus what might be interpreted as laziness and lack of ambition in a population is actually the result of insufficient and poor-quality diets.[11] Apathy and inactivity are also characteristic of individuals with severe protein-calorie deficiency.

The problem of caloric and protein inadequacy in the general population deserves special consideration, since this issue currently represents a controversial area in the nutrition community. In general, for populations as a whole, where per capita food intake is inadequate, caloric deficiency is a major problem. In the case of protein the problem is more complex, since both quality and quantity of the protein in food are important. In most developing countries, the primary source of calories and protein for populations is one of the cereal grains, generally wheat, rice, maize, sorghum, or millet. All of these are relatively low in protein value (approximately 7-10%), and few are nutritionally adequate in themselves for man. Almost all cereal grains are unbalanced amino acid mixtures which are deficient in one or more of the essential amino acids. This can be overcome by ingestion of appropriate mixtures of cereals and by supplementation of the diet with legumes, fruits, vegetables, and nuts, as well as modest amounts of eggs, fish, meat, or milk. The more varied a diet, the less likely a risk of specific nutrient deficiencies. In the developing world, however, diets are monotonous for low-income families, and there is little opportunity for diet enrichment.

The quantities of cereal grains eaten to meet caloric needs are so large that the protein needs of older children and adults can be largely met from this source. In most populations where the staple food is a cereal, severe protein deficiency, although rare, is hardly ever seen in the absence of energy or total food inadequacy.[12] A possible exception to this situation may be in populations that subsist on cassava, plantains, yams, or bread fruits, all foods that are extremely low in protein content. Another exception to this is infants and preschool children, whose ability to consume large quantities of food low in caloric density is limited by the size of their stomachs (bulk constraint). The high prevalence of infectious disease in this age group, which decreases food intake, exacerbates this problem. Legumes with 18% to 25% protein have been the traditional source of more concentrated protein to provide adequate nutrition for these vulnerable groups and a margin of safety in the diets of persons of all ages. Examples include the corn and bean diets of Mexico and Central America, the use of soybeans and rice in many Asian countries, and the consumption of various grams such as chickpeas and pigeon peas with wheat in India. Any drop in legume production or increase in legume prices, therefore, has serious nutritional consequences in developing countries.[13]

USE OF NUTRITIONAL STANDARDS

Given the nutritional problems of individuals and population groups in the developing world, which were discussed in the preceding section, what specific nutritional guidelines should be followed to attack these problems? Simply stated, how much of what type of food or how much of what nutrient(s) should be provided for whom? In order to answer these questions, it is necessary to identify the nature and magnitude of the nutrient deficiencies and the deficient individuals, and nutritional standards do exist for this purpose.

Dietary allowances or nutritional standards, except those for energy, have been recommendations for levels of intake of nutrients sufficiently *in excess of average* nutritional requirements to meet the physiological needs of nearly all of the population—a public health or statistical concept. They are intakes which, on the basis of the available scientific evidence and in the judgment of the committee developing them, are compatible with the maintenance of the health of most people. They are not amounts required by all individuals, and they are not recommendations for an ideal diet. They are recommendations directed toward ensuring the nutritional health of *groups* of individuals or *populations,* must therefore be high enough to meet the needs of most of those with the highest requirements, and hence must exceed the needs of most people. Thus persons consuming diets supplying less than the RDA of a given nutrient are not necessarily consuming an inadequate amount of the nutrient, since the standards are set high enough to afford a margin of safety to cover individual variation in a population. Yet the greater the proportion of individuals in a population who habitually have intakes of nutrients below the RDA, the greater is the risk that some of them will be consuming nutritionally inadequate diets. And the more the habitual intake falls below the allowance and the longer the period of low intake, the greater is the risk of deficiency.[14]

Recommended or safe practical allowances are intended to apply to healthy individuals and are largely based on studies conducted on carefully selected, healthy individuals living in temperate climates and studied in a stable, protected environment. The majority of the world's population, however, especially those in developing countries, is exposed to factors which are likely to operate in concert to increase nutrient needs. An example is acute and chronic infections, including parasitic infections, which can affect the intake, absorption, and loss of specific nutrients. In addition, there are significant nutrient losses in sweat due to high environmental temperatures often in association with moderate to heavy physical work for the populations of most developing countries. Populations of these countries are also more likely to consume diets high in phytates, oxalates, and other plant factors which reduce the absorption of various minerals. Such populations often have caloric intakes that are periodically or chronically inadequate, and this can have effects on other nutrient requirements due to the interrelationship of nutrients.[15]

The quantitative effects of the above factors on nutritional requirements have not been taken into account in the formulation of the standards.[16] The question to consider is, Are the standards thus inappropriate for use in the developing world, or are the standards suitable and applicable as guidelines until more refinements are made in their formulation and the environmental factors are quantified, or should the standards developed for healthy individuals be used while improvements are made in the environmental conditions which prevent optimum utilization of the diet?

Despite their limitations and the need for refinements in the measures,[17] nutritional standards, as they currently exist, can serve as useful *guidelines* or *goals* for population groups provided their limitations are recognized. Although our knowledge is fragmentary of the quantitative effects on physiological needs of various environmental factors which impair nutrient utilization, we do know that such factors would increase requirements. Thus, until such information is available, it should still be appropriate to use the current standards as targets or goals of feeding programs despite the fact that actual individual needs may be even higher.

Such an approach may be acceptable at the population level, since the standard used would probably meet the nutrient needs of many in the population, but it may be inappropriate at the individual level. In the latter case, nutrients in excess of those predicted by the standards may be necessary to eliminate signs and symptoms of deficiency because of factors which interfere with optimum utilization of the diet. At the population level, however, we should not arbitrarily recommend an increase in protein and energy intakes in a region over that estimated by the RDAs merely because there is a high prevalence of infection. Such a practice is costly and the benefits uncertain. Furthermore, given the prospects of a limited food supply and the likelihood of greater limitations on resource allocations in the future, such a policy is impractical. Given, then, the above gaps in knowledge in the formulation of nutritional standards and the fact that the standards are only estimates of physiological requirements, of what use are they in formulating policy to address food and nutrition problems?

As pointed out by a recent joint FAO-WHO expert group,[18] probably the most important standards for international and national planning are those for protein and energy, since the quantity, quality, and cost of food supplies are determined in large part by the need for these nutrients. These standards can be properly used in two ways: (1) to provide a standard against which an existing dietary intake of a population, as determined by survey data, can be assessed; and (2) to provide a nutritional target for improvement where a nutritional problem exists. The way the requirement standards are used should be determined by the end purpose, i.e., either as an assessment tool or a target.

A survey of the intake and requirements of households in communities or of groups of individuals of a given age-sex category can indicate nutritional risk, i.e., the probability of deficiency in the populations studied, but deficient individuals or households cannot be identified from this information alone. At the population level, the standards can be used to compare intakes of different population groups and to evaluate the mean intake of the same population with time. They can also be used to estimate the food energy and protein needs of communities and nations in order to compare food supply availability with population needs in the formulation of food balance sheets. Yet all these balances can show is whether or not a nation has enough food potentially to meet its needs, *not* who or how many may be malnourished since this depends on the nature of food distribution. Similarly, the standards can be used as a guide for planning food supplies. Clearly, in any plan to feed populations, provisions for wastage in processing, preparation, and storage, as well as food habits and inequitable distribution of the food, must be taken into account.

The most promising indicator of the extent of nutritional inadequacies in large population groupings is the deficit in caloric intake.[19] Caloric deficiency also often signals insufficient intake of specific nutrients such as proteins, minerals, and vitamins. Allowances for calories are fairly rigid, since they include no margin of safety. The energy requirement is the intake considered adequate to meet the energy needs of a healthy person of a specified age and sex. It is an average value, and thus half of the individuals will need more and half less energy than is specified. In contrast, the RDAs are intended to cover the needs of 97.5% of the population. Caloric requirements can be relatively precisely determined for populations provided information on the variables that affect requirements, such as age, sex, body weight, height, and physical activity patterns, are taken into account. Estimates of average per capita caloric intake are satisfactory indicators of the relative caloric adequacy of overall food supplies. This is because people cannot consume much more than their caloric requirements without becoming progressively obese.

Protein standards are not as meaningful indicators as calories, since protein requirements depend on many specific variables such as protein quality, health conditions, and the caloric adequacy of the diet.[20] Also, the overall per capita availability of protein cannot be used as an indicator of the extent of malnutrition in a country because individual protein intakes often exceed physiological needs by a factor of 2 or 3 if availability and purchasing power permit. Figures of overall protein consumption, therefore conceal large-scale inequities among different population groups. Thus protein availability must be substantially in excess of physiological requirements if the less privileged sectors of the population are to receive enough.[21] Similarly, other nutrients are not suitable indicators, since deficiencies of specific nutrients are more often a serious local, regional, or age-specific problem rather than a widespread phenomenon among population groupings which consume adequate caloric diets.

There are certain limitations to the use of calories as an indicator of nutritional adequacy. Countrywide data on caloric deficits *underestimate* true deficits, since they compare physiological caloric requirements with the calories supplied from the total amount of food consumed by the population. Yet it is clear from the dietary intakes of individuals in industrial nations that food is not consumed merely to meet requirements. Such a macro-level calculation takes no account of food distribution among regions and individuals and leads to the erroneous conclusion that many people are consuming food above requirements.

Whole country estimates of deficits are more appropriate indicators of the extent of malnutrition rather than estimates of food needed since they do not provide figures on the *magnitude* of the total caloric deficit. More precise estimates of caloric deficiency require the use of less aggregate data. Using caloric consumption estimates by income groups, Reutlinger and Selowsky[22] show how approximate estimates of the size of the population consuming inadequate calories and the extent of the caloric gap can be made. Yet comprehensive food consumption data by income and other groupings are available for only a few countries. Calculations of caloric deficits by income groups do not address the problem of nutrition intake *within* the family, but data on nutrient intake by age groups are extremely difficult and expensive to generate.

Approaches used to predict gross food supplies (calories) and the quality of the food supply (nutrients) must be based on different theoretical frameworks. If food availability, purchasing power, and other socioeconomic factors permit, caloric intake will be proportional to need such that the average intake of a population can be compared directly with the average requirements predicted for the population. For almost all other nutrients, there is no reason to think that intake would be proportional to requirements. Thus, in order to assess risk of deficiency for most nutrients except calories, the variability of both nutrient

Individual needs: nutritional guidelines for policy? 221

requirements and *usual* nutrient intake among individuals must be considered.[23]

Reutlinger and Selowsky's approach is an excellent example of how nutritional standards have practical application as guidelines or targets for planning total food supplies. This approach is suitable for a macro-level or population-level attack on food problems. The specific nutrient deficiencies and the special problems of vulnerable groups cited in the previous section, "The Malnutrition Problem," cannot be addressed in this way. Variations in nutrient needs for different ages and sexes even if appropriately estimated can have little importance in calculations made for feeding groups of mixed age and sex, since such calculations ignore the practical aspects of food distribution.

There are limitations in applying nutritional standards to *specific* nutrient problems, since the standards are not designed for use in appraising the nutritional status of individuals. All nutritional standards (except for calories) are well above any estimate of average requirement, and thus consumption of a nutrient below the specified levels is not evidence of malnutrition. In addition to dietary intake information, clinical, biochemical, and anthropometric measures are necessary to assess the nutritional status of individuals. Such an approach identifies who is deficient for what nutrients in relation to a set of standard measures. The next step is to determine how much of what food or nutrient should be provided.

If an attempt were made to treat all deficient individuals in a population separately, the task would be formidable and costly. In this situation, community or national programs aimed at the at-risk or deficient individuals represent a suitable alternative. Such an approach is food fortification, which in many situations represents an ideal way of meeting certain nutrient deficiencies.[24] Fortification programs will affect individuals already consuming an adequate diet, but such a blanket approach may be, in a given situation, the most feasible and economical way of meeting the nutritional requirements of the at-risk members of a population. Here nutritional standards are used to determine the amount of the nutrient which would cover the needs of nearly all members of a population.

Combating protein-calorie malnutrition in a community is a complex problem which in the long term will require more than just the provision of food. While the most severe forms of PCM, kwashiorkor and marasmus, should, if possible, be treated on an individual basis with high-protein, high-calorie-density foods, the mild to moderate forms, which constitute the majority of cases, are more difficult to treat. This is because supplementation of diets with protein and amino acid fortification of foods must depend on the measurement of the protein-deficiency problem. Whereas anemia can be diagnosed by objective measures, no such suitable device exists for determining the existence of protein deficiency and the quantitative protein needs of the individual. Thus, in the absence of clear objective signs of protein deficiency at an early stage, the question of fortification of foods or the formulation of blended products must depend significantly on standards for dietary protein requirements.

A blanket approach to this problem is not necessarily the proper strategy because it can be very expensive. Also, the range in protein requirements based on age and sex is very broad, and it is young children with continued episodes of infection who are the most vulnerable. Attempts have been made to improve the protein quality of food staples by the addition of protein concentrates or isolates or deficient amino acids. The evidence that such an increase in protein quality significantly improves the nutritional status of the vulnerable groups in the population is inconclusive. It is likely that most adults in the developing world would benefit more from increased dietary energy than from an increase in protein quality alone. Thus the provision of foods designed in recognition of the needs of specific population groups may be desirable under certain circumstances. Formulated or blended weaning foods, such as CSM (corn-soy-milk) and WSB (wheat-soy-blend), which were included in the U.S. Food for Peace Program, were developed to meet the needs of the weaning infant and preschool child, which were not being met by existing food programs. While in this case the food is targeted directly to the vulnerable groups, such a program can be beset by many difficulties.[25]

If used properly, nutritional standards can serve as *guidelines* in planning food supplies and assessing the adequacy of the diet of population groups. They can also be used in conjunction with other measures to identify the at-risk members of a population and the nature and magnitude of nutrient deficiencies. In addition, they can serve as *goals* in programs aimed at improving the nutritional status of individuals and populations. An element of judgment is involved in determining levels of nutrients or amounts of food which will meet the needs of the vulnerable groups in programs which affect many individuals. Yet the need to use a blanket approach is the consequence of the magnitude of the problem.

Individual needs often are not met because of distribution problems and individual variation in nutrient requirements due to age, sex, and environmental factors which impair nutrient utilization. Yet just as an element of judgment is needed to quantify nutrient needs, an element of judgment is needed to decide what is the best way to meet that need. This is where policy dictates program design.

NUTRITIONAL GUIDELINES FOR POLICY

Unlike famine or starvation situations, the shipment of food commodities *per se* to developing countries will not solve the malnutrition problem. In a famine, food must be provided to the affected population to avert massive starvation and death so it is a life-death issue and a logistical problem. Policy decisions would not be based on nutritional criteria, since countries cannot be classified according to different types or forms of starvation. Economic, political, and moral considerations and obligations would determine which countries received food shipments.

Individual needs: nutritional guidelines for policy? 223

The malnutrition problem is due to inadequate or poor-quality diets, so here the focus should be on improving diets by providing more or better nutrition. It is the difference between relieving hunger and raising the nutritional status of a population. Any policy aimed merely at providing food to combat malnutrition will be treating the problem as a disaster relief effort which, by its very nature, is a short-term solution to a temporary acute problem. Malnutrition is a complex chronic "environmental" problem and cannot be treated exclusively as a food problem.

Before any consideration of nutritional guidelines can be made in the formulation of food policy, including both U.S. export policy and the food policy of governments in developing countries, there must be a firm commitment by the policy decision makers to address specifically the problems of those who do not have adequate diets and who are inaccessible to the food market. Only then can food and nutrition policy be based on human need and not exclusively on balance of payments, international trade, and commodity surpluses. Only when the value of food production and food aid is estimated in terms of calories and other nutrients and not solely in cash terms will nutrition play a role in policy formation. A food policy should be based on a specific nutritional *goal* or set of *objectives* with specifications as to time frame, budget and resource allocation, and sectoral or departmental responsibility at the national level. Nutritionists can provide information on the nature, magnitude and extend of food and nutrition problems, alternative strategies to attack these problems, resource needs and financial costs, and the probability of success and come up with a set of concrete recommendations. Yet policy decisions rest with the political leaders, who must rate the problems as high- or low-priority issues.

Food needs are generally regarded as effective demand and its elasticity and are expressed on a world scale in terms of commodities.[26] Such a practice however, ignores the practical aspects of food distribution and individual differences in nutrient need. The science of nutrition has advanced sufficiently in recent years to enable nutritionists to analyze the food situation, to define "demand" more accurately, and to relate it to human nutritional needs. For example, if sufficient data are available, nutritionists can determine the magnitude of a country's caloric deficiency (even by region or income groups). With the aid of an agricultural economist, estimates can be made of the amount of grain or other foodstuffs which should be imported or planted and the costs involved in meeting the caloric needs or filling the caloric gap in the country.

Whether the information is incorporated into the agricultural production plans of the nation or whether the food is to be imported is a policy decision which will be determined by the local conditions in a country. In either case, any program adopted to increase per capita food availability should be designed with a specific goal in mind, e.g., to increase the caloric intake of a specified group by a specified number of calories. Consideration, therefore, must be given not only to the provision or production of the food but also to how it reaches the target group.

Plans to increase local or national food production or to import food should be formulated in recognition of the specific nutrient needs of the area and how these needs can best be met. For example, in agricultural production planning aimed at increased food production, consideration should be given to the *source* of calories. In most developing countries, 60% to 80% of food calories are supplied by two, three, or four staple foods which are generally cereal grains. While in theory it is possible that the remaining 20% to 40% of dietary sources of calories might be rich in other nutrients and thus ensure overall adequacy for the population, in practice this is seldom true. Often the complementary energy sources, e.g., sugar, are also low in nutrients. For this reason, the nature of staple foods usually determines the type and severity of malnutrition in a country and can even explain regional differences in the nutritional status of a population in the same country. Thus "when a very limited number of foods provides a very major proportion of the calories, the nature of these foods is of crucial importance and any policy on the staple foods must be watched not only with regard to the caloric value but also with regard to the overall nutritive value of the staples."[27]

The above concept should be incorporated into economists' models, which at present suggest an ideal diet made up of a homogeneous mixture of the dominant regional cereal (usually one variety) and one variety of soybean. According to the models, this mixture, expressed as quantifiable food tonnage, is to be fed to humans or farm animals, to travel, or to be distributed locally depending on market channels and incomes.[28] While nutritional criteria should be incorporated into food production plans, the quantitative aspect of food production (with its economic return) does not easily become a partner to the qualitative need (with its health return).[29]

For specific nutrient deficiencies, nutritionists can provide quantitative estimates of the number of individuals in a population at risk of having, e.g., vitamin A deficiency and can suggest possible programs of attack on the problem. Vitamin A deficiency can be dealt with in a variety of ways ranging from nutrition education or fortification to increased production and availability of vitamin A-rich foods.[30] Yet before any attack on the vitamin A problem can be made in a country, eradication of the disease should be a stated objective of government policy. Which method of attack is undertaken will depend on the specifications of the policy objectives, namely, to decrease the incidence of vitamin A deficiency by what amount, in how much time, and in what group of individuals. It will also depend on resource and budget constraints and on factors which may be unique to a region or country.

The basis of nutritional judgments in policy formation cannot be made on health alone. The effects of food policy decisions on other sectors must be taken into account. Just as the cause of malnutrition problems is multifactorial, any program directed at its eradication is bound to have effects on social and economic factors, and these must be recognized in program design. Nutritional factors, as well as economic, ecological, and social factors, should be considered in agriculture development planning as well as in public health improvement programs. In addition, however, any policy measures related to agricultural development or food production must be carefully assessed in relation to the effects they themselves may have on employment and hence on income distribution and purchasing power. For example, any increase in total caloric or protein supplies to meet even a generous allowance or requirement level will not solve the inequities in food distribution as long as the disparity in purchasing power is not remedied.

Inasmuch as specific nutritional deficiencies are often confined to a special and perhaps small group within the population, food and nutrition policies must often be *directed* toward the identified needs of specific groups within the community. Just as in the case of policy and programs at the national level, however, any policy measures related to the improvement of the health and nutritional status of vulnerable groups in the population or directed at the eradication of a specific nutritional problem should be designed and evaluated in recognition of the effects they may have on social, economic, and ecological factors.

There is considerable need for coordinated programs which take into account the interrelationship of health with nutritional and social factors. Programs aimed at the improvement of nutritional status and the control of infectious disease should be instituted together, since they are mutually reinforcing and more economical if provided in a coordinated manner than separately. In addition, family planning programs should be integrated with the above two objectives.[31] Where appropriate, nutrition education could be a component of an integrated program as well, e.g., in promoting breast feeding, orienting food demand, and encouraging improved utilization of food supplies and better distribution of the available foods within the family. Unless all the factors that influence or affect program objectives are taken into account in planning and program design, the development and implementation of a sound nutrition policy will be considerably limited.

Programs aimed at both long-term planning and short-term improvement should be components of any food and nutrition policy. Long-term planning should take into account both micro- and macro-level needs. Programs should be designed which include improvements in agricultural production, health and sanitation, in particular health care delivery, mass communication in terms both of roads and of information dissemination or schooling, and income distribution. Although the nutritional component or objective of such programs is not readily discernible, such program measures are necessary as the groundwork for the permanent solution of the malnutrition problem. For example, it is well recognized that income policies are crucial to raising the nutritional standards of large numbers of individuals. Yet income increments alone will not solve the problem.[32] In other words, factors which will foster economic and social development will also improve the nutritional and health status of the population and vice versa.

In addition, programs directed at short-term improvement should be incorporated into policy design and program implementation. Such programs generally focus on specific individual needs or isolated problems. For example, a policy to eradicate vitamin A deficiency could begin with a program of massive doses of vitamin A for children until fortification, nutrition education, or agricultural production programs aimed at long-term and lasting improvement are underway. Development objectives of improved health and nutritional status of the population will proceed more rapidly if efforts at both the national or population level and at the individual or community level are simultaneously made, since they can be mutually reinforcing and synergistic.

MORAL IMPLICATIONS OF NUTRITION POLICY

In addition to nutritional, health, economic, political, and social considerations, to what extent should and to what extent can moral issues be incorporated into the formulation of food and nutrition policy? Should the goal of food and nutrition policy be to provide a minimally adequate diet for all? Is there such a thing as a minimally adequate diet or an ideal diet? Is there a level of dietary intake which is necessary for optimum health and a different level (quantitatively and/or qualitatively different) which is representative of "the good life"?

In developing countries, it is known that children and adults in a population are able to adapt to a reduced level of energy and iron intake by decreasing their physical activity and possibly by lowering basal metabolic rates. Should such a diet be considered minimally adequate, or should a minimally adequate diet allow all individuals to maintain a higher level of physical activity? If the latter is the case, what should that level be?

Diet adequacy and health status are assessed by the evaluation of various measures derived from the study of individuals who are judged to be "healthy and normal." The standards are thus subjective and controversial, since they are based on a predetermined definition of health and normal activity. Individuals who represent the "ideal condition" live in environments where there are no barriers against food intake, little stress from infectious diseases or other environmental factors, and no constraints on physical activity. Should the diet which allows these individuals to maintain "normal" values for the assessment indicators be considered an ideal diet, a minimally adequate diet, or a diet which is compatible with both maximum health and "the good life"? Should the goal of nutrition policy be to provide a diet which allows individuals to be "normal" on all biochemical tests, to grow normally according to standardized growth charts, and to be free of any known clinical signs or symptoms of disease, or should the diet be something "better"?

At what point between this "nutrition and health equilibrium state" and overnutrition does an ideal diet lie? Overnutrition, with its attendant problems of obesity, atherosclerosis, diabetes, and coronary heart disease, is by definition a malnutrition problem and hence not a condition of optimum health. Should food and nutrition policy be formulated not only to assure a minimally adequate diet for all but also to prevent an overabundance of food which could lead to a malnutrition problem at the other end of the health spectrum?

The questions posed above are difficult to answer because such terms as "ideal" diet and "minimally adequate" diet depend on one's definition of health. In contrast to conditions of undernutrition and overnutrition, which are characterized by a definite set of signs, symptoms, and measures incompatible with health and well-being, the terms "minimally adequate diet" and "ideal diet" are not quantifiable. Both lie somewhere between undernutrition and overnutrition but exactly where is unclear. The goal of nutrition policy at best should be to prevent either of the two extremes of the spectrum.

Are there any moral imperatives which can establish a priority scale of nutrition problems? Is it more desirable to reduce protein-calorie malnutrition among zero- to two-year-olds, eradicate vitamin A deficiency, or eliminate nutritional deficiencies from the diets of pregnant and lactating women? There is no easy answer to this question. No single measure has been developed to assess the benefits of achieving these different objectives.[33]

Perhaps a criterion to consider here is which objective can do the most good for the most people. If such factors as time, money, resource availability, and logistics are taken into account, the choice is relatively simple. A vitamin A fortification program could be more feasible economically and could reach more people than a program designed to provide food supplements to young children or pregnant/nursing women. Yet an approach which benefits many could also do harm to others. Excessive intake of vitamin A, which is stored in the body, can have serious pathological consequences. One questions whether the criterion of benefiting the most people is morally sound for nutrition policy. A program which could reach the most people and benefit many might not be addressing the nutritional problem which is greatest in magnitude and severity in terms of long-term consequences and risk of death.[34]

Is it possible on moral grounds to establish a priority scale as to which subgroups in a population should receive additional food (calories) given a limited amount of resources and money? Should highest priority be given to the infant and preschool child who is a vulnerable target for PCM with its attendant consequences of impaired physical and mental growth and development and possibly death? Could school children benefit more from the additional food by being more alert and attentive in the classroom (and thus being able to learn skills which can be translated into efficient productivity later in life) and having fewer bouts with infection and hence less absenteeism (higher return on educational investment)?[35] Should the food be given to the pregnant/nursing woman whose own health status, which is likely to be impaired by closely spaced pregnancies, could be improved, who would be less likely to have a low-birth-weight child, whose breast-milk quantity and quality could be improved, and who would not be limited in her physical ability and therefore could provide more adequate child care? Or should male adult laborers be given additional food so that their productivity and work efficiency could be significantly increased? (This would depend on job availability and type of job.) The argument for supplementing this group is both that the country would benefit from increased work output of the labor force and that the family of the laborer would benefit from additional income or purchasing power and hence the ability to purchase more food and "better nutrition."[36]

From a nutrition and health standpoint, infants and preschool children and pregnant/nursing women are likely to benefit the most from additional food (calories). On moral grounds, the additional food could prevent irreparable or irreversible harm to health in these latter two groups. For adult laborers and school children, any damage from malnutrition has already been done during the early years of life, and it is unclear that additional food alone can reverse the physical and biochemical changes in these age groups. To decide between the two vulnerable groups raises the issue of where one intervenes in the life cycle. Should we feed today's newborns and infants who may already be permanently and irreversibly impaired physically and mentally from the consequences of PCM during the first years of life, or should we provide for next year's infants by supplementing the diets of female adolescents of reproductive age and pregnant women?

A child born of normal birth weight has a better chance of surviving the first two years of life than a child born of low birth weight.[37] This child, however, is still susceptible to PCM if there is abrupt weaning and inadequate diet supplementation and the child is born into an unsanitary environment with a high prevalence of infectious disease, both of which are likely in developing countries. In both vulnerable groups, food alone will not assure a successful outcome, since other environmental factors may cancel out the benefits of the food. It may be more compelling to prevent irreparable damage in the unborn child and reduce the risk of developing PCM during the first year of life by supplementing the pregnant mother, and thereby increasing the likelihood of a normal-birth-weight child. Yet on moral grounds, can today's newborn and infant be overlooked just because the damage *may* have already been done? Based on the scientific evidence that some of the consequences, both physical and behavioral, of PCM can be reversed with appropriate diet and treatment,[38] it is impossible to make a choice between supplementing pregnant women or infants. Ideally, nutrition policy should be formulated in recognition of the interrelationship of the needs of both groups and integrated programs which benefit both groups should be an objective of such policy.

What moral imperatives can be invoked to decide "who shall eat" where there is prolonged mass starvation in an entire country and limited food supplies within the country? This raises the whole issue of practicing triage not on a country-to-country basis, but within a country on an individual basis. One could argue on nutritional and health grounds that the adult population has more nutrient reserves (larger lean body mass, body fat cell mass) than young children and could endure without food for a longer period of time than would be true for young children, again with less or no irreparable damage. Yet political and economic motivations might argue in favor of the adult population, who are needed to plant the crops, irrigate the fields, build the roads, and provide the food for tomorrow, all of which foster development. Morally, it would seem the objective should be to prevent death and thus young children and pregnant women should receive first priority in food distribution. Just as it is unrealistic to believe that nations will "die" if policy decisions based on triage concepts are made to prevent shipments of food to an entire starving nation, one cannot think in terms of letting all young children die in order to save the adult population.[39]

In most cases, nutritional guidelines for policy clearly converge with moral imperatives. Nevertheless, it would be naive to think that moral considerations *per se* play a significant role in program design. It may not be ethical or humanitarian, but health and nutritional considerations are incorporated, if they are, into policy and program design only on the basis of economic and political motivations. While moral principles warrant attention to the needs of individuals in a population, decision makers who are formulating policy are concerned with the welfare of the nation as a whole and understandably their own welfare and viability as leaders, and they often overlook the individual needs of the people. In other words, they recognize the political and economic value of food but cannot appreciate the nutritional worth of food.

SUMMARY

Despite the limitations of nutritional standards, the state of the art of nutrition allows a better assessment of the health and nutrition situation in a country than could be worked out by economists or politicians alone. Just as the nutritional needs of some individuals are not adequately taken into account by the standards, the same may be true in the formulation of national objectives of food and nutrition policy. The nutritional concepts of vulnerable or target groups should therefore be incorporated into policy such that all programs, whether food aid or nutrition education, are *targeted* toward specific groups or nutrient deficiencies. Thus national food policy should recognize nutritional needs not only at the macro- or population level but also at the micro- or individual level, and both should be addressed simultaneously.

Nutritional guidelines should be incorporated into food policy, but there is no one set of guidelines or a blueprint which applies equally well to all countries. There is certainly no reason to establish a guideline that all governments should attack the malnutrition problem by providing diet supplements to infants and preschool children. While two countries may have similar food grain deficits in a given year from an economist's point of view, the nature, magnitude, and extent of the nutrition problems may be quite distinct due to differences in local conditions. Thus policy and program design would be different.

Nutritional considerations alone cannot determine the most appropriate strategy for attacking a nutrition problem, e.g., whether to increase food aid, fortify food, establish integrated nutrition, health, and population programs, or foster genetic breeding of crops. Nutritionists can identify the vulnerable groups in a population, the specific nutrient deficiencies of individuals and national, regional, and community groups, and suggest alternative strategies to combat these problems. In the end, however, consideration of economic social, political, and ecological factors, in particular budget, resource, and time availability and constraints, *must* play a decisive role in policy decisions and program design.

Malnutrition problems are not due to food inadequacy alone. Their solution requires dramatic changes in the economic, agricultural, social, and health sectors. Thus health and sanitation programs, income and price policies, educational programs, land reform, and programs aimed at improvements in food delivery are all programs which, if instituted in recognition of nutritional needs and the effects of such programs on all sectors, can have a positive impact on the nutritional and health status of the population. Therefore, food and nutrition policy should be integrated with development planning. And U.S. aid, whether in the form of food, money, or technical assistance, should help foster such development objectives.[40]

Finally, there is a humanitarian dimension to world food and nutrition problems, which is discussed in various chapters throughout this book. In theory, moral considerations should play a significant role in policy decisions. In practice, however, such factors *per se* are not taken into account at the national planning level. Only recently has nutrition been recognized in policy formulation in some countries. And the motivation to incorporate nutrition into policy has been primarily economic and political. The possibility that PCM could cause permanent damage to mental development also stirred some politicians to action. Nutrition cannot be sold to governments on humanitarian grounds. Since moral dicta and nutritional principles generally converge, the most that can be hoped for is that nutritional considerations will play a more dominant role in policy formulation, and thus moral issues while not explicitly addressed will be implicitly applied.

NOTES

1. N. S. Scrimshaw, C. E. Taylor, and J. E. Gordon. *Interactions of Nutrition and Infection*. Geneva: World Health Organization, 1968.

2. Food and Agriculture Organization. *Assessment of the World Food Situation, Present and Future.* World Food Conference document E/CONF. 65/3. Rome: FAO, 1974.

3. *Ibid.*

4. N. S. Scrimshaw and Moisés Béhar. Protein Malnutrition in Young Children. *Science,* 133: 2039, 1961.

5. Derrick B. Jelliffe, Patricia Jelliffe, Charlotte G. Neumann, and Aaron Ifekwunigwe. Tropical Problems in Nutrition. *Annals of Internal Medicine,* 79: 701, 1973.

6. E. Pollitt and C. Thomson. Protein-Calorie Malnutrition and Behavior: A View from Psychology. In R. Wurtman, ed. *Nutrition and the Brain.* New York: Raven Press, in preparation. (A comprehensive review of work in this area.)

7. Scrimshaw, Taylor, and Gordon, *op. cit.*

8. Ruth Rice Puffer and Carlos V. Serrano. The Role of Nutritional Deficiency in Mortality: Findings of the Inter-American Investigation of Mortality in Childhood. English edition of the *Boletin de la Oficina Sanitaria Panamericana,* VII (1):1, 1973.

9. J. M. Bengoa. The Problem of Malnutrition. *WHO Chronicle,* 28:3, 1974.

10. Dimensions and Causes of Hunger and Malnutrition. *Food and Nutrition,* I(1):23, 1975. (Extract of paper presented at the United Nations World Food Conference, 1974).

11. Nevin S. Scrimshaw. Applications of Nutritional and Food Science to Meeting World Food Needs. In *Prospects of the World Food Supply: A Symposium.* Washington: National Academy of Sciences, 1966, p. 49.

12. P. V. Sukhatme. Protein Strategy and Agricultural Development. *Indian Journal of Agricultural Economics,* 27:1, 1972.

13. Committee on World Food, Health and Population. *Population and Food: Crucial Issues.* Washington: National Academy of Sciences, 1975, p. 10.

14. Alfred E. Harper, Recommended Dietary Allowances: Are They What We Think They Are? *Journal of the American Dietetic Association,* 64 (2):151, 1974. Alfred E. Harper, Recommended Dietary Allowances (Revised–1973). *Nutrition Reviews,* 31(2):393, 1973. D. M. Hegsted, Problems in the Use and Interpretation of the Recommended Dietary Allowances. *Ecology of Food and Nutrition,* 1:255, 1972. World Health Organization. *Energy and Protein Requirements.* WHO Technical Report Series No. 522, Geneva, 1973.

15. P. O. Astrand, Nutrition and Physical Performance. In Miloslav Rechcigl, Jr., ed. *Food, Nutrition and Health: A Multidisciplinary Treatise Addressed to the Major Nutrition Problems from a World Wide Perspective.* In G. H. Bourne, ed. *World Review of Nutrition and Dietetics,* vol. 16. Basel: S. Karger, 1973, p. 59. C. Gopalan and S. G. Srikantia. Nutrition and Disease. In Miloslav Rechcigl, Jr., *op. cit.,* p. 98. C. E. Taylor and Cecile DeSweener. Nutrition and Infection. In Miloslav Rechcigl, Jr., *op. cit.,* p. 204.

16. Vernon R. Young and N. S. Scrimshaw. Human Protein and Amino Acid Metabolism and Requirements in Raltion to Protein Quality. In E. C.

Bodwell, ed. *Proteins for Human Consumption.* Westport, Conn.: AVI Publishing Corp., in press. Vernon R. Young and Nevin S. Scrimshaw, Nutritional Evaluation of Proteins and Protein Requirements. In Nevin S. Schrimshaw, Daniel I. C. Wang, and Max Milner, eds. *Protein Resources and Technology: Status and Research Needs.* AVI Publishing Co., Westport, Connecticut, in press, 1977. Vernon R. Young and Nevin S. Scrimshaw. Unsolicited draft manuscript.

17. V. R. Young and N. S. Scrimshaw, *op. cit.* Nevin S. Scrimshaw. Strengths and Weaknesses of the Committee Approach: An Analysis of Past and Present Recommended Dietary Allowances for Protein in Health and Disease. *New England Journal of Medicine,* 294(3):136, 1976. P. V. Sukhatme. The Protein Problem: Its Size and Nature. *Journal Royal Statistical Society Acta,* 137(2):166, 1974.

18. Energy and Protein Requirements: Recommendations by a Joint FAO/WHO Informal Gathering of Experts. PAG *Bulletin,* V(3):30, 1975.

19. Shlomo Reutlinger and Marcelo Selowsky. *Malnutrition and Poverty: Magnitude and Target-oriented Policies.* International Bank for Reconstruction and Development, April 1975, Washington, D.C.

20. *Ibid.*

21. World Health Organization, *op. cit.*

22. Reutlinger and Selowski, *op. cit.*

23. George H. Beaton and Lynn D. Swiss. Evaluation of the Nutritional Quality of Food Supplies: Prediction of the "Desireable" or "Safe" Protein: Calorie Ratios. *American Journal of Clinical Nutrition,* 27:485, 1974.

24. Alan Berg. *The Nutrition Factor: Its Role in National Development.* Washington: The Brookings Institution, pp. 107-118, 1973.

25. *Ibid.,* pp. 160-180.

26. See the chapter by Lyle Schertz in this volume.

27. J. M. Bengoa. Significance of Malnutrition and Priorities for Its Prevention. In Alan Berg, Nevin S. Scrimshaw, and David L. Call, eds. *Nutrition, National Development and Planning.* Cambridge, Mass.: M.I.T. Press, 1973, p. 103.

28. Johanna T. Dwyer and Jean Mayer. Beyond Economics and Nutrition: The Complex Basis of Food Policy. In Philip H. Abelson, ed. *Food: Politics, Economics, Nutrition and Research.* A special *Science* compendium. Washington: American Association for the Advancement of Science, 1975, p. 74.

29. J. M. Bengoa. Significance of Malnutrition.

30. Berg, *op. cit.*

31. Michael C. Latham. Nutrition and Infection in National Development. In Abelson, *op. cit.,* p. 69.

32. See the chapter by Lyle Schertz in this volume.

33. Peter Hakim and Giorgio Solimano. *Nutrition and National Development: Establishing the Connection.* Discussion Paper No. 5, M.I.T. International Nutrition Planning Program, M.I.T., Cambridge, Mass., July 19.

34. Compare the contrasting approaches in the chapters by Peter Singer and Thomas Nagel in this volume.

35. The nutritional and health value of additional calories for this age group is inconclusive in relation to their school performance.

36. There is no evidence to support this as the likely chain of events, especially in families most in need. Furthermore, additional calories could benefit only workers in highly labor-intensive jobs, so there is the question of whether families of urban workers, who are employed in mechanized factories or similar occupations, could benefit.

37. Moisés Béhar. The Importance of Accurate Measures of Malnutrition. In Berg, Scrimshaw, and Call, *op. cit.*, p. 147.

38. Pollitt and Thomson, *op. cit.*

39. See the chapter by Henry Shue in this volume.

40. See the chapter by John Field and Mitchel Wallerstein in this volume.

Beyond humanitarianism: a developmental perspective on American food aid

John Osgood Field & Mitchel B. Wallerstein

Of course the people were not actually starving—you can keep them from starving on mandioca, and malnutrition is much safer for the rich than starvation. Starvation makes a man desperate. Malnutrition makes him too tired to raise a fist. The Americans understand that well—the aid they give us makes just that amount of difference. Our people do not starve—they wilt.

—From the novel *The Honorary Consul*
by Graham Greene

The profound promise of our era is that for the first time we may have the technical capacity to free mankind from the scourge of hunger. Therefore ... we ... proclaim a bold objective—that within a decade no child will go to bed hungry, that no family will fear for its next day's bread, and that no human being's future and capacities will be stunted by malnutrition.

—Secretary of State Kissinger
at the World Food Conference,
Rome, November 1974

We wish to acknowledge with particular gratitude the research assistance of David F. Pyle, formerly with CARE in India and Turkey and currently a doctoral candidate in political science at M.I.T. We received helpful comments on a predraft outline of this paper from Thomas R. Saylor, Lewis Gulick, and Marion Frazao. An earlier draft elicited valuable criticism from our colleagues Philip C. Abbott, F. James Levinson, and Robert E. Stickney and from the Hon. Edwin M. Martin and Professor Kenneth L. Robinson of Cornell University. Henry Shue and Peter G. Brown have both encouraged and guided our efforts with generous attention. While thanking so many kind people, we remain solely responsible for the content of this chapter.

As recently as five years ago, the following three statements were widely believed to be true:

1. Development is essentially a process of increasing economic output. Viewed developmentally, the distribution of wealth in a society is less important than are the implications of distribution for further investments in growth.
2. Malnutrition is an indicator of underdevelopment, the solution to which ultimately lies in the process of development itself.
3. Food aid, when not linked to strategic and diplomatic purposes, is basically humanitarian. Its role in development is marginal.

In all likelihood, each of these propositions would have been accepted without serious qualm by most specialists concerned with development, nutrition, and food aid. So might a fourth proposition:

4. Except in the most tangential way, the three topics have little to do with one another, with experts in one being largely uninvolved professionally with experts in the other two.

In short, nutritionists did not concern themselves with development, developmentalists paid scant attention to nutrition, and people in the food aid business were very much more pre-occupied with issues of logistics and delivery than with nutritional impact and cost effectiveness.

Today each of these statements would engender lively controversy. There has been a coming together as well as a change in perspective. The very concept of development has been broadened to include a vast range of concerns associated with human well-being which had previously been dismissed as "welfare." In this climate, the new field of nutrition planning has emerged, focusing on malnutrition from a distinctly developmental point of view. Moreover, food aid is being scrutinized in terms of its developmental significance, particularly with regard to producing nutritional change. Malnutrition is now seen not merely as a reflection of underdevelopment but also as a barrier to development, affecting human capabilities, productivity, and even the willingness of couples to practice family planning.[2] The connecting links between food aid, malnutrition, and development are not firmly established by any means, but they are being taken seriously intellectually and they are becoming evident in the articulation of public programs.

These revisionist rumblings notwithstanding, the impression remains strong that food aid has little developmental significance, that its benefits are matched by its negative consequences, and that—at the heart of the matter—food aid is inappropriate to the fundamental food-related need of most low-income countries, which is to expand their own agricultural production in order to feed their growing populations. The type of aid most relevant to that need is technical assistance. In the opinion of many experts, food aid is at best a temporary palliative, a cushion, a "contingency" resource.[3] The real developmental work lies elsewhere.

The thesis of this essay is that food aid can make a meaningful contribution to development if it is targeted explicitly against protein-calorie malnutrition and if nutrition interventions utilizing food aid are, in turn, embedded in a multifaceted thrust against the low productivity, high fertility, and pervasive poverty of rural populations.[4] To be sure, one would not employ food aid toward the solution of most vitamin and mineral deficiencies unless these derived from an underlying condition of basic protein-calorie malnutrition. Nor is food aid automatically the best means of addressing malnutrition. It is most relevant to situations of inadequate food intake. Yet inadequate intake is not always the principal determinant of malnutrition,[5] particularly when food utilization is impaired by parasitic infection and respiratory disease. (In most low-income countries, however, problems of undernutrition reflecting inadequate intake go hand in hand with problems of morbidity; food aid is then appropriate if, by itself, insufficient.) Finally, an implicit assumption of food aid is that the food provided supplements what is normally available. This is not always the case either. Especially with regard to children, food aid may be substitutive, with less given to the benefited child from home supplies as a result.[6]

Nevertheless, food aid is—on balance—a valuable resource for impacting protein-calorie malnutrition in the vast majority of cases characterized by indigenous food scarcities and by large numbers of people lacking the purchasing power to generate effective demand for what food is available. It goes without saying that national governments bear principal responsibility for the nutritional well-being of their populations. Food aid is simply the most direct form of external assistance for meeting nutritional needs. It is potentially a driving wedge for stimulating broader changes in rural life as well.

Programming food aid for such purposes as these would constitute a significant departure from prior practice. In the past, most food aid (72%) has taken the form of Title I[7] concessionary sales to governments, with only limited follow-up concerning who gets it once transferred. In these instances American food has contributed to development indirectly by augmenting the resources available to a government, thereby enabling the government to do with the food whatever it wishes (including reexporting it).[8]

Similarly, more targeted food aid, especially the humanitarian assistance channeled through voluntary agencies under Title II, has also tended to be distributed without concern for what happens, or does not happen, as a result of it. Title II donations have gone to people in need, but the definition of need has usually been imprecise and the testing of results something of a rarity.[9] In each case, the developmental benefits of the aid have been vaguely prescribed (if prescribed at all) and casually analyzed.

Food aid can do better. Donors such as the United States Agency for

International Development (USAID) and the American voluntary agencies which distribute Title II food abroad (CARE, Catholic Relief Services, Church World Service, and many smaller organizations) have become very much more concerned about the effectiveness of food aid programs, what impact they have and what contribution to development they make, than used to be the case. At the same time, the governments of many low-income countries which receive food aid have begun to take a hard second look at their development strategies with a view to addressing the poverty and low productivity of rural areas, development's neglected country cousins during the initial enthusiasm for rapid industrialization.[10] On both sides of the aid relationship the opportunity exists to chart a new course for American food assistance, using it creatively as an instrument of change while directing it to the people in greatest need. The opportunity is to go beyond humanitarianism by making food aid a resource for rural uplift, beginning with the eradication of severe protein-calorie malnutrition and related nutritional deficiencies.

Whether or not this opportunity is seized will depend on the level of commitment made by the U.S. government to use food specifically for development. Over the years food aid has been a stepchild of large domestic surpluses which no longer exist. Moreover, there are alternative claims on exportable American food supplies.[11] Foreign sales at market prices have become critical to the U.S. balance of payments;[12] much food aid serves the strategic and diplomatic requirements of American foreign policy, quite apart from whatever else it may seek to accomplish;[13] and humanitarian relief efforts in times of acute need absorb a consequential share of the total supply.[14] At least four qualities characterize these claims: they are compelling, appropriate (that is, deserving of support), inevitable, and likely to increase the pressure on available foodstuffs in the foreseeable future.

There are also reasons why developmental objectives might be expected to fare poorly in competition with other international purposes of food aid. Thus while strategic interests, the need to woo friends and shore up accommodating leaders, and humanitarian relief all possess attractive features (they are, typically, short term, intensive, highly visible, and symbolic as well as instrumental), development is invariably longer term, complex and diffused (even technical), of low visibility, and less symbolic than instrumental. The very unspectacular nature of food for development leaves it a "back burner" enterprise, ongoing but rarely of cardinal concern.

This is not to say that developmental food aid lacks advantages when contrasted with alternative uses. Food trade, for example, is predominately with rich countries; and when food is sold to poor countries, its pricing tends to favor consumption by the wealthy few rather than by the underprivileged many. Political uses of food are irresistible; but as Congress has come to appreciate, unless checked they can overwhelm other purposes which are also deemed to be in the national interest.[15] Humanitarian food shipments are the proverbial "bottomless pit." Whatever their utility for crisis liquidation, misapplied (as in school feeding) they can be never ending because little of long-term consequence happens as a result.[16] None of these uses addresses the developmental needs of low-income countries at all adequately.

If American food is to play a useful developmental role, it will be necessary to define that role much more explicitly and precisely than has been true in the past. What is needed is little short of a developmental theory of food use: a set of reasonable expectations concerning what might be achieved and a testing out and refinement of those expectations from programmatic experience. The discussion which follows is a prologue to such a theory. It is an attempt to conceptualize the developmental significance of food aid in terms of malnutrition and rural change, after which it explores some of the policy implications of thinking about food aid in this fashion.

Throughout the 1950s and during most of the 1960s, development theory emphasized the expansion of capital stock and investment in capital goods production. Rapid industrialization was widely accepted as the most expeditious path to development for low-income countries. Billions of aid dollars were spent to promote economic growth, most of them going to the urban industrial sector of recipient countries. Agriculture was typically shortchanged, and in some cases the rural hinterlands were forgotten entirely. The so-called "early development school"[17] viewed expenditures on social programs (health, nutrition, etc.) as welfare, equating them with consumption rather than with investment. Planners at the time spoke confidently of a "trickle down" effect that would distribute the benefits of increased production.

Two evolutionary departures from this growth-oriented model of development have taken place over the past decade and a half, resulting in a significant erosion of the early consensus concerning development. One departure reflected the fact that industrialization has not proceeded as smoothly as had been anticipated under the banner of capital accumulation. The other emerged in response to the failure of development to improve the life circumstances of the great majority of people in low-income countries, most of whom have remained largely unaffected by the gains made.

As early as the latter 1950s, Theodore Schultz and others began to formulate notions of "human capital," arguing that investments in people could be just as important for development as investments in heavy goods and equipment.[18] The emphasis on productivity as the essence of development persisted, but the conception of social expenditures as legitimate developmental concerns gained widespread acceptance.[19] In a variety of issue contexts, from education to health, the idea of "bubble up"—unleashing human creativity—assumed a fashionability rivaling that of conventional "trickle down" theory. Nutrition advocates, to cite one example, sought to identify ways in which malnutrition constrains human productivity potential.[20]

More recently, the very centrality of productivity in thinking about development has come under challenge. Building on the human capital idea while departing philosophically from it, a new "modern development school"[21] has emerged proclaiming the primacy of popular well-being and the quality of life.[22] The objective of development, according to this school, is not productivity or growth *per se*. Rather it is "the sustained reduction of deprivation."[23] Enhancing productivity is not dismissed in this conception; it is reduced from an end unto itself to a possible means for achieving "the successive relaxation of systemic obstacles to the full realization of ... human potential," or—simply— "depauperization."[24] Equity and growth are not so much conflicting goals as they are alternative but compatible ways of improving the human condition, which is now the *sine qua non* of development. What is new in this perspective is not that it rejects traditional theory, but that it requires development planning "to show a direct and immediate concern for deprivation and to demonstrate the link between its reduction and increased levels of production."[25]

Complementing this incorporation of humanism into development has been a growing realization of the extent to which various components of human deprivation go together, reinforcing one another negatively and making it extremely difficult for isolated interventions against them to produce the impact desired. Malnutrition, infant mortality and rampant morbidity, illiteracy and ignorance, low productivity and marginal livelihood, large family size and unresponsiveness to family planning programs cohere so strongly that they form a veritable syndrome of poverty, cultural and structural, that is highly resistant to change. Planners have come to appreciate the synergisms involved and to perceive the need for multisectoral planning and integrated interventions.[26] If the problems are synergistic, the solutions must be as well for progress to occur.

The interest in malnutrition as a developmental problem had its origins in the concern for human productivity appended to traditional development theory. However, this interest has been sustained and broadened within the "deprivation" framework. Probably no form of human deprivation is more tragic, morally distasteful, and inhibitive of change than is pervasive, chronic malnutrition with all its side effects. Physical stunting, deteriorating health and susceptibility to disease, impaired learning and reduced capacity for work, possibly even irreversible brain damage—these are the longer-term effects of malnutrition which come into play when its most serious immediate effect—death in early childhood—is surmounted. By circumstance and by disposition, the malnourished and others comprising the peripheral poor are passive. They do not gamble with new ideas and techniques, and they do not avail themselves of new opportunities. Their conservatism is a product of their vulnerability. Development, in the form of expanding wealth, typically passes them by. People on the margins of survival are neither beneficiaries of development nor participants in the process. They live in another world.

It is possible to argue, of course, that programs to alleviate the multiple sufferings of the poor in low-income countries are not developmental programs at all, that they are little more than the familiar welfare efforts of the past wrapped in new labels, and that foreign aid designed to assist such programs—child feeding, for example—is also as humanitarian today as it was before the deprivationists were around to elevate it to the status of developmental aid. One can be quite hard-nosed in insisting that development, for it to mean anything at all, has to mean the generation of wealth first and foremost. Just as distribution is not growth, greater well-being is not development unless it can be shown to contribute to productivity.

What the "new development school" has done, essentially, is to turn this last definitional statement around. Improved productivity is not development, or at least the totality of development (it certainly is not its most important aspect), unless it contributes to greater popular well-being. China's standard of public health, possibly the highest of all underdeveloped countries, is as much development, given the situation prior to 1949, as is Japan's industrial output.[27] Reducing the incidence and severity of malnutrition in Cuba is a form of development no less worthy than India's dramatic increases in agricultural production.[28] Given the sad experience of economic stagnation in countries like Sri Lanka and Uruguay, few in the deprivation tradition would dismiss considerations of growth out of hand. Nevertheless, their emphasis is on people as against product.

The fervor of the deprivationists is fueled, moreover, by two poignant considerations: the widely recognized fact that low-income groups have benefited little, if at all, from conventional productivity-oriented development, and the growing sense that a reduction in population growth requires, as a precondition, clearly perceived opportunities for improved well-being on the part of the people involved.[29] Indeed, if the "child survival hypothesis"[30] is even partially correct, combating malnutrition becomes an important ingredient in making family planning a more acceptable and pervasive practice than it now is.[31] Seen in this light, what on the surface might appear to be welfare—providing food supplements to the children of indigent families, improving their health, and otherwise promoting their survivability—is really part and parcel of development.

The strength of the "deprivation addendum" to development theory is that it makes people the focus of development, not irrelevant bystanders or cogs in the wheel. Its weakness is that it comes very close to equating development with welfare quite apart from the resource base and productive capacity upon which welfare ultimately rests. Almost anything can be claimed as development if phrased properly. Moreover, if every contribution to well-being is a contribution to development, then even humanitarian food aid eaten by someone who needs it is a contribution to development. Humanitarian and developmental aid become indistinguishable, and the concept of development loses all meaning.[32]

In a very real sense, this stretching of the notion of development, this blurring of conceptual distinctions, has bedeviled nutrition advocates for some time. Establishing the case for investments in nutrition, or in nutrition-oriented aid, as a developmental undertaking has not been easy. As often as not, the claims have either been disputed or they have been ignored.[33] Nutrition planning remains a fledgling enterprise for this reason, while food aid addressed explicitly to malnutrition constitutes a novel conception of purpose (when famine is not involved) with considerable uncertainty as to where it fits in with broader development efforts.

What the deprivationists need to acknowledge more prominently than they have is the importance of durability. Improvements in the human condition which cannot be maintained under normal circumstances are hardly signs of development. Combating malnutrition may be a legitimate developmental concern, but enhanced nutritional status that is dependent on external charity to maintain it is not development. Eliminate the aid, and the gains will be reversed. At the very least, the reduction of deprivation has to be sustainable, and the ability to sustain it has to be indigenized.[34] For food aid to be developmental, therefore, other kinds of change—more traditional, productivity kinds of change—are necessary. In addition, the aid has to be programmed to produce change, a simple notion but one commonly forgotten in practice.

Food aid has played a somewhat more ambiguous developmental role than most other types of aid. The developmental objectives of what has traditionally been a surplus disposal program were not always clearly specified or enforced. Moreover, Title II donations were—and are still—regarded as principally humanitarian in nature, being largely utilized in child-feeding programs. Title I concessionary sales were, or so it seemed, more developmental in intent and effect, providing recipient governments with added resources, "freeing up" their foreign exchange for other types of imports, cushioning against shortfalls in domestic agricultural production, and dampening inflationary tendencies and price fluctuations triggered by local food shortages. On the other hand, food aid has also been accused of a number of negative effects: lowering the domestic price of food in recipient countries, thereby serving as a disincentive to agricultural production; shielding governments from the need to face up to hard decisions in the rural sector, particularly with regard to land reform; and accentuating urban-rural differences by enabling governments to concentrate on industrial development at the expense of agriculture.[35]

From a deprivational point of view, of course, the feeding programs made possible by Title II have a clear developmental significance above and beyond the relief they provide. Ideally at least, food-for-work schemes are the most vivid example of assisting development "from below." Unemployed and underemployed people are put to work doing all sorts of things: road construction, building irrigation facilities, undertaking soil conservation measures such as bunding and terracing, erecting schools and warehouses, digging tube wells, reforestation, rural electrification, and the like—all highly labor-intensive undertakings designed to enhance the viability and productivity of marginal rural areas and peoples.[36] Unfortunately, many food-for-work projects have been poorly planned or implemented and have yielded disappointing results. Yet when well conceived, food-for-work represents a transfer of real income to the less privileged strata of rural society (programs exist in urban slums as well but are less common), the development of needed infrastructure, and possibly the best means available of recruiting poor people into a process of change from which they themselves can benefit directly (the food and pay they receive) and indirectly (in terms of what is done to improve the local environment and economy).

Properly programmed, child feeding contributes to the reduction of deprivation and hence to development no less than food-for-work. The most obvious respect in which it does so is with regard to malnutrition. If food aid does nothing else, it should at least combat malnutrition. This is its comparative advantage vis-a-vis all other forms of assistance. Yet until quite recently most on-site and take-home feeding programs for children were not thought of as nutrition programs in any rigorous sense. Food was given, but little effort was made to allocate it to those children at greatest nutritional risk—preschoolers between the ages of 6 months and 36 months. Moreover, monitoring nutritional status among the beneficiaries of food aid was more the exception than the rule, and food shipments were rarely coupled with other interventions designed to improve the way people live. The actual results of child feeding over the years, therefore, have remained somewhat obscure.

This uncertain impact need not be the case; and under the new target-group-performance criteria adopted by USAID and the voluntary agencies in approving child-feeding programs it is not likely to be the case in the future. The cardinal virtue of food aid as a weapon against malnutrition is that it can be channeled directly to designated groups among the poor. One does not have to wait for anticipated "trickle down" effects so typical of capital grants. Although not immune to deflection, including hoarding and black market profiteering, food aid is more easily targeted, with speedier pay-off, to people in need than is true of most forms of assistance.[37]

Food aid, in sum, is double-barreled. It enables other things to happen, such as road building and school construction, thereby serving the same purpose as money, while being a valuable resource in its own right (one cannot eat money). Indeed, it is possible that the low elasticities of demand for staple nutritious foods consumed by preschool children make nutrition supplements preferable to cash grants in many instances. It would appear that small children do not benefit nutritionally from increased income nearly as much as adults do, a factor that needs to be taken into account whenever alternative forms of assistance are under review.[38]

Title II food aid, in particular, responds to a basic human need, and for this reason it is potentially a part of any serious attempt to impact the poverty syndrome. Moreover, Title II programs tend not to possess the same limitations commonly attributed to Title I. When food aid is allocated to disadvantaged strata, people typically lacking effective demand for food adequate to satisfy their needs, it neither depresses market prices nor serves as a disincentive to increased agricultural production. It does not even inflate food prices by adding demand to a largely inelastic supply. So targeted, food aid merely fills the gap between purchasing power and need. It is otherwise at least neutral in its economic implications. Similarly, far from being an invitation for governments to ignore rural development, Title II donations can be a vital component of the broader strategy to achieve major economic gains and lessen deprivation in the countryside.[39]

Nevertheless, distinguishing developmental uses of food aid from political (strategic and diplomatic) uses, on the one hand, and humanitarian uses, on the other, entails a modest amount of conceptual agility. The three are extremely difficult to disentangle, for some overlap is built into the conceptions themselves. Developmental objectives are often promoted by the U.S. for political purposes, with the choice of countries to which developmental food aid is sent conditioned by the broader concerns of American foreign policy. Similarly, insofar as developmental aid helps people in need, as Title II food shipments almost invariably do, there is an element of humanitarianism involved which can always be invoked if the developmental objectives of the aid are not realized. Both developmental and humanitarian food aid are a form of relief, and both are intended to reduce deprivation. In truth, there is no reason why all three objectives of aid cannot apply simultaneously.

Wherein, then, lies the difference? How is one to recognize food aid as developmental quite apart from whatever else it may be?

Politically inspired food aid is designed to produce an *effect*—to create good will, to help a friendly government, to secure support on some issue, to enhance American access to an international market, or whatever. Developmental food aid is designed to produce *change*—increases in capacity, productivity, opportunity, well-being, viability, and the like. Political aid seeks benefits for the donor; developmental aid, for the recipient. The success of political aid is often a matter of interpretation. The success of developmental aid is a matter of degree; the change to be encouraged can be specified and measured quite precisely.

The difference between developmental and humanitarian uses of food aid rests on what is supposed to happen as a result. Humanitarian assistance is best viewed in one of two ways. It is either a form of crisis liquidation intended to redress a particularly unfortunate situation (famine and other disasters) by helping people affected by the crisis return to the *status quo ante*. Or it is longer-term aid which is intended to be helpful and without which a marginal situation would be even worse. Humanitarian aid is essentially a holding operation. When it is not short-term relief, it has a way of becoming an ongoing, seemingly endless enterprise with little sense of what it is supposed to accomplish and with almost no effort made to test its impact. School feeding, which over the years has absorbed close to half of Title II commodity expenditures, is a classic example.

By contrast, developmental food aid is designed for specific purposes which go beyond the *status quo ante* and which do not permit the aid to become part of an unchanging environment. Unlike humanitarian donations, developmental food aid has clearly identified objectives stated in terms of the nature and magnitude of the change to be produced and how the change is to be brought about (the sequence of events and causal linkages involved).[40] The principal emphasis is on impact, not delivery. Something is supposed to happen as a result of the aid within a specified period of time and according to an explicit intervention strategy. Developmental food aid assumes statements of anticipated effect, and it further assumes a reasonably rigorous monitoring and evaluation of program operations in order to bring means and ends, approach and intended impact, into line with one another. There is no better antidote to vague assurances of intent, sloppy programming, unexpected events and influences, and the false security of "doing good" than an ongoing, well-conceived procedure for the review of program effectiveness.

Also unlike humanitarian aid, developmental aid invites, indeed it requires, measurement of its results. The question that must be asked is, "By doing what we are doing are we producing the change that we said we wanted to bring about?" The critical *assumption* of developmental aid is that if change is not occurring satisfactorily, the aid should be reprogrammed in order to improve performance or it should be terminated.[41] The *ideal* of developmental aid is that, by virtue of attaining its proclaimed objectives, it self-destructs or is redirected toward the solution of other problems.[42]

Fortunately, measurement is not a serious problem in the types of deprivation reduction for which food aid is most relevant. Assuming that malnutrition is the most immediate target of child-feeding programs, one can in fact measure changes in nutritional status quite simply to determine whether food aid is having the impact intended, and, if not, why not.[43] Similarly, if an objective of a food distribution program is to improve health status more broadly by encouraging use of existing health services, that too can be measured readily, even by paramedical personnel.[44] If food aid is made available through public works programs designed to improve the agricultural output of small farmers (as via construction of ancillary irrigation ditches) or to develop better means of marketing their crops (by paving roads), one can—in fairly standard, simple, and straightforward ways—assess whether the goals are being reached.

In short, the "how you know it's development" question is answered by the identification of purpose and by the specificity of the programming undertaken. The "how you know if development is occurring" question is answered by the measurement of change (once it is established that the change involved is legitimately developmental). Food aid is a particularly appropriate resource for assisting development when it is addressed explicitly to malnutrition. Improving the nutritional status of vulnerable groups is developmental in its own right under the reduction of deprivation concept. It is also developmental inasmuch as malnutrition functions as a constraint on other types of change (acceptance of family planning, for example), thereby diminishing the effectiveness of related governmental programs in the social sector. Moreover, when nutrition interventions are part of a more comprehensive strategy designed to energize the rural environment, reducing deprivation and enhancing productivity become reinforcing objectives with the prospect of being sustainable as well.

None of these notions is especially novel. Yet the surprising thing is how rarely food aid has actually been thought of or analyzed in this fashion. The developmental significance of most food aid in the past two decades has been vague at best, while from the standpoint of deprivation the people most in need—the bottom 20% to 40% of the income ladder and, nutritionally, preschool children and pregnant and lactating mothers—have not benefited from the food to any appreciable degree.

Happily, this legacy is now being overcome. The nutritional and agricultural activities sponsored by USAID have greatly expanded in the past 2 years, while the American voluntary agencies engaged in food aid have begun to think of their work as being more developmental than relief-oriented and to program accordingly. Recent legislation is supportive of these priorities, notably in seeking to ensure continuity of effort and to prevent short-term political considerations from dominating the choice of countries to be assisted.[45] In a very real sense, we may begin to talk in terms of the development of developmental food aid.

Conceptualizing food aid as an agent of change has implications for the way it is programmed. Particularly if food aid is to serve the people-oriented developmental purposes identified in this chapter, it will be necessary for both donor and recipient countries to upgrade their performance and integrate their efforts to a degree not otherwise required. Donating food is not enough, nor is receiving and distributing it. Developmental food aid along the lines indicated is unlikely to achieve its potential in the absence of multisectoral planning and coordinated interventions aimed at the poverty syndrome.

The past is instructive on this point. If there is one outstanding lesson to be learned from the history of Title II assistance to date, it is that isolated inputs are not sufficient. Food aid accomplishes little when it is introduced into an otherwise unchanged environment. And yet food aid has often been a well-intentioned "shot in the dark," the very existence of which has been reason enough for the recipient government to allocate its own resources to more productive or pressing sectors elsewhere in the economy. In fact, the international and voluntary agencies which distribute most Title II foodstuffs frequently act as substitutes for government, functioning at the grass-roots level of a poor society essentially alone. The result is that food is given to needy people (in the general sense) but little else takes place to liberate them from the multiple constraints of their poverty. If the track record of food aid is quite spotty in this regard, the reason is the "stopgap" quality of much of what has gone on.

It is this "stopgap" quality which can no longer be accepted. For food aid to be more than humanitarian, it must—in the first instance—be programmed to produce change in nutritional status. Beyond "nutritional first aid,"[46] it should be an integral part of a broad-gauged intervention strategy whose purpose is to restructure the environment in which marginal productivity and livelihood dominate.[47] Without a sustained governmental effort in this direction, the immediate nutritional benefits derived from supplementary feeding will remain unsupported, and in all likelihood the gains will prove short-lived barring continuous assistance from external sources. It is only cumulative change that unites reduction of deprivation with increased productivity, allowing each to be part of the other and both to be self-sustaining. The principle of food-for-work needs to be extended, therefore, and transformed into a comprehensive governmental program for rural development.[48]

How seriously the United States takes the developmental purposes of its food aid will determine what requirements it sets forth in order for countries to qualify for this type of assistance. Obviously, not all food aid need be (or can be) utilized in the ways recommended here. Food aid has many purposes, and significant constraints on poverty-oriented development planning are likely to persist in many countries where the United States has an interest. Moreover, food aid is usually too small a share of the total available food supply in recipient states to be an effective source of leverage, while placing conditions on aid can be distasteful, to say the least. "Strings" have a way of being misunderstood and deeply resented. They often appear to be an arrogant holdover from the colonial era, a negation of the recipient country's sovereignty and an insult to its self-respect. Strings and related pressures can also be counterproductive if applied indiscriminately.

On the other hand, it is difficult to imagine how food aid can be an effective agent of change unless certain conditions apply. It seems necessary, for example, that a government seeking aid be committed to the reduction of deprivation, that it be involved (or become involved) in promoting change in the rural sector, that it provide a planning and programmatic framework into which the donated food (and other assistance) can be incorporated, and that it be willing to monitor its progress and act decisively against correctable shortcomings in program implementation. At the very least, developmental food aid cannot be an excuse for inaction. It must also avoid being dissipated on palliative programs leading nowhere.[49] If the political will to undertake rural reform is present but the administrative capabilities to achieve it are not, the aid can contribute to improving capability and eventually performance. (One can develop a delivery system by having something to deliver.) If the capability is there but the will to use it is not, the aid either should not be granted or should be withdrawn after a reasonable trial period. In short, when developmental aid does not assist development, it is best redefined or dispensed with entirely lest it become, like so much humanitarian aid, a "bottomless pit."

All this sounds quite forbidding. It need not be. Developmental aid is best provided in a spirit of cooperation with the recipient country and with a mutual willingness to learn from experience, making adjustments as necessary in order to optimize results. The strings involved are not in the nature of source tying (i.e., aid requiring the recipient to purchase from the donor), but rather in the nature of "equity tying" (the goal being primarily to assist the poor). All that is really required for aid to be granted is a pledge of serious intent and earnest effort. All that is really required for aid to be continued is evidence of progress, in terms of what is being done and what impact it is having.[50]

Seen in this light, the decisive criterion for granting developmental food aid is neither the magnitude of need, defined by some ranking of countries, nor the promise of rapid progress. Need is not meaningfully summarized in national aggregates. Malnutrition and rural backwardness are just as oppressive in large parts of Brazil as they are in most of Bangladesh. On the other hand, to favor countries where the prospects for rapid success are greatest is to reduce food aid to the level of a common investment. In all likelihood, a small number of large, relatively affluent countries would get most of the aid, leaving little or none for the large number of small, relatively impoverished countries—hardly a suitable response to the long-term problem of global malnutrition. If the requirements mentioned here are deemed appropriate, developmental food aid should go to countries, be they dynamic or backward, where programs exist, or are planned, to combat malnutrition and to promote rural change. Until more is known about the whole complex process, a country's commitment to these objectives is a better basis for allocation than is an economic profile or projection of return on investment.[51]

Of course, any requirements imposed on other countries by the United States as a condition of aid would be meaningless unless matched by certain commitments made in return. The logic of developmental assistance is twofold: the aid must be available in quantities sufficient to help produce the kinds of change desired, and there must be continuity of effort in order to enhance the prospects for success.

It is probably wishful thinking to expect dramatic increases in the amount of food which the U.S. government will make available for aid purposes given its depleted reserves, its understandable concern for domestic prices, and its desire to cultivate commercial markets abroad.[52] Even so, developmental food aid assumes at least a minimum level of assistance guaranteed on a multiyear basis, both in the aggregate and with reference to specific programs in specific countries. For American food aid to be an effective instrument against malnutrition and for it to play a role in broad-gauged, integrated attacks on rural poverty and overpopulation, it must be in reasonably dependable supply. The sudden, rather drastic cuts which took place in 1973 and 1974, at a time of record need, cannot be permitted to recur.[53]

Just as important as floor levels and approximations of multiyear budgeting is the need to insulate developmental food aid as much as possible from political manipulation. The choice of countries for which developmental assistance of any kind is provided, or not provided as the case may be, is bound to be heavily influenced by political considerations, but the entire food aid program suffers and its developmental objectives suffer most when the primacy of politics is abused, as it was in the final years of the Vietnam war. Qualification tests based on political criteria are also counterproductive. In 1974 food aid to avert famine in Bangladesh was delayed, with tragic consequences, principally because of concern in Washington that Bangladesh might be disqualified from receiving P.L. 480 support after having sold jute to Cuba earlier in the year.[54] The aid in question was more humanitarian than developmental, but the point is clear: such political restrictions defeat the purpose of developmental food aid, which is to assist development, in many cases threatening to undermine what has already been achieved.

Adequate levels of support and the continuity of effort required to achieve developmental objectives cannot be sustained when food aid becomes a political football. This is what is so disturbing about the Ford administration's decision, disclosed in early 1976, to review *all* economic aid against the voting record of recipient countries in the United Nations and other forums, with those countries opposing the American position on matters of political importance being punished with cutbacks.[55] Whatever merit such a response might have in other respects, its developmental implications are likely to be disastrous. Insulating food aid from excessive politicization is a necessary condition for its developmental potential to be realized.[56]

In sum, the kind of developmental food aid with which we are concerned here rests on several assumptions about the orientation of recipient countries and equally about the willingness of the United States to be a serious aid partner. Neither set of assumptions can be taken for granted. Even when the situation is viewed with guarded optimism, it seems unlikely that a very large proportion of P.L. 480 commodity shipments can, realistically, be allocated in such a way for the foreseeable future. Some further upgrading of present programs supported by food aid is feasible (much is already being done), and there are certain to be targets of opportunity on the horizon inviting a creative response. In the main, however, food aid will probably continue to serve several masters simultaneously, and its developmental uses for nutrition in league with broader efforts at rural uplift are likely to be more the exception than the rule for the immediate period ahead.[57]

On the other hand, for a variety of reasons numerous low-income countries have begun to revise their developmental priorities in favor of agriculture and to take a second, anxious look at rural poverty. An opportunity exists, therefore, to begin programming food aid more ambitiously than ever before in order to help achieve greater equity and productivity. The question for the United States is how important such goals are when juxtaposed with other foreign policy objectives.

There is nothing magical about food aid. Other forms of assistance also promote development, even with reference to nutrition. Food aid is an automatic response neither to malnutrition nor to rural poverty, particularly inasmuch as feeding programs tend to require a large and expensive administrative apparatus to sustain them. Money can often accomplish the same ends as food while being more flexible in application. Clearly, to the extent that there is only so much aid to be given, it makes little sense to become locked into a large food aid component of the total package.[58]

On the other hand, the principal problem facing food aid at the present time is not that there is too much of it but that supplies are erratic and purposes unclear. Moreover, food aid really should not be viewed as an alternative to other types of aid, but as a resource to be used, as appropriate, in concert with other types of aid for the attainment of substantive objectives. It bears repeating that food aid serves development best when it is integrated with other inputs. The United States happens to produce an abundance of food. Food aid is, therefore, a logical form of aid in a food-short world.[59] If alleviating malnutrition is an objective of U.S. foreign assistance (for whatever ultimate set of reasons), the role of food aid is probably inescapable if, by itself, insufficient.

It is easy to be impressed with the American Food for Peace Program. Since its inception in 1954, $27 billion have been spent to relieve suffering, assist the needy, and "promote development" in low-income countries. One hundred and two million people were fed under Title II alone in 1966, and the figure has not gone below 74 million people for any year since then. In all, 157 countries have received P.L. 480 assistance in the 22 years of the program's existence.

So long as American food resembled a free good available in seemingly endless quantities, food aid could be—and was—a generous method of disposal. Moreover, because the compulsion to dispose typically exceeded concern for the practical consequences of doing so, little was required in the way of specifying intended impact or of measuring actual results. The giving justified itself. Food aid lessened the pressure on domestic stockpiles, created a favorable image for the United States, kept people alive, and added to the limited resources of developing countries while in the longer run cultivating overseas markets for American farm products.

The situation has changed dramatically with the end of large American reserves and the growing international demand for food. To a degree unknown in the surplus era of the 1950s and 1960s, food aid must now compete for the available supply of disposable commodities with alternative uses. At the same time, reconciling the several purposes of food aid has itself become increasingly difficult. Commercial sales abroad, which have more than tripled in the past 20 years, would have food follow the dollar sign. Political imperatives would have it tied to the vicissitudes of international diplomacy. Humanitarian impulses would respond to disasters and to crying need, which is pervasive. Given such claims under conditions of relative scarcity, the distinctly developmental objectives of food aid can easily be eroded or lost sight of entirely, particularly as they have been traditionally identified in a rather diffuse, even amorphous manner. It is little wonder that those involved in food aid have begun to take a hard look at what actually happens as a result of their efforts.

This period of vulnerability and reappraisal is also, quite possibly, a moment of opportunity to do something really consequential with food aid: to apply it systematically to combating malnutrition, as recommended at the 1974 World Food Conference, while embedding nutrition interventions in a broader matrix of programs designed to curb population growth and to promote greater productivity and well-being among the rural poor. An international momentum exists at present to redirect aid to the achievement of these ends, not as an act of charity, but as a vital and necessary contribution to development. USAID and the American voluntary agencies which distribute food overseas are part of this momentum, and low-income countries appear to be increasingly receptive to it. The combination of food aid, more rigorously programmed, and technical assistance is perhaps the most direct means by which the United States, pending creation of an international food reserve system, can assist low-income countries to confront the poverty syndrome with all its costly and destabilizing implications.

Conceptually, at least, food aid, malnutrition, and development have come together. The need now is for programmatic experience to sharpen our sense of the linkages involved and to provide a guide for action.

NOTES

1. As conventionally employed, the term "food aid" refers to the shipment of food to other countries at concessionary rates or as a donation. Food aid is distinguished from food trade at market prices and also from technical assistance and various financial arrangements for promoting agricultural development in low-income countries.

2. Leading statements on these themes appear in Alan Berg, Nevin S. Scrimshaw, and David L. Call, *Nutrition, National Development and Planning* (Cambridge, Mass.: The M.I.T. Press, 1973), and Alan Berg, *The Nutrition Factor: Its Role in National Development* (Washington, D.C.: Brookings, 1973).

3. For example, see the chapter by Ambassador Martin in this volume, especially pp. 325-326; also the chapters by Charles Shuman, pp. 147 and 160, and Victor Ferkiss, p. 178.

4. Food aid is just as relevant to urban populations as a resource against malnutrition and as a form of payment or subsidy. (In fact, the bulk of food aid

has gone to urban residents.) Our focus is on rural areas because of the greater magnitude of the problem there and also because rural development is "preventive medicine" for the same problems intensifying in an urban setting. Indeed, a theoretically major benefit of emphasizing rural development is that doing so will reduce the incidence of migration to urban centers by virtue of making the countryside more viable for the rural poor.

5. See F. James Levinson, *Morinda: An Economic Analysis of Malnutrition among Young Children in Rural India,* Cornell-M.I.T. International Nutrition Policy Series, Cambridge, Mass., 1974.

6. Whether supplementary feeding programs are really supplementary for the target groups has been questioned often, although the data base for making an informed assessment either way is extremely hard to come by.

7. Title I of Public Law 480—the Agricultural Trade Development and Assistance Act of 1954—and Title II (mentioned below) are the principal vehicles by which food aid is made available to other countries. For an excellent summary of the mechanics, history, and statistical data of P.L. 480, see James E. Austin, "The Food for Peace Program: A Shrinking Cornucopia?" Manuscript 4-375-276, Harvard School of Public Health, Department of Nutrition, and Harvard Business School, 1975.

8. Reexporting food aid is technically against the law, as is exporting comparable quantities of domestic production in light of food aid. Both, however, have been known to occur. Research is currently in progress at M.I.T. examining the economic effects of food assistance in recipient countries. For a preliminary statement of findings see Philip C. Abbott et al., "U.S. Food and Nutrition Policies and International Food Needs: An Analysis of Strategy Alternatives," First Year Report to the Science and Technology Policy Office, National Science Foundation, by the International Nutrition Planning Program, M.I.T., and Harvard University, July 1975, especially p. 146.

9. For a detailed review which recommends greater emphasis on nutrition see "Food For Peace: An Evaluation of PL 480 Title II," vol. 1, "A Global Assessment of the Program," and vol. 2, "Evaluations of Eight Country Programs," report to the Office of Program Evaluation, Agency for International Development, by Checchi and Company, Washington, D.C., July 1972. The "Checchi Report" is a landmark analysis which has had considerable influence on thinking about the programming of food aid.

10. For a particularly lucid analysis of this reappraisal see James P. Grant, "Development: The End of Trickle Down?" *Foreign Policy,* 12 (Fall 1973), pp. 43–65.

11. Approximately one-third of total U.S. grain production is currently exportable. In the past several years domestic consumption of grains (directly for humans and indirectly as feed) has accounted for between 67% and 80% of what is produced annually. For a perceptive analysis of American options in dealing with world food issues see Lyle P. Schertz, "World Food: Prices and the Poor," *Foreign Affairs,* 52 (April 1974), pp. 512–537.

12. Foreign sales at market prices exceeded $12 billion in 1973 for all agricultural commodities, accounting for about 25% of total U.S. export earnings. Commercial sales increased dramatically to $21 billion in 1974, a level maintained in 1975 and continued in 1976.

13. For example, in fiscal year 1974 more than two-thirds of Title I commodities, or almost half of all commodities shipped under P.L. 480, went to Cambodia and South Vietnam. Egypt is a newly favored recipient, joining such traditional stalwarts as South Korea, Taiwan, and Pakistan. The implications of future world food needs for American policy are assessed in Central Intelligence Agency, *Potential Implications of Trends in World Population, Food Production, and Climate,* OPR-401, August 1974, 50 pp.

14. For example, Biafra in 1969, $30 million worth of food; Bangladesh in 1972, $87 million (with $59 million more in 1973); and the Sahel in 1974, $50 million plus. Perhaps the most ambitious relief effort was during the Bihar famine of 1966-67, when the United States donated one-fifth of its wheat crop to India (Berg, *op. cit.,* p. 216; other figures calculated from "U.S. Overseas Loans and Grants and Assistance from International Organizations," Obligations and Loan Authorizations: July 1, 1945-June 30, 1973, Statistics and Reports Division, Office of Financial Management, Agency for International Development, May 1974, pp. 12, 84-129).

15. See the chapters by Thomas Reese Saylor and Daniel E. Shaughnessy in this volume.

16. Superficial "triage" and "lifeboat" theories thrive on the frustration and sense of futility that such perpetual generosity can arouse. See, for example, Garrett Hardin, "The Tragedy of the Commons," *Science,* 162 (December 13, 1968), pp. 1243-1248, and "Living on a Lifeboat," *Bioscience,* 24 (October 1974); also Wade Green, "Triage," *New York Times Magazine,* January 5, 1975, and the response by Alan Berg, "The Trouble with Triage," *New York Times Magazine,* June 15, 1975.

17. The label, by Jelliffe, is a nutritionist's construct not commonly used by development economists (Derrick B. Jelliffe, "Summation," in Berg, Scrimshaw, and Call, *op. cit.,* p. 380).

18. See, for example, Theodore S. Schultz, "Investment in Human Capital," *American Economic Review,* 51 (March 1961), pp. 1-17.

19. The underutilization of labor in production processes has been a major concern for some time, particularly in agriculture. Because labor input per worker is low in terms of both man-hours and efficiency, the economies of most low-income countries are "labor extensive" more than they are "labor intensive" (Gunnar Myrdal, *The Challenge of World Poverty: A World Anti-Poverty Program in Outline* [London: Penguin, 1970], p. 97). The result is low yields per acre in the rural sector, a circumstance rectifiable by appropriate investments in agricultural technology (new seeds, etc.) and by rural extension services oriented to smaller farmers.

20. Nevin S. Scrimshaw and John E. Gordon, *Malnutrition, Learning, and Behavior* (Cambridge, Mass.: The M.I.T. Press, 1968). Human productivity remains a lively concern. See also Pedro Belli, "The Economic Implications of Malnutrition: The Dismal Science Revisited," *Economic Development and Cultural Change,* 20 (October 1971), pp. 1-23, and comments on Belli's article by W. T. Wilford, Richard H. Franke and Gerald V. Barrett, and Frederick M. Peterson, with a reply by Belli, in *ibid.,* 23 (January 1975), pp. 337-357. Other leading analyses include Samir Sanad Basta, "Iron Deficiency Anemia in Adult

Males and Work Capacity," doctoral dissertation, Department of Nutrition and Food Science, M.I.T., February 1974; Marcelo Selowsky and Lance Taylor, "The Economics of Malnourished Children: An Example of Disinvestment in Human Capital," *Economic Development and Cultural Change*, 22 (October 1973), pp. 17-30; F. James Levinson and Philip C. Abbott, "Economic Consequences of Malnutrition," *Archivos Latinoamericanos de Nutricion*, XXIV (September 1974), pp. 339-348; and "The Relationship of Nutrition to Brain Development and Behavior," National Academy of Sciences, National Research Council, Washington, D.C., June 1974, 15 pp.

21. The label is again Jelliffe's; *op. cit.*, p. 380.

22. Exactly what "well-being" consists of is not always clear in the literature. The core of it would seem to be having enough to eat, good health, and suitable shelter.

23. Leonard Joy, "Design and Modification of Sectoral Projects and Programmes in Relation to Achieving the Targets," and P. R. Payne and L. J. Joy, "A Note on the Logic and Terminology of Planning," papers prepared for the Joint FAO/WHO Committee of Experts on Nutrition, Ninth Session, Rome, December 11-20, 1974.

24. Irma Adelman, "Development Economics: A Reassessment of Goals," paper presented at the Annual Meeting of the American Economics Association, San Francisco, December 1974, pp. 10-12. For a similar perspective by a clinical nutritionist see Michael C. Latham, "Nutrition and Infection in National Development," *Science*, 188 (May 9, 1975), pp. 561-565.

25. Joy, *op. cit.*, p. 3. Berg's *Nutrition Factor* straddles the two revisionist traditions. The increasing concern with issues of distribution on the part of economists is reflected in Hollis Chenery et al., *Redistribution with Growth* (New York: Oxford University Press, 1974), and in the papers prepared for the Princeton-Brookings Income Distribution Project in 1974.

26. See, for example, Government of India, Ministry of Education and Social Welfare, Department of Social Welfare, *Integrated Child Development Services Scheme* (New Delhi, July 1975), 51 pp.

27. For a particularly insightful analysis of public health in China see Joe D. Wray, "Health and Nutritional Factors in Early Childhood Development in the People's Republic of China," paper prepared for the report of the Early Childhood Development delegation visit to the People's Republic of China, November-December 1973, February 1974, 78 pp. See also *Report of the Medical Delegation to the People's Republic of China, June 15-July 6, 1973*, National Academy of Sciences, Institute of Medicine, Washington, D.C., 1973, 213 pp.

28. See, for example, Vincente Navarro, "Health Services in Cuba: An Initial Appraisal," *New England Journal of Medicine*, 287 (November 1972), pp. 954-959, and James D. Gavan and John A. Dixon, "India: A Perspective on the Food Situation," *Science*, 188 (May 9, 1975), pp. 541-549.

29. F. James Levinson, draft manuscript (untitled), October 15, 1975, p. 9.

30. Stated simply, the hypothesis holds that reducing the incidence of high infant and early childhood mortality will increase motivation to limit births in poor families and thus lead to fertility decline. See, for example, Carl E. Taylor,

Jeanne S. Newman, and Narindar U. Kelley, "The Child Survival Hypothesis," unpublished manuscript, Department of International Health, School of Hygiene and Public Health, Johns Hopkins University, 1975, 23 pp.

31. This argument is analyzed and in large measure supported in Joe D. Wray, "Will Better Nutrition Decrease Fertility?" paper presented at the Ninth International Congress of Nutrition, Mexico City, September 1972, 25 pp.; James E. Austin and F. James Levinson, "Population and Nutrition: A Case for Integration," *Milbank Memorial Quarterly,* Spring 1974, pp. 169-184; and the chapter by Michael F. Brewer in this volume.

32. We are grateful to Peter G. Brown and Henry Shue for bringing this problem into bold relief for us (correspondence, January 9, 1976).

33. For a perceptive critique by two nutrition planning specialists, see Peter Hakim and Giorgio Solimano, "Nutrition and National Development: Establishing the Connection," Discussion Paper No. 5, M.I.T. International Nutrition Planning Program, July 1975.

34. The importance of development's being self-sustaining is a common theme. See, for example, Lester E. Gordon, *Economic Planning and Technological Change in Less Developed Countries,* Economic Development Report No. 233, Development Research Group, Center for International Affairs, Harvard University, June 1973, 21 pp.; and with particular emphasis on rural development, Uma Lele, *The Design of Rural Development* (Baltimore: Johns Hopkins University Press, 1975).

35. Inevitably the record is mixed. For two recent assessments see Paul J. Isenman and H. W. Singer, "Food Aid: Disincentive Effects and Their Policy Implications," AID Discussion Paper No. 31, October 1975, 36 pp., and *Disincentives to Agricultural Production in Developing Countries,* Report to the Congress by the Comptroller General of the United States, ID-76-2, November 26, 1975.

36. What John P. Lewis identified as a "third sector" of employment below modernizing agriculture and modernizing industry is especially appropriate for food-for-work schemes. See his "The Public Works Approach to Low-End Poverty Problems: The New Potentiality of an Old Answer," *Journal of Development Planning,* 5 (1972). Earlier programs are reviewed in Lawrence W. Witt, "Development through Food Grants and Concessional Sales," in Carl K. Eicher and Lawrence W. Witt, eds., *Agriculture in Economic Development* (New York: McGraw-Hill, 1964), pp. 339-359. A more recent assessment appears in the "Checchi Report," *op. cit.,* notably vol. 1, chap. VI.

37. This argument differs from the position advanced by Ambassador Martin in this volume, pp. 325-326.

38. See Levinson, *Morinda,* especially table 24. In the author's own words, "the effects of income per se on the food consumption of the young children are far less pronounced than for the population as a whole. The income elasticities of consumption for calories, even among the 18-24 month age group . . . is only .082, meaning that if a family somehow succeeded in doubling its income . . . the child's caloric intake would increase by only 8 percent. (The increase in an adult's caloric intake might be 10 times that great.) The young child's protein, Vitamin A, and iron intake would increase even less. This would suggest that . . .

a simple income supplementation program unaccompanied by other interventions is unlikely to have a major effect on (children's) food intake" (p. 53). Reutlinger and Selowsky have analyzed data from the Calcutta Food Survey of 1969 suggesting that higher, not lower, elasticities pertain for younger children than for older children and adults among the urban poor. The favorable intrafamily redistribution of nutrients that accompanies improved income differs from Levinson's findings, but the outcome is much the same inasmuch as the higher elasticities for younger children are outweighed by the nutritional insult that afflicts the small child when his mother enters the labor force. When family income increases as a result of female employment, as is often the case, the small child may suffer a "negative income effect," since the marginal propensity to spend on food for the infant fails to compensate at all adequately for the lessened or ceased breast feeding that typically occurs. (Shlomo Reutlinger and Marcelo Selowsky, "Undernutrition and Poverty: Magnitude and Target Group Oriented Policies," International Bank for Reconstruction and Development, Bank Staff Working Paper No. 202; Washington, D.C., April 1975; data from United States Agency for International Development, *A Study of Food Habits in Calcutta* [Calcutta: Hindustan Thompson Associates, 1972].)

39. Ironically, the way to promote agricultural development may be to ship food. According to John W. Mellor, there is reason to believe that a developmental strategy emphasizing rural areas requires the type of underwriting best provided by food aid. With the expansion of rural employment, one of the features of such a strategy, there will be a sharply rising demand for food given the greater expendable wages made possible and the fact that poor people typically spend a large percentage of income increases on food. The demand for food is likely to increase more rapidly than the production of food in the short run. (The latter often declines in the transition from subsistence to cash cropping.) Hence the need for food aid. Indeed, the promise of food aid might actually encourage low-income countries to adopt a rural strategy. These ideas are developed at length in Mellor's most recent book, *The New Economics of Growth: A Strategy for India and the Developing World* (Ithaca, N.Y.: Cornell University Press, 1976).

40. Nutrition planners, influenced by James M. Pines of Transcentury Corporation, often think in terms of "project hypotheses" charting expectations concerning these sequences and linkages.

41. A third response to disappointing performance is, of course, to lower one's sights if they are too ambitious given the nature of the problem, the target groups identified, the resources at one's command, and the circumstances conditioning what can be achieved. The importance of evaluating program performance is now being emphasized by the voluntary agencies. See, for example, CARE's *Multi-Year Planning System,* CARE, Inc., manual, 1973, especially sec. 5.

42. For a similar perspective see the remarks by C. Gopalan in W. M. Cherry, O. L. Freeman, C. Gopalan, O. Matzke, and H. M. A. Onitiri, "Round Table: The Future of Food Aid," *Ceres,* 33 (May-June 1973), pp. 36-39.

43. High infant and early-childhood mortality is the most general statistical indicator that malnutrition is, or remains, a serious problem. Anthropometric

measurements tend to be the most practical tests of nutritional status under field conditions in low-income countries. USAID and other international agencies have studied the matter at length, as have various governments and private scholars. See, for example, CDC/Atlanta, "Simplified Field Assessment of Nutritional Status in Early Childhood: Some Practical Suggestions for Developing Countries," report prepared for the Office of Nutrition, USAID, May 23, 1975, 19 pp.; also P. M. Shah, *Early Detection and Prevention of Protein Calorie Malnutrition* (Bombay: Popular Prakashan, 1974). When adequate food intake does not produce satisfactory results, the reason is likely to involve parasitic infection and/or respiratory disease. In this regard see especially Nevin S. Scrimshaw, Carl E. Taylor, and John E. Gordon, *Interactions of Nutrition and Infection*, WHO Monograph Series, No. 57, World Health Organization, Geneva, 1968, 329 pp. For a general assessment of nutritional guidelines for policy purposes see the chapter in this volume by Linda H. Haverberg.

44. Wray, "Health and Nutritional Factors"; Tara Gopaldas et al., *Project Poshak*, vols. I and II (New Delhi: CARE-India, 1975).

45. In 1974 Congress stipulated that not more than 30% of Title I assistance could be allocated to countries not on the United Nations' list of countries "most seriously affected" by the global economic crisis and further required that no more than a tenth of annual P.L. 480 appropriations could be expended for a single country. Legislation passed and signed in December 1975 is in the same spirit and provides for continuity of distribution under Title II (see note 53 below).

46. Jose M. Bengoa, "Significance of Malnutrition and Priorities for Its Prevention," in Berg, Scrimshaw, and Call, *op. cit.*, p. 124.

47. See John P. Lewis, *Quiet Crisis in India: Economic Development and American Policy* (Garden City, N.Y.: Anchor, 1964), notably chap. 6.

48. There is no lack of things to be done requiring government sponsorship: e.g., rural public works and the employment they generate, agricultural extension services to increase the productivity of small farmers, the setting up of credit cooperatives to encourage needed investments and of market cooperatives to break the back of local money lenders and otherwise improve the bargaining power of marginal producers (farmers, fishermen, pottery makers, weavers, and so on), expanded health care and family-planning services as well as opportunities for education, and even land reform. For an elaboration see Myrdal, *op. cit.*

49. Diffusion of effort is an ever-present possibility. Some programs are intended more to salve the conscience of the rich than to satisfy the hunger of the poor. In Mellor's words, "It may make the rich feel good that they are doing something for the poor, when what is really needed is for the rich to go along with the kinds of development programs that will expand employment, incomes, and consumption of the lower income classes. However, the latter course very often involves much more substantial social, political, and economic change than the rich are willing to tolerate and certainly more than is involved in most nutritional programs put forward" (John W. Mellor, "Nutrition and Economic Growth," in Berg, Scrimshaw, and Call, *op. cit.*, p. 73). According to Dandekar and Rath, a 15% reduction in consumer expenditure by the top 5% of the

income ladder in India and a 7½% reduction by the next 5% on the ladder would permit a redistribution of income sufficient to provide all but 10% of the Indian population with a nutritionally adequate diet (V. M. Dandekar and Nilakantha Rath, "Poverty in India: II. Policies and Programmes," *Economic and Political Weekly,* January 9, 1971, p. 142). No redistribution of this magnitude has been attempted, although India is a world leader in testing out nutrition interventions.

50. A shared sense of purpose is no panacea, of course. The Johnson administration's "short tether" policy toward India tied P.L. 480 assistance to certain agricultural and population policies in a manner analogous to what is advocated here. The result was a backlash of resentment, reflecting the built-in sensitivity of a close aid relationship as much as the somewhat abrasive manner in which the American position was articulated.

51. This argument is consistent with the misgivings expressed by Shaughnessy in this volume, concerning Congress's penchant in recent years for stipulating limits on Title I aid to countries not on the United Nations MSA ("most seriously affected") list or countries above a certain per capita GNP. See pp. 96–97 in particular.

52. The analysis by Lawrence Witt in this volume supports this inference.

53. Title II shipments, for example, dropped from 5.6 billion pounds in fiscal year 1972 to 4.6 and 2.9 billion pounds in fiscal year 1973 and fiscal year 1974 respectively. With so much food aid going to South Vietnam and Cambodia in fiscal year 1974 expecially, several countries received less than one-fifth as much food as they had in the mid-1960s despite famine conditions in South Asia and the Sahel. The decline in availability of Title II commodities occurred at a singularly unfortunate time in one other respect. Many of the voluntary agencies which distribute Title II food had begun to recognize the long-term futility and cost ineffectiveness of providing purely humanitarian food relief and were shifting the emphasis of their programs so as to achieve better nutritional impact within a framework of broader developmental initiatives. The cutbacks in 1973 and 1974 impeded this progress. Congress has recently made a decisive contribution to continuity of effort by enacting an annual minimum of 1.3 million tons of food grains for use in Title II programs (Public Law 94-161, Sec. 208, December 20, 1975).

54. Emma Rothschild, "Food Politics," *Foreign Affairs,* 54 (January 1976), p. 296. An amendment to P.L. 480 passed and signed into law in 1975 actually prohibited Title I sales to countries trading with Cuba or North Vietnam, although the prohibition could be waived at Presidential discretion.

55. *New York Times,* January 9, 1976, pp. 1, 5. The celebrated cablegram sent by UN Ambassador Moynihan to Secretary Kissinger and all American embassies several days prior to his resignation identified Tanzania as one country to which $28 million in aid had been suspended because of "Tanzania's unhelpful voting record at the last General Assembly" (*New York Times,* January 28, 1976, p. 8). Ironically, Tanzania is as oriented to rural development, distributive equity, preventive medicine, and popular well-being as any country in Africa.

56. For a thoughtful elaboration of this point see the statement "No Strings Attached" by the Rev. Theodore M. Hesburgh, president of Notre Dame, on the "Op. Ed." page of the *New York Times,* February 4, 1976 (p. 31).

Similar sentiments were expressed by the Senate Foreign Relations Committee in its report on the current economic aid bill (*New York Times,* January 9, 1976, p. 5).

57. This view is shared by many experts, including Kenneth L. Robinson (correspondence, February 23, 1976).

58. This paragraph draws upon correspondence from Ambassador Edwin M. Martin concerning an earlier draft of this chapter (letter of April 1, 1976).

59. Saylor, in this volume, reaches the same conclusion; p. 201.

15 Slowing population growth with food aid
Michael F. Brewer

Food and population size have long been associated with each other. Malthus was echoing a well-documented tradition of thought about their relationship when he cautioned that limited food supplies eventually would curb population growth. Contemporary students continue to assign food and nutrition prominent roles in explaining the growth dynamics of human populations.

Aside from international migration, growth of a country's population is the result of its birth and death rates. The period of rapid growth in human numbers that each of the developed countries has experienced in the past, and that less developed nations currently are undergoing, reflects relative changes in those rates. Technological innovations and social change that historically accompanied national development have had, over time, the net result of reducing both. During the typical "demographic transition" the death rate falls before the birth rate. Rapid population growth ensues until the birth rate also falls. The central question of this chapter is whether an increased food supply can hasten or induce the coincidence of birth- and death-rate decline.

Various explanations have been advanced as to what causes change in these demographic variables, including several hypotheses about what happens to birth rates while death rates are changing.

Declining mortality accompanied the development of the industrial nations during the last century, and continues to characterize them. Various technological, social, and institutional changes associated with the development process, it is argued, reduced incentives for large families and made the means of birth control more widely available. A gradual decline in the birth rate followed. The reduction of both rates was slow, requiring about a century and a half to reach present levels. Substantial population growth occurred during the process, but at a moderate enough rate to be accommodated by the expanding economies of the industrial countries—at least until recent years.

In the less developed nations, the demographic transition did not follow this pattern. The decline in mortality was much more abrupt and occurred later than it had in the industrialized world. More importantly, there has not yet been a significant decline in birth rates, except in South Korea and a few small countries such as Costa Rica and Taiwan—with the important possible exception of mainland China. The result has been a rapid increase in population throughout most of the underdeveloped world.

If the traditional explanations of the demographic transition process are valid, it follows that the underdeveloped world, given time, will spontaneously go through its own transition in birth rates. Whether the population growth that occurs in the meantime can be accommodated by the societies and economies of Third World countries is a question of major international significance, and is of direct concern to the United States. Our government's expectations on the subject will be reflected in its foreign policies and international activities.

Historical evidence used to bolster orthodox transition theory generally comes from the West, with England frequently cited as an illustration. At mid-nineteenth century it was the richest country in the world. Its economic expansion enabled many low-income people to join the middle class. Caring for large families at middle-class standards proved to be an expensive proposition, however, making difficult the accumulation of disposable income that was useful, if not essential, for moving up the social scale. As smaller families became prevalent among middle-income groups a "democratization" of birth control occurred, spreading this technology among all classes of the national population. The activities of Annie Basant and Charles Bradlaugh in late-nineteenth-century England, and a generation later of Margaret Sanger in the United States, brought advocacy of birth control into the open, where it has since remained.

Demographic transition theory relies upon the entire process of economic and social development. Overcoming gross food shortages, improved sanitation, and other public health services are viewed as principal "triggers" for the decline in death rates. Causes for the drop in birth rates are more complex and diffuse. The driving force behind the drop in birth rates often is identified as those individuals in the national population who are relatively healthy, who enjoy fairly broad opportunities for self-fulfillment (especially through employment), and who desire smaller-size families to exploit those opportunities. The physical, social, and economic circumstances under which these agents of change live—circumstances that in less developed countries can be heavily influenced by the availability of food—provide the incentives for desiring smaller families. In time, as the bulk of the population begins to enjoy improved health and similar opportunities, the small-family concept gains public sanction, eventually becoming a social norm, and national birth rates decline.

While intuitively appealing, the traditional demographic transition "model" is loosely framed and ambiguous with regard to important definitions, units of measurement, etc. Furthermore, notable exceptions have been observed in particular countries to demographic characteristics the model would "predict." This lack of specificity and questionable empirical support has raised questions about using demographic transition theory as a basis for framing international development and population policies of the U.S. and other developed countries. For example, food aid might prove self-defeating, because its direct effect would be to reduce death rates, and if the predicted decline in birth rates did not follow promptly, even more rapid population growth would result. This and related concerns have permeated policy debate, and prompted the conviction that humanitarian food aid programs and international population programs should be linked, synchronized, or coordinated—but demographic transition theory fails to provide guidance for how this can be accomplished.

THE CHILD SURVIVAL HYPOTHESIS

A more explicit relationship between food and nutrition, on one hand, and population change, on the other, has recently been asserted. William Rich of the Overseas Development Council has presented a general statement of this variant of the demographic transition in a monograph titled *Smaller Families through Social and Economic Progress*.[1] The central idea has been labeled the "child survival hypothesis." Its basic proposition is that high fertility rates in many rapidly growing underdeveloped countries are the result of parents' wishes to have a certain number of their children (usually sons) survive the parents' own old age. The particular size of "completed family" desired, it is contended, depends upon such factors as the number of surviving descendants needed to provide parental old-age support and, in cultures where children are perceived as economic assets, what constitutes an efficient-sized family labor force. The number of births required to achieve these parental objectives will differ with the prevailing infant mortality, longevity, and morbidity characteristics of the populations involved.

The thesis maintains that the prevailing birth rate, coupled with mortality and morbidity characteristics of the population, generally yields child survival expectancies, or probabilities, consistent with the size of completed family that parents want. Increasing the chance of child survival by improved nutrition, public health, sanitation, etc., so the argument runs, will lead to a perception by parents that fewer pregnancies and births are necessary to secure the desired size of the surviving family. The thesis argues that if food aid and nutrition programs achieve increased infant survival, parents will desire fewer children and will be motivated to use birth control to achieve that result. If this demand can be met by family-planning programs, vasectomy clinics, etc., the net result will be lowered fertility. The thesis does not overlook the immense logistical problem of delivering effective fertility control services, but it does contend they are easier to surmount if there exists widespread desire for smaller-sized families. Although it does not specify the length of time required for birth rates to fall after mortality has been reduced, the thesis implies that food and nutrition program intervention can bring about reduced child mortality and subsequent lower fertility more rapidly than could be done by conventional family-planning efforts under conditions of high mortality. The thesis thus implies relatively less priority should be accorded to traditional population programs and relatively more to nutrition and related public health measures. Its validity has been the subject of controversy.

In suggesting that declines in fertility will occur naturally, if not automatically, once child survival has been increased, the new thesis reflects doubt about the efficacy of traditional family-planning programs. Acknowledging that contraceptive services are needed if parents are to realize their desire for smaller-sized families, the new thesis leads to the conclusion that population programs should become an adjunct to food, nutrition, and public health enhancement efforts. It suggests a more "passive" type of program than the population efforts of U.S. foreign aid in the recent past.

This sanguine thesis also is politically convenient, in the face of strident demands the Third World countries recently have been making for a larger share of worldwide development. These arguments were loudly articulated at both the World Population Conference and the World Food Conference, sometimes implying that an equitable distribution of capital and wealth is a sufficient, as well as necessary, condition for simultaneously "solving" population and food problems. The child survival thesis appears responsive to that line of thought. It implies that overseas aid from the United States and other developed countries should emphasize increasing available food supplies to the less developed countries, along with public health services, and other activities to reduce mortality—activities that are less controversial than fertility control programs.

In short, the child survival hypothesis generally is consistent with the traditional notion of demographic transition; it provides a rationale for international assistance that would escape the hard criticism leveled at past U.S. international population programs; and it encourages activities politically less vulnerable to the increasingly adamant development demands of Third World nations.

If valid, the hypothesis suggests significant changes in the content and staging of U.S. aid programs. Greater emphasis than in the past would be placed on food and humanitarian activities, less on family-planning programs. Both types of activities would be coordinated in function and timing within each country—an administrative accomplishment international aid agencies have yet to demonstrate. The thesis further suggests that family-planning efforts will be most effective if they follow other programs designed to increase food supply and nutritional levels. The tone of preemptive urgency characteristic of U.S. population programs over the past decade would be tempered accordingly.

Slowing population growth with food aid 263

QUESTIONS OF EVIDENCE

With its substantial policy implications, the child survival hypothesis warrants critical examination. To help interpret some recent research on the general subject, it can be reformulated as a series of related, causal links. An increase in food aid from the United States that improves the nutritional status of a particular underdeveloped country is considered the activating variable—the exogenous force in the model. A chain of consequences are hypothesized, including an increase of the survival rate of infants and children (and incidentally, mothers as well); a decrease in the family size desired by parents; an increase in their demand for and use of contraception or other fertility control measures; and finally a reduction in national fertility. This series of hypothesized events along with several "side conditions" that need to be met if each event is to induce the anticipated subsequent results can be depicted as follows:

THE CAUSAL LINKS IMPLIED BY THE CHILD SURVIVAL HYPOTHESIS

A. *An increase in U.S. food aid to LDC that improves its nutritional status*
   Required side conditions:
   - The additional food is distributed at least equally among the entire population, preferably with priority to those components with high fertility who also suffer malnutrition.
   - Food aid programs are carried out in ways that neither reduce indigenous agricultural production nor disposable real income of the malnourished.

B. *Decrease in infant and child mortality*
   - B linked more closely to C if there is concomitant economic development and expanded employment opportunities.

C. *Decrease in family size desired by parents*
   - Attitudes to those parents who perceive need for fewer pregnancies to attain desired family size transferred to the general population in order to widely sanction the norm of smaller families and family planning.

D. *Increase in the demand for family-planning information and services*
   - Family-planning services enjoy public sanction and are made widely available at a reasonable cost.

E. *Reduced fertility of the LDC population.*

The validity of each causal link can be assessed by examining recent research findings.

The A-B Link: Can Food Assistance Reduce Infant and Child Mortality?

The enhancement of nutritional status, discussed by Haverberg elsewhere in this volume, frequently requires the reduction of parasites and disease as well as increasing the intake of food energy. If existing sanitation, medical, and public health conditions do not permit the former, then increasing food assistance *per se* may not be sufficient to achieve enhanced nutritional status. In analysis that follows, it is assumed that food aid *can* effectively change nutritional status.

For international food aid to result in higher rates of child survival, and subsequently in reduced fertility, one must assume the recipient country distributes the supplement to its own food supply in a pattern which increases the nutritional status of malnourished groups experiencing high child mortality and high fertility. In many less developed countries, these attributes describe the rural poor.

Food delivery to this segment of the population poses logistical and political-administrative challenges that an LDC may not be able to meet. Obsolescent port facilities or limited surface transportation systems may severely constrain the ability of a country to receive food shipments, and make its subsequent distribution both time-consuming and expensive. Governmental corruption or a traditionally monopolistic structure of the food-marketing system may represent additional obstacles. The equal distribution of food to people living in numerous rural communities invariably is more expensive than if their settlement pattern consisted of larger cities, and it is problematic whether the rural poor can rally the political support needed to secure such a distribution. For these reasons, a central government agency may be unable to distribute food to malnourished, high-fertility groups. If curbing population growth is a primary objective of food aid, program efficiency requires this capacity.

To be sure, Title II of P.L. 480 contains provisions for food distribution by private groups, who may use their own distribution facilities to directly reach the intended recipients. In 1974 privately distributed food amounted to only 18 percent of the dollar value of total U.S. food aid.[2] If the objective of the aid program is as pervasive as affecting national fertility, a high distributional priority favoring the target group must be assigned to food shipments under both Title I and Title II.

The long-run impact of supplemental food aid on indigenous food production and its distribution also is important and must be at least neutral. If it is negative, the nutritional achievements of international food aid will be offset, possibly to the extent that a net reduction of available food results. Past experience under Public Law 480 provides evidence that the donation of food without cost to developing nations depresses commodity prices in local markets, eliminating an essential production incentive. Various mechanisms may be used to overcome this price-depressing impact of food aid. The present discussion presumes they can be successfully incorporated into future programs.

A substantial body of information, much of it discussed by Haverberg, supports the proposition that improved nutrition of mother, infants, and children reduces both their mortality and morbidity. Summarizing findings about pregnancy wastage of mothers in less developed countries, a recent National Academy of Sciences report[3] concluded:

> The importance of giving special attention to the nutritional improvement of adolescent girls cannot be over-emphasized.[4]

And speaking about older women, it added:

> Health and nutrition of mothers at the upper end of the child-bearing years or of parity order need special protection as long as complete avoidance of pregnancy is not assured at those ages. The goal of contraceptive protection in these groups of women would seem to be a reasonable concurrent target.[5]

The B-C Link: Will a Decrease in Infant and Child Mortality Reduce the Size of Desired Family?

Limited research has addressed the extent to which a reduction in infant mortality affects parental desires for family size. A study conducted in East Pakistan[6] found that the expected number of children a mother will bear in a 5-year period increased about half a child after she experienced the loss of an infant. Expected birth probabilities increase relatively more rapidly if a mother is in the 20-to-29 age bracket—they compensated more fully for the death through increased fertility.

Using data from the 1960–62 demographic survey of East Pakistan, this study also reveals something about son preference:

> The reproductive response of a mother to the death of her child is somewhat more pronounced if she loses a boy than if she loses a girl. . . .[7]

A 1974 study of Sierra Leone, West Africa,[8] found replacement more than made up for the mortality experienced, and led to the speculation that high rates of infant mortality stimulate "insurance" births as well as having a "replacement effect" on fertility. Younger-aged mothers experienced the highest fertility after the death of a child.

The extent to which, and mechanisms by which, experience of child mortality within a family affects the desired family size norm of the general population have not yet been specified. A 1972 study speculates on this relationship in the following:

If the only effect of a reduced level of infant and child mortality were on those couples who actually experienced child loss, the rate of natural increase would rise following a reduction in infant mortality. This is because couples who lost children did not fully compensate for that loss. On the other hand, if a high level of infant and child mortality in the community affects the behavior of couples who do not experience a child loss, elevating their fertility, then a reduction in infant or child mortality might reduce the rate of natural increase. The findings of our study give ground for belief that the community level of infant and child mortality have an independent effect on fertility; nevertheless they do not give conclusive proof for such a hypothesis.[9]

Various explanations can be advanced to suggest this causal association—which the child survival thesis implicitly asserts. Investigating the thesis empirically is difficult, requiring controls on observed populations that rarely are present or possible to effect in less developed countries.

Preferences are difficult to detect and often are unstable. The Pakistan study cited above examines fertility response to the death of a child. The thesis in question, however, argues that a change in the perceived optimum family size is a response to the survival of a child who otherwise would have died. There is no *a priori* reason to expect symmetry in parental response to these two situations. Furthermore, the evidence advanced in the East Pakistan study[10] is *completed* family size, not parental desire for smaller families. However, it seems reasonable to assume that the behavioral change is preceded by a parallel preference change.

The role of lactational amenorrhea further complicated testing this and subsequent element of the child survival hypothesis. Evidence supports the contention that lactation restrains ovulation. Infant mortality removes this natural dampener on fertility, and thus some portion of the greater fertility observed among women who experienced an infant death may simply be attributable to their shorter periods of lactation.

One can only conclude that available evidence is too general to permit rigorous testing of this link in the child survival hypothesis. While generally consistent with the relationship advanced, the data cannot be said to confirm its validity.

The C-D Link: Does a Smaller Family Size Norm Increase the Demand for Birth Control Services?

Considerable evidence relating to a change in desired family size and use of birth control has been collected—usually in order to evaluate family-planning programs. These investigations typically are aimed at women, and attempt to measure the proportion of those specifically informed about the advantages of smaller families who subsequently accept family-planning services—in short, response to family-planning information and education programs. As one would expect, the findings are diverse, reflecting the cultural setting of the individuals observed and the specific character of the family-planning program. The scope and magnitude of such studies vary greatly, as does the rigor with which they have been conducted. Many have been criticized because they do not observe the "persuaded" individuals over time to determine how long they continue to use these services. Nevertheless, it seems safe to conclude from these studies that some women exposed to the virtues of small families will modify their desired family size and seek the means to achieve it. While behavior of individuals whose desired family size has been reduced by exposure to population information and education provides support for the C-D link of the child survival hypothesis, there is little basis for gauging the magnitude of the relationship or the time required for its manifestation.

Similar conclusions about an entire population, however, are another matter. If the child survival thesis is to provide a basis for international assistance policy, sufficiently large numbers of couples must use family-planning practices to affect national fertility. The demographic transition scenario cited above suggests that there must be public sanctioning of birth control in contemporary Third World countries as well as a reduction in the prevailing norm of desired family size. This may be achieved by government proclamation, a major information and education effort, or as the result of various kinds of incentives.

The D-E Link: Will More Family Planning Reduce Fertility?

The impact of family-planning programs on birth rates or other measures of national fertility has been widely discussed, and the difficulty of deriving explicit conclusions noted. A recent survey of 32 studies examining this relationship arrived at the following summary:

> ... 24 concluded the family planning program did reduce fertility for the target population as a whole. Of the 32 studies, only seven were judged to have strong methodologies; six of those concluded that family planning programs did lower fertility, the singular exception was the Wyon and Gordon study[11] of the Khanna project. The authors argue that the Khanna Program offered high quality services, yet it did not result in lowering of fertility. Since it operated in the 1950's it depended primarily on foam tablets and condoms, (with some use of withdrawal, rhythm, and abstinence) and hence did not have available the more sophisticated technologies available today.
>
> The six studies, which used a strong methodology and did find family planning led to a reduction of fertility, all dealt with the Taiwanese program. More sophisticated methodologies may be in use in that country because of greater availability and quality of data.[12]

The main methodological problem in this type of research is to estimate how fertility might have changed in the absence of family-planning programs—

the extent to which other socioeconomic factors might have modified the reproductive behavior of the population. While the data suggest affirmation of the hypothesis, many of the findings are uncomfortably ambiguous. This has led a number of prominent individuals, including the chairman of the recent Commission on Population Growth and the American Future, John D. Rockefeller, to express disappointment at the results of what he termed the "family planning approach." At the World Population Conference he went on to clarify that he did not intend to be negative about family planning *per se,* but rather urged that it be carried out within the context of a general program aimed broadly at the socioeconomic development of the less developed countries.[13]

Other Pertinent Research Findings

The most specific applied research dealing with the child survival hypothesis involves statistical estimates of the correlation between changes in infant mortality and completed fertility (the B-E links discussed above). Three recent studies[14] estimate the direction and magnitude of the relationship (with infant mortality being the dependent variable). Of these, one study dealt with data from Puerto Rico, the other two with multinational data. All found a positive relationship of fairly significant magnitude. In fact, a survey of research exploring the relationship between 10 independent variables and completed fertility concluded that "infant mortality," along with "female education" and "increase in income to the poorest 40 percent of the population" had most significant influence.

The quantitative estimate—referred to as the "elasticity of infant mortality with respect to completed fertility"—is given in the accompanying table.

A critical aspect of the child survival hypothesis is the time required for the infant mortality decline to induce a reduction in fertility. A recent statistical analysis[15] of data from 53 countries in Asia, Africa, and Latin America showed that the median interval between the onset of a decline in mortality rates to the onset of fertility decline is 11.4 years. It also indicated that the more rapid the decline in infant mortality, the shorter the interval before fertility begins to decline. This is a very short time lag indeed, compared to the historical demographic transition of the developed nations. If the estimate is accurate, it holds strong implications for program design. Here again, the difficulty is to weed out influences of other factors that would have altered fertility in the absence of a reduction of infant mortality. Public health programs, water purification, and maternal and child nutrition programs are often concomitant parts of the widespread modernization of a country, and probably affect fertility jointly with other cultural and economic changes. If this is the case, additional expenditures for food aid and assistance may be redundant if undertaken solely for the purpose of reducing fertility.

Summary of findings on the correlates of fertility: direction of relationship, averages of elasticities, and adequacy of research

Independent Variable	Nature of the Relationship with Fertility*	Elasticity (computed average from studies cited)	Adequacy of Research
Income and its Distribution			
Income	?	−.24[a] (6)[b]	Fair
Income Distribution	−	−.36 (1)	Poor
Socioeconomic Change			
Economic Development	?	−	Poor
Socioeconomic Status	−	−	Poor
Education and Literacy	−	−.15 (1)	Fair
Female	−	−.25 (9)	Good
Male	+ or 0	−	Fair
Employment			
Male	+ or 0	+.09[c] (1)	Fair
Female	−	−.19[d] (2)	Fair
Rural	+ or 0		
Urban	−		
Children	+		Poor
Value of Children			
Age at Marriage	−	−	Poor
Type of Marriage	?	−	Poor
Costs of Children and Childbearing	−	−	Fair
Son Preference	− or 0	−	Poor
Infant Mortality	+	+.33 (3)	Fair
Other Variables			
Urban-rural Differentials	0	−.11[e] (3)	Fair
Religion	0	−	Poor

*(+) symbol is used if the relationship to fertility is direct, (−) symbol if the relationship to fertility is inverse, (0) symbol if there is no relationship to fertility, and (?) symbol if the relationship to fertility is indeterminant.

[a] Elasticities for per capita income and income per worker.
[b] Numbers in parentheses indicate number of elasticities found.
[c] Elasticities for male earnings.
[d] Elasticities for female earnings and female labor force participation.
[e] Elasticities for percent of population in urban areas.

Source: *The Policy Relevance of Recent Social Research on Fertility,* Occasional Monograph No. 2 Interdisciplinary Communications Program, Smithsonian Institution, 1974, p. 65.

This rather spotty record of supporting evidence suggests that enhanced infant survival does contribute to reduced population growth. But it confirms only general statements of association, not specific cause and effect linkages. Nor does it demonstrate that reduction of infant mortality is a necessary or sufficient precondition for fertility declines. Activities that reduce infant mortality such as food and nutrition programs, however, are thus consistent with both the population and the humanitarian objectives of U.S. aid. But the evidence is not conclusive that food and nutrition are more efficient than other programs for this purpose.

QUESTIONS OF ETHICS

Among ethical questions inherent in any international program of food aid is the propriety of using those programs to reduce fertility. Involved is the forthrightness of articulating U.S. international development objectives, and the justification of the U.S. manipulating individual behavior in other sovereign countries.

Demographic trends reflect the aggregate results of many individual decisions. If past fertility trends are to be changed without coercion, the circumstances under which individual decisions are rendered must be modified: Either new options must be created, the comparative advantages of existing ones altered, or different criteria used to evaluate expected outcomes. In instances where advantages of reduced fertility exist but are not widely perceived, more adequate information about those advantages may result in the desired shifts in fertility. In other instances, new options and incentives need to be created—for instance by increasing employment opportunities for women, or reducing economic uncertainty through social security or similar programs.

To the extent that population programs also expand options, they are bound to have positive effects on individual welfare. And programs based on rational, individual decision making can broaden a population's participation in national development. If campaigns to reduce fertility are designed to open wider opportunities for individuals, citizens may acquire greater capacity to make decisions in a host of other areas as well. In short, family-planning behavior by individuals can be a potent resource for change, rather than merely the consequence of change. Perhaps it would prove more efficient, as well as more forthright, to so regard it. Such a perspective would favor an emphasis on educational programs to inform individuals, organizations, and public groups about alternatives to high fertility, how they can pursue those options, and the public as well as private consequences of so doing.

The tendency in the United States to regard fertility control programs for the less developed countries as an intervention in a deterministic behavioral systems has been criticized as "manipulative" and "dehumanizing" by LDC spokesmen. A defensive argument of "saving them from themselves" can be made, yet that claim to superior wisdom—which may manifest itself as simple paternalism or, more assertively, as coercion—appears open to ethical question.

The distinction may be subtle, but it is not trivial. It represents a watershed between those who accept fertility control as essential in light of the critically urgent need to stem population growth and those who would see information and education as the cutting edge of U.S. population programs for the less developed countries. If an effective program of information and education can bestow on the individual a sense of self-esteem, responsibility, and capacity for positive participation in addition to modifying traditional fertility patterns, then strategies for subsequent stages of development can build on this new capability.

The fertility control approach that has characterized programs of the Office of Population of AID in recent years has been criticized as coercive—it has been alleged that the United States has required family-planning programs as a condition for other assistance. Such a provision recently was explicitly proposed,[16] though it failed passage, as an amendment to the 1975 House Food Aid Bill. While the avoidance of precisely that criticism is one of the apparent advantages of the child survival hypothesis, does the use of food aid as a more benign instrument for reducing fertility remove the ethical issue? If food aid and other humanitarian programs are aimed at increasing individual choice, and accordingly place major emphasis on population information and education, it would seem that the charge of manipulation and coercion can be effectively refuted.

QUESTIONS OF POLICY

What does this examination of the child survival hypothesis permit one to conclude about U.S. food aid policy? Three guidelines can be deduced, and two fundamental questions about U.S. international assistance strategy can be posed.

Criteria for Food Aid

To maximize the contribution food aid can make toward reducing fertility, the eventual household recipients should be the malnourished, high-fertility and high-mortality components of the national population. Assuming that these will usually be the poor, and very likely rural people to whom food delivery is both costly and difficult, some fairly strong requirements about the ultimate distribution of food within the recipient country are indicated. Such requirements can exceed neither the physical capacity of port and transportation systems nor the administrative capability of poorer countries. Possibly a food distribution plan and procedure would be an appropriate prerequisite for receiving food aid. Such a requirement would be neither possible nor useful when such aid was in response to localized emergencies such as earthquakes or floods. For chronically food-short countries, however, such a plan might identify physical or administrative obstacles to the efficient utilization of food aid, and suggest ways to overcome them. Enhancing the ability of a developing country to distribute food to its own population appears an appropriate use of foreign assistance funds.

To avoid further intensifying a country's food dependence, the arrangements under which such aid is provided and distributed within the recipient country should avoid disrupting its domestic food and agricultural markets, and especially avoid reducing commodity prices to levels that discourage agricultural production. A variety of measures may be used to avoid such undesirable results of food aid. For example, the sale of U.S.-contributed food, coupled with a program that supplements the income of poor individuals, may prove effective. In other cases a complete isolation of food aid from commercial commodity markets may be applicable. Specific arrangements would have to be tailored to the circumstances of the recipient country.

And finally, to capitalize on any incentives toward smaller-sized families that increased food supply and improved nutrition might generate, population information, education, and family-planning services should be available. This suggests close synchronization between population programs and food aid. Population activities will be more effective, and presumably also more acceptable, if developing countries view reduced fertility as an active factor in promoting change rather than its passive consequence.

Questions of Strategy

The child survival hypothesis and its supporting evidence discussed above pose two basic questions about U.S. international population and development strategy. The first is whether a strategy that places major emphasis on food and nutrition will prove too expensive to undertake. Assuming its validity, the key behavior-changing incentives in the child survival hypothesis result from improved nutritional status of the population. It is argued elsewhere in this volume that malnutrition is properly considered a disease—to be overcome only by improved public health as well as by more and better-quality food. If the former requires the array of medical, sanitation, and administrative measures typical of past development programs, its cost could be very high—relative to the cost of increased food aid. The budget required for pursuing demographic objectives in all Third World countries by an elaborate health and nutrition strategy might easily exceed what the U.S. Congress and the governments of other developed countries will provide. This would be especially true if increased parental employment is a necessary condition for the B-C link of the hypothesis to operate. In short, although the hypothesis suggests there may be a "shortcut" to demographic behavior traditionally associated with the full accoutrements of a "developed" society, the evidence available does not demonstrate that reduced population growth can be purchased inexpensively with the coin of U.S. food assistance. Less popular and perhaps ethically less acceptable programs may have to be adopted out of budgetary considerations.

A second question relates to the risk entailed by relying upon the child survival thesis. The empirical evidence discussed above leaves a substantial level of uncertainty associated with the hypothesis, and especially the period of time over which improved nutrition allegedly will result in reduced fertility. The compound rate at which populations grow imposes increasingly large social and private costs for every year fertility remains high. Prudence would suggest that the inherent risk of a food-nutrition strategy be reduced insofar as possible. Less palatable but more dependable programs may be deemed in the best interest of both the U.S. and the recipient Third World. India's recent program of enforced sterilization of parents after three children may suggest the Third World itself is unwilling to accept that level of risk.

These choices will not be easy. At the present time legislation before the U.S. Congress tends to follow what the child survival hypothesis implies about foreign aid. Food distribution and population programs are linked, and attention is devoted to the problems both of distribution of contributed food within the recipient country and of shielding its domestic agricultural markets from adverse impacts of food aid. The recent U.S. posture on these matters evidences a renewed dedication to the general development of poorer countries—along seemingly broader lines than in the past. While any food aid programs should be designed and administered so as to have as positive an effect on reducing fertility as possible, it would appear imprudent, given the weak evidence supporting the child survival hypothesis, to depend on improved nutritional status as the principal route to that objective. There remains ample room for larger and accelerated population programs by the U.S. in the Third World, especially those with an emphasis on population information and education activities.

NOTES

1. William Rich, *Smaller Families through Social and Economic Progress,* Monograph No. 7, Overseas Development Council, Washington, D.C., June 1974.

2. *Food for Peace: 1974 Annual Report on Public Law 480*, 94th Congress, 2nd Session (House Document No. 94-352), Government Printing Office, Washington, D.C., 1976.

3. Sub-Committee on Nutrition and Fertility, Committee on International Nutrition Programs, Nutrition and Fertility Inter-relationships, *Implications for Policy and Action* (interpretive report of conference held in Washington, D.C., November 15-17, 1973), National Academy of Sciences, Washington, D.C., 1974.

4. *Ibid.,* p. 7.

5. *Ibid.,* p. 8.

6. Paul T. Schultz and Julie DaVanzo, *Analysis of Demographic Change in East Pakistan: A Study of Retrospective Survey Data,* Rand Corporation, Santa Monica, California, 1970.

7. *Ibid.,* p. 8.

8. Donald W. Snyder, "Economic Determinants of Family Size in West Africa," *Demography*, vol. II, no. 4, 1974.

9. Daniel M. Heer, "Determinants of Family Planning Attitudes and Practices" (report summarizing full study conducted in Taiwan, 1969-72, under AID Contract No. AID/CSD 2478), Harvard University, 1972, pp. 165-6—cited in Interdisciplinary Communications Program Smithsonian Institution, *Policy Relevance of Recent Social Research On Fertility*, Occasional Monograph No. 2, Washington, D.C., September 1974.

10. Schultz and DaVanzo, *op. cit.*

11. John B. Wyon and John E. Gordon, *The Khanna Study: Population Problems in the Rural Punjab*, Harvard University Press, Cambridge, Mass., 1974.

12. Interdisciplinary Communications Program, Smithsonian Institution, *op. cit.*, p. 45.

13. Rockefeller, John D. *Population Growth: The Role of the Developed World*, International Union for the Scientific Study of Population, 1974, pp. 4-5.

14. Reported in Interdisciplinary Communications Program, Smithsonian Institution, *op. cit.*

15. Carl E. Taylor, Jeanne S. Newman, and Narindar U. Kelly, "The Child Survival Hypothesis," Department of International Health, School of Hygiene and Public Health, Johns Hopkins University, 1975.

16. See discussion of the "Litton Amendment" to H.R. 9005, *Congressional Record*, September 10, 1975, pp. H 8585f.

16 Nutritional dilemmas of transforming economies

Norge W. Jerome

INTRODUCTION AND SUMMARY

Introduction

No discussion on food policy is complete without some reference to the tragic and costly effects of public and private economic development programs on millions of individuals throughout the world. The demands of economic development programs have often triggered rapid changes in the traditional system of food production, processing, distribution, and consumption, and a decline in the group's nutritional status. Among the victims of "economic progress" are peasants, small farmers, tribal groups, rural-backwoods dwellers and in-migrants to cities.

Food policy designers must be guided by past policies and programs which have jeopardized tribal and rural peoples by displacing them, changing their economies and their modes of producing, securing, distributing, and consuming foods, and, consequently, their nutritional status. Unquestionably, contemporary food and population problems are rooted in the past.

One billion and a half persons residing in Africa, Asia, and Latin America suffer from hunger and malnutrition (Berg, 1973:5). A significant portion of this malnourished group once lived in economic systems geared to the groups' basic needs. Often, the transformation from a subsistence to a cash-based economy failed to meet the basic subsistence and nutritional needs of the local people. New alliances with large, remote, and complex market networks were often

---

The author wishes to acknowledge the assistance of Ms. Pamela Kisslinger in gathering some of the material for this chapter. Special thanks is offered Miss Carol Carter for assisting in the preparation of this manuscript for publication.

based upon unbalanced commercial transactions between unequal groups. In addition, new developments in the agricultural sector led to population shifts and their attendant change in the acquisition, distribution, and consumption of foods. Hunger and malnutrition often developed.

When the subsistence system of hunter-gatherers is compared with economies of modern peasants in the Third World, it appears that the former type of economy provided an adequate (if not luxurious) diet for its population. The transition from a basic subsistence economy of the hunter-gatherer type to that of a subsistence-cash economy as exemplified by the peasant or small farmer, herdsman, or fisherman (who make up one-third of the human population) is often attended by food scarcity and malnutrition. Transition from one economic level to another requires major alteration in all aspects of the traditional system, including the nutritional content of the diet.

It has been well documented that peoples residing in changing subsistence economies who lack the requisite cash and social and political relations necessary for securing food for themselves and their dependents are particularly vulnerable to chronic malnutrition. Small peasants and agricultural and industrial laborers (wage earners) in low-income countries fall within this deprived and malnourished group. They are also the major recipients of direct food aid from high-income countries.

Tribal peoples once existed in dynamic equilibrium with their environments. They were able to satisfy their basic material needs by matching these needs with the products of the environment. As is the case with all peoples and cultures, the perception and satisfaction of needs are dependent on local environmental possibilities and distal marketing strategies. In labeling hunter-gatherers "the original affluent society," Sahlins (1972) accepts the common understanding of affluence—that the material wants of those affected are easily satisfied. Of course, as he quickly points out, wants may be "easily satisfied" by producing much or desiring little. Economy in the use of resources, or the desire for little, represents the hallmark of tribal peoples' affluence.

Consumption patterns of tribal cultures and the industrialized world are strikingly different. Bodley (1975: 4-5) asserts that "primitive cultures make but light demands on their environments and can easily support themselves within their own boundaries." The opposite situation prevails for the industrial civilization or the "culture of consumption," as he terms it. However, economists have traditionally viewed transformations from a subsistence to an industrialized economy as an indication of "progress" or "development." This ethnocentric viewpoint reinforces "culture of consumption" values and negates or deemphasizes those values and activities linked with conserving environmental resources. This type of value system also prevents observers from understanding the systems of production, distribution, consumption, and replenishment in small-scale economies and in economies undergoing transformation through "development" schemes. Moreover, this limited viewpoint disregards the importance of cultural and ecological possibilities and limitations, regional and subnational variations, local consumer technology and economics, and the food and energy resources and distribution systems of the local area.

Throughout recorded history, man has demonstrated his ingenuity by successfully producing food under every environmental condition. In response to environmental exigencies, cultural dictates, population growth, and biological imperatives numerous and often ingenious schemes have been devised to extract or produce an adequate diet and surplus foods. Currently, the reality of the ominous Malthusian prophecy has cast serious doubts on man's continued ability to provide food for the ever-increasing world population. A reassessment of strategies seems in order.

Berg (1970) has captured one of the basic issues in the current food-population dyad by stating that malnutrition cannot be approached as a peripheral welfare problem. There is growing recognition that improved nutritional standards represent a basic prerequisite for development in Third World nations (Berg and Muscat, 1972). The idea that nutritional well-being is basic to economic development is being gradually accepted by policy makers and economic planners. Many are attempting to apply this concept of development to the food-population-development problem. By viewing food and food use contextually and understanding their relationship to economics, business, health, and other aspects of human life, it may yet be possible to stabilize and enrich the various food production systems of the world.

A multidisciplinary approach to the problems of nutrition provides one of the best means of conceptualizing the issues and finding solutions to the problems. Obviously, the traditional unidisciplinary approach has had limited value. The food and nutrition issue has been tackled from many singular perspectives, e.g., from the standpoint of economics, agriculture and agribusiness, politics, marketing, health, and the military. However, there is a growing recognition that no one discipline can do justice to the complexities of the current world food, nutrition, and population problem. This chapter has been developed from that recognition. It combines nutritional and anthropological perspectives in order to arrive at a general holistic design of the ecology of food production and food use. This perspective captures and conveys the dynamics of food use in relation to nutritional adaptation and malnutrition.

Summary

In accordance with the ecological approach to nutrition studies presented by Simms et al. (1972), this chapter will elaborate on the dynamic interactions of the total ecosystem which permit a population to adapt to or benefit from its resources. Adaptation may be expressed through nutritional balance or through malnutrition. Examples of populations demonstrating the dynamic interplay of forces and manifestations of adaptive responses will be presented.

By looking at the interplay of forces in various environments which lead to specific types of nutritional adaptation, a clearer, holistic picture of man's adaptive processes will emerge. The ecological perspectives that Rappaport (1971a) describes for anthropology are especially pertinent to the study of nutrition. His approach is to determine whether "behavior undertaken with respect to social, economic, political, or religious conventions contributes to or threatens the survival and well-being of the actors, or whether this behavior maintains or degrades the ecological system in which it occurs" (Rappaport, 1971a:7). Following him, we may return to the original anthropological frame of reference which was to integrate the biological, physical, and cultural environments (Baker, 1962) that lead to a holistic understanding of cultural man.

The chapter discusses and exemplifies the ways that various peoples have responded and adapted to their ecosystems in their attempt to satisfy food needs. It also describes a variety of ecological settings, cultures, and economies and shows how economic systems (which include food production, distribution, and use) can adapt to the environment at one level of development yet show evidence of maladaptation at another. Malnutrition and food shortages represent but two of the many responses of an economic system maladapted to an ecosystem. This occurs when the intricate preexisting state of balance had not been taken into account. An understanding of natural systems of food acquisition, diet selection, and nutritional balance will aid in establishing guidelines, if not policies for food aid in developmental programs.

The chapter begins with a discussion of relationships between the ecosystem, diet, food use, culture, nutritional adaptation, nutritional health, and malnutrition (pp. 280-284). It continues with examples of a wide range of economic systems and myriad adaptive responses from small-scale economies, i.e., hunters and gatherers to contemporary industrial societies. For each economic system, the chapter focuses on various forms of adaptation to the ecosystem, the nutritional status that ensues, and conditions contributing to the nutritional status of the groups described. These include the nature of the physical environment, diet, population size, economic development, food productivity, "cultural" practices associated with food production, distribution, and consumption, the extent of foreign intervention, and the culture's perceived relationship with the physical environment (pp. 284-300).

Hunter-gatherers are among the few population groups with little or no control over their diet; they depend primarily on the foodstuffs of their local environment for their nutrition. Strategies for survival include methods for maintaining an adequate and constant food supply. Some groups suffer from nutritional stress periodically because neither the local environment nor the strategies for food production provide for an adequate food supply during seasonal or other changes. The Copper Eskimo and Guayaki Indians are examples of these societies (pp. 285-286). The ! Kung Bushmen of the Kalahari Desert and the Hadza of Tanzania also depend upon the local environment for their food supply. However, unlike the Copper Eskimo and Guayaki, they subsist in rich environments and exercise a great degree of selectivity in securing their diet. Their nutritional status is very good (pp. 286-289). The section on hunters and gatherers continues with a discussion on the influence of the rate of change on nutritional equilibrium, and the impact of modern technology and purchased foods on diet and nutrition in subsistence economies (pp. 289-290).

Pastoralism is discussed within the context of a subsistence system (pp. 290-291). It represents a movement away from the total reliance on locally available foods toward conscious food production in a harsh environment. The Jie of Uganda exemplifies a pastoralist group with a subsistence system combining transiency, food production, and the accumulation of wealth in a harsh environment without unnecessarily exploiting the environment or compromising the group's nutritional status.

Agriculture is viewed as another form of relationship between man and nature; the subject is discussed from this standpoint on p. 292. Agriculture combines three unique features—conscious food production to provide surpluses, cultivation of nonlocal plant crops, and sedentarism. Agriculture may either adapt to or exploit the environment. The method selected can alter the environment, economy, diet, and nutritional status of the population maximally or minimally.

Subsistence agriculture can adapt to the environment and produce an adequate diet, as shown for the Tsembaga of New Guinea (pp. 292-293). Tribal groups including subsistence agriculturists often control their surplus foods and engage in transactions which permit a generalized reciprocity among specific well-known groups. By contrast, peasants have no control over their surpluses and must transact business with distant, unknown, commercial enterprises. This often ends in unbalanced transactions.

The transition from an ecologically sound subsistence farming economy to a cash-based cropping system often leads to a loss of control over cash crops and surplus foods and results in a reduction in the amount of food available for home consumption. Nutritional intake is thus affected. Transformed agriculture-based economies and unbalanced transactions between peasants and economic elites are key issues in food policy considerations. This topic is discussed on pp. 293-298.

Industrialized agriculture (agri-industry) includes the type of large-scale farming found in modern, industrialized nations e.g., the U.S.A., and that developed as a result of international aid programs in developing countries e.g., the green revolution. Industrialized agriculture has had a different impact on these groups. Except for a few home-grown products consumed by the farm family, there is little reason to believe that consumption patterns of the farm household in modern, industrialized nations differ significantly from those of the society as a whole. However, despite an increase in food production as a result of the application of modern agricultural techniques in some areas of the developing world, the gap between the rich and poor has widened. Often there has been a lack of convergence between agricultural innovations and the local ecology and the wholesale transfer of technologies into developing economies. Many developing countries have been unable to integrate capital- and energy-intensive technologies into their existing systems. In addition, only a limited number of farmers could afford to invest in high-yield grains. As a result of transferred technologies, laborers have been displaced by machines, and this has led to disruptions in traditional social institutions and relationships (pp. 298-299).

Four major policy implications follow from this chapter. Each is related to the basic principle of fully understanding the extant intricate relationships among elements in an existing sociocultural, economic, and nutritional system before attempting to modify it.

1. Since people can be worse off nutritionally and economically as a result of "economic progress," a viable policy for national or regional economic development should include goals and standards for nutritional health.
2. Economic and nutrition policies should be based on an objective assessment of the ongoing sociocultural, economic, and nutritional systems. Knowledge of what people have, how they have achieved it, what value they place on it, what they desire for individual and group welfare, and their strategies for achieving those goals should precede prescriptions for development programs.
3. Economic and nutrition policies and programs should be monitored closely and frequently by local communities to determine whether the goals are being achieved. Appropriate adjustments and modifications should follow.
4. The modification of any system must include only those elements which harmonize with the existing system. For example, the inappropriate transfer of technology should be avoided at all costs.

NUTRITIONAL ADAPTATION VS. MALNUTRITION

The term "nutritional adaptation" refers generally to the ability of the human body to rally or respond positively to the insults of nutritional stress; e.g., a shortage would lead to the most economic use of available nutrients by altering the body's metabolic activity while permitting it to function (Mitchell, 1964). With limited nutrient intake for a given period of time, the body efficiently utilizes what is available and adapts to lowered intake. However, this form of adaptation is time-specific; when nutrients are limited for prolonged periods, the response could be maladaptive and may lead to death of the species.

While examples of nutritional stress illustrate the dynamics of nutritional adaptation, they sometimes tend to present a limited picture. Nutritional adaptation also refers to the change in requirements in the individual in response to age, sex, activity, and environment and in whole populations according to a range of socioenvironmental factors. This is reflected in the variations of established recommended daily dietary allowances for different populations (Young, 1964:306-322).

Within a broader framework nutritional adaptation applies to any instance or setting where an individual or population had adjusted to the nutrients available in the diet, either metabolically or behaviorally, thereby expressing functional nutritional well-being. Naturally, a wide range of nutritional health is manifest under these varying conditions. Nutritional adaptation will apply to all peoples who have adapted to their ecosystem so as to experience functional nutritional health. Thus the small stature of prewar Japanese represents an example of adaptation to the available supply of nutrients.

At the opposite end of the continuum are those individuals and populations who have not been able to sufficiently adapt to the available quantity and quality of nutrients, thus failing to manifest functional nutritional well-being. Such people suffer malnutrition.

The Role of Diet

Nutritional adaptation and malnutrition both depend primarily on the actual diet consumed. The diet develops in response to the food potential of the physical environment and the cultural mechanisms and dictates for coping with or controlling food acquisition, distribution, and consumption. A nutritionally adaptive diet depends on the interaction of these two agents. The physical environment must offer the potential for providing food—either indigenously or through human efforts—and the cultural environment must adapt to this potential by utilizing available resources without destroying them in the process. Further, cultural factors almost always work to limit the dietary choices; "food prohibitions, learned eating preferences, and culturally defined limits on what is considered edible limit the individual to a fraction of what is actually palatable, reasonably nutritious and satisfying" (Garn, 1968:49).

The ecological approach to nutrition negates the simplistic environmental determinism explanation of diet in favor of one that integrates the dynamics of both the physical and cultural environments. However, it will become clear that the influence of the physical environment and the degree and emphasis vary with the habitat, level of technology, and subsistence base. Regardless of the focus, in no instance is it accurate to speak of either the physical environment or the culture determining the diet.

Sahlins would exchange the notion of environmental determinism for one of "environmental possibilism; which holds that cultures act selectively, if not capriciously, upon their environments, exploiting some possibilities while ignoring others; that it is environment that is passive, an inert configuration of possibilities and limits to development, the deciding forces of which lie in culture itself and in the history of culture" (Sahlins, 1964:132). However, the potential for cultural selectivity varies in relation to environmental potential, the variety of edible foods, the level of technology, and the extent of foreign intervention. Whereas the Copper Eskimo subsist primarily on the local food supply and exercise limited selectivity (Damas, 1972), members of modern industrialized societies also consume primarily local foods and exercise a great deal of selectivity (Jerome, 1970 and 1976). Regardless of the degree of selectivity a culture exercises in its choice of diet, cultural factors are always involved in food-related activities.

Cultural Factors in Nutritional Deficiency Disease

A wide range of nondietary factors contribute to nutritional adaptation and malnutrition. These are cultural factors that influence what is used as food, by whom, in what amounts, under what circumstances, and a host of social relations regulating food production, supply, distribution, and consumption. Also governing food use by omission are rules about a wide variety of dietary items which must be avoided by specific individuals under specified conditions.

Throughout much of the folk world, people attribute spiritual and ideational factors to illness and disease. These ideas have also been applied to nutritional deficiency diseases.

Protein-calorie malnutrition (kwashiorkor and nutritional marasmus) is widespread throughout most of the developing nations. It is generally associated with weaning foods of low nutritional value. It is further precipitated by infectious and parasitic diseases, which are commonly treated by lowering the already deficient nutrient intake (particularly when complicated by diarrhea). However, for many cultures, the cause of kwashiorkor is believed to be completely nondietary; kwashiorkor is believed to be brought on instead by breach of taboos. For example, among the northeast coastal Bantu kwashiorkor ("chirwa") is endemic. However, "chirwa" is not associated with the lack of high-protein weaning diet, but caused by the breach of a taboo. This taboo forbids the parents from sexual intercourse during the period of gestation or before the child is weaned. It is believed that should a pregnancy occur, the unborn fetus would "steal the strength" from the mother's milk and the nursing child would suffer. Actually, such a taboo is adaptive, in that it helps space pregnancies, and is beneficial to the mother and child's health. However, it becomes maladaptive when the guilt associated with the breach of the taboo, manifested in the child's case of kwashiorkor, inhibits the parents from taking appropriate action to regain the child's health (Gerlach, 1964).

Another example comes from Buganda (a section of Uganda). Kwashiorkor ("obwosi") is not associated with nutritional deficiency in the young child. The Buganda understanding of kwashiorkor is that it is caused by the jealousy that the unborn fetus feels toward the suckling sibling and directs that jealousy by making the child sick. Therefore, when the mother becomes pregnant, the nursing child is often separated from the mother, taken into custody by a grandmother or other relative who often neglects the importance of a highly nutritious diet, thereby precipitating the kwashiorkor which was meant to be prevented by sending the child away. Coupled with the psychological trauma of separation from the mother, the condition often worsens (Burgess and Dean, 1962; Cravioto, 1966; Amann et al., 1972). The kwashiorkor that results from separation is termed "omusana," which is believed to be caused by the cold nights that the child spends away from its mother (Burgess and Dean, 1962:25).

The examples cited clearly indicate that folk ideas and beliefs, and behaviors emanating from these beliefs, work in conjunction with nonideational factors to equate diet prescriptions. Edibles are given, withheld, or provided in limited amounts based on ideas of their appropriateness for specific individuals at specific times. Often, the behavior (if not the belief) has or did have a sound rational basis and had its root in the historical or ecological experience of the group.

Folk Beliefs Associated with Diet

A myriad of folk beliefs associated with intrinsic magical and semimagical properties of foods have characterized the food habits of all peoples. Some foods offer prestige (white bread and polished rice), others security (milk in the U.S., rice in Asia), and still others a sense of group identification ("ethnic" foods) (Jerome, 1970). Frequently, beliefs concerning the intrinsic value of foods are associated with critical periods in the life cycle, i.e., pregnancy, lactation, disease. Often such beliefs are neutral in their nutritional impact, e.g., the Papago avoidance of salts and sweets by the mother until the umbilical cord falls off the infant (Gonzales, 1972), or the avoidance of timid animals or repulsive-looking food to protect the infant from growing up timid or ugly (Hughes, 1963). Of particular interest are those foods which are avoided in accordance with some taboo, thereby possibly eliminating a much-needed nutrient from the diet, especially at critical periods. These food taboos include the prohibition of eggs in avoidance of childbirth complications and sterility (HEW, 1973), the avoidance of milk by lactating mothers, the Burmese reduction of meat and fowl during pregnancy (Mead, 1955), the Papago diet of maize and wheat flour gruel for the first days following childbirth, the Tewa prohibition of milk for 4 weeks after childbirth (Gonzales, 1972), the Navajo preference for serving coffee and soft drinks to children on the assumption that milk is a "weak" food (Reisinger et al., 1972), and the Zulu taboo against consuming milk from cows not owned by kin (Cassel, 1957). Because all cultures attach symbolic significance to their food, the examples of associated properties are virtually limitless.

In addition, foods are often granted special healing properties. According to the doctrine of signatures, the physical characteristics of a plant indicate its specific healing properties. For example, heart-shaped leaves possess healing powers for the heart, or red plants cure blood diseases. Often, foods are attributed qualities less easily identifiable. The hot and cold theory of disease prevalent in Mexico and South America is a classic example of this. Just as applicable is our current popular obsession with the semimagical healing powers of vitamins C and E, "organic" and "natural" foods, and a host of other foods, herbs, and supplements.

Patterns of Food Use

In addition to beliefs associated with the inherent properties of food, each culture also institutionalizes its own food use patterns. These include methods of production, storage, and preparation, the system of food distribution, and consumption styles of the individual and group.

Methods of preparation carry nutritional implications in terms of nutrient retention or loss; for example, parboiling rice retains important nutrients. The specific mix or combination of staple grains or legumes may enhance or reduce the protein content of the diet. Similarly, other combinations may reduce the diet's mineral content. Ingredients added during preparation may destroy certain nutrients.

The system of food distribution within the family may also have serious nutritional consequences. The order of eating, the identity or status of individuals allotted first choice in food selection, and the method of serving food to individual household members all have important nutritional consequences. For example, in Ethiopia (as in many East Africa nations) the father is granted priority in meal selection, followed by guests, the mother, the older children, and finally the youngest children (Habte, 1969). No special foods are fed to the weaned child, who during the critical growth years must consume the least desirable, leftover adult foods.

Numerous ideational and behavioral forces influence the actual diet consumed, and to a large extent determine an individual or group's nutritional status.

HUNTERS AND GATHERERS

The nutritionist interested in the anthropological aspects of diet (or the anthropologist interested in nutrition) will find hunter-gatherers of particular interest for two main reasons. Accounts of hunter-gatherers existing today or from the recent past offer clues to the subsistence activities of prehistoric populations, and perhaps suggest the type of diet and health standards experienced by early man. Naturally, direct correlations cannot be made, since habitats, cultural dictates, experience, and social organizations vary. However, hunting and gathering still represent man's experience in living for more than 99 percent of human history.

Hunter-gatherer groups depend primarily on the foodstuffs of their local environment. They are among the few population groups with very little control over their dietary options; as a result, they are less exploitive of the environment in their efforts to survive and live. While they depend on the food sources of the immediate physical environment, they also develop strategies for maintaining an adequate and constant food supply. The mechanisms or cultural dictates associated with securing food from the local environment usually promote the type of equilibrium considered desirable by the group. Quimby notes that "when the technology of a hunting culture is perfected in relation to its habitat, it can be said to be in equilibrium with its environment" (Quimby, 1968:293).

The Copper Eskimo represent one group residing in an extremely hazardous environment who adapted successfully to the very limited food resources. The Arctic tundra habitat offered only white spruce and willow as vegetation, and the vast majority of the diet was derived from animal sources. Traditionally, the caribou and ringed seal were the most highly prized catch, though there was some hunting of smaller animals such as the fox and wolf and fishing for lake trout and char. It is apparent that the extent of diet selectivity was dictated by environmental limitations and further constricted by seasonal variations of food availability. Religious sanctions and taboos associated with food further reinforced the practices born out of a meager environment; e.g., to avoid displeasing the chief spiritual deity, who might discontinue the food supply, contact between land and sea mammals was prohibited.

Yet even within the scope of what appears to be strict environmental determinism in a harsh environment, important cultural factors affecting diet emerge. First, the technology (developed in response to environmental imperatives) is designed for the specific type of food production found in the region. Bows, arrows, harpoons, lances, kayaks, snow knives, shovels, drills, and adzes of the Eskimo tool kit facilitate fishing and hunting in the Arctic tundra (Damas, 1972). Second, the culturally devised reciprocal food distribution system (termed "piqat") assures a constant food supply for all people. For example, the successful seal hunter would bring his catch home to be divided among his family and his partners' families. If all of his partners were present for distribution, the hunter received only the least desirable sections—the fat, entrails, and skin. In return, he received more choice sections of meat from his partners' catches. This system of food exchange offers more than security of food; it also enhances community relations and promotes the solidarity and cooperation necessary in a marginal environment.

However, even with the cultural mechanisms for acquiring and distributing food, famine occurred fairly frequently. The practice of female infanticide helped limit the population size, but the cyclical supply of adequate food failed to provide year-round security. When the physical environment could provide adequate food, the people thrived. Since they relied on only local food sources, seasonal changes reduced the food supply. The inconsistent food supply prohibited metabolic or cultural adaptation, resulting in periods of nutritional stress.

The Guayaki Indians represent another example of a hunter-gatherer group dependent upon an unproductive environment for its total food supply. Inhabiting the tropical forests of Paraguay, the Guayaki respond to their environment, which offers few edible fruits or other vegetation, by concentrating their activity on hunting. Clastres (1972) reports that the economic life of the Guayaki is a continual food quest. Hunting is the focus not only of economic activity but also of socioreligious life and ritual activity. Besides hunting and the generally unproductive fishing or gathering, the search for much-prized honey and larvae constitutes the Guayaki subsistence activities, which start anew every day, due to lack of surplus and storage facilities. For the Guayaki, the diet composition is directly related to the limited food sources, and cultural adaptations decrease the chance of any one member going hungry. Clastres confirms their lack of options for diet selectivity by stating, "the life of the Guayaki depends directly upon a familiarity with their natural habitat . . . these Indians eat all animals of the forest, almost without exception" (the exception being the avoidance of birds with mythological significance) (Clastres, 1972:154).

The limitations of the environment as indicated by a scarcity of plant sources have been virtually overcome by the group's undiscriminating selection of animal foods. This assures the Guayaki an adequate and constant food supply. Yet, as with the Copper Eskimo, the effective exploitation of the environment depends on the degree of their technological development; the bows and arrows of the hunters, plus spears, digging sticks, baskets, pottery, and other containers, are designed to exploit the food potential of the environment. The simple technological complex is consistent with the nomadic life-style that prohibits a large inventory of material possessions. Also as with the Copper Eskimo, the system of game distribution includes rules prohibiting a hunter from consuming his own catch. The hunter's catch is divided among tribal members; each hunter relies on the catch of others for his own consumption. Again, this not only offers security in food but reinforces tribal relations (Clastres, 1972).

To avoid the conclusion that a hunter-gatherer subsistence base implies minimal diet selectivity in marginal environments, examples of hunter-gatherer groups subsisting in rich environments and exercising a great degree of selectivity from environmental possibilities will follow.

A classic example of such a group are the !Kung Bushmen of the Kalahari Desert. Lee (1972) has successfully destroyed the myth that all hunter-gatherer groups lived in constant peril of starvation and were forced to spend the majority of waking hours in the food quest. Instead, he presents the following picture, which he claims is common of hunter-gatherers. The !Kung Bushmen are well adapted to their environment and enjoy high health standards while expending minimal time and energy doing so. In addition to the stable food supply, the dry climate and high elevation result in freedom from most infectious diseases endemic in tropical Africa.

While the ! Kung Bushmen are both hunters and gatherers, the major portion of the diet is derived from reliable and nutritious plant sources. Though meat is highly relished, its supply is scarce and unpredictable and acts as a supplementary treat to the diet. The ! Kung diet consists of over 100 species of edible plants in the Dobe area, though 23 species constitute 90 percent of the diet by weight, with the mongongo, baobob, and marula nuts taking highest priority. The abundance of food sources evidently allows a great deal of diet selectivity; less palatable foods are consumed only in times of scarcity. Factors contributing to this relatively rich diet are (1) primary dependence on vegetable food over animal, (2) thorough knowledge and understanding of the local environment, and (3) reciprocal food distribution that pervades the Bushmen's social life. Further evidence of food security derives from the proportion of time spent in leisure. The women average 2 to 3 days per week in the food quest and enjoy their leisure time visiting camps, sleeping, entertaining, or doing embroidery.

! Kung Bushmen's subsistence activities demonstrate an appreciation of the man-environment relationship. They make no distinction between natural resources and social wealth; the land is communally owned and available to all. Therefore, there is no need to amass a surplus of food, since their habitat is their natural storehouse. This method of food production and distribution tends to reduce food anxiety, for there is an implicit confidence in the ability of the environment to provide for the group. Sahlins (1972) generalizes this confidence to all hunters, stating that "storage would be superfluous" when the true surplus is everywhere. A stored surplus, like an abundance of material goods, would only limit their mobility. The variety and abundance of naturally available foods makes the tedious agricultural work of their Bantu neighbors quite unattractive. Thus the ! Kung Bushmen stand out as an example of a hunter-gatherer group which totally relies on its naturally occurring food sources, yet exercises a great degree of cultural discrimination and selectivity while extracting a highly nutritious diet.

The Hadza present another example of a hunter-gatherer group exercising great selectivity in gathering plant foods of their rich environment. Eighty percent of their diet by weight consists of vegetable foods; meat and honey constitute the remaining 20 percent (Woodburn, 1968).

The diet of the Hadza consists of meat, yam, wild, raw berries, and other fruit. Infant feeding is permissive, and nursing is prolonged until the mother becomes pregnant again. Fat, marrow, gruel of baobob seeds and honey are introduced at an early age and the infant consumes the full adult diet by 18 months (Jelliffe et al., 1962).

The search for food and its distribution among members of the group are loosely organized. Men and women gather food individually and eat at the gathering site; only the women bring home surpluses. Hunting is an individualized male activity; the hunter eats his fill at the kill site and brings home only the leftovers. In this way, men and women are independent of each other in obtaining food; food exchange is not an important part of their way of life (Woodburn, 1968). The rich and stable environment, with its reliable food resources, has dictated this type of individualized food acquisition and loose distribution system. The Hadza are a well-nourished people.

Jelliffe and his associates (1962) conducted an investigation of the nutritional status of the Hadza children. The children received high nutritional ratings. There was no clinical evidence of protein-calorie malnutrition, rickets, scurvy, or vitamin B deficiencies. Jelliffe and his associates reported Bitot's spots (a vitamin A deficiency symptom) in 13 percent of the "preschool"-age children and in 17.3 percent of the older children. Twenty-seven percent suffered from malaria and 30 percent from conjunctivitis. The lack of extensive nutritional deficiencies endemic in neighboring areas demonstrates the successful adaptation to the environment.

Cockburn (1971) arrived at similar results in his examination of 62 Hadza children. The children were well nourished with healthy teeth. The incidence of malaria and conjunctivitis was similar to that reported by Jelliffe et al. Cockburn further showed that four children had taenia, and three had giardia; none had roundworm or hookworm, but there were many with ringworm. He concluded that the children were afflicted with infections that could thrive in a small mobile population. Polgar (1964), Black (1975), and Cockburn (1971) agree that parasitic infections of hunter-gatherers (louse, pinworm, yaws) were adapted to prehominids.

No single environmental, technological, or cultural factor dictates the system of acquiring, selecting, and distributing foods of hunter-gatherer groups. Systems of food acquisition and use represent an intricate interplay of environment, technology, and culture. Innovations in any single component of the finely articulated system could reverberate throughout and cause disruptions.

The Copper Eskimo and Guayaki represent groups habiting very different marginal environments who both manage to usually extract an adequate diet from the limited possibilities. Strict institutionalized distribution systems are adaptive to the insecurity of the food supply. The ! Kung Bushmen and the Hadza both occupy relatively rich environments and are afforded a great degree of dietary selectivity. Both groups subsist primarily on vegetable foods with meat as a delicacy. Yet the social organizations differ dramatically. The ! Kung enjoy sharing their food, particularly meat, and food passes freely between camps. The food quest of the Hadza and much of their consumption are individualized.

The adaptations of the hunter-gatherer groups are characterized by a slow rate of cultural and environmental changes. The reliance on indigenous food sources entailed a minimum of direct environmental manipulation, which resulted in minimal alternations in the ecosystem. Dunn (1968) has captured the essentials of life among hunting and gathering peoples in the following statement: "the group utilizes environmental resources intensively but with minimal permanent disturbance of the environment; the individuals are well adapted to the conditions of the ecosystem in which they belong; the individual lives in intimate contact with his fellows and the environment" (Dunn, 1968:223).

The Impact of Change on Diet

Among hunting and gathering peoples, change developed in response to crisis conditions, e.g., sudden environmental changes such as drought or floods, or in response to the influx of new ideas carried in from other cultures. A slow rate of change permitted greater possibilities of maintaining the equilibrium essential to nutritional well-being. Malnutrition is rare, although there are instances of starvation (more so in the Arctic regions than the tropics). Nutritional disease is considerably less frequent than among agricultural groups, who depend on one or two staple food crops for nutritional sustenance (Dunn, 1968). At this traditional subsistence level, each survival strategy resulted in diets that provided adequate nutrients for the population for a majority of the time. "To date," state Lee and Devore (1968:3), "the hunting way of life has been the most successful and persistent adaptation man has ever achieved."

Kemp's report (1971) on diet and food use in an isolated Eskimo village of hunters in the southern coast of Baffin Island in the eastern Canadian Arctic vividly illustrates how change in technology may cause disruptions in a well-adapted life. During the 13-month period of reporting in 1967-68, the villagers acquired 44 percent of their calories in the form of protein, 33 percent in the form of carbohydrate and 23 percent in fat. Almost all the protein (93 percent) came from game; 96 percent of the carbohydrate was store food. This traditional diet was fairly well balanced, nutritionally; the relatively high-protein diet was obtained from hunting. Nutritional problems arose with the decline of hunting. In one household in September 1967, when the family worked for wages, the caloric input remained at 2,700 kilocalories per person per day, but 62 percent of the calories were carbohydrate and only 9 percent were protein. As calories from purchased foods replaced calories from the hunt, flour consumption increased and meat consumption decreased. This resulted in a change in the traditional distribution of protein, fat, and carbohydrate calories.

Although the diet had been altered by the new mode of securing foods, the introduction of non-Eskimo technology, energy, and world view also altered traditional social mechanisms which controlled food distribution and the individual's relations with the ecosystem. "Today" states Kemp (1971:114), "ritual control of the forces of nature and of the food supply has almost disappeared; technology is considered the mainspring of well-being. Prayers may still be said for good hunting and traveling conditions. . . . hunting decisions may also be affected by dreams. None of these activities, however, has the regulatory powers of the intricate symbols and beliefs of earlier times. . . . the mutual trust between man and his food supply has evidently been lost in the report of the high-powered rifle and the rumble of the outboard motor."

PASTORALISTS

Pastoralism developed as an adaptive response to the exigencies of an arid, marginal ecosystem. It has been defined as "a cultural adjustment to semi-arid open country in which native vegetation will support large ruminants but in which hoe agriculture without advanced technologies cannot be sustained satisfactorily" (Goldschmidt, 1968:240). Pastoralists' subsistence represents a movement away from the total reliance on locally available foods toward a conscious effort at food production. This requires appropriate use of environmental elements, particularly water, and the development of ingenious strategies for survival in a relatively uninhabitable land. "The pastoralists," states Baker (1974:172), "live in a high risk situation, they have evolved a risk-minimizing strategy proven over time and based on holding the maximum number of productive animals in the face of heavy losses. They never keep all the animals together but spread them over different grazing areas and keep a range of animals able to utilize various niches in the ecosystem. The price of an innovation may well be death for, if it fails, there is no reserve capacity."

Current pressures to disrupt pastoralist tribes and relocate them on sedentary ranches has greatly decreased their numbers, yet for over 3,000 years they inhabited the area from the Atlantic shore of the Sahara to the steppes of Mongolia with additional representation among North and South American Indians (Sahlins, 1968; Griggs, 1974). Despite the movement away from pastoralism it has been suggested that pastoral nomadism was the best possible use of the land in contrast to the prohibitive costs of cultivation and irrigation (Griggs, 1974).

Pastoralists can be divided into two groups, the nomads and the seminomads. The nomads do not occupy a permanent dwelling and do not practice agriculture, while the seminomads set up semipermanent settlements near water with part of the tribe (usually women and children) cultivating crops (Griggs, 1974). Goldschmidt (1968) has outlined the following pastoralist characteristics: (1) mobile, with the associated limited material possessions, (2) militarism, particularly in regards to raiding and protecting their herds, (3) male-dominated patrilineal societies, (4) little or no concept of land ownership, and (5) dependence on an inadequate water supply. Pastoralists often live in a symbiotic relationship with nearby sedentary villages. Sahlins (1968) includes political cohesion in his list of characteristics. Communities enter into regional arrangements of internal peace, collective defense, and periodic redistribution of natural resources.

The diets of pastoralists generally consist of the meat and by-products of their herds, including milk and milk products, and blood; the animal-based diet is supplemented with vegetable foods grown, gathered, or traded. Naturally, slaughtering of livestock is uncommon, as the primary source of wealth is the herds. The arid land prohibits high-yield agriculture and offers limited indigenous food supplies.

The Jie of Uganda

The Jie of Uganda are typical of pastoralists in that they show one group's subsistence strategy in its adaptation to a dry, barren environment. Jieland is divided into two climatic zones—the relatively moist west and semidesert east. Seasonally, they experience a rainy season between March and August and a dry season for the remainder of the year. Jie settlements are located in the center, bordering on the two climatic zones. All land is communal pasture. Gulliver's statement (1968:264) on Jie subsistence strategy is apt: "they make the best use of their meager natural resources by pastoral transhumance between east and west regions, which they use for their herds in the rainy and dry seasons, respectively."

The Jie combine the raising of livestock with the cultivation of crops. Livestock is of primary importance in Jie life. The herds are esteemed not only as a relished food source but also for their aesthetic value. They participate in the ritual life of the Jie and serve as a basis for much social interaction. Economic activities are divided sexually; the men take full responsibility for the livestock and the women take charge of all agriculture. All economic activity is individually based.

The diet consists primarily of sorghum, meat, milk (especially for children who can consume as much milk as desired), milk products, blood (taken from the necks of living animals), finger millet made into beer, and peanuts. This traditional diet, which has met with few changes in the twentieth century (Gulliver suggests this is due to the uselessness of the land for Western exploitation), is a remarkable example of the resourcefulness that converted arid, tropical land into a productive, inhabitable area.

Though limited by a harsh environment and dependent upon sparse rainfall so necessary for the survival of livestock and crops, the Jie have been able to create food sources for themselves. Unlike hunter-gatherers, they produce some of their foods. They have successfully integrated food production, nomadism, and the accumulation of wealth (livestock) in a harsh environment. The Jie subsistence system exemplifies a change in the man-nature relationship which does not unnecessarily exploit the environment yet provides nutritional sustenance for the population.

AGRICULTURAL SYSTEMS

Agriculture combines three unique features—conscious food production to provide surpluses, sedentarism, and independence from indigenous plants. It represents but one other type of relationship between man and nature and will be viewed within the following broad categories: (1) the transition to subsistence agriculture, (2) transition to a cash cropping economy, and (3) industrialized agriculture particularly in relation to the developing nations.

Agriculture introduced a subsistence strategy requiring active food production and less dependence on indigenous plants. As agriculture developed, man encountered profound changes in his environment. Many of these changes were predictable, but others were unpredictable; the results were both positive and negative.

From a cultural standpoint, agriculture involved rearranging patterns of social organization to correspond with a sedentary life and a more complex economy. New forms of technology for cultivating food crops and for processing, storing, and distributing foods also required different social arrangements. The social relations of hunter-gatherers were determined primarily by seasonal cycles and fluctuations in available food and water, while agriculturists had to adapt their social institutions to the complexities of the agricultural economy (Cohen, 1968).

The physical environment underwent major changes under agriculture. Indigenous species were replaced with preferred types, which upset the natural balance of the ecosystem. Agricultural techniques were developed in response, but not always in adaptation to the environment. Often these resulted in overcultivation and overgrazing and subsequent erosion of the land. However, these changes are maladaptive and avoidable. In his discussion of agricultural system Griggs implicitly demonstrates how the various agricultural techniques had originally been devised to adapt to and not exploit the environment (Griggs, 1974). For example, he illustrates how shifting agriculture is adaptive to the tropical rain forest environment and is perhaps the most effective use of the land given a low population density.

Subsistence Agriculturists

The subsistence agriculturists are distinguished from other forms of rural cultivators by a number of criteria. Technology is generally simple. Production is intended for household consumption rather than for commercial sale. The production unit is self-sufficient in that producers control the means of production (Wolf, 1966; Mellor, 1969). There is no interdependence with outside groups for food, so market networks do not exist, and social relations involving food production are primarily ceremonial and ritual. The Tsembaga of New Guinea, who practice subsistence agriculture, or "swiddening," and swine husbandry, provide a good example of subsistence agriculturists. Their form of agriculture makes relatively light demands on energy inputs, yet provides for almost all their dieteary needs (Rappaport, 1971b).

The Tsembaga could name at least 264 varieties of edible plants, representing 36 species. The staples are taro and sweet potatoes, but they cultivate a wide variety of legumes, leafy vegetables, and other tubers. Maize and sugarcane are also grown. The wide variety of cultigens and the system of planting permit the best use of space, soil, and light and discourage plant-specific pests. This system of cultivation is therefore ecologically sound in its pristine autonomous system. It is also nutritionally sound. The garden produce provides the men with 2,600 kilocalories per day and the women with some 2,200 kilocalories. The average Tsembaga male is 4 feet 10½ inches tall and weights 103 pounds; the average adult female is 4 feet 6½ inches tall and weights 85 pounds. The combination of "swiddening" and swine husbandry and the production and use of a wide variety of foods provide a subsistence base that is productive, self-sufficient, and nutritionally adequate.

The Sanio-Hiowe of Papua, New Guinea, represent another example of productive subsistence agriculturists. Sago production is a highly productive subsistence technology in the simply organized economy of the Sanio-Hiowe. The high energy return of sago work allows the women working only 1 day in 4 or 5 to provide 85 percent of the calorie intake of their community. A woman can produce sufficient sago in 1 day to provide for 16.7 people (Townsend, 1974).

The use of simple technology in the production of food and the noncommercial nature of transactions involving food production hold true for many other groups. The mini agricultural systems of the subsistence agriculturist demonstrate stability, self-sufficiency, efficiency, productivity, and richness—characteristics consistent with health and well-being.

The Peasantry and the Transition to Cash Economies

Throughout much of the developing world agricultural communities are making the transition from subsistence farming to a cash-based cropping system. Such transformations in agricultural and economic systems often lead to a reduction in the amount of foods available for home consumption and concomitant reduced nutritional intake. The groups directly affected are primarily peasants, who constitute the majority of the agricultural population, and farmers of very small holdings who cannot afford to convert to cash crops or adopt modern agricultural techniques on the farms.

Peasants are distinguished from subsistence agriculturists primarily by the positions they occupy in the large society (Foster, 1966; Wolf, 1966). They form part of a larger, compound society and are mutually dependent on the larger society. This interdependence is the key factor distinguishing peasants from tribal peoples; the latter do not have economic arrangements with groups in the larger society. Wolf (1966) has described peasants as rural cultivators who raise crops and livestock in the countryside for household consumption—not as a business or enterprise in the economic sense. However, their surpluses are transferred to a dominant group of rulers that uses the surpluses to underwrite its own standard of living and for distribution to still other groups in the society. Tribal societies, on the other hand, exchange surpluses directly among members of their own groups. The loss of control over surplus food sharply distinguishes peasants from tribal peoples and is key to the unbalanced transactions between peasants and the economic elites.

The peculiar social and economic relations between peasants and the dominant group have led to some life views which Foster (1965) has termed "image of limited goods." This outlook conceptualizes every aspect of the environment as "limited" and "finite" in number. That is, there is a limited quantity of resources, possessions, emotions, energy, etc., which are depleted when used. Therefore, if one individual progresses economically, this implies that another will experience hardship; love shown for one's child takes away that much love from one's spouse. This attitude develops into an individualistic orientation combined with a constant awareness of community members. In order to avoid suspicion and disapproval, surplus wealth is generously spent on community celebrations. Because individual achievement receives negative sanctions, opportunities for economic growth are often met with resistance.

Foster believes that developmental efforts should be directed to changing the world view from one of "limited good" to an open system where the individual can "feel safe in displaying initiative" (1965:310). Of course, one can only "feel safe in displaying initiative" if one perceives that he is safe vis-a-vis the dominant power structure of the larger society.

Tax (1957) disagrees with the categorical classification of peasants as a conservative, unadaptive people; he sees them as cautious people who feel they know better than outside developers what is best for them. These developers often become frustrated with the peasants' resistance to change.

The dominant powerful group in the larger society sets the stage for social relations, economies, and food production, distribution, and consumption of the peasantry. The dependent relationship between peasants and the larger economic system may serve to divert village resources from the community to the economic elites and so equalize economic statuses and diet intakes of the peasants. Results of a study conducted by Plattner (1974) in several highland Guatemalan Indian peasant communities indicated that parents' wealth was not related to children's heights. Apparently, the diversion of food and nutrients from the site of production in the village to distant markets adversely affected the nutritional status of all village children including those of relative wealth. This study had assumed that the economic status of parents would be reflected in the quality of the diet and in the growth of children (Plattner, 1974).

Obviously, the transition to a cash economy is not a sign of inevitable malnutrition. Yet, unfortunately, for many societies this has been the case. When the energy traditionally expended on hunting, gathering, and fishing and on the cultivation of food crops is redirected to the production of a market commodity, the local food supply is often reduced and diet quality suffers. Often, the most fertile land is used for the cash crop (coffee, cotton, cocoa), thus lowering the production capacity of the land under food cultivation. The change to a cash economy also means that a large part, if not the majority, of food is purchased instead of produced. The high cost of protein-rich foods often makes them prohibitive, thereby forcing the people into an affordable high carbohydrate diet which is often much less nutritious than the original diet. Thus, under the guise of economic progress or the gain of material wealth, the nutritional status becomes vulnerable. This ironic turn of events is what Hughes calls "the hidden cost of development" (Hughes and Hunter, 1970:452). The following examples will illustrate this point.

Collis (1962) recounts the effects of cash cropping in a Nigerian village. The transition to growing cocoa for a cash profit carried promises of prosperity. Cocoa offers a high yield per acre per energy output. The crop was grown in the rich valleys, and food crops were grown in the less fertile highland. Eventually cocoa planting moved uphill, seriously diminishing the already waning food supply. Since food crops do not grow well under shaded branches, food production is reduced even further. Because of the resort to purchased foods, when money runs out cheap carbohydrate foods such as cassava and yam form the basis of the diet. Furthermore, instead of being well off and happy, the villagers were dull, apathetic and sick, and the villages dirty and run down. Collis offers this comment: The cash crop "tends to kill their traditional life, merely putting money in their pockets for a short period in the year, during which time they enjoy themselves. When the money gets scarce, months before the next harvest, they find themselves short of everything" (Collis, 1962:223).

The West Nigerian villagers have a high parasitic rate of malaria and loa-loa and a high infestation rate of ascaris and hookworm. Fifty-four to sixty percent of the children one to fourteen years of age suffer from spleen enlargement. Kwashiorkor is prevalent, precipitated by inadequate weaning foods, diarrhea, and infectious or parasitic diseases.

A similar report on the consequences of the introduction of sisal agriculture comes from northeastern Brazil (Gross and Underwood, 1971). The principal economic activities prior to the introduction of sisal centered around cattle raising and subsistence farming. With the introduction of sisal as a profitable export crop, small landowners partially or completely abandoned subsistence agriculture in order to plant the profit-making crop. The commonest form of sisal cultivation in Brazil is transplantation of vegatively reproduced suckers, which require about 4 years to reach maturity. Small sisal growers had to enter the labor market to obtain supplementary work during the 4 years required for the plants to reach maturity. Generally, the men entered the labor force to work at decorticating the sisal. Decortication involves a mobile, manually fed rotating rasp driven by a diesel motor and requires high human labor inputs. Harvesting takes place the year round.

At harvest time, small landowners usually found that the price of sisal had fallen sharply since planting, or that they could not harvest at a profit because decorticating unit owners discriminated against small fields. The only source of income for such persons became labor on decorticating units. The change from subsistence agriculture to cash crop (sisal) was advantageous only to the small percent of persons who owned equipment and could control production and prices. The laborers' wages were generally inadequate to meet the subsistence needs of their families. Energy costs of sisal laborers were so great in relation to wages that their nonproductive dependents were deprived of calories and an adequate diet. The evidence indicated that if they did not deprive their families, they could not function as wage earners. The rapidly growing children were especially affected. Clearly, the nutritional status of the group had suffered through the introduction of the cash crop.

Gross and Underwood (1971) discuss the implications of the drain of labor from one part of the world to contribute to the welfare of another: "Sisal production is part of a system whose effect is to expropriate energy in the form of manual labor in one part of the world and apply it to the general welfare of another people thousands of miles away."

The final example shows the impact of the transition to a cash economy on the Miskito Indians of Nicaragua. The traditional subsistence economy as described by Nietschmann (1972) was a well-adapted hunting and fishing economy supplemented by the fruits of slash and burn agriculture. Nutritional needs were well met. However, this picture dramatically changed with the entrance of foreign "developers" and tradesmen. After Western contact, the Miskito changed from being satisfied with their adequate subsistence and developed new needs and desires. The market emerged for selling sea turtles and hawkbills, and in the enthusiasm and promise of prosperity the people abandoned their subsistence fishing and agricultural activities to devote their time to commercial fishing. This led to overpredation of the new source of wealth (Neitschmann, 1972; Weiss, 1974).

The impact on the diet was dramatic. Cash from the sale of the turtles was used to purchase food. However, the Miskito could only afford to purchase low-protein, high-carbohydrate staples of rice and flour. In addition, the reciprocal food distribution system of the subsistence economy vanished, thereby destroying a valued traditional institution and a strategy for achieving a balanced diet.

In general, a cash crop or wage economy has had a disastrous effect on the nutritional adequacy of the diet. The balance achieved under a subsistence economy can be disturbed by a reduction in the amount and quality of food crops produced in favor of cash drops, and by a further reduction in the amount of foods produced and processed at home.

The transition to cash cropping has affected aspects of the ecosystem besides nutritional standards; it has also taken its toll on the environment. For example, the Sahelian drought of 1972-74 represents one vivid example of the extent of environmental impact on a transitional economy. Though a drought is seemingly an uncontrollable natural calamity, certain imprudent actions precipitated the crisis. According to Wade (1974a), the Sahelian drought and desertification were caused by years of overgrazing and overplanting without adequate fallow periods. Cash crops (cotton and peanuts) had been grown on the most fertile land, leaving only the poorest land for food crops. The less fertile soil could not take the strain of intensive cultivation, resulting in poor crop yield, soil exposure, erosion, and eventually desert. In addition, the deforestation led to a loss of nitrogen in the soil, and the overgrazing of pastures created boreholes. The combination of these events left the Sahelian environment without any resistance to the mere suggestion of drought.

Lilimani's description of the economic impact on malnutrition in Kenya, where one-third to one-fourth of the families consume less than 60 percent of the "minimum daily requirements" (MDR) in preharvest periods and one-fifth consume less than 80 percent in postharvest times, sums up the transition problems in many developing countries:

> The rural population consists of subsistence farmers who, together with the urban wage earners, business contractors and tradesmen, do not have sufficient purchasing power to buy the surplus proteins and thus obtain a healthy, nutritious diet. The country must export protein foods as part of the Agricultural Export Plan and it also must request protein aid. A person who cannot understand this fact cannot comprehend the problems of the transition period to a monetary economy or the whole paradox of development [Lilimani, 1969:45].

One solution, offered by Dr. C. Munoz of WHO, is to convert food crops into cash crops through increased production (Munoz, 1969). Small landholders need to be advised on the appropriate types of food to grow in their areas in order to provide more and varied foods and a balanced diet. Surpluses sold at the market would bring in hard currency, which, through education, can be used to improve the nutritional standards and to invest in high-yield agriculture.

A study conducted by the UN Food and Agricultural Organization (FAO) indicated the actual change in diet as a result of increased income levels, in part a consequence of the transition to a monetary economy (Willet, 1973). The findings are pictured in the accompanying table.

The rise in fat content was attributed to increased consumption of separated fats, milk, meat, fish, vegetable fats, and oils. Carbohydrate consumption was

Per Capita Income Level	% of Calories from Given Sources			
	Fat	Carbohydrates	Protein	
			ANIMAL	VEGETABLE
$ 100	15	75	2	8
$ 600	30	60	—	—
$2,600	40	50	>8	2

marked by a decrease in cereals, pulses, roots, and tubers, and an increase in sugar. It is important to note that the total of protein calories does not increase with income, but the source of protein shifts. The change in carbohydrate source—sucrose instead of roots, tubers, and grains—is also worthy of note.

Industrialized Agriculturists

Industrialized agriculture may be conveniently divided into two types: (1) the large-scale farming of modern, industrialized nations, e.g., the United States, and (2) large-scale farming developed as a result of international aid programs in developing countries, e.g., the Green Revolution.

Large-scale farming in modern, industrialized nations requires little discussion. In general, this type of farming is usually a capital- and energy-intensive business enterprise designed as a commercial venture. It requires complex machinery and often incorporates a wide range of knowledge and skills in agricultural science and business to achieve high productivity. Except for a few home-grown products consumed by the farm family, there is little reason to believe that consumption patterns of the farm household differ significantly from those of the society as a whole.

The situation is different in developing countries. The introduction of advanced agricultural techniques in developing nations has met with a wide range of responses. It appears that while food production increased in many areas of the developing world where modern agricultural techniques have been applied, the local population failed to benefit by the increased food supply. The status of the poor and ill-fed either did not change or changed for the worse. Only the relatively wealthy could afford to take advantage of the agricultural innovations. Basically, these failures stem from a lack of convergence among agricultural innovations and the local ecology and the wholesale transfer of technologies into areas unable to integrate them into the existing systems.

There were some benefits, however. Improved agricultural techniques have succeeded in raising overall food production levels. Since 1947, India has experienced an increase in agricultural productivity of 3.5 percent per year while the population has grown at a rate of 2.5 percent (Franda, 1974). It has been claimed that the high-yield crops are an overall improvement over traditional varieties, even without the use of fertilizers (Wade, 1974b).

However, the impact of the Green Revolution on the overall nutritional standard of the majority of traditional farmers appears quite negative. The criticism that modern methods have widened the gap between the rich and poor seems to be based on empirical fact. The initial costs of investing in high-yield seeds, fertilizers, pesticides and herbicides, and modern equipment is beyond the reach of most small farmers and peasants. Furthermore, the high-yield varieties are adaptive to specific ecological zones. This greatly limits the utilization potential over large areas. For example, the new "miracle" rice available in Asian countries (excluding China) is adaptive to only 20 percent of the available crop land. High-yield wheat strains developed for use with irrigation or high rainfall constitute only 6 percent of the wheat sown in Western Asia and North Africa (Freebairn, 1973).

The Green Revolution has also had an impact on traditional social institutions. In particular, the system of mutual obligations and responsibilities between landowners and laborers has been disrupted, thereby "undermining village social welfare systems established over centuries" (Freebairn, 1973:103). Workers have been replaced with the expansion of mechanized techniques, creating a system of capital-intensive production at the expense of labor-intensive production.

Other limitations include the unavailability of credit for the small landholder who desires to participate in improved agricultural techniques. The combination of high credit risk for lenders and the length of time and risk required to actually profit from the investment leaves the small holder in an immobile position with little leverage to enjoy what he feels is rightfully his (Mellor, 1969). In the Indian Punjab, it appears that the farmer with less than 10 acres participating in the Green Revolution suffers from an actual decline in economic position (Freebairn, 1973). Overall, it appears that the efforts of the Green Revolution succeeded in raising production but failed in meeting many of the basic needs of the local population.

Programs are being developed to overcome some of the problems associated with the Green Revolution. For example, the International Crop Research Institute for the Semi-Arid Tropics (ICRISAT) is working on developing high-yield seeds which are resistant to insect and disease predation and which can grow with little fertilizer (Franda, 1974). Other international agricultural research programs designed to extend the Green Revolution have been described by Wade (1975). A recent report by Greenland (1975) describes a program of the International Institute of Tropical Agriculture (IITA) in Nigeria. It is aimed toward developing farming systems that enhance the ability of the small farmer to benefit from improved crop varieties. Greenland correctly advocates that before attempting to replace the traditional "shifting" system of agriculture, it is important to analyze carefully those factors that make it stable and those factors that often make the shifting cultivator adhere to it when offered alternatives. Obviously, the type of analysis advocated will include the interplay of technological, social, cultural, biological, and physical factors in a dynamic ecosystem.

IMPLICATIONS FOR POLICY

Throughout this discussion, emphasis has been placed on economic change as it relates to and affects the ecosystem and the individual's economic circumstance and nutritional status. In particular, we have been interested in assessing the nutritional consequences of development. In many instances, it has been shown that economic development has had an adverse effect on the extant equilibrium of particular ecosystems including nutritional equilibrium. Economic development has also had a negative effect on subsistence farmers, fishermen and herdsmen, and small landowners and their families found in many parts of the world.

It is clear that as man has entered into more complex economic systems, the risks and consequences have taken a toll on his nutritional well-being. Often, the rate of change has been so rapid that it has prohibited adequate biological and cultural adaptation.

Currently, there is great pressure to develop programs for combating malnutrition and increasing economic development. Domestic and international aid agencies are setting up programs throughout the developing world to attack the triple problem of overpopulation, malnutrition, and economic stagnation. It has been suggested that this desperate search for solutions to a gigantic problem manifests the lack of comprehensive planning in previous developmental schemes and very limited understanding of relationships within specific economies and ecosystems. Programs now in effect have emphasized the transfer of sophisticated technology used in modern industrialized countries to relatively small-scale economies and the investment of heavy capital by relatively capital-free economies. Technical advisers have tended to be inconsiderate of the implications of their "improvements" on these countries and their peoples, environments, technology, infrastructure, culture, social system, and level of education. They have also tended to be insensitive to the goals and expressed needs of the groups they have been purportedly assisting or advising.

The four major policy implications are restated as follows:

1. A viable policy for national or regional economic development should include goals and standards for nutritional health, since nutritional well-being and economic development are intricately related in our contemporary world.
2. Policies and prescriptions for program development must be based on sound knowledge of what people have, how they have achieved it, what value they place on it, what they desire for individual and group welfare, and their strategies for achieving those goals.
3. Economic and nutrition policies and programs should be monitored closely and frequently by local communities to determine whether the goals are being achieved. Appropriate adjustment and modifications should follow.
4. The modification of any system must include only those elements which harmonize with the existing system. Inappropriate transfer of technologies, methodologies, and resource utilization should be avoided at all costs.

REFERENCES

Amann, V. F., D. G. R. Belshaw, and J. P. Stanfield (eds.), 1972. Nutrition and Food in an African Economy, vols. 1 and 2. Kampala, Uganda: Makere University.

Baker, P. T., 1962. The Application of Ecological Theory to Anthropology. American Anthropologist, 64:15-22.

Baker, R. 1974. Famine: The Cost of Development? Ecologist, 4:170-175, 1974.

Berg, A., 1970. Nutrition as a National Priority: Lessons from the India Experiment. American Journal of Clinical Nutrition, 23(11):1396-1408.

Berg, A., and R. Muscat, 1972. Nutrition and Development: The View of the Planner. American Journal of Clinical Nutrition, 25(2):186-209.

Berg, A., 1973. The Nutrition Factor. Washington, D.C.: The Brookings Institution.

Black, F. L., 1975. Infectious Diseases in Primitive Societies. Science, 187:515-518.

Bodley, J. H., 1975. Victims of Progress. Menlo Park, Calif.: Cummings Publishing Company.

Burgess, A., and R. F. A. Dean (eds.), 1962. Malnutrition and Food Habits. New York: The Macmillan Company.

Cassel, J., 1957. Social and Cultural Implications of Food and Food Habits. American Journal of Public Health, 47:732-740.

Clastres, P., 1972. The Guayaki. In Hunters and Gatherers Today, edited by M. G. Bicchierri, pp. 138-174. New York: Holt, Rinehart and Winston, Inc.

Cockburn, T. A., 1971. Infectious Disease in Ancient Populations. Current Anthopology, 12(1):45-62.

Cohen, Y. A. (ed.), 1968. Editor's Note to R. McC. Adams, Early Civilizations, Subsistence, and Environment. In Man in Adaptation: The Biosocial Background, p. 363. Chicago: Aldine Publishing Company.

Collis, W. R. F., J. Dema, and A. Omolulu, 1962. On the Ecology of Child Nutrition and Health in Nigerian Villages, parts I and II. Tropical and Geographical Medicine, 14:140-163, 201-229.

Cravioto, J., 1966. Malnutrition and Behavioral Development in the Pre-School Child. In Pre-school Child Malnutrition: Primary Deterent to Human Progress, pp. 74-84. Washington, D.C.: National Academy of Science-NRC.

Damas, D., 1972. The Copper Eskimo. In Hunters and Gatherers Today, edited by M. G. Bicchierri, pp. 3-50. New York: Holt, Rinehart and Winston, Inc.

Dunn, F. L., 1968. Epidemiological Factors: Health and Disease in Hunter-Gatherers. In Man the Hunter, edited by R. B. Lee and I. Devore, chap. 23. Chicago: Aldine-Atherton.

Foster, G., 1965. Peasant Society and the Image of Limited Good. American Anthropologist, 67:293-315.

———, 1966. Social Anthropology and Nutrition of the Pre-School Child. *In* Pre-School Child Malnutrition: Primary Deterrent to Human Progress, pp. 258–266. Washington, D.C.: National Academy of Science-NRC.

Franda, M. F., 1974. Food Research in India. South Asia Series Field-Staff Reports, vol. XVIII, no. 9. American Universities Field Staff, Inc.

Freebairn, D. K., 1973. Income Disparities in the Agricultural Sector: Regional and Institutional Analysis. *In* Food, Population, and Employment: The Impact of the Green Revolution, edited by T. T. Poleman and D. K. Freebairn, pp. 97–119. New York: Praeger Publishers, Inc.

Garn, S. M., 1968. Cultural Factors Affecting the Study of Human Biology. *In* Man in Adaptation: The Biosocial Background, edited by Y. A. Cohen, pp. 48–55. Chicago: Aldine Publishing Company.

Gerlach, L. P., 1964. Socio-Cultural Factors Affecting the Diet of the Northeast Coastal Bantu. Journal of the American Dietetic Association, 45(5):420–424.

Goldschmidt, W., 1968. Theory and Strategy in the Study of Cultural Adaptibility. *In* Man in Adaptation: The Cultural Present, edited by Y. A. Cohen, pp. 238–242. Chicago: Aldine Publishing Company.

Gonzales, N., 1972. Changing Dietary Patterns of North American Indians. *In* Nutrition, Growth and Development of North American Indian Children, edited by W. M. Moore, M. M. Silverberg, and M. S. Read, pp. 15–34. Washington, D.C.: Government Printing Office.

Greenland, D. J., 1975. Bringing the Green Revolution to the Shifting Cultivator. Science, 190(4217):841–844.

Griggs, D. B., 1974. The Agricultural Systems of the World: An Evolutionary Approach. London: Cambridge University Press.

Gross, D. R., and B. Underwood, 1971. Technological Change and Calorie Costs: Sisal Agriculture in Northeastern Brazil. American Anthropologist, 73(3):725–740.

Gulliver, P. H., 1968. The Jie of Uganda. *In* Man in Adaptation: The Cultural Present, edited by Y. A. Cohen, pp. 262–284. Chicago: Aldine Publishing Company.

Habte, D., 1969. Proceedings of the East African Conference on Nutrition and Child Feeding. Washington, D.C.: Government Printing Office.

HEW, 1973. Report on the Health, Population, and Nutrition Activities of the Agency for International Development, Department of State, for Fiscal Year 1972.

Hughes, C. C., 1963. Public Health in Non-Literate Societies. *In* Man's Image in Medicine and Anthropology, edited by I. Galdston, pp. 157–233. New York: International Universities Press, Inc.

Hughes, C. C., and J. M. Hunter, 1970. Disease and "Development" in Africa. Reprinted from Social Science and Medicine, 3:443–488. Pergamon Press.

Jelliffe, D. B., et al., 1962. The Children of the Hadza Hunters. Journal of Pediatrics, 60(6):907–913.

Jerome, N. W., 1970. American Culture and Food Habits Communicating through Food in the U.S.A. *In* Dimensions of Nutrition, edited by J. Dupont, pp. 223–239. Colorado Associated University Press.

———, 1975. On Determining Food Patterns of Urban Dwellers in Contemporary United States Society. *In* Gastronomy: The Anthropology of Food and Food Habits, edited by M. L. Arnott, pp. 91–111. The Hague: Mouton Publishers.

Kemp, W. B., 1971. The Flow of Energy in a Hunting Society. Scientific American, 225(3):104–115.

Lee, R., and I. Devore, 1968. Problems in the Study of Hunter-Gatherers. *In* Man the Hunter, edited by R. B. Lee and I. Devore, pp. 3–12. Chicago: Aldine-Atherton.

Lee, R. B., 1972. The ! Kung Bushmen of Botswana. *In* Hunters and Gatherers Today, edited by M. G. Bicchieri, pp. 327–367. New York: Holt, Rinehart and Winston, Inc.

Lilimani, 1969. Proceedings of the East African Conference of Nutrition and Child Feeding. Washington, D.C.: Government Printing Office.

Mead, M. (ed.), 1955. Cultural Patterns and Technological Change. New York: The New American Library.

Mellor, J. W., 1969. The Subsistence Farmer in Traditional Economies. *In* Subsistence Agriculture and Economic Development, edited by C. R. Wharton, chap. 7. Chicago: Aldine Publishing Company.

Mitchell, H. H., 1964. Nutritional Adaptation. *In* Nutrition: A Comprehensive Treatise, vol. II, edited by G. H. Beaton and E. W. McHenry, pp. 351–384. New York: Academic Press.

Munoz, C., 1969. Proceedings of East African Conference on Nutrition and Child Feeding. Washington, D.C.: Government Printing Office.

Nietschmann, B., 1972. Hunting and Fishing Focus among the Miskito Indians, Eastern Nicaragua. Human Ecology, 1(1):41–67.

Plattner, S., 1974. Wealth and Growth among Mayan Indian Peasants. Human Ecology, 2(2):75–87.

Polgar, S., 1964. Evolution and the Ills of Mankind. *In* Horizons of Anthropology, edited by Sol Tax, pp. 200–211. Chicago: Aldine Publishing Company.

Quimby, G. I., 1968. Habit, Culture, and Archaeology. *In* Man in Adaptation: The Cultural Present, edited by Y. A. Cohen, pp. 291–296. Chicago: Aldine Publishing Company.

Rappaport, R. A., 1971(a). Nature, Culture, and Ecological Anthropology. *In* Man, Culture, and Society, edited by H. L. Shapiro, pp. 1–31. London: Oxford University Press, Inc. (Warner Modular Publication).

———, 1971(b). The Flow of Energy in an Agricultural Society. Scientific American, 225(3):116–132.

Reisinger, K., K. Rogers, and O. Johnson, 1972. Nutrition Survey of Lower Greasewood, Arizona Navajos. *In* Nutrition, Growth and Development of

North American Indian Children, edited by W. M. Moore, M. M. Silverberg, and M. S. Read, pp. 65-90. Washington, D.C.: Government Printing Office.

Sahlins, M. P., 1964. Culture and Environment: The Study of Cultural Ecology. *In* Horizons of Anthropology, edited by S. Tax, pp. 132-147. Chicago: Aldine Publishing Company.

———, 1968. Tribesmen. Englewood Cliffs, N.J.: Prentice-Hall, Inc.

———, 1972. Stone Age Economics. Chicago: Aldine Publishing Company.

Simms, L. S., B. Paolucci, and P. M. Morris, 1972. A Theoretical Model for the Study of Nutritional Status. Ecology of Food and Nutrition, 1(3).

Tax, S., 1957. Changing Consumption in Indian Guatemala. Economic Development and Culture Change, 5(2):147-158.

Townsend, P. K., 1974. Sago Production in a New Guinea Economy. Human Ecology, 2:217.

Wade, N., 1974(a). Sahelian Drought: No Victory for Western Aid. Science, 185(4147):234-237.

———, 1974(b). Green Revolution: Creators Still Quite Hopeful on World Food. Science, 185:844-845.

———, 1975. International Agricultural Research. Science, 188:585-589.

Weiss, B., 1974. Selling a Subsistence System. Presented at the 73rd Annual Meeting of the American Anthropological Association, Mexico City, November 23, 1974.

Willet, J. W., 1973. Food Needs and the Effective Demand for Food. *In* Food, Population, and Employment: The Impact of the Green Revolution, edited by T. T. Poleman and D. K. Freebairn, pp. 44-52. New York: Praeger Publishers, Inc.

Wolf, E. R., 1966. Peasants. Englewood Cliffs, N.J.: Prentice-Hall, Inc.

Woodburn, J., 1968. An Introduction to Hadza Ecology. *In* Man the Hunter, edited by R. B. Lee and I. Devore, pp. 49-55. Chicago: Aldine-Atherton.

Young, E. G., 1964. Dietary Standards. *In* Nutrition: A Comprehensive Treatise, vol. II, edited by G. H. Beaton and E. W. McHenry, chap. 5. New York: Academic Press.

Distributive criteria for development assistance
Henry Shue

> *Real generosity toward the future lies in giving all to the present.*
> Albert Camus, *The Rebel*

As the International Development and Food Assistance Act of 1975 was introduced onto the floor of the U.S. House of Representatives in the form of H.R. 9005, the Chairman of the Committee on International Relations said: "It is one of the best bills ever to come from our committee. It is the first foreign assistance bill in my memory which came from the committee without a dissenting vote, and without an opposing minority report.... This bill is a far-sighted attempt to express America's leadership in helping poor people in poor countries to improve their lives."[1] What, exactly, is involved in "helping poor people in poor countries"?

In this chapter I attempt three tasks: an explicit formulation of the basic principle for governing the distribution of aid which appears to be implicit in the 1975 Assistance Act, an examination of a fundamental objection to the aid strategy based upon the principle as formulated, and the presentation of a solution to the difficulties brought out by the objection.

An early version of this chapter was presented to the "Working Group on Moral Issues in the Distribution of Food," sponsored by The Academy for Contemporary Problems, Columbus, Ohio, and a later version was presented to a conference on "Justice 200 Years Later," sponsored by Ohio University, Athens, Ohio. I am grateful to members of both groups for their suggestions and especially to Peter G. Brown of the former and Mark R. Wicclair of the latter.

TO MAKE THE POOREST PRODUCTIVE

It is important to be clear about the sort of interpretation of the distributive principle in the act which will be presented. I will try to express the spirit rather than the letter of the law. Thus I will not maintain, for example, that any particular legislator had in mind precisely the formulation of the principle which I derive. The claims for what I am doing are that it is part of a process of interpretation which will be necessitated by any thoughtful implementation of the legislation and that this particular interpretation is true to the overall thrust of the legislation.

Exactly what the implications of the law will be in a given country depends, of course, on the detailed circumstances in that country. But before anyone begins the important task of applying the principles in the law to specific cases, the equally important task of thinking through the relative priorities among the basic objectives of the law must be completed. I hope to contribute to this analysis of basic objectives.

Although I will not be conducting a detailed examination of the text of the law, it is essential to have a typical passage before us. In an amendment to Title I of P.L. 480 (the "Food for Peace" program) the following statement is made about how the proceeds of concessional sales of U.S. agricultural commodities are to be spent by a less developed country: "In negotiating such agreements with recipient countries, the United States shall emphasize the use of such proceeds for purposes which directly improve the lives of the poorest of their people and their capacity to participate in the development of their countries."[2]

It is clear that the 1975 Assistance Act is intended to help the very poorest people of less developed countries (LDCs) become economically productive participants in their societies. But the act first recognizes that those who are the worst-off need help before they can be productive. Thus, although the act is aimed at increasing the output of "the poorest of their people," it contains a determination first to help to provide for the basic needs which, unfulfilled, prevent a person from developing the capacity to lead a productive life.

The act has two goals and a clear priority between them. The goals are fulfilling the needs of the poorest and increasing the productivity of the poorest, and it is recognized that, for the poorest, basic needs must be fulfilled before productivity can be increased. So the general rule for allocating assistance seems to be as follows:

> Assist the poorest group first (even if it is currently unproductive) and then promote a form of development by this group which will increase its output.

The significance of this general principle is most easily underlined by contrast with an alternative principle which reverses the emphases on the two main considerations, improving the lives of the poorest and promoting increases in output:

> Assist the group with the greatest existing capacity for increased output (irrespective of its current economic level).

Thus, according to the law, the groups to be assisted first are to be chosen on the basis of existing need, not existing capacity. Now in practice the implications of the principle embodied in the law and the contrasting principle presented above might not turn out to be significantly different. In some particular country, it might be the poorest who also had the greatest unused productive capacities, so that aid to the poorest would also turn out to be aid to those who could produce the greatest increases in output. But even though these theoretically contrasting principles can sometimes overlap in practice, they can also sharply diverge, depending upon the specific situation in a particular country. Accordingly, it is essential to be definite at the theoretical level about what the priorities are.

A definitional problem which requires immediate attention is some further specification of the meaning of "poorest." Although the word itself might suggest a purely economic criterion, another possibility would be a nutritional one. The practical problem is that an income criterion and a nutritional criterion would not always select the same people, and those chosen for assistance by a nutritional criterion might be generally worse off than those chosen by an income criterion. The reason is that some peasants with little or no monetary income, who would therefore qualify as worst off by an income criterion, nevertheless eat something approaching an adequate diet because they grow their own food. The point of the Assistance Act, however, appears to be to reach those who are, on the whole, materially worst off.

The solution would appear to be the use of a nutritional criterion to define the very worst-off group and then the use of income to define all successive levels. Thus the principle would become:

> Assist first the group whose members have the severest nutritional needs (even if it is currently unproductive) and then promote a form of development by this group which will increase its ouput; next assist the group with the lowest incomes who were not already included in the worst-off group, promoting increases of output by that group; then the group with the next lowest incomes, and so on.

As formulated, the distributive principle gives weight to both fulfilling needs and increasing output, but in a very definite order. The first group to be assisted is chosen on the basis of need, but efforts are then made to increase its output before assistance is allocated to the second neediest group, whose output is then increased before funds for assistance are allocated to the third worst-off group, and so forth.

Presumably the funds available would often be used to create new jobs and to increase the wages for existing jobs. But since many of the nutritionally worst off are too unhealthy to hold jobs, and many are in areas in which jobs cannot be created at a reasonable cost quickly enough to employ all those capable of work, much of the funds would be used as nonwage income supplements to bring the consumption of food by the unemployed and underemployed up to an adequate level.

TODAY'S WORST-OFF VS. TOMORROW'S WORST-OFF— JUSTICE AMONG GENERATIONS

But, it could be objected, is this policy not throwing efficiency entirely to the winds? The same funds which could go to the members of today's nutritionally worst-off group as income-supplementing transfer payments to be spent now could also be invested. If some form of investment for these funds would produce a greater increase in the total output of the society, it is less efficient to allocate them as transfer payments to the worst-off for their present consumption. In fact, this defense of efficiency might say, it is in the long-run interest of the worst-off that the total output of their own society should be maximized through wise investment so that there will be the largest possible quantity of jobs to employ them, wages to be paid them, goods for them to purchase, exports to strengthen their currency, etc. In contrast to the strategy dictated by the distributive principle implicit in the 1975 act, which we may call the direct assistance strategy (DAS), there is then what we may call the long-term development strategy (LDS), which would use the available funds for long-range investment instead of for present food consumption.

However, an appeal to the supposed long-run benefits of efficiency for the worst-off is obviously misguided as a defense of LDS from the perspective of the interest of those who will starve unless their present incomes are supplemented. Since they will die in the short run, long-run benefits will not reach them. The question is, For how many other categories besides the category of the starving would the policy which is most efficient overall be the inferior policy? Clearly, it is also mistaken to think that long-term benefits could compensate for continued short-term deficiencies for the seriously malnourished. Many of the effects of malnourishment, especially the malnourishment of pregnant and lactating mothers and of infants, are irreversible and debilitating or incapacitating. Irreversible brain damage can make the availability of employment in the long run cruelly irrelevant, and irreversible intestinal damage can make the later provision of an adequate diet, which the body simply cannot assimilate, sublimely pointless. For the malnourished, as well as the starving, the effects of income insufficient to purchase an adequate diet over the short term are too destructive to be outweighed for them by any long-term benefits of efficiency.

But the defense of LDS in the name of efficiency can readily be reformulated. Let us grant, it may be said, that it cannot be in the long-term best interest of *the present worst-off themselves* to operate the economy with maximum efficiency at all times, including the present and immediate future. The inferiority of LDS to DAS over the short term is conceded. But maximum efficiency is in the long-term best interest of everyone else—everyone who does not suffer severe irreversible damage in the short run—and this includes those who might be called *the future worst-off:* those who turn out to be at the bottom of the socioeconomic pyramid in succeeding generations. If we invest efficiently now, we can lay the base for a healthier economy for the future with more jobs, higher wages, more consumables, etc., for whoever is then worst off. Thus even those who, in the future, are worst off, judged *relatively,* can be *absolutely* much better off than the starving worst-off of today. Insofar as the legislation is intended to benefit as many of society's worst-off as possible, benefiting several generations of the worst-off of the future is preferable to benefiting only the worst-off of today. In its most extreme form, the thesis is that we may need to allow some starvation today in order to eliminate not only starvation but also malnutrition tomorrow. Surely it is better on the whole that a few should starve now so that none need starve later, according to a defender of LDS.[3]

But this generational trade-off version of the appeal to efficiency suffers from at least three sorts of difficulty. First, the generations do not change like the guards at Buckingham, with all the sick old people marching off at one corner as the healthy new infants march on at the other corner. Although "the fair savings problem" and "the problem of justice between generations," which take distinctions between generations very seriously, are comfortingly familiar to economists and philosophers—insoluble theoretical problems seem loyal, like old friends who never go away—there are serious weaknesses in their conceptualization. In the abstract, whether the health of "the next generation" outweighs the sickness of "the present generation" seems a splendid puzzle, but it is not clear whether the abstract terms can be meaningfully translated into concrete terms. Malnourished pregnant women tend to give birth to damaged babies, and malnourished lactating mothers tend to rear weakened infants. A difficulty about delineating generations is that one generation is the source of the next, and the poor health of the first tends to set a low maximum on the possible level of health of the second.

The problem is, of course, not merely the damage done the fetus in the womb. It is not even entirely physical—it is also a matter of the socioeconomic situation of the infant. Except by means of extraordinary bureaucratic contortions, there is no way to provide an adequate diet for the infants in households whose other members have inadequate diets. It is important not to overstate the point about the nutritional level of the infant's household: it would be possible for a government to distribute specially formulated food designed specifically for infants, although it would take a virtually totalitarian governmental apparatus to be sure that the infant formula was actually consumed only by infants. And it is not a matter only of the infant's diet, but of its entire upbringing. People impoverished enough to be malnourished (leaving aside the special case of the malnourishment of surfeit, the dietary imbalances of affluence) are normally in no position to be good parents. Even if their brains are not damaged from malnutrition in their own infancy, they suffer from the lethargy of caloric insufficiency and the uninformed darkness of illiteracy. They probably lack the energy to act on what they know, and they certainly lack the information to act with foresight. To an enormous degree the deficiencies of malnourished impoverished parents hang on the necks of the "new" generation. Consequently, the implementation of any decision to write off one generation and then eliminate malnutrition in the next would be bedeviled by the obscurity of the formula for separating generations.

On the other hand, it is perfectly possible to reverse a policy at some arbitrary time, say at the end of a quarter century, letting the chips fall where they may. So a solution to the difficulties in a policy which assumes a neat separation of generations may be stated in terms of allowing malnutrition and starvation to continue for a certain period, for example, 25 years, by refusing to supplement the income which the present worst-off are able to earn, in order to invest the available funds in the most efficient manner, for the sake of a better life for the worst-off of the future. For the sake of the argument, this policy is described in the most appealing terms possible: the funds are not simply to be used in a manner which is more efficient, but in the most efficient way; and the fruit of the added efficiency is not to benefit the very or the moderately well-off, but the worst-off, of the next quarter century.

But there is the more important difficulty that while one would naturally want to be sure in the case of such a policy that the mechanisms for distributing the benefits to the worst-off of the future were as firmly in place as the mechanisms for imposing the sacrifices on the worst-off of the present, such firmness about the future distribution of these very costly gains is in fact out of the question. No government is in any position to commit its successor 25 years hence to any particular allocation of expenditures, even in nations with long-established procedures for continuity and change in government. In the sort of LDC in which the worst-off are malnourished, chances are that successions in leadership itself, not to mention procedures for budget formation, have not been regularized. Consequently, any *quid pro quo* with a 25-year delivery period must be viewed as inordinately tenuous, especially in light of the gravity of the initial sacrifice: purposely allowing malnutrition, which could be eliminated, to continue.

A defender of the allegedly more efficient alternative LDS might plead here that a "mere practical problem," or "matter of implementation," is being exaggerated as if it were a fundamental objection in philosophical principle. But the fact that people who make a commitment are not simply unable to guarantee its performance, but are actually very unlikely even to be able to influence whether the commitment is kept, must weigh heavily, irrespective of its classification as "practical" or "in principle," a classification which is very dubious in this case.

It might also be said that the period of 25 years was chosen arbitrarily and that over a shorter period a commitment could be expected to be fulfilled. This is correct, although no economic investment sufficiently fundamental and far-reaching to justify the sacrifice involved would be likely to produce its "pay-off" in very much less time. The challenge would be to allow enough elapsed time for a major accomplishment without allowing enough time for the strings of control to attenuate. Perhaps it could be done, but it appears very unlikely.

In any case, let us turn to the third difficulty, which is clearly a matter of principle. The acceptability of LDS is affected by the precise nature of its justification, which has so far remained ambiguous. The central question is, Why is it that we must perform so efficiently now for the sake of the future worst-off? Put more clearly, the question is, What feature of the future worst-off gives them a claim on present resources which is not only (1) stronger than the claim of the present worst-off but also (2) so much stronger that the present worst-off are to suffer certain and severe harm for the sake of probable benefit for the future worst-off? It is worth noticing two types of possible answers, although the first answer need not be taken seriously.

First it might conceivably be maintained that the needs of the future worst-off will be somehow more severe, but such a thesis is not plausible. Short of death by torture, starvation and the heavy misery of malnutrition and its consequent diseases are sufficiently close to the nadir of human experience to make further hedonic comparisons moot.

Second, it might be, and indeed increasingly is, argued that the future problems will quite simply be worse quantitatively. The population will have expanded, and consequently needs of the same severity as now will be felt by far more people. This contention does deserve to be taken very seriously. Unfortunately, it is complicated by the fact that whether its prediction about the future turns out to have been true depends to a considerable extent on our action or inaction in the present. Presumably there are approximately as many correct alternative predictions about future population as there are alternative policies for the present, but in order to keep the issue intellectually manageable we may temporarily restrict consideration to the two predictions which are the correlates respectively of the two policies at opposite poles, LDS and DAS: (1) if the incomes of those new starving or malnourished are *not* supplemented by the amount necessary to obtain an adequate diet, the population of malnourished or starving after 25 years will be m; (2) if the incomes of those now starving or malnourished *are* supplemented by the amount necessary to obtain an adequate diet, the population of malnourished or starving after 25 years will be n. Now, the question is, Which is larger, population m or population n? And although there is inadequate space here to explore the copious data, the answer appears to be that, while the relation between improved nutrition and improved (i.e., reduced) fertility is not adequately understood, the weight of current evidence suggests that over a long enough period improved nutrition tends to produce lower fertility by means of reducing infant mortality.[4] If this is so, population m

(result of LDS) may be greater than population n (result of DAS). To at least this extent the "efficient" policy LDS will have been self-defeating.

But this does not establish that the policy of postponing direct assistance for the worst-off with inadequate incomes until after a period of economic development is mistaken. For alternative present policies would produce not only different sizes of population but also different amounts of economic resources. Once again, consider the simple dichotomy of LDS and DAS respectively: (1) if the incomes of those now starving or malnourished are *not* supplemented, the economic resources will be r; (2) if the incomes of those now starving or malnourished are supplemented, the economic resources will be s. Hence the choice, as far as the future worst-off are concerned, is between (1) using resources r for population m and (2) using resources s for population n. In short, which is greater, r/m or s/n? If we continue to assume that $m > n$, then $r/m > s/n$ only if $r > s$, and significantly so. In any case, obviously, unless $r:s > m:n$, the "efficient" policy is not even efficient.

Even the most Job-like reader must by now have entertained the thought that our abstract analysis has long since left all available data far behind. No responsible economist would claim to be able to estimate r or s, much less $r:s$, for any LDC. But the depth of our ignorance is just the point. Any decision to opt for LDS with r/m instead of DAS with s/n is choosing the certainty of death and suffering now for the sake of possible future gains the dimensions and probabilities of which are largely speculative. It is no good to suggest that, instead of the present sort of logical analysis, computer simulations of various scenarios could be run. They could indeed, and with utmost internal rigor. But, since what we do not know are the relative probabilities of the alternative basic assumptions, we do not know on which scenario to base our policy choice.

It may appear that this argument is basically obscurantist and that it assumes that we know next to nothing about the future and should ignore what little we do know. On the contrary, although foresight does seem considerably more scarce than futurology based on arbitrarily chosen assumptions, we must cherish any genuine foresight we can secure. And the argument here is more complex than a simple appeal to ignorance. At least as significant as the uncertainty about the magnitude of future needs and resources is the severity of the present sacrifice demanded by any policy which neglects the fulfillment now of at least the nutritional needs of those whose present needs are greatest. Any alternative policy is proposing that the malnourished be allowed either to die or to continue to exist without a supply of physical energy adequate for a life of normal activity or normal length. If they were being forced to forego a summer home, a second car, or holiday travel for the sake of uncertain benefits for future generations, it would be another matter, and a much higher level of uncertainty would be acceptable. The acceptable level of uncertainty depends on the severity of sacrifice. The combination of (a) the uncertainty that future needs would actually be of a greater magnitude relative to future resources as a result of our concentrating on present needs and (b) the severity of the sacrifice imposed upon the present worst-off by our choosing not to fulfill their basic needs seems to undercut any justifying assumption that the worst-off of the future have so much greater a claim on present resources than the present worst-off have that the present worst-off should be neglected for the sake of the future worst-off. Reliance on LDS does not appear to be justified.

Unfortunately, neither does reliance on DAS, because the consideration of uncertainty combined with severity of consequences cuts both ways. It is not only LDS but also DAS which has uncertain long-range consequences. The most obvious difference between the two policies is that in the case of the policy of providing food for the consumption of today's hungry, it is the benefits which are immediate and therefore relatively certain, while in the case of the alternative policy of neglecting present consumption for the sake of long-range investment, it is the costs which are immediate and therefore relatively certain (and very severe). But just as LDS might turn out to have benefits over the long run which might be thought to outweigh its present costs, the policy of using up available funds on the food consumption of the existing worst-off might turn out to have costs over the long run—in the form of long-run benefits from alternative investments foregone—which would outweigh its present benefits. How do we know that the hidden long-run costs of assisting today's malnourished instead of making long-term investments are not so great as to outweigh by far the immediate benefits? Since the costs of DAS are determined by the benefits foregone by such a policy, and the benefits foregone are precisely the long-range benefits of the type of investment made under LDS, the uncertainty of which has been so strongly emphasized, there must be every degree of uncertainty about the balance of costs and benefits in the case of the one policy which there is in the case of the other. And since, by hypothesis, the total benefits to be derived over the long run from LDS are greater than the total benefits of DAS, more will have been foregone than achieved if LDS would have worked but DAS was chosen.

This equality of uncertainty is important, because it is easy to convince oneself (1) that a policy of allowing a relatively small amount of starvation now in order to prevent a relatively large amount of starvation later (by using available funds for long-range agricultural development instead of for current feeding programs) is a radical and cruel policy, since the resultant starvation is "clear and present," but (2) that a policy of using available funds to feed today's hungry, even if the alternative investments foregone might have made it possible to have eliminated far more hunger in the future, is careful and humane, since the resultant starvation is hidden in the future. But such a policy might be, not careful, but merely myopic.

The same degree of uncertainty must infect calculations about the long-term consequences of both LDS and DAS. This is for the simple reason that the long-range costs of having pursued DAS are just the benefits, if any, which would have resulted from pursuing the sort of investment included in LDS instead. So if we are uncertain what would be gained by LDS, then we cannot be confident about what would be lost by DAS. But if the uncertainty about LDS gives us no basis for preferring DAS, the uncertainty about DAS similarly gives us no basis for preferring LDS. With regard to long-term consequences there is simply a stalemate.

This means that there is a stalemate overall. The immediate effects of DAS obviously are overwhelmingly superior to the immediate effects of LDS. But since we do not know the price in lost long-term benefits, we cannot say that DAS would be superior overall. We do not know.[5]

THE BETTER-OFF VS. THE WORST-OFF—JUSTICE WITHIN GENERATIONS

The tragic dilemma of a choice between certain starvation now and possibly much greater starvation later is created only if the available funds are inadequate both to provide direct food aid today and to invest for greater food production tomorrow. To this point we have not challenged the assumption that the only source of additional investment for the sake of the future worst-off would be a decision not to increase the food consumption of the present worst-off. But why should all sacrifices necessary on behalf of the worst-off of the future be made by the worst-off of the present? Perhaps some of the burden for the sake of the future worst-off should be borne by the present better-off. If we are willing to contemplate with full seriousness purposely refraining from alleviating malnutrition, perhaps we should consider some reduction in present consumption by the better-off, both the better-off within LDCs themselves and the better-off of wealthy countries like the United States.[6]

Before we try to answer this new question about the just distribution of present burdens, it is important to underline the two crucial respects in which it differs from the earlier question about the distribution of benefits across generations. First, the new question concerns a distribution at a given time rather than a distribution among different times. And, second, the current question concerns the distribution of burdens rather than the distribution of benefits.[7] Contemporary theories of justice are particularly thin with regard to the latter aspect of justice: from whom are redistributions to come? Rawlsian theory has the difference principle to specify a ranking of those to whom benefits are to go, but no standard at all to indicate a ranking of those by whom any necessary burdens are to be carried. Indeed, Rawlsian theory is written as if, at least over the long run, everyone can benefit from a constantly expanding pie.[8]

We have been assuming here, on the contrary, that if the lot of future generations of the worst-off is to be made better than it will be as things are going now, some sacrifices will need to be made by the present generation. And we have so far critically examined an argument designed to show that these sacrifices should be made by the present worst-off, the malnourished. Now we will consider the possibility of sacrifices by the present better-off. If adequate funds could be transferred from the better-off, it might be possible to implement both DAS and a long-term development strategy which, unlike LDS, did not depend on withholding food from today's hungry for its capital.

However, there is a deeply felt objection to any significant redistribution of wealth, which needs to be considered. The objection rests on a general premise about incentives. The premise is that economic development will occur only if incentives are available to motivate people to contribute to society as well and as much as they are able. From this premise it is concluded that, far from its being reasonable to demand sacrifices from the better-off, it is necessary to provide them the possibility of making further gains in return for their additional contributions to development.

However, even if the premise is accepted, the conclusion does not follow, for two reasons. First, it is necessary to distinquish social positions from the particular people who happen to occupy them at any given time.[9] It may be that the social structure of a growing society needs to contain positions to which higher incomes, prestige, and other attractive features are attached so that those who are capable of contributing more to growth than others can contribute will have a potential reward to motivate them.[10] But it is an entirely separate matter whether the present occupants of the privileged positions have earned their existing privileges by the superior quality or greater quantity of their past contributions to their society or will continue to earn future privilege by future contributions. Insofar as an incentive defense of wealth or privilege is concerned, it is not only permissible but critically necessary that the privileged positions be enjoyed only by those who have demonstrably contributed and are continuing to contribute to the society's development. Otherwise, social contribution becomes only one of several routes to wealth and privilege, and they will serve less effectively as incentives to superior contribution if there are other, less onerous methods of securing them. Therefore, an appeal to an incentive psychology, far from serving as a defense of just any existing distribution of wealth and privilege, could serve as one possible basis for a schedule of redistribution. Wealth could be taken from those who have made no special contribution to the advancement of society and made available as an incentive for those who are willing and able to contribute.

The details of any plans to redistribute the available wealth in order to increase its incentive effects would require a separate treatment. The relevant point here is simply the following. The need for incentives is a consideration in favor of creating inequalities of wealth in the social structure, but it is in no way a basis for a blanket endorsement of whatever distribution of wealth among particular individuals already happens to exist. Whether those who are in fact better off at any given time are entitled to their extra wealth depends, as far as incentives for contributions are concerned, on the actual extent and level of their contributions. So the importance of the availability of incentives to motivate social contributions cannot be invoked as a general objection against imposing sacrifices on any of those who are currently better off. Those who have the wealth may not have earned it.

The second reason why the need for incentives cannot buttress a general argument against demanding sacrifices from those who are currently better off is as follows. Once we grant the need for incentives, we have granted the need for inequalities.[11] But the real question is how large the incentive inequalities are to be. To maintain that no sacrifices may be demanded of the better-off would be to advocate allowing whoever occupied the better-off positions to dictate the terms on which they will contribute to society. But there is no reason to allow such unilateral dictation.

Incentives are, after all, relative. Someone who will receive relatively more than others provided that he or she makes a better or larger (or more dangerous, or whatever) contribution has an incentive for making that superior contribution. Some people can have incentives even while the absolute level of the advantages of the positions they occupy is reduced, provided that the occupants of those positions will nevertheless receive relatively more than everyone who will not or cannot make the superior contribution. Therefore, the need for incentives is not a sufficient reason not to require absolute sacrifices by the existing better-off or not to reduce the advantages presently attached to certain positions. It is necessary only to keep the relative advantage of the positions great enough actually to motivate people to act as desired in order to occupy those positions.

How much relative advantage is enough to motivate? It is critically important to realize that incentives are also relative in a second respect: the amount of incentive which is enough to motivate is relative to the expectations about incentives of the people who are to be motivated. If those to whom a given amount of incentive is offered know beyond any doubt that they cannot hope for any greater incentive by holding out for more, then the incentive offered, even if extremely small in absolute (and relative) terms, may be sufficient to motivate them. What is essential for minimizing incentives is that there should be certainty about the limit on how much can be hoped for. People may then settle for the most which they can possibly obtain, even if the absolute amount of the incentive is quite small.

Therefore, any abstract objection to demanding sacrifices from the existing better-off which appeals to the need for incentives fails. The better-off could be required to make absolute sacrifices while being offered the incentive of small relative advantages for additional contributions in a context in which it was clear that expectations of still greater incentives were certain to be frustrated.

It was necessary to discuss incentives because the need for them is presented as an objection to requiring sacrifices for future generations by the better-off rather than by the malnourished worst-off. However, as far as incentives are concerned, it seems entirely feasible to require sacrifices by the existing better-off while improving the position of the existing worst-off in accord with DAS, at least until the gap between the worst-off and the better-off is closed to such a degree that the better-off lose their relative advantage. That degree of reduction in inequality is nowhere in prospect.

The incentive objection was raised against the suggestion that the better-off of the present generation be asked to sacrifice for the sake of the worst-off of future generations. Although the objection fails in its full-blown form, the considerations it invokes do serve to establish a maximum limit on rational demands upon the better-off for sacrifices: it would be self-defeating to fail—by eliminating incentives—to motivate the better-off to do as much as they can to improve the position of the worst-off of future generations. However, this limit applies, not to the absolute position of the better-off, but to their relative position: the better-off positions must be allowed a sufficiently great relative advantage so that those wishing to occupy those positions will do as much as they can. Such relative advantages are compatible, however, with considerable sacrifice of preexisting absolute position. Most specifically, the need to provide some relatively advantaged positions in society as incentives for greater contributions by some citizens is not an objection against imposing some absolute sacrifices on behalf of the worst-off of future generations upon the better-off, instead of the worst-off, of the present generation.[12] Indeed, aid which does not emphasize such transfers from the better-off functions as a subsidy for existing inequalities.

Therefore, we would not be forced to choose between the direct assistance of today's malnourished embodied in DAS and investments for the future worst-off if legislation like the International Development and Food Assistance Act of 1975 were accompanied by measures within LDCs which transfer wealth from the consumption of today's better-off to investments for tomorrow's worst-off and by measures within wealthy nations like the United States which transfer wealth from today's better-off here to investments for tomorrow's worst-off in the countries where malnutrition will otherwise be worst. The choice need not be reduced to one or the other of the two unacceptable extremes, condemning today's hungry for the sake of tomorrow's hungry or risking an enlargement of tomorrow's hungry for the sake of today's. It is the paucity of the wealth available for assistance to the worst-off of any generation which preserves the dilemmas of distribution which this chapter has addressed.

NOTES

1. 121 *Congressional Record* H 8571 (daily ed., September 10, 1975).

2. 89 Stat. 852, Sec. 205. I will not discuss the alternative means by which the U.S. can "emphasize" the purposes it favors, although the evaluation of such means is essential to any complete assessment of the legislation.

3. It may appear that I am attacking a straw man of my own manufacture. And indeed relatively few advocate explicitly that the poor of the future should be assisted at the expense of the poor of the present, although some supporters

of "lifeboat ethics" are saying literally this. See Garrett Hardin, "Carrying Capacity as an Ethical Concept," in *Lifeboat Ethics: The Moral Dilemmas of World Hunger,* edited by George R. Lucas, Jr., and Thomas W. Ogletree (New York: Harper & Row, 1976), 120-137. But many influential voices advocate assisting all the poor, present and future, with an amount of funds which is not to be enlarged by any change in the existing distribution of wealth. This is an equivalent proposal, as we shall see.

4. This is, of course, an encapsulation of the "child survival hypothesis" of recent demography. See Carl E. Taylor, Jeanne S. Newman, and Narinda U. Kelly, "The Child Survival Hypothesis," Baltimore: Department of International Health, School of Hygiene and Public Health, Johns Hopkins University, 1975 (mimeographed). There is much controversy about whether an increase in the rates of child survival is *sufficient* for an increased willingness to produce fewer children. On the other hand, no nation in history is known ever to have experienced a significant long-term reduction in fertility rates without an increase in child survival rates. Compare the chapter by Michael F. Brewer. Also see Henry Shue, "Food, Population and Wealth: Toward Global Principles of Justice," *Proceedings of the American Political Science Association,* 1976.

5. Note the contrasting conclusion reached in the chapter by Nagel, pp. 60-61, and endorsed in the chapter by Singer, p. 53 (note 23).

6. I take no position here about the relative degrees of responsibility of the better-off in the LDC and the better-off in another, much wealthier country. For three sharply divergent treatments of this issue, see the chapters by Peter Singer, Samuel Gorovitz, and Joseph Sneed.

7. I have adopted this phrasing from Christopher Ake, "Justice as Equality," *Philosophy and Public Affairs,* 5:1 (1975-76), 71-72.

8. See John Rawls, *A Theory of Justice* (Cambridge, Mass.: Belknap Press of Harvard University Press, 1971), *passim.*

9. I first realized the theoretical significance of this distinction as a result of the discussion of "strata" and "positions" in Douglas Rae, "Maximin Justice and an Alternative Principle of General Advantage," *American Political Science Review,* 69:2 (1975-76), 642.

10. I am ignoring the thesis that developed societies ought to do much less to stimulate growth. If it is correct, it would further buttress the case against maintaining existing incentives.

11. The inference from incentives to inequalities is not valid in the completely general form in which it is stated. There is one type of case in which an incentive does not consist of the superior position in an inequality. If an effort by someone would cause an increase in the total size of the pie which is to be distributed, his own share of the increase could serve as his incentive for making the effort, even if his share were no larger than anyone else's.

12. These interconnections between the distribution within the present generation and the distribution among generations seem to me to militate against the Rawlsian position that the principle of just savings can be formulated first so that it can then be employed as a constraint upon the difference principle (See Rawls, 293-298). The solutions to the problems of justice among generations and justice within generations appear to need to be formulated conjointly.

 Focus on nutrition: who should pay for what?

The Hon. Edwin M. Martin

I believe that humans can be different from other animals in ways which make me proud of participating in the difference and that one valuable expression of that difference is the acceptance of the principle that each has an equal right to an opportunity to live a full life fulfilling to the extent possible his or her potential.

I would stress "equal" because, of course, the "fullness" chosen by each must be limited by its effect on that of all others. Moreover, the degree of "fullness" each can have is controlled by what each generation can extract from its natural environment, and by the regard paid to preserving such resources for future generations. This seems obvious and logical but cannot be translated into very concrete terms and is, of course, wholly unquantifiable.

I would stress also in this statement the right to opportunity, not to enjoyment. The conversion of one to the other requires an individual effort for which only the individual is directly responsible though society may play an important conditioning role.

As world society now operates, equal opportunity requires that each person have access to a minimum supply of goods and services. What should compose such a minimum package will vary from place to place and from person to person. How much of anything is required to satisfy the requirement of a "minimum" is difficult to quantify objectively and will also vary considerably. But it would be wholly unacceptable to permit these difficulties to prevent action.

It has been generally accepted that the elements of an education in reading, writing, and arithmetic are part of such a package. Nearly all societies have or are trying hard to provide it.

In the richer countries, the idea that medical care is in the same category is spreading. I suspect that most societies would accept the principle and that lack of performance is more a matter of resources than desire.

It seems to me impossible to deny that a minimum diet is equally important to any concept of equality of opportunity. In fact, it is a prerequisite to all others, for without it, education or medical care or any other measure has only a limited, if any, value. Therefore I conclude easily that enough food to be adequately nourished is essential to equality of opportunity and we all have an obligation, moral or otherwise, to try to realize this goal, even if this requires that people with incomes well above the average, especially in the so-called developed countries, share their material goods to some degree with those less fortunate, wherever they may live. Most would probably go beyond a bare minimum and support provision of enough food to permit living in a state of "nutrition and health equilibrium" that is consistent with their chosen life role.

Once this conclusion is accepted, the center of discussion shifts, usually, to the nature of the sanctions behind this "obligation," with particular reference to their value in persuading the well-off that they should transfer resources to the poor in adequate amounts. I have put the "obligation" in terms of a right possessed by all humans to equity or to equality of opportunity. This "obligation" is frequently referred to as a "moral" one, but this seems to me to be more the use of a respected word to add weight than a substantive point. No one wants to be labeled "immoral" or "antimoral." The real issue is why we believe it is right or "moral" for all humans to have this equal opportunity. This is important both to reassure those who have adopted this position that they are right and as an argument to persuade others to share their views and thus to accelerate action.

How would I propose to persuade others to subscribe to this position and act on it? Here I am in difficulty. Since I share with most people an ignorance of the principles of philosophy, ancient or modern, none of the sometimes elaborate demonstrations of their universal validity are to me logically or emotionally convincing. They all seem to rest in the end either on Divine Revelation or on some form of "intuition," whether as to "moral" truth or some other kind. The former is undoubtedly persuasive for many, and we should be thankful for it. As to the latter, I am not too well versed in animal psychology, but I am unconvinced that one can transfer the concept of behavioral intuitions in animals, often so impressive in their detail, to moral principles in man.

Even for myself, I am pretty much at a loss to explain why I believe what I do. The best I can make of it is that it results from the cumulative impact of a religious, rather puritan, upbringing, economically somewhat straitened circumstances which induced sympathy for underdogs, and a nervous system that was rather fragile in the face of suffering and death.

If my skepticism is at all valid, I find it rather implausible to undertake a campaign to persuade masses of well-off people by a process of ethical or moral logic that although up to now their intuitions have not led them to decide to share their wealth to any substantial degree with the less fortunate in their own country, let alone throughout the globe, they should from now on experience an uncontrollable desire to do so to satisfy their moral obligations to themselves if not to others. Most of them just weren't as fortunate as I was in the influences of early childhood.

Does this mean there is no way to increase the willingness of more of the affluent to share more generously their wealth to achieve a world without malnutrition, the goal described by Secretary Kissinger in his keynote speech to the World Food Council in November 1974 in the following words: "all Government should accept the removal of the scourge of hunger and malnutrition, which at present afflicts many millions of human beings, as the objective of the international community as a whole, and should accept the goal that within a decade no child will go to bed hungry, that no family will fear for its next day's bread, and that no human being's future and capacities will be stunted by malnutrition"?

There is a large amount of rhetorical overoptimism no doubt in the time span allowed to achieve these eloquently phrased objectives. Nevertheless, the World Food Conference incorporated the language unchanged in its first resolution, and one must recognize that the obstacles to its accomplishment are not technical or natural, but political, depending on redistribution decisions. They are hence subject to man's control (assuming that one can grant man free will outside nature).

I do not think we are left without a persuasive rationale to do better than we have. What is too often overlooked is the vital contribution of good nutrition to productive efficiency of both the individual and his society. If we accept the goals of rising material prosperity, at least for the poor if not for everyone, and of avoiding wasteful expenditure to be able to spend more on activities that benefit people, we must cooperate to eliminate malnutrition. A vast proportion of what many criticize as laziness or negligence or stupidity, resulting in gross worker inefficiency, is the result of present malnutrition or of protein or other deficiencies in the womb or very early childhood. Even when surveys report high rates of unemployment or underemployment, there may in fact be labor shortages which limit output increases because so few have the strength to put in a full day of hard work.

A large percentage of medical expenditure is wasted, especially in developing countries, on people, especially children, who would not be sick, or would be much more quickly cured, if the attacking bacteria or virus or parasite were dealing with the defenses of a healthy body and not one seriously weakened by lack of food. On top of this, of course, are the days of work lost unnecessarily from such illnesses.

Equally as serious are the wastes of money and, even more important, of scarce teacher time on children whose minds are dulled by hunger and whose illnesses constantly interrupt their attempts to get ready for a useful and rewarding life. In many developing countries the high dropout and repeater rates make it several times more expensive to graduate one high school student than in developed countries, despite far lower expenditures per student year.

Considering that over 90% of malnourished people live in developing countries and that the great majority of those with incomes high enough to be targets for a "sharing" campaign live in developed countries, the central question, although not the only one, becomes, Why should people in developed countries want to share more of their resources with developing countries to promote the productive efficiency and improve the income levels of the latter? There are several possible reasons which operate together or individually with different force on different people or societies. Supporting the commitment to equality of opportunity with its dependence on economic improvement, but I believe in some ways distinguishable from it, is the "humanitarian" motive, derived essentially from our feeling uncomfortable, or even guilty, at the thought or sight of suffering. Others may still think in cold war terms of the need to compete for national loyalties with the centrally planned economy countries. Economic progress with our help may attach peoples more closely to our ideology. In addition, economic progress itself weakens to some extent the drive for radical social changes to the right or left, changes which I think most of us would regret. For many in the so-called free market countries, the best justification for economic progress in the developing countries is the expansion of markets for their exports which it assures and, increasingly, the development of reliable sources of scarce raw materials and, in some case, cheap manufactures. Both follow from increased economic growth and sophistication and from the effect of that on political stability. All of these have played important roles in motivating resource transfers in the past and some continue to do so.

However, I would rather stress that if we look ahead for a few decades, we must recognize that a growing number of our problems in maintaining and improving our quality of life can only be dealt with by measures which must have international collaboration in their design and implementation. To achieve the level of cooperation necessary, other countries, not necessarily all of them but most of the major ones, including the leaders of the developing world, must share some of our interests in and concerns about the future. Even the smaller countries must be willing followers, for not only will most major decisions need majority support in one or other of the UN bodies, but recent history suggests that we cannot be sure where and when new discoveries will give a minor player a major role. Most Third World countries must be able to foresee that in not too many years their societies must grapple to some degree with the same problems we and an increasing number of them already face. Those that do have them already will feel the probability of the same dangers we now fear. This does not mean they must have, or see within early reach, the same GNP per capita that we have now. What is required is that theirs is rising fast enough to raise their hopes as well as fears for the future. Thus it becomes necessary for them to consider steps to avoid interruptions to that growth and side effects limiting the improvements in important aspects of their quality of life to which they can justifiably look forward. Only then can we go into international forums with some hope of finding understanding of and acceptance for the new forms of international cooperation and action we must achieve to save ourselves.

Some may wonder how in reality fewer malnourished people will change governmental attitudes toward rich countries like our own. One should have no illusions that the poor have any significant political influence, even where they are most numerous, or that this will be changed much by making them less poor, even in a functioning democracy. They are too busy keeping themselves and their families alive and often too ill informed to play a political role. But the existence of large populations in absolute poverty presses on political leaders in several ways. Often it hurts their national pride to see foreigners point their fingers at their country and cry "shame" for the poverty that is everywhere visible. This accounts in part for the high priority given by nearly all countries to social services of all kinds in their capitals.

More important in the long run is the effect of conspicuous poverty in radicalizing the educated, usually starting in the university. Some are children of poverty, resenting their background. Most are people from better backgrounds who become sworn enemies of the status quo for any one of a variety of reasons but usually stimulated by the evidence of poverty and hopelessness all around them. They provide the leadership for the urban mobs of the poor, feared by many governments. They are the rural guerrillas and the terrorists, all with a major capacity to cause political disturbances. And in too many cases, elitist governments will seek to control them by repression, which is seldom very effective, and by denouncing foreign elites rather than by serious remedial action. And, of course, the most productive foreign target from their standpoint, now that there are so few colonies, is the U.S.

Cooperation with us becomes political dynamite at home; rejecting our proposals is a gain on the home front even though short term. But how many governments are guided by the long term?

What are those issues so vital to us on which we need help? Put concretely, apart from the obvious need to protect the global environment by a variety of actions, the whole structure of international trade and finance is becoming constantly more delicate, requiring more and more international intervention of the wisest sort to keep it operating efficiently. Cooperation in rationing scarce nonrenewable resources should be of especial concern to the U.S., as growing scarcities will force more and more attention on our responsibility for an excessive proportion of their global consumption. To substitute gradual adjustment for drastic change forced on us by confrontation tactics will be a major challenge to our ability to secure understanding from other countries.

But perhaps the most critical issue to the future of all of us is the controls we can establish over the use for the benefit instead of the destruction of mankind of our power to manipulate the atom. It should not be necessary to expand on the dangers which can be avoided only by effective international cooperation in this matter, and I say "cooperation" rather than "control" advisedly. Policemen in this field will be helpless in the face of nations or citizens who do not accept the need for law and order, who feel that they have no real stake in the future of mankind.

At least equally important to the future of all of us is the need to bring the population explosion under control. There can be no doubt that progress in general development, economic and social, is vital to progress in reducing birth rates. This alone would justify massive help in raising the living standards of the poor.

As an extra dividend, there is increasing evidence that better nutrition can have a very specific effect on family decision making, the key forum in which limitation of family size must originate. Not only does the decline in infant and child mortality which results from better nutrition enable parents to count on more grown children from fewer births, but parents who have risen enough above absolute poverty to be adequately nourished can begin to have some hope for a better life, at least for their children if not for themselves. Once this stage is reached, they will be justified in starting to think and *plan* for the future. It will be clear to most that they can do more for a few children than for many. Enabling families to look up at what can lie ahead for themselves and their children, and not to have to look only down at how to get food for today, will start a revolution with many rewards, not least with respect to that vital goal of a manageable family size.

This may seem a lengthy digression, but without the wide acceptance of some such line of reasoning in the rich countries I see no prospect of persuading those with the means to do so to provide adequate help to any program to assure equality of opportunity from any angle, including that which I am discussing here, nutrition. Whether an "obligation" derived from these motives of long-term self-interest can qualify as a "moral" one does not interest me. A long-term perspective insofar as it is perhaps more concerned with our children than ourselves, having regard to the interests of subsequent generations and incapable of affecting the interests or desires of those now living, comes the closest to an unselfish and hence moral act that I can visualize. Of course, it increasingly, I think, brings praise from one's contemporaries, which is gratifying.

Not unrelated to this focus on a greater contribution to development in the poorer countries, where most malnourished people live, as a better justification for the attack on hunger than "moral obligation," I would also argue that food aid, though necessary, should not and cannot be our primary instrument in that effort. First one must be clear about the nature of food aid and the location of the problem. There are two quite distinct kinds of help lumped under "food aid." The bulk of it involves the issuance of purchase orders to governments, which then purchase the food, mostly grains, in commercial markets, bring it into their ports, and sell it in the open market or on a subsidized basis through something like fair-price shops. But also, though on a much smaller scale, governments, the World Food Program, and private, voluntary agencies distribute food to selected malnourished groups or individuals, often in a form more or less designed to meet their specific nutritional problems. Typical are programs such as food-for-work, school lunches, and supplemental feeding for nursing and pregnant mothers and the preschool child. The latter form can only be effective if accompanied by a substantial body of administrative talent to identify those needing help and to see to it that it gets to them.

The problem to be dealt with by food aid of the first sort has several characteristics. Most developing countries do not produce the food that their people should eat, but are in varying degrees dependent on imports, largely of grains. The more prosperous ones earn enough foreign exchange to purchase what they need on world markets. In some cases, agricultural production has been focused on export crops on the theory that the foreign exchange earned could more than pay for needed food imports, but too often that foreign exchange is diverted to other purposes, usually industrialization or national prestige expenditures, and the country requires food aid. Other countries are too poor in foreign exchange and have too large food deficits to be able to close the gap by commercial imports. The latter countries have the greatest need for food aid.

Food aid is in most cases an expensive alternative to local production. Shipping costs are one aspect. But even where the cost of shipping grain overland to a major port city is as great as transporting it by water, there will often be the alternative of shipping fertilizer instead of grain, with a relative cost of 1 to 6 or even 8, dependent on world prices and the efficiency of its use in the developing country.

The efforts of developing country governments to feed their people better through grain imports, food aid or otherwise, tends to favor urban consumers not requiring selective-feeding programs. There is just not the administrative or transport capacity to get food from ports to a widely scattered rural population whose needs are different from one part of a country to another and from year to year. Moreover, in times of food shortage the political urgency of feeding the urban poor is everywhere judged to be greater than that of getting food to rural areas. A dramatic proof of this is the almost universal tendency of those living in rural areas, where crops have failed, to migrate to the nearest city.

The other form of food aid, involving the selection of special types of food for delivery to special groups of people needing supplementary feeding, is even more expensive because of the high costs of the personnel required to make it effective. But dealing, as it tries to do, with special nutritional problem cases, general increases in food supplies through imports or local production are not apt to be an adequate substitute. This type probably also reaches out into smaller communities and rural areas more effectively than imports of food in bulk will do.

From this analysis, I would conclude as follows:

1. Insofar as food aid is necessary to fill a gap between local production and local need, any form of resource transfer to the developing country can help it equally to feed people better. Foreign exchange can be spent for any type of import. If provided for food, it releases a resource to import something else; if provided for military equipment, more food can be paid for. From this it would appear that P.L. 480 Title I food aid shipments make no uniquely humanitarian contribution to preventing malnutrition. The results all depend on the will of the developing country. If one wishes to be especially helpful to governments that are believed to be making a sincere effort to improve the well-being of their people, and especially their poorest people, including their level of food intake, it is necessary to so direct all resource transfers from abroad, not just food aid.

2. For the 75% of the malnourished in developing country rural areas, helping them raise locally more of the food they should be consuming but aren't should have a very high priority not only because it adds to food self-sufficiency nationally but also because general-purpose food aid will help them little and that expensively. It follows from this that insofar as there is competition for donor resources between such food aid and investment in increased food production in developing countries, the latter should be preferred. General food aid should be financed only to the extent that countries have such large food deficits in any one year and such a limited foreign exchange availability that a serious deterioration in nutrition levels becomes the likely alternative. Maintaining these food aid prospects on this highly contingent basis has the further advantage of stimulating developing country governments to give a higher priority to the rural sector generally, and to basic staple food production in particular, in their price, tax, and investment policies.

3. Since present trends in food production and consumption will cause the food gap to double or perhaps triple over the next 10 years, without much possibility that the countries with the biggest deficits—India and Bangladesh alone will account for a third of the gap—can pay for the increased food imports required just to maintain present nutrition levels, we must choose between a rapidly rising aid level to these countries and helping them to become more, rather than less, self-sufficient in basic foods. The latter not only is the more efficient alternative but will contribute to development and rising incomes, as well as permit an equal aid effort to achieve more in terms of increased production since less of it will have to be spent for current consumption goods like food.

4. There is no good alternative at the present for specialized nutrition programs, financed and at least partially staffed from abroad, though pressure must be exerted for increasing local leadership and personnel if not financial participation. In fact, if personnel can be found locally or from abroad and organized into efficient operating organizations, and the availability of the necessary foods could be guaranteed on a multiyear basis, it would be desirable to expand these types of activities for the indefinite future.

If one can accept the above description of the problem, what is one to do about it? The following suggestions are put in general terms for the most part, but this is much more in the interest of simplicity of presentation than as a reflection of reality. The latter is extraordinarily diverse as to both the causes of nutritional deficiences and their remedies, a fact of which concrete actions must take full account.

Our first task must clearly be to persuade people of the importance of good nutrition to both quality of life and development. Without acceptance of that as a fact, we cannot hope either to persuade the well-off to share or to convince the developing country leadership to take the key decisions of policy and resource allocation without which sharing can have little effect, and even that only as a palliative.

It is curious that nutrition in all countries is treated largely as a goal to speak well of but not worthy of doing much about. I suspect it labors under several handicaps. There is a common preoccupation with production as alone worth serious attention, a bias only now losing a little ground in the richer countries with the growth of consumer pressure groups. Isn't it strange that we never read about growth in gross national consumption, but only in gross national production? Thus the food problem is treated as 95% a production issue, and only passing reference is usually made to consumption, for which read, of course, nutrition.

Then there seems to be a tendency for men of action, the decision makers, to relegate nutrition to the hands of the do-gooders, to make it a matter for the humanitarians, not worthy of the attention of those who spend their time dealing with the "real" world of hard facts. Or it is assumed that housewives have in some way been mysteriously endowed with the capacity to provide the family with the foods it needs as economically as possible.

Finally, nutrition is sometimes seen, rightly but not often enough, as a result of poverty, and poverty as something to be cured by GNP growth through the dubious assumption of trickle-down, rather than realizing that poverty-induced malnutrition is also a cause of poverty, with improvement possible in many cases through the increased productivity which a direct attack on malnutrition can stimulate.

But political leaders may be representing their constituencies in a sound democratic way by slighting nutrition-oriented programs. For the public seems almost equally uninterested, whether it is Americans buying quack diet books guaranteed to cure any ailment, meat lovers ignoring their cholesterol levels, families discriminating against pregnant and nursing mothers and their youngest children in distributing a scarce supply of protein-rich foods, or medical and paramedical students learning little or nothing about the nutrition-health relationship.

Everyone needs to take nutrition more seriously if we are to have a healthy world society populated by healthy and energetic people. To achieve this awakening will take more than exhortation. There must be greatly expanded programs of field research, economic and social and cultural as much as medical, into nutrition deficiencies, their specific causes, and their consequences for human well-being. Of course, this research will serve a dual purpose, proving not only illustrations of why action is necessary but the locationally specific information the operator needs to plan remedial programs.

First-class educational institutions everywhere must see that their graduates know something about the importance of nutrition, based on the concrete evidence of this field work. Of special importance will be teachers, as children in school are a particularly important conveyor belt for ideas, not only for the next generation but into their homes for this one. But economists and planners and managers must learn enough to understand the wide impact of poor nutrition on development and to see where action to reduce it can be fitted into the programs and projects they are drawing up and implementing.

Assuming we have a new, awakened interest in nutrition—and the World Food Conference's excellent resolution on the subject suggests that we may have passed a turning point—to what actions should that new interest be directed? Two groups I would disregard as of too little importance in the total picture to be worth any of our still limited supply of enthusiasm for the subject. First are those who can afford to eat what they should but don't. Some may say they don't know what they should eat, but these people also can be assumed to have access to the best information. Good nutrition is for these people a matter of personal will, not social intervention.

The second group are those whose poverty prevents them from buying a good diet, and probably makes it difficult for them to know how best to use locally available foods, but who live in countries with adequate resources and institutions to remedy these situations without serious strain. All that is required is the public will to do so. This includes all of the developed countries and many of the richer developing ones. In them, there still will be an urgent need to increase public understanding of the importance of taking the necessary actions, including active education programs in the broadest sense to ensure that income supplement activities, like food stamp programs, do have nutritional benefits commensurate with their costs.

But nearly 90% of the malnourished are undoubtedly to be found in the remaining developing countries, where they represent 25% of the population and a somewhat higher percentage of the children. As noted above, 75% of these live in rural areas; three-fifths of them are to be found in South Asia alone, where their basic food is rice. For nearly all of them the root cause of their malnutrition is poverty, aided of course by ignorance. Improvement in any case depends on increased incomes and cheaper food.

From an action standpoint, it will often be useful to divide the malnourished conceptually into three groups: the three-fourths in rural areas, the one-fourth in urban areas, and the occasional sufferers of sudden calamities. All would benefit from an adequate global supply of food, year in and year out, thus avoiding the jumps in price due to scarcity which hit hardest those spending normally more than 50% of their income for food. To achieve this, we must all try to produce more of the basic staples that make the difference for most people between enough and not enough to eat, usually grains. Developed countries not only must be more reluctant than in the past to pay their farmers not to produce the basic grains but must also guarantee their farmers a price which will cover current costs, a profit, and a return for their skills. And the major exporters and importers of grains must agree promptly on an international system of national grain reserves as they were urged to do at U.S. prodding by the World Food Conference. Harvests will vary in size from year to year for the foreseeable future due to weather or other factors, and we must have stocks with which to supplement low yields when necessary to keep prices at reasonable levels and have grain on hand to meet emergencies promptly. One can easily justify something close to a public utility treatment for as important a commodity as basic foods, with price stability through reserves matched by guarantees of reasonable returns. In addition, it is of special importance that the USSR find means to moderate the wide fluctuations in its output which in recent years, characterized by rapid growth in consumption, have levied such large and unpredictable demands on world grain supplies. And, of course, we must all cooperate with funds and brains to increase the output of countries whose yields fall farthest short of their potential, namely, the developing countries. Larger outputs from their fields will become more and more indispensable as the decades go by.

Underpinning all this effort to use what we know more widely and effectively must be a much-increased research investment, not only applied but basic. Food plants are still pretty inefficient machines for using space by any normative criteria.

Both urban and rural groups will benefit from the general development progress in developing countries which for a variety of reasons must be achieved. But its impact on the incomes of the malnourished is apt to be slight in most countries; the "trickle-down" will reach few of those at the poverty level about whom we are concerned and then only slowly.

This will be true unless, of course, more countries adopt development strategies focused more directly on the poor. Few seem ready to be added to the short list of those which have made greater income equality an effective priority goal. Besides, few have enough wealth to enable radical redistribution to help much. Probably the most one could press for with hope is the adoption of more progressive tax systems, in fact as well as in law, coupled with less regressive public expenditure programs, now biased heavily in most countries in favor of the urban middle classes, the holders of political power. This approach could help most directly to improve nutrition by using tax collections to subsidize food prices to low-income consumers and the prices of inputs purchased by poor farmers to produce their food. A common problem will be to control who ultimately benefits from the lower prices, easier again in major urban areas.

No one should expect overnight miracles along these lines, especially in improving the equity of tax collections. A good many countries do have, though, schemes to subsidize both inputs for food production and the prices of basic foods to poor, usually urban, consumers. Their extension in ways that protect the incentives of farmers to produce more can be pushed by donors of both food aid and aid-to-food-production projects. It will also be facilitated by a widening recognition among developing country leaders, though still not as strong as among most donors, that future political stability as well as economic progress depends on more attention to equity factors in their planning processes.

Indirectly, but more importantly, many countries, pushed by donors through their choice and design of aid projects, as well as by more general consultations on growth policies, are seeking to help the poor by making their investments, public and private, more labor-intensive and focused more sharply on poor farms and small enterprises, creating more jobs and better incomes for the presently unemployed and underemployed. Concrete programs to this end in urban and rural areas have been developed for a number of countries, guided by the results of surveys by teams under the auspices of the ILO World Employment Program. These programs having started really only in this decade, results thus far have been slow and small, but momentum is growing.

I am forced to conclude that essential as they are, measures to maintain global food supplies at adequate levels and thus stabilize their prices, as well to increase the incomes of the poor through general development and income redistribution devices, are not likely to achieve much more over the next decade than holding malnutrition rates close to the level of 1970, a reasonably good year. That is not enough. Increased and better-directed food aid can help out, but, for the reasons outlined, is not a very satisfactory or efficient means. I, therefore, come to improving the cost efficiency of food systems as the most promising, though neither fast nor easy, way to enable more of the poor to afford enough to eat.

Increased "cost efficiency" is an absolute necessity, for lower prices to consumers must be accompanied by better incomes to farmers, both because this is essential to stimulate adequate increases in output in developing countries and because farmers are so large a proportion of the malnourished poor. But what is required is not just a rising volume of cheap food but one whose nutritional quality is improving as well.

However, in seeking increased cost efficiency, one cannot always calculate "costs" and "benefits" solely by orthodox financial measures. Rather, one must also take a long look, and a wide look, and sometimes accept higher costs than normal market criteria would dictate because of the indirect benefits they will bring, benefits whose value may in some cases be expected to increase considerably over the years, as the number of people to be fed will go on increasing inexorably for a long time to come. This is made especially necessary for food production by reason of the fact that investments tend to be rather permanent, with long lives. The "long look" is required by the fact that the earth's supply of land, fresh water, and nonrenewable resources cannot be increased. Expenditures now, and some resultant increase in current food costs, to preserve arable land for future use by reducing erosion, salinization, etc., may prevent soaring costs later to compensate for land scarcity. Substituting labor for fossil-fuel energy may also have long-term advantages in addition to creating more jobs, providing an additional justification for the labor-intensive technologies which the "wide look" requires in view of the present serious underemployment in most rural areas and the certainty that for several decades at least the rural labor supply will continue to grow at a rapid rate. The "wide look" also may require that countries with desperate foreign exchange shortages seek a greater degree of food self-sufficiency than strict adherence to the dictates of theories of the international division of labor could support.

Apart from these policy considerations, efforts to increase cost efficiency will run up against several practical problems. All but the richest developing countries face sharp limits on the amount of foreign exchange they can put into development investments, and their debt positions make borrowing on hard terms impossible. Most of them also have narrow tax bases and thus suffer from shortages of the local currencies required in such large proportions by most food production projects, especially if they try to be especially labor-intensive.

Another restraint met in many countries is the shortage of trained people able and willing to work in rural areas. Every effort must be made to train more and to give better compensation and higher prestige to personnel working with farmers. Without progress in this, it will often be necessary to settle for a simple new technology rather than the best one from the standpoint of cost efficiency.

On both points donors, including the U.S., have a major role to play, making more highly concessional aid available, being willing to cover more local costs—a hard decision for many to make so far—and stepping up their training efforts.

Current concern about food supplies and growing interest in nutrition and equity are producing progress by both donors and recipients along the lines suggested. But all possible pressure must be maintained by all those concerned about the future.

There are thus a wide variety of considerations of which account must be taken in the drive for increased cost efficiency, some more important for one crop or in one area than for other crops or areas. In fact, such a formidable set of exceptions and constraints to improved cost-efficiency as the overriding goal might suggest that on balance little can be done to improve on present costs and prices. On the contrary, I think there remain a great number of ways by which major improvements are possible. They are not listed in order of priority for that will differ from place to place.

1. Food plants grown from present seeds are, as noted earlier, inefficient converters of solar energy, water, and nutrients into edible products. Research on grains has been extensive but is quite recent on growing them under the tropical conditions of most developing countries with their special soils, weather, diseases, and insects. Past research has focused almost entirely on export crops. Moreover, serious work is just beginning or has not yet begun for some of the less universal foods, even though they are of great importance in certain areas. This is especially true for legumes and root crops. Well-oriented research by multidisciplinary teams can not only expand output but cut costs materially below present levels. More of our money and brains must be devoted to this effort not only through the present extensive system of international centers but also through strengthening national research institutions, the essential transmission belts of new discoveries to local farmers and farmers' key problems back to the research teams.

2. But without waiting for the benefit of new research, improved cultural practices are known and available for use which could greatly increase present yields of many basic food staples without additional cash for inputs. Where fertilizers and artificial water are used in food production, a number of field studies on various continents suggest that often as much as half of the input is wasted and does not contribute to plant growth. One hundred percent efficiency is never possible, but far better conversion ratios are within reach of most of the farmers whose productivity is now low, sometimes with small additional investments, often without any.

3. But cash inputs will cut the cost per unit of output even further. The inadequate use of fertilizers with high-yielding varieties of rice and wheat is well known. But, especially as fertilizer use increases, we are a long way from using in most developing countries anything like the quantity of pesticides that would be profitable to apply to reduce crop losses. In time, this will become less important as new seeds with improved gene resistance to the major pests and diseases are released, but as of now most farmers do not have the skills or credit or sources of supply to take proper measures to protect their increased investment in land, labor, water, and fertilizer against pests and diseases. Similarly, in many areas adequate labor is not available for weeding, or it is made difficult by locally desirable technologies, such as minimum-tillage cultivation. Greater use of chemical herbicides can divert large quantities of water and nutrients from weeds to food plants with important cost savings. If farmers can have these new technologies explained and their results demonstrated, have the credit provided them to purchase the new inputs, and then be given reasonable assurance against their natural fear of crop failure with debts unpayable and perhaps even survival itself at stake for the poorer farmers, present levels of technology could revolutionize average yields and drastically cut costs.

4. In many tropical and subtropical countries land and water are being wasted by the failure to do the planning and provide the credit, inputs, and marketing facilities necessary to grow two or three crops, combining the use of abundant and free solar energy with the new seeds which are not only early-maturing but nonphotosensitive.

5. A most important reduction in food costs for the bulk of the malnourished—the 75% living in rural areas—could be made if the measures just described for increasing output and cost efficiency on farms were applied as a matter of priority to the production of the most needed subsistence crops on the poorer farms where so many of the malnourished live. Growing yourself what you should eat will save large transport, storage, and marketing costs, so large in

fact that at present the scattered poor farmers can seldom afford to purchase food produced a long distance away and hence no system exists to supply it to them. Raising output on the richer farms in an area may be helpful from a national standpoint, but there is little income trickle-down, and sales tend to be made to traders supplying urban markets. After the wheat revolution in the Punjab which resulted in huge surpluses for shipment all over India, there was still 35 to 45% malnutrition in many Punjab villages. Partly this reflected the inability of the landless laborer to get enough income to buy the food he and his family needed. Ensuring that adequate subsistence foods are planned for, even in projects for growing crops for export, livestock, or nonfood products, should also help by keeping local prices low despite some shifts of land from subsistence crops to the new purposes. All this seems logical enough, but one gets the impression that the needs of the local inhabitants seldom figure in the detailed crop patterns incorporated in agricultural projects to be financed by concessional aid.

6. In the very near future, it will be possible to purchase seeds whose genes will substantially increase the nutritional value of several key grains with little or no added cost through the incorporation of higher quantities of needed proteins. This may not show up on the cost-benefit ratios of the project analysts but it will represent a revolution in nutritional cost efficiency.

7. Present levels of waste in the postharvest handling of foodstuffs present a major, widely recognized opportunity to reduce consumer costs and increase supplies. Primary processing by village rice mills is one promising target. Probably the majority of them turn out at least 5% less rice from paddy than modern, readily available mills can do—an enormous difference in total rice supply. Most of the grain storage is at the farm and village level, where around 70% of the harvest is consumed. Safe tropical storage is not technically easy, especially in humid climates. Nor is it easy to convey new technology to widely scattered farmers, involving as it usually must not only the proper construction of storage receptacles from local materials but also the use of chemicals, largely imported and hence facing complex distribution and cash cost difficulties. But the pay-off for consumers could be great indeed.

8. In most developing countries, general development progress can increase the efficiency of the production and distribution of farm inputs and of the transport and marketing systems for the food produced. The present inefficiencies of the latter, especially, add greatly to storage losses as a reason for high food prices, especially for urban populations. Much larger specific efforts, primarily with donor help, are justified by the importance of lowering food costs. Farm-to-market roads, main transport arteries, and occasional market buildings have attracted donors in many countries. But one has the impression that the institutional aspects of the marketing system are not well understood when in private hands and normally inefficient when assumed by cooperatives or governments. It is not unique to this sector, but largely reflects the general shortage of management talent in most developing countries as well as the low

priority widely accorded to distribution capacity as compared to production facilities.

9. Waste resulting in higher nutritional costs is also an enemy to be attacked in the home purchase, preparation, and distribution of foods. Knowledge of what foods to buy to secure the best possible diet with the purchasing power available does not exist for many parts of the developing world even among the experts, let alone the housewives. A vast effort is required, usually referred to as a global nutrition surveillance program, to determine what deficiencies are most common in each area and what are the most available and economical remedies. Then one can mount a program of education of the ultimate purchaser, either directly or through children in school or both. It is a herculean but essential task if we are to make any significant progress toward the very ambitious goal set by Secretary Kissinger. In particular, it is necessary to make clear the adequacy of a well-selected vegetable diet without dependence on the much more expensive— not just dollarwise but scarce-resource-wise—animal foods, especially for urban populations. And it is equally important to make the family aware of the special requirements of pregnant and nursing women and very young children for an adequate volume of protein. Maldistribution within the family has been shown time and time again to be a major cause of inefficiency in the use of the scarce food dollars of poor sectors of the population. I would go one step further, though, in this difficult business of family education. Everyone should be taught at school and through the mass media the general lesson that poor nutrition aggravates all sorts of illnesses in most debilitating ways, as well as reducing seriously the working efficiency of this and the future generation. Knowing this, families may make better choices in spending any additional income that they secure than many do now.

10. The final point in this decalogue of measures to improve the cost efficiency of the food systems in developing countries involves even more specifically the ultimate consumer. It is not widely recognized outside expert circles how much food is wasted because of the tens of millions of people of all ages who suffer from diseases and parasites that divert to their uses food that should be meeting the consumer's essential requirements. Progress in the campaigns against these endemic afflictions will have an important nutritional pay-off.

How fast can we, in fact, hope to pursue these various programs to successful conclusions, assuring a stable supply of the foods needed to cure malnutrition at prices that low-income families can afford? I fear it will be a slow process even with the best will in the world, and that to be sure of adequate progress in the war on malnutrition we shall have to fall back on food aid in too many countries for too long. As of now, most food production projects in which donors and developing nations are participating jointly have a medium-term span of some 7 to 10 years from initial identification as something worth doing to substantially full production maturity. To one concerned about malnutrition and aware that the upsurge in investment in agriculture in developing countries only started in significant volume in 1974 that seems slow indeed. But many experts feel that the newly popular comprehensive area development projects,[1] excellent as they appear in principle, even at this pace may be trying to do too much too fast, with expansion of physical facilities outpacing the changes required in farmers' attitudes, skills, and institutions.

Hence some effort is now also being given to searching for areas in food deficit and poor developing countries where substantial increases could be secured more quickly by supplying to already knowledgeable and probably better-off than average farmers the one or two inputs which have been the only ones missing of the complete package needed for high yields per acre. It is not possible now to say what will be possible along this line, but it should be noted that the benefits are apt to accrue more to income growth and to the national balance-of-payments situation than to the malnourished.

At the other end of the scale one must, I think, devote some resources to research and project planning that is designed primarily to feed the inflated population of the year 2000 and beyond but is unlikely to help much before. Basic research and investigation of "crazy" ideas are eminently worthwhile from this standpoint, even if 90% of the projects have to be scrapped. At the same time, we need to push ahead with the complicated planning required to exploit fully the land and water resources of areas with such major potentials as the Gangetic Plain, the central and southern Sudan, and the Senegal River Basin, to mention only three.

The major obstacle to faster progress along any of these lines is people, dedicated people with brains. Many kinds of brains are scarce: research brains, fact-gathering brains, planning brains, communication brains, and, above all, management brains. Not that there aren't plenty of people with first-class brains in developing countries, but not enough have wanted to or had the opportunity to acquire skills relevant to food production, especially the skills that are only learned from the trial and error of daily practice over many years.

This is especially serious because while it is easy to build irrigation systems, it is desperately difficult to convert a farming community to the use of the new technologies or to establish the viable village and district institutions without which the newly available water will be largely wasted. Only daily people-to-people contacts over extended periods, often many years, can ensure that when a project is finished its physical contributions will be properly used and maintained for the indefinite future. This is a task for which patience and dedication are as important as brains, perhaps more so. That is why I come back to my basic theme. Only if there is a national recognition of the vital importance of good nutrition to national progress and well-being, and of the importance of increased local production for the achievement of that goal, and of the relevance of the investment program to raising food output *and* improving the nutrition of all, poor as well as rich, can it be hoped to secure that degree of loyalty we must ask for from all participants in the improvement of the food system, to say nothing of the acceptance by peoples of donor nations of their obligation to "share" to the extent necessary to achieve such a worthy goal.

Here again, as in the case of the main obstacle to achieving the Kissinger goal, we face the basic issue of political commitment. The whole drive for a better world, including progress in the "developing" countries, has been left far too much in the hands of economists and technicians. Without a political sytem which can select sound goals, evoke strong loyalty to them, and then manage efficiently, through its bureaucracy, the manifold public programs required to achieve them—and in most developing countries the absence of alternative institutional structures requires government to take a high proportion of the important tasks—little progress will be possible. What kind of a political system will best meet these difficult challenges in each country no outsider can presume to say. But those in developed countries interested in progress in the developing countries should be much more concerned than most of them have been to find ways to help each country build the political institutions best suited to it—a most delicate job, calling for experimentation, trial and error, and hence for patience and tolerance as well as skill. How much travail have we in the West gone through to achieve our successes, limited as they have been? Being truly helpful calls also for an understanding, only acquired in the past 10 or 15 years with respect to technical matters, that what works for us may be quite inappropriate for others, especially true as regards political questions.

Meanwhile, our international leaders, intellectual and political, in and out of government and international agencies, must earn their standing by keeping constantly before the decision makers, whether chiefs of state, legislators, or farmers—all are essential participants—the urgency of actions to improve nutrition and to safeguard an adequate food supply over the decades ahead.

NOTE

1. These projects attempt to provide a farming district of considerable size and a high percentage of poor farmers whatever is required to increase yield: assured inputs, including water, fertilizer, pesticides and seeds, credit to buy them, marketing facilities for the increased output, and, above all, technical assistance in developing and persuading farmers to adopt an appropriate package of inputs and practices, usually managed by a specially created public authority, outside the usual bureaucracy. Where considered necessary to stimulate farmer response, they may include roads, education and health programs, and the creation or strengthening of local farmer institutions such as cooperatives.

Index

Accidental acquisition theories of ownership, 67-69
Acreage, reduction in, 81, 82
Agency for International Development (AID), 27, 81, 99, 151, 237, 242, 250
   Office of Population, 271
Agriculture: *see also* Food aid; Nutrition
   credit, 150, 160, 299
   Green Revolution, 15, 18, 151, 157, 279, 298-299
   management, 151
   price controls, 150, 155, 156, 158-159
   profitability of, 150
   research, 151
   subsistence, 279, 292-293
   transition to cash-based cropping system, 293-298
   weather, 14-15, 17-19, 83, 84, 154
Agriculture, Department of, 26, 27, 32, 99, 146
Agriculture and Consumer Protection Act of 1973, 206
Allocation of social goods, 172-175
Amann, V. F., 283
Amazon Indians, 40

Anarchy, State and Utopia (Nozick), 41, 72
Anemia, 216, 221
Argentina, 25
Ariboflavinosis, 216
Aristotle, 166
Assessment of the World Food Situation, 213
Augustine, St., 112

Baffin Islanders, 289
Baker, P.T., 278, 290
Balance of payments, 7, 88, 237, 335
Bangladesh, 36, 179, 216, 248, 326
Barbados, 179
Basant, Annie, 260
Bentham, Jeremy, 129
Berg, A., 275, 277
Beri-beri, 216
Bigotry, 129, 133, 134, 137, 141
Birth control, 47, 97, 145, 260, 261, 266-268, 270-271
Birth rates, 9, 61, 145, 259-273
Birth weights, 214, 228
Black, F. L., 288
Black market profiteering, 242
Bodley, J. H., 276
Bradlaugh, Charles, 260

Brazil, 15, 25, 30, 216, 295–296
Breast feeding, 214, 216
Brewer, Michael F., 8, 259–274
Brown, Peter G., 1–10, 45, 65–78, 191
Buganda, 282
Burgess, A., 283
Burke, Edmund, 166
Burma, 25, 96, 283
Burundi, 179

Calhoun, John C., 166
Calories, 32–33, 213
   protein-calorie malnutrition, 215–217, 219–221, 227–228, 230, 236, 282
Cambodia, U.S. food aid to, 203, 204, 205
Canada, 25
Cape Verde, 179
CARE, 237
Cassel, J., 283
Cereal production: *see* Grain production
Charity, 56–57
Chickpeas, 217
Child and infant mortality, 8, 9, 215, 262–269
Child survival hypothesis, 8–9, 240, 261–273, 324
Chile, 15, 213, 204, 205
   U.S. food aid to, 100–101, 204
China, 22, 260
Church World Service, 237
Citizenship, 43
Clark, Ramsey, 211
Clastres, P., 286
Cockburn, T. A., 288
Cohen, Y. A., 292
Collis, W. R. F., 295
Colombia, 15
Colonial exploitation, 55
Commercial loans, 80
Commodity Credit Corporation (CCC), 153, 209
Competition, 150, 169
Concessional sales, 80, 148, 149, 202, 208, 209, 236, 241

Consequentialist views, 44–48, 129
Consumption, 20–24; *see also* Food aid (U.S.)
Contraception: *see* Birth control
Copper Eskimo, 278, 282, 285–286, 288
Corn, 88, 151, 152, 217
Costa Rica, 260
Cravioto, J., 283
Credit, 150, 160, 299
Crop-reporting services, 160
CSM (corn-soy-milk), 222
Cuba, 138, 240, 248

Daft, Lynn, 186
Damas, D., 285
Dean, R. F. A., 283
Death rates: *see* Mortality rates
Détente, 28
Devaluation of dollar, 22
Developmental perspective on food aid, 234–258
Devore, I., 289
Diet: *see* Nutrition
Direct assistance strategy (DAS), 308–314
Disaster relief, 80, 85, 209–210, 243
Distribution, 6–7, 21–22, 305–317; *see also* Food aid (U.S.)
Dollar, devaluation of, 22
Domestic markets, insulation of, 24–28
Drought, 14–15, 19, 297
Duel marketing system, 200–201
Dunn, F. L., 288–289

Early development school, 238
East Pakistan, 265, 266
Egypt, 25, 96
   U.S. food aid to, 101
El Salvador, 216
Embargoes, 25, 71, 159, 167
Endemic goiter, 216
Entitlement theory of justice, 41–42
Eskimo, 278, 282, 285–286, 288
Ethiopia, 36, 284
Exchange rates, 20, 22
Export quotas, 25, 159

Export taxes, 159, 176
Exports: *see* Food aid (U.S.)
Extramarket channels, 6-7

Family planning: *see* Birth control
Family ties, 43
Famine relief argument, 37-53
  consequentialist objections to, 44-48
  nonconsequential objections to, 38-43
Favoritism, 134, 137
Feed grains, 25, 26, 29, 88, 152-153
Ferkiss, Victor, 5, 7, 156, 164-182
Fertility, 3, 261-273
Fertilizers, 36, 332
Field, John Osgood, 3, 9, 10, 234-258
Food, as national property, 65-78
Food and Agriculture Organization of the United Nations (FAO), 20, 32, 146, 219, 297
Food aid (U.S.), 5-8, 10, 26-27, 79-93
  balance of payments, 7, 88, 237, 335
  Cambodia, 203, 204, 205
  Chile, 100-101, 204
  developmental perspective on, 234-258
  distributive criteria, 305-317
  early programs, 81
  Egypt, 101
  excess production capacity, 81-82
  famine relief argument, 37-53
  feed grains, 25, 26, 29, 88, 152-153
  food reserves: *see* World food reserves
  foreign policy and, 203-205, 237
  free market approach, 5-7, 147-163, 167, 168, 172-173
  future programs, possibilities for, 84-85
  historical context for, 202-204
  impact of expanded food demand, 83-85
  India, 149, 188, 203
  Indochina, 95
  in-kind (tied), 87
  International Development and Food Assistance Act, 74, 205, 210, 305-317
  interventions in market, 164-182
  Korea, 100, 204
  political aspects of, 60, 94-102, 138-139, 191, 248
  population growth and: *see* Population growth
  Public Law 480, 26, 27, 60, 81, 94-101, 129, 138, 139, 148-149, 188, 199, 202-211, 248, 249, 264, 306, 326
  quantities of exports, 89-90
  radical inequality and, 55-61
  S. 1654, 205-206, 208-211
  social concern, growth of, 80-81
  South Vietnam, 203, 204, 205
  utilitarian framework for policy analysis, 103-128
Food Aid Convention (1968), 81
Food fortification, 221
Food for Peace Program, 101, 102, 148, 211, 222, 249; *see also* Public Law 480
Food reserves: *see* World food reserves
Food-for-work projects, 241-242, 246, 325
Foreign Assistance Act of 1961, 139
Foreign Assistance Act of 1973, 204
Foreign Assistance Act of 1974, 204
Foreign Assistance Act of 1975, 95, 211
Foster, G., 294
Franda, M. F., 298
Free markets, 5-7, 147-163, 167, 168, 172-173
Freebairn, D. K., 299
Freedom, concept of, 165-168

Gangetic Plain, 335
Garn, S. M., 281
General Agreement on Tariffs and Trade (GATT), 28, 184
General principle of distributive justice, 114-125
Goldschmidt, W., 290

Gonzales, N., 283
Gordon, John E., 267
Gorovitz, Samuel S., 5, 129–142
Grain production: see also Food aid (U.S.)
   India, 18, 24
   price levels, 19, 30, 188, 192, 193
   Union of Soviet Socialist Republics, 18–19
   United States, 19, 21
   world 16, 17, 19
Grain reserves: see World food reserves
Grain surpluses, 81–82, 84, 148, 153, 190, 192
Green Revolution, 15, 18, 151, 157, 279, 298–299
Greenland, D. J., 299
Griggs, D. B., 290, 292
Gross, D. R., 295, 296
Gross national product (GNP), 2, 61, 96–97
Guayaki Indians, 278, 286, 288
Gulliver, P. H., 291

Hadza of Tanzania, 278–279, 287–288
Hannah, John, 146
Hardin, Garrett, 47, 60, 61, 71
Haverberg, Linda, 3, 212–233, 264, 265
Hoarding, 242
Hughes, C. C., 283, 295
Human Action (Mises), 161
Human capital, concept of, 238–239
Humphrey, Hubert, 152, 204, 205, 211
Hunter, J. M., 295
Hunter-gatherers, 276, 278–279, 284–290
Hybrid corn, 151

Identification, 132
Ik tribe, 39–40
ILO World Employment Program, 330
Imbalance, defined, 213
Import taxes, 159
Income distribution, 2, 10, 21–22, 54–61, 74–75, 187, 314–317

Income transfers, 7, 188
India, 179, 240, 326, 332
   Bangladesh and, 36
   government intervention in agriculture, 157–158
   grain consumption, 21
   grain production, 18, 24
   Green Revolution, 298, 299
   population growth, 46
   U.S. food aid to, 149, 188, 203
   vitamin A deficiency, 216
Indochina, U.S. food aid to, 95
Indonesia, 216
Infants, 214, 215, 217, 227–228
In-kind (tied) aid, 87
In-kind transfers, 80
Intelligence, 67
Interagency Staff Committee, 99–100
Internal agricultural development, 7, 9–10, 60, 84
International Bank for Reconstruction and Development (IBRD), 27, 36
International Crop Research Institute for the Semi-Arid Tropics (ICRISAT), 299
International Development and Food Assistance Act of 1975, 74, 205, 210, 305–317
International food reserves: see World food reserves
International Institute of Tropical Agriculture (IITA), 299
International Wheat Agreement, 28, 81
International Wheat Council, 184
Irrigation, 30

Jefferson, Thomas, 131, 133
Jelliffe, D. B., 287, 288
Jerome, Norge W., 10, 275–304
Jie of Uganda, 279, 291
Johnson, D. Gale, 146, 153–154
Johnson, Lyndon B., 203
Jones, B. F., 185, 186
Justice, theories of, 38–42, 67–69

Kant, Immanuel, 129, 130
Kemp, W. B., 289–290

Kenya, 179, 297
Khanna Program, 267
Kinship, obligations of, 43
Kissinger, Henry, 3, 152, 158, 254, 321, 334
Korea, U.S. food aid to, 100, 204
Kung Bushmen of the Kalahari Desert, 278–279, 286–288
Kwashiorkor, 215, 221, 282–283

Labor theory of property, 71–75
Labor theory of value, 165, 173
Lactational amenorrhea, 266
Laissez-faire system, 57
Lee, R., 289
Legumes, 217
Liberal theory of society, 165–170
Lifeboat (triage) theories, 47, 48, 60, 172
Lilimani, 297
Livestock production, 2, 19, 25, 26, 29, 30, 83, 88, 152–153
Locke, John, 72, 172
Long-term contracts, 70–71
Long-term development strategy (LDS), 308–314
Loyalty, 133–134, 136–137, 141

Maize, 216
Malawi, 179
Malnutrition, 3, 6, 32–34, 213–217; see also: Food aid (U.S.); Nutrition
Malthus, Thomas R., 259
Management, 151
Marasmus, 215, 221, 282
Market food ration system, 200
Marshall Plan, 81, 95
Martin, Edwin M., 3, 7, 9, 10, 319–336
Marx, Karl, 112
Mauritius, 179
Mead, M., 283
Meat consumption, 7, 48, 152–153
Mellor, J. W., 292, 299
Mexico, 15
Milk producers, 155
Mill, John Stuart, 129, 130, 134–135
Millet, 216

Minimum daily requirements (MDR), 297
Mises, Ludwig von, 161
Miskito Indians of Nicaragua, 296
Modern development school, 239, 240
Moral desert, 40–41
Morrill Act of 1862, 151
Mortality rates, 8, 9, 215, 259–269
Most seriously affected countries (MSAs), 96
Mozambique, 179
Munoz, C., 297
Muscat, R., 277

Nagel, Thomas, 2, 4, 54–61, 139
Natural rights, 113
Navajo Indians, 283
Nazism, 43
New Guinea, 279, 293
Nicaragua, 296
Nietschmann, B., 296
Nigeria, 295, 299
Nonconsequentialist views, 38–43, 129, 136
North Vietnam, 138
Nozick, Robert, 41, 169, 171
Nursing women, 214, 227–228, 325
Nutrition, 8–10, 32–34, 212–233, 280–284, 319–336
  cultural factors, 282–283
  diet, role of, 281–282
  folk beliefs, 283–284
  Green Revolution, 298–299
  guidelines for policy, 222–226
  of hunter-gatherers, 278–279, 284–290
  impact of change on diet, 289–290
  increased cost efficiency, drive for, 331–334
  moral implications of policy, 226–229
  of pastoralists, 279, 290–291
  of peasants, 293–298
  protein-calorie malnutrition, 215–217, 219–221, 227–228, 230, 236, 282
  subsistence agriculture, 292–293
  transforming economics and, 275–

304
   transition to cash-based cropping system, 293-298
   use of standards, 217-222

Ocean floor, 73-74
Office of Management and Budget, 99
On Liberty (Mill), 134-135
Organic theory of society, 166-168, 172
Organization for Economic Cooperation and Development, 184
Organization of Petroleum Exporting Countries (OPEC), 90, 92, 193
Overnutrition, 213, 226-227
Ownership
   meaning of, 66-67
   theories of, 67-75

Pan American Health Organization, 215
Papago, 283
Parasitic infections, 218, 288, 295
Pastoralism, 279, 290-291
Paternalism, 111
Peace Corps, 151
Peasantry, 293-298
Pellagra, 216
Philippine Islands, 216
Pigeon peas, 217
Plato, 112, 166
Plattner, S., 294
Point Four Program, 95
Polgar, S., 288
Political aspects of food aid, 60, 94-102, 138-139, 191, 248
Pollution, 72
Population growth, 3, 8-9, 46-47, 60, 61, 145-146, 177, 259-274
   child survival hypothesis, 8-9, 240, 261-273, 324
   ethical questions of food aid, 270-271
   policy questions of food aid, 271-273
Preferences, 110-113
   weighing conflicting, 114-125
Pregnant women, 214, 227-228, 325

Preschool children, 214, 215, 217, 227-228, 242, 325
Price controls, 150, 155, 156, 158-159
Price levels of grain, 19, 30, 188, 192, 193
Production, 14-20; see also Food aid (U.S.)
Production-estimating services, 160
Productivity, 238-239
Profit incentive, 151-152
Property, food as national, 65-78
Property rights, 165, 166, 168-171
Protein-calorie malnutrition, 215-217, 219-221, 227-228, 230, 236, 282
Public goods, 110, 122-124
Public Law 94-161, 96
Public Law 480 (1954), 26, 27, 60, 81, 94-101, 129, 138, 139, 148-149, 188, 199, 202-211, 248, 249, 264, 306, 326
Punjab, 333

Quimby, G. I., 285
Quotas, 25, 159

Racism, 43
Radical inequality, 55-61
Rand Corporation, 192
Rappaport, R. A., 278, 293
Ratchet effect of escalating prices, 188
Rawls, John, 38, 67-68, 114-125, 170
Recommended daily allowance (RDA), 217-219
Red Cross, 80
Redistributive tax, 58
Reisinger, K., 283
Research, agricultural, 151
Reutlinger, Shlomo, 191, 220-221
Rice, 158, 185, 216, 217, 298-299, 332, 333
Rich, William, 261
Rockefeller, John D., 268
Rwanda, 179

S. 1654, 205-206, 208-211
Sadat, Anwar el, 101

Sahelian drought, 14-15, 19, 36, 297
Sahlins, M. P., 276, 281-282, 287, 290
Sanderson, Fred H., 192
Sanger, Margaret, 260
Sanio-Hiowe of Papua, New Guinea, 293
Saylor, Thomas Reese, 7, 10, 199-211
Schertz, Lyle, 3, 6, 13-35
Schultz, Theodore, 238
Scurvy, 216
Selowsky, Marcelo, 220-221
Senate Committee on Agriculture and Forestry, 204-205
Senegal River Basin, 335
Shaugnessy, Daniel E., 7, 94-102
Shue, Henry, 1-10, 305-317
Shuman, Charles B., 2, 5, 7, 145-163
Sierra Leone, 265
Simms, L. S., 277
Sisal, 295-296
Singer, Peter, 4, 36-53, 56, 69, 134, 136, 141
Slavery, 133
Smaller Families through Social and Economic Progress (Rich), 261
Sneed, Joseph D., 8, 103-128
Social contract theory of society, 165
Social democracy, 114
Soft loans, 80
Somalia, 179
Sorghum, 88
South Africa, Republic of, 178
South Korea, 260
South Vietnam, U.S. food aid to, 203, 204, 205
Soybeans, 26, 217
Special relationships, 134-136
Species solidarity, 172
Specific deficiency, 213
Sri Lanka, 179, 240
Starvation: *see also* Famine relief argument; Malnutrition; Nutrition
    defined, 213
State, Department of, 99, 187, 189, 199, 203, 205
Sterilization, 47
Stocks, reserve, 184-185, 189

Subsidies, 158, 160
Subsistence agriculture, 279, 292-293
Sudan, 335
Surpluses, 29, 36, 81-82, 84, 148, 153, 190, 192
Swank, C. William, 6, 7, 183-195
Sweden, 213

Taiwan, 260
Tanzania, 179, 278-279, 287-288
Tariffs, 159, 176
Tax, S., 294
Taxation, 58, 150, 157, 159, 176, 329
Territoriality, 172
Tewa, 283
Thailand, 25
Theory of Justice, A (Rawls), 67, 114
"Tragedy of the Commons, The" (Hardin), 71
Treasury, Department of the, 99, 100, 202
Trezise, Philip H., 185, 186
Tsembaga of New Guinea, 279, 293
Turnbull, Colin, 39, 40

Uganda, 279, 291
Undernutrition, 213, 227
Underwood, B., 295, 296
Union of Soviet Socialist Republics
    government intervention in agriculture, 158
    grain consumption, 21
    grain production, 18-19
    importing of U.S. grain, 23, 26, 159
    livestock production, 19, 29, 30
United Nations, 131, 140, 190, 248
United States: *see also* Food aid (U.S.)
    devaluation of dollar, 22
    domestic food programs, 26
    exports to U.S.S.R., 23, 26, 159
    food as national property, 65-78
    grain consumption, 20
    grain production, 19, 21
    insulation of domestic markets, 25-26
    surpluses, 29, 36, 81-82, 84, 148, 153, 190, 192
Universal Declaration of Human Rights,

131
Uruguay, 240
Utilitarian theories of ownership, 69–71
Utilitarianism, 38, 69–71, 129, 130, 131
  framework for policy analysis in food aid, 103–128
Utopianism, 168

Vietnam War, 133
Vitamin A deficiency, 216, 224, 226, 227

Wade, N., 297, 298, 299
Wallerstein, Mitchel B., 3, 234–258
War, 133
Wealth, distribution of, 2, 10, 21–22, 54–61, 74–75, 187, 314–317
Weaning foods, 222, 282
Weather, 14–15, 17–19, 83, 84, 154
Welfare state, 57
Wheat, 28, 88, 158, 185, 216, 299, 332, 333
Willet, J. W., 297

Witt, Lawrence, 7, 79–93
Wolf, E. R., 292, 294
Woodburn, J., 287, 288
World Bank, 27, 36
World Court, 140
World Food Conference (1974), 28, 146, 152, 153, 183, 184, 200, 250, 262, 321, 328, 329
World Food Program, 81, 87, 98, 202, 324
World food reserves, 6, 7, 152, 153–154, 158, 179–180, 183–195
  evaluation of, 187–194
  proposals for, 184–187
World Health Organization (WHO), 219
World Population Conference, 262
Wortman, Sterling, 152
WSB (wheat-soy-blend), 222
Wyon, John B., 267

Yemen, 179
Young, E. G., 281

Zulu, 283